ESSAYS IN SOCIAL HISTORY

VOLUME 2

Edited
for the Economic History Society

by
PAT THANE
and
ANTHONY SUTCLIFFE

CLARENDON PRESS · OXFORD
1986

Oxford University Press, Walton Street, Oxford OX2 6DP

Oxford New York Toronto
Delhi Bombay Calcutta Madras Karachi
Kuala Lumpur Singapore Hong Kong Tokyo
Nairobi Dar es Salaam Cape Town
Melbourne Auckland

and associated companies in
Beirut Berlin Ibadan Nicosia

Oxford is a trade mark of Oxford University Press

Published in the United States
by Oxford University Press, New York

Introduction and Selection © The Economic History Society 1986

British Library Cataloguing in Publication Data
Essays in social history.
Vol. 2
1. Great Britain—Social conditions
I. Thane, Pat   II. Sutcliffe, Anthony
III. Economic History Society
941.07   HN 385
ISBN 0-19-873078-0
ISBN 0-19-873077-2 Pbk

Library of Congress Cataloging in Publication Data
Flinn, Michael W. (Michael Walter), 1917-   comp.
Essays in social history.
Vol. 2 edited by Pat Thane and Anthony Sutcliffe.
Includes bibliographical references and index.
1. Great Britain—Social conditions—Addresses,
essays, lectures.   2. Great Britain—Economic conditions
—Addresses, essays, lectures.   3. Social history—
Addresses, essays, lectures.   I. Smout, T. Christopher,
joint comp.   II. Economic History Society.   III. Title.
HN385.F56   306'.0941   75-311699
ISBN 0-19-877016-2 (v. 1)
ISBN 0.19-877017-0 (v. 1 : pbk.)
ISBN 0-19-873078-0 (U.S. : v. 2)
ISBN 0-19-873077-2 (U.S. : pbk. : v. 2)

Set by Colset Private Ltd.,
Printed in Great Britain
at the University Press, Oxford
by David Stanford
Printer to the University

Contents

Contents

Introduction

This is the second volume of essays in social history to be published by the Economic History Society.[1] It reflects an awareness that the field of social history remains an important growth area within both the social and the historical sciences. In his editorial foreword to the newly launched *Pelican Social History of Britain*, J. H. Plumb remarks that 'the historical imagination . . . has become intoxicated with social history', so that work in the field has 'mushroomed like an atomic explosion'. For Plumb, 'the time is more than ripe for an attempt at synthesis'.[2] Our ambitions are more modest. In this collection we aim to feature some of the best work on British social history to have appeared in essay form in the past decade, since the publication of the previous volume. These essays in themselves provide some of the likely raw material for syntheses in progress or in prospect. Our introduction aims to relate this work to wider developments in recent British social historiography.

I

Our predecessors, like ourselves, were aware that social history, however far back its origins might be traced—through G. M. Trevelyan into the nineteenth century—was undergoing a fundamental reconstruction, in what Keith Wrightson has recently identified as 'the wave of new thinking about English social history which swept through the universities of the English-speaking world in the 1960s and 1970s'.[3] The rejection of Trevelyan's mode of history was the most emphatic statement in E. J. Hobsbawm's thoughtful essay on the nature of social history which Flinn and Smout placed first in their collection.[4] What would replace the older social history was less clear; even Hobsbawm's vision of a coming 'history of society' was as much exhortation as prediction. Now, a decade and a half after the original publication of that article,[5] the shapes assumed by the new social history are easier to discern.

These newer forms and concerns are striking in their variety. However, if Trevelyan's mode of history has been abandoned, his purpose of writing for a popular audience with an educative rather than an antiquarian or a narrowly professional intent, to inform people about the characteristics of their own society, has not. This has, indeed, been one of the formative traditions of British social historiography, through the work of Toynbee, the Webbs, the

Hammonds and R. H. Tawney, sustained over a century not only by the writings of these and others (in this collection the essays of Williams and Samuel belong in this tradition) but by a succession of institutions devoted to popular education, in which Britain has been especially rich, and in whose teaching history has always played a prominent role: the university extension movement, the Workers' Educational Association, adult colleges such as Ruskin College, more recently the Open University. It remains the purpose of historians of a variety of political persuasions. Admittedly, it has perhaps been strongest among historians associated with the labour movement and thus has produced an emphasis on the history of the working class.[6] However, a broader social history flourishes in the work of such as Briggs and Marwick, and one as likely now to be seen on videotape as on paper. Trevelyan was read by torchlight in the blackout or by candle-light in the power cuts; today the presentation of social history adapts to technological change. That change, of course, is part of our disturbing late twentieth century experience; the idea of progress is at its lowest ebb for fifty years. Yet the growth of social history does not depend on progress; on the contrary, need and demand for it may become greater as a depressed and confused world turns towards its past.

The British tradition of popular social history has, however, been only one of many strands which have gone into the making of recent social historiography. When the previous volume was in preparation no clear direction for the field had been established. In North America the largely quantitative 'new social history' (much influenced by the highly quantitative bias of much American sociology) was already highly self-aware and organized through journals and symposia. In Britain there was no such self-conscious bid for leadership. The Economic History Society supported the publication of research within the area of social history, thus continuing an established tradition, for British—unlike American—economic history grew out of the specialism of history rather than out of economics, and its practitioners had never encouraged a sharp divide between the study of the economy and its social context. Such a division may have become stronger in Britain in the past decade, but it is nevertheless not complete. The Society's offshoot, the Urban History Group, promoted much that could be defined as social history. Neither organization, however, felt a primary commitment to social history. The journal which devoted most space to what would be conventionally defined as social history, *Past and Present*, aspired to a more comprehensive approach to the past, on the model of *Annales E.S.C.*, which excluded explicit recognition of social history as a separate field. *The International Review of Social History*, published in the Netherlands, provided another outlet for the growing volume of British work in social history in the later 1960s and early 1970s. However, its international and Marxian interests prevented its providing a rallying point for, or becoming a formative influence upon, the field in Britain, where it was growing faster than elsewhere in Europe. The broad approaches of these institutions and publications may, however, have been a source of strength rather than of weakness for British social history, preventing too rigid a self-definition and keeping alive intellectual links with other approaches to historical experience.

The especially rapid growth of social history from the later 1960s owed much to an alliance of British historical empiricism, as reinvigorated especially by E. P. Thompson,[7] with a still self-confident sociology and with politics broadly of the Left, in a period of rapid growth of universities and other institutions of higher education and of the numbers of younger historians within them. This occurred in an atmosphere of growing criticism among younger people of many social conventions, including conventional approaches to history. Professional history appeared to them to have cut itself off from the study of questions essential to the understanding of the construction of the present. Hence many younger scholars were attracted by the even faster-growing social sciences, especially to sociology, or/and to Marxism, either to their specific study or to their application to history. Such scholars were unwilling to accept a subordinate or marginal position for their interests and sought further to define social history and to encourage its growth. Hence came the launch in 1976 of the journal *Social History* by Janet Blackman, Keith Nield and Geoffrey Crossick, then relatively junior members of the Department of Economic and Social History at the University of Hull; the foundation of the Social History Society by Professor Harold Perkin in the same year; and the development and growth of History Workshop, based on Ruskin College, Oxford. This was first organized around annual conferences and then, also in 1976, *History Workshop Journal* was launched, initially subtitled 'a Journal of socialist historians' but, since 1982, 'a Journal of socialist and feminist historians'.

II

These eclectic origins of the recent growth of social history have produced eclectic results. How can these be ordered and assessed and what are the likely future lines of development? What, above all, does social history mean, and why is its definition apparently more elusive than those of other branches of history? The problem arises from the sweeping breadth of its potential range. The sheer variety of what can be described as social history perhaps explains why few attempts at assessment have recently been made on the lines of E. J. Hobsbawm's contribution to the previous volume. So we must attempt the task ourselves. Our starting point is a simple taxonomy of four interpenetrating and overlapping, but nevertheless conceptually distinct, modes of social history: social history as 'total history', as a branch of the social sciences, as a history of human groups and as an integrating praxis.

The idea of total history, according to the director of the French national archives, forms part of the spirit of our age.[8] The origins of the aspiration to total history, or to a 'history of society' in the sense understood by Hobsbawm, is conventionally ascribed to the French *Annales* tradition stemming from the 1920s. Yet a prominent contemporary *annaliste*, François Furet, while questioning the very existence of an '*annales* school', has commented that 'the idea of total history is elusive', by reason of the very breadth of its potential grasp.[9] His own definition is probably the clearest that can be achieved:

> naturally it no longer denotes the nineteenth-century view of history as a privileged discipline designed to encompass all the significant manifestations of man in society and to interpret the development of these manifestations as so many necessary stages in the history of mankind. 'Total history' merely expresses the ambition of providing a fuller perspective, a more exhaustive description, a more comprehensive explanation of a given object or problem than can be provided by the social sciences whose conceptual and methodological innovations it has borrowed.[10]

Aspirants to 'total history' may study just one society, community or problem comprehensively in a single period. In the study of the ancient world, for example, a 'history of society' perspective has increasingly displaced more traditional political history, partly owing to the growing body of archaeological evidence which can fruitfully be incorporated into an analysis of social structure and relationships.[11] Alternatively, total historians may survey a theme or problem over a long time-span, for example Alan Macfarlane's controversial but stimulating attempt to identify a major continuity in the development of features of British society from the thirteenth century to the very recent past, effacing the orthodox turning-points of political and economic history in the sixteenth, seventeenth and eighteenth centuries, emphasizing, in particular, continuity in property and family relationships.[12]

'Total history' is a more practical ambition for social than for economic, political or intellectual historians. As Hobsbawm pointed out, by reason of the breadth of their potential concerns and the difficulty of clearly demarcating the social as distinct from the political, economic or intellectual spheres: '. . . the social or societal aspects of man's being cannot be separated from the other aspects of his being, except at the cost of tautology or extreme trivialization'.[13] Asa Briggs also proclaims: 'Social history is the history of society. It is concerned with structures and processes of change. Nothing is irrelevant to it. Nor can any evidence, even the most ephemeral, be ignored'.[14] Yet this both raises the danger for social history of obsession with the trivial and raises the question of its relationship with social theory and, more broadly, with the other social sciences. Without a clear analytical framework, a firm formulation of the questions to be asked and the problems to be explored, all history risks, as Furet warns, sinking into a morass of randomly related factual statements; hence the inclination of 'total history', as he suggests, to 'borrow' from neighbouring disciplines when suitable organizing concepts appeared to be lacking from the historical tradition.[15]

The legacies of nineteenth-century positivism and idealism which sustained earlier 'total' historians, such as H. G. Wells and Arnold Toynbee, are now somewhat impoverished. Historical materialism, based in varying degrees upon the work of Marx, remains much more influential, but even among Marxists there are now doubts and debates concerning the extent and nature of its applicability, even to British history from which Marx's own universal model was derived. This reassessment has arisen from increasing awareness both of the particularity of British history and of complexities and variations in the development of all societies of which the model took little account.[16] An early product of this debate and shift within Marxism was *Past and Present's* abandonment of the sub-title adopted at its foundation: 'a journal of scientific history', its encouragement of a variety of theoretical approaches, in particular in recent years those drawn from anthropology, and its adoption of a catholic definition of history as the study of 'the transformations which society undergoes by its very nature'.[17]

Mutual borrowing among history and the neighbouring social sciences has indeed grown in the past decade for the institutional, intellectual and political reasons already noted. It has been due also to a sense among some historians of history's apparent theoretical and conceptual limitations and, on the part of the other social sciences, to a growing awareness that the time dimension was a serious absence from their own work or was incorporated with such disregard for empirical observation as to be of little value.[18] It could be added that implausible attempts by social scientists to incorporate the time dimension have, notably in respect of the history of the family, had the effect of stimulating historians to ask new questions in order to do a better job and have indeed opened up some research areas to historians for the first time.[19] At the same time, closer acquaintance with the preoccupations especially of sociology, combined with the emergence of new political and social movements in the present, has drawn historians into new fields, including the study of women, ethnic and racial minorities, religious groups, and others not easily subsumable within the categories of social stratification previously conventional among historians. Nor did history seem to provide the tools for analysing the complex relationships connecting such groups and the remainder of society.

History has gained from the ideas, approaches, and methods derived from neighbouring disciplines through the opening up of new fields of enquiry and new and fruitful ways of answering old questions, as several essays in this volume illustrate. Our predecessors believed that the discipline with which social history would become most closely allied was sociology.[20] However, in the past decade disillusionment derived from the apparent excessive detachment of sociological theory from empirical reality, with structural – functionalist simplifications of complex social relationships and changes, and sociology's own loss of confidence that it could provide the total understanding of society to which its more ambitious practitioners once aspired, has, perhaps excessively, diminished its influence. Rather, there has been more recently a growing, and perhaps also temporary and overoptimistic, association between social history and social anthropology. This has been largely due to recognition of a large area of common interest and to a greater apparent similarity of method with anthropologists than with sociologists—a combination of empirical observation with conceptualization of individual and group action.

Yet though historians frequently invoke the value of anthropology it is less often clear what, other than this methodological congruence, they mean. Natalie Davis has best described its role in relation to history: 'Anthropology can widen the possibilities, can help us take off our blinkers and give us a new place from which to view the past and discover the strange and surprising in the familiar landscape of historical texts'.[21] Its uses are well illustrated in Medick's contribution to this volume. Work acknowledging a debt to anthropology has been growing rapidly on such social phenomena of the past as the family, including Medick's own, that of Natalie Davis on popular culture, ritual and gender roles,[22] that of Keith Thomas, Alan Macfarlane and others on magic, witchcraft and popular religion[23] and on more recently developed interests among historians, such as ageing, death and the history of age groups from childhood on.[24] Such work is difficult partly because sources may be unhelpful or non-existent, but also because historians may not always be sure what they are looking for, or may be seduced by the apparent familiarity of past phenomena into mistaking their meaning. The example of anthropology may be of especial value in assisting historians to enter the past as though it were a foreign and unfamiliar culture—as Williams pleads for recognition of the unfamiliar in early nineteenth-century Wales[25]—free from the presupposition that because this is our own society it must be essentially familiar, prepared that is, to experience the 'culture shock' familiar to anthropologists and to have their presuppositions overthrown. This is easier to propose than to practise; and merely to discover and to describe the past is not enough. As Medick points out, one of the functions of limited studies of past communities is to generate hypotheses, concepts, theories and methods testable and usable elsewhere. If they are not seen in this light, as Medick emphasizes, if the historian sees his or her purpose as merely the presentation of empirical data, we perpetuate the unsatisfactory division of labour whereby the historian supplies the facts and the social scientist theories without grounding in understanding of real events. This may, as indeed it has on occasion, lead to further distortion

through the crude application of social science theories and concepts to the
past by historians groping for a theoretical framework, but unsure how to
find one or how to employ it, a relationship between neighbouring disciplines
of mutual incomprehension because neither really understands the
procedures and preoccupations of the other. This has been a problem of
recent historiography, notably with regard to the crude use of concepts
borrowed from sociology such as 'social control' in the study of religion,
crime, social policy and other aspects of social relations, not to mention the
uses of class and other social structural concepts, of which more later.

Medick is well placed for such criticism, being experienced, as few British
historians yet are, in anthropology and sociology as well as in history. He
illustrates his point by taking up a frequent criticism of the work of the
E.S.R.C. Cambridge Group for the Study of Population and Social
Structure. Their empirical work has valuably dispelled the sociological
illusion of a uniform transition from extended to nuclear family forms during
the process of industrialization in western Europe.[26] They have undermined
previously untested assumptions of this kind drawn from modernization and
structural – functionalist theory, but, as Medick points out, they have
attempted to replace it with no new theory or concepts concerning the
relationship between social and economic change. They could indeed do so
only with difficulty, in view of their greater concentration upon descriptive
study of household structure over time than upon relationships within
households or between households and the wider society. A further problem
with this approach is that it obscures the possibility that apparent continuities
in structure, of the kind Laslett has revealed, may disguise major changes in
the content and significance of these structures.

Medick is unusual in giving convincing content to his criticism by
demonstrating, as also does Levine's contribution to this volume, that
changes did occur within structurally similar households in relation to
economic change during the process of early industrialization. His point is,
however, capable of wider application and is now being taken up by
historians in other fields. Apparent continuities in institutions, in forms of
behaviour (such as political protest) and in terminology, may obscure
changes and ambiguities in content and meaning.

This raises the problem, which historians, and others, have largely
ignored, of the possible limits to, and pitfalls of, borrowing among the social
sciences. The gains are considerable, but the problems of cooperation among
disciplines which have grown out of different intellectual traditions, with
different preoccupations, interests and skills, have perhaps been glossed over
too easily. It is too readily assumed that since social scientists are all at some
level engaged in the same intellectual exercise of seeking to understand social
change, cooperation among them presents no problems. It is, however,
significant that the best recent interdisciplinary contributions to social

history, utilizing the conceptual or methodological resources of more than one discipline, have come from those actually trained in more than one discipline.[27] Perhaps historians, rather than looking to other disciplines for assistance, should think more seriously about the independent contribution which they can make to the difficult endeavour of documenting and interpreting social change, and lack of it, without doing violence to its complexities. To clarify the *differences* among the social sciences and to specify what each can contribute to this task may at this stage be more helpful than the conventional invocation of their similarities.

III

The aspiration to 'total history' and association with other social sciences has encouraged an inclination among social historians towards grappling with larger-scale historical questions. However, most practising social historians have, more modestly, been concerned centrally with the study of human groups and experiences from which they have, at most, generated tentative general conclusions; and by no means all have sought consciously to apply theories and methods drawn from other social sciences. Most obviously, they have been concerned with the areas of history generally avoided by political, economic and intellectual historians. This leaves for social historians the whole area of non-market consumption and production including the reproduction of labour power. Central therefore to its area of inquiry are the individual and groupings of individuals on the basis of kinship, common interest and cultural tradition. These groupings, as institutions, generate records which allow the historian to perceive, however dimly or indirectly, the experience of the individual, including those least likely to leave personal records; those who—mainly owing to their low status—remain almost unglimpsed in the sources normally used by political historians and as ciphers in the work of many economic historians.[28] This cannot be the entire purpose of the social historian, but E. P. Thompson's aspiration to 'rescue the poor stockinger, the Luddite cropper, the obsolete hand-loom weaver, and even the deluded followers of Joanna Southcott, from the vast condescension of posterity,'[29] epitomizes the attraction and potential of this area of inquiry.

This study of human groups, their composition, activities, experiences, mentalities and culture, has provided the main dynamic for the general growth of social history since the late 1960s, reinforcing the preference, already referred to, for the history of the masses. Similar developments occurred in other countries, notably in the United States, and more slowly and with weaker institutional support in continental Europe. Within each country they took distinctive forms within a conjuncture established by historical experience, existing tendencies of public policy and the historiographical inheritance of each national society. In the United States, for example, ethnic origins and experience, and social and residential mobility, were the main preoccupations of a polyglot and pluralistic society made increasingly aware of the tension between the ideal, or myth, of the melting-pot and the struggles of disadvantaged groups – notably in the 1960s and early 1970s of Afro-Americans—for social recognition and economic advancement.

British social historiography meanwhile was dominated by concern with class. Conceptions of class have rarely been clearly or simply Marxist, rather combining a diluted and often confused Weberianism with empiricism or even prejudice to produce a largely cultural conception of class. Attention has been directed largely towards the working class, with other classes treated as existing principally through their impact upon the working class and given until recently little consideration in themselves; the relations between classes being treated somewhat mechanically, often with concepts imported from sociology such as those of 'deference' or 'social control'. The justification for this focus upon the working class, if not for some of the concepts employed, was precisely their neglect in the pre-existing historiography. The difficulty of studying groups who rarely in the conventional sources spoke directly for themselves led to the development of new resources for historical research, of techniques such as oral history and the use of such documentary sources as autobiographies and diaries.[30] Such approaches have done much to redress the previous neglect of subordinate social groups. They may, indeed, have moved too far in the direction of neglecting more dominant groups and from consideration of the relationships between the two, though, as we shall point out later, this neglect appears to be coming to an end.

IV

Relationships among significant social groups cannot be understood in purely social terms, since they encompass economic and political relationships. Social history has been criticized for becoming too specialized, for building barriers between itself and economic and political history and hence rendering itself incapable of contributing to the analysis of central issues in recent history, in particular of the process whereby power, in its many manifestations, is constructed and sustained.[31] There is truth in such criticisms, and there is little to be said for a social history which so limits itself. In attempting to avoid this trap social history must necessarily interpenetrate political and economic history. Indeed, at its best, its ambition is to bring about their integration. Hence Hobsbawm's comment that 'a survey of social history in the past seems to show that its best practitioners have always felt uncomfortable with the term itself'.[32] This has not been a defensive posture, rather a statement of the desirability and possibility of this integrative role. It is desirable because, although there may be areas of social *integrating function of social history.*

experience of interest to historians which in no way bear upon economic or political experience, they are hard to think of, unless they are trivial. One of the functions of social history is precisely to try to integrate the other specialisms, to seek out and analyse the complex relationships among the separate but associated political, economic and social processes, to provide dimensions of explanation not normally sought by specialists in other fields; indeed much of the stimulus to the growth of social history has derived from a sense of unanswered questions and unexplored levels of explanation in other fields.

This is not to claim any superior status for the kinds of explanation which social history can offer, still less to deny the need for the conventional empirical studies of the other specialisms: of high politics for example or of the functioning of particular firms or of trade flows; nor is it to assert that everything which goes by the name of social history achieves, or even aspires to, this integrating task. But understanding the vast complexity of the past must be a co-operative endeavour, in which a variety of skills and interests are brought together to encompass its many dimensions. Social historians have developed distinctive concerns, methods and concepts which they contribute to this enterprise.

They have done so with notable energy in the past decade, utilizing all of the approaches discussed in this introduction, which we have tried to represent in this volume. Least represented here is the aspiration to 'total history', which, of its nature, least readily lends itself to brief essay form. All the essays, however, whatever their differences of preoccupation, approach, and method, demonstrate an unwillingness to allow any preoccupation with the identity of social history to weaken their contribution to the understanding of issues of central concern to all modern historians. Levine and Medick, for example, discuss the dynamics of early industrialization in relation to demographic and family patterns; Williams and Reid its uneven progress in relation to popular protest and cultural change. Whilst Samuel describes the complexities of the rural economy, Elizabeth Roberts contributes to the contentious question of the assessment of standards of living; Crossick to analysis of the economic and political roles of the lower middle class; Dyos and Reeder to the study of the process of urbanization. Rubinstein calls in question conventional assumptions about where wealth and power were concentrated in the nineteenth century, as Hay also raises questions about the role of economically powerful groups of employers in the political process and, with McLean, contributes to understanding some of the social pressures and assumptions behind important aspects of political decision-making.

We have tried to represent the range of recent developments, regrettably incompletely for lack of space. We have omitted all the exciting developments in early modern history, since we felt that a token article or two could not do it justice, despite acute awareness of the ways in which historians' deepening understanding of the eighteenth century and before is changing our perception of the period of industrialization with which the volume is chiefly concerned;[33] though the contributions of Levine, Medick, Williams and Reid indicate some of this. The excessive preoccupation of social historians with the nineteenth century, until recently, carried with it the danger of looking at its history through the wrong end of the telescope, searching for recognizable roots of the present with presuppositions drawn from present concerns. The expansion of the historiography of the early modern period should enable us better to understand the nineteenth century on its own terms, to appreciate what it shared with its past and the degree to which it was shaped by that past, as well as with its future.

This is the more important because, as several of our contributors demonstrate, one of the more important recent changes in our understanding of nineteenth-century history is the recognition that social, economic and political change was much slower, more regionally diverse, more uneven, less unilinear than has sometimes been assumed. A new type of society did not spring up fully formed at some point in the nineteenth century; and what remained from its past were not mere archaic survivals but active agents of change, profoundly influencing the new. A longer-term perspective may help us to shake off the nineteenth-century belief in progress which still, however unwillingly, holds us in its grip, and help us better to understand, for example, early nineteenth-century movements, such as Chartism, to think through the implications of Gwyn Williams's comment that 'The ideology of democracy is pre-industrial';[34] to ask indeed whether society in 1914, or even in 1984, was more 'democratic' in any real sense, actually allowed people more control over their own lives, even in the narrow political sphere, than that of the 1760s, with its turbulent vestry meetings, hustings, petitions and riots.

Even for the narrow historical period to which we have confined the volume (the post – 1918 period remains, as it was ten years ago, under-represented because still under-researched, though this appears at last to be changing[35]) we have left out much—most seriously, religion, without which nineteenth-century society is almost impossible to understand. Religious belief, in its great variety, was a real force shaping people's lives and actions, dividing them as decisively as class and status, in ways in which historians in the unusually secularized Britain of the present can too easily underestimate and only with difficulty comprehend, and the full significance of which they are still far from grasping. Analysis of the history of religion places a severe strain upon strict Marxist or even Weberian methodologies, encouraging recourse to approaches drawn from anthropology and from ethnology, phenomenology, semiology, psychology and, with caution, psychiatry. We have given religion insufficient prominence in this volume, chiefly because much of the best work exists in book rather than article form.[36] Its importance surfaces, however, in some of the contributions; Williams's striking opening description of the Rhydowen chapel, for instance, forcefully symbolizes the centrality of non-conformity in modern Welsh culture.

Crime and its control have also been excluded. The growing study of crime has contributed to our understanding of changing forms of behaviour, of social-political relationships and attitudes to them; but much of this work is accessible in recent publications.[37] Also fast developing and at last becoming more closely integrated with other aspects of history, and also omitted from this volume, for reasons of space, is the social history of health and medicine whose study is beginning to contribute to the social history of the twentieth century, as of earlier periods.[38]

We have tried to include work representative of most other important recent trends among modern social historians of Britain. David Levine's study of Shepshed is one example of the fulfilment of our predecessors' expectations of the work of the E.S.R.C. Cambridge Group for the Study of Population and Social Structure, and an example of fruitful borrowing of techniques from another discipline, despite the criticisms noted above. Levine demonstrates the value of modern quantitative techniques for providing answers to historical questions otherwise answerable only with the greatest difficulty, or not at all, owing to the quantity of necessary data and the problems of linking them in the pre-computer era. In this instance the question is the important one, which has long baffled historians, of the precise reasons for the rapid population growth after 1750. Levine's answers have recently been supported by Wrigley and Schofield's larger-scale study.[39] Another merit of Levine's work is that he avoids the problem which disfigures some quantitative studies of so abstracting the data from their historical context that their meaning becomes obscured or distorted. He is able to use the data to illuminate more than strictly demographic aspects of life in Shepshed, in particular the relationship between economic change, changes in family relationships and strategies for survival at low levels of subsistence.

Levine's work, however, raises the question, as does that of Wrigley and Schofield, despite their wider scope, of whether explanations of social change on a national scale can be generated from the limited local studies which, as Levine points out, such detailed quantitative work necessitates; this problem is especially important in view of the extreme local variability in economic and cultural characteristics indicated by other studies in this volume and elsewhere.

Like Medick, Levine demonstrates that micro-studies can generate concepts and approaches of wider applicability. Much has also been done by urban historians to link social history to local environments. Shaped and guided in Britain to a very large extent by the late H. J. Dyos, urban history acquired a distinct identity and consciousness from the early 1960s and, for all its conceptual limitations, opened up and prepared much of the ground which social history has taken over. Local studies allowed historians, in this field also, to operationalize models of social change which they later transposed onto the national stage.[40] However, the article by Dyos and Reeder on the suburbs and the slums of Victorian London does more than offer these two environments as mirrors of class and income differences. It puts forward a model of social and economic relations in which the environment and the economic mechanisms which sustain it enter into social processes as a distinct variable. Through Dyos's work we can be persuaded never to neglect the links between social action, the local community, and the physical expression of that community, connections which look forward to an ecological history in which man will be securely located in the physical environment which his planet offers him. Thus, a comprehensive social history incorporating land and buildings, together with climate, may yet emerge.

Medick's examination of gender roles in peasant and proto-industrial households, as already suggested, complements and extends quantitative work on household structure by exploring the complex world of relationships within and among households. Similarly Davidoff enters the otherwise closed world of relations between master and servant, husband and wife, in nineteenth-century England. Her study of ritual and etiquette within the household suggests how the sensitization of the historian to sources and forms of interpretation, once the recourse primarily of the sociologist or anthropologist, has increased our capacity to penetrate essential features of past human experience. Her study reveals changes in relationships structurally least changed by industrialization; her use of sociological theory enables her to present these relationships as dynamic and two-sided in place of previous more static accounts of social relationships.

The experience of servant or wife was common to most women in the nineteenth century. Davidoff's was an early and influential product of the growth of women's history which accompanied the revival of feminism in the 1970s. Scattered though such work remains, it has begun to change our perception of the roles of women in modern society to a point at which few serious historians would now entirely fail to incorporate women's experience into their work where they legitimately might, as was routinely the case a decade ago.

Women's history has moved on from the hagiographical studies of heroines and of past movements for emancipation, especially for the vote, which once characterized it, to analysis of the wider social and economic experience of women; their contributions, for example, to the economy as producers full and part-time, paid and unpaid,[41] some of which also emerges in the essays of Levine, Medick, Samuel and Roberts; and as consumers, which Roberts illustrates especially well. As she points out, women as managers of scarce household resources crucially determined family living standards and hence, to some degree, social status. The woman's skill at 'managing' could make an essential contribution to the productive capacity as well as to the health and comfort of the male wage-earner and to his security and 'respectability', of which so much is made in discussions of the 'labour aristocracy' and other aspects of stratification within the working class.[42] Hence the study of women's roles has contributed to changes in the way that economists as well as historians define 'work', with the recognition of the importance for the economy of certain forms of non-market labour; to changes also in their analysis of certain forms of consumption, and to increased understanding of the processes whereby social status is constructed. Presumably wives also played an important role in the construction of lower middle-class life styles, which Crossick describes in this volume, although he does not explore this point. In such ways women's history is ceasing to be an undesirably separate area of study and is being integrated into, and is contributing to, the understanding of aspects of history which, as most of them do, concern both women *and* men.

In addition studies of middle-class housewives,[43] of 'emigrant gentlewomen', the energetic, resourceful female colonial pioneers,[44] and of the independent-minded women in philanthropic organizations and pressure groups[45] have begun to dispel the stereotype of the helpless Victorian woman, one of the many popular stereotypes with which 'the Victorians' are peculiarly beset. For all the great importance of integrating the history of women with the history of society there is also a specific task—to which these studies have contributed—of elucidating the specific roles and experiences of women in the past and of examining the processes whereby their unequal access to positions of economic, political and social influence has been constructed and sustained; though such study must also, of its nature, tell us much about male experiences, attitudes and fears.[46] There has been some progress in the study of the social construction of male and female roles, for example through exploration of the emergence and influence of the concept of 'separate spheres' and the ideology of the family in the early nineteenth century and its later reinforcement.[47]

Work on women's history is serving to reinforce our growing awareness of the complexity of social processes during the period of industrialization, including the problems involved in assuming any simple relationship between economic experiences and political action. Even the 'women's movement' of the 1900s is coming to be seen as a complex of sometimes conflicting aspirations, divided not only among women of different social position but among the different aims of women of similar social position; between, for example, those who wanted equal opportunities with men and those who believed that it was possible for women to be equal in social value with men whilst fulfilling different social roles. Women's history indeed now covers, as it should, such a wide range of topics and theoretical stances that it cannot simply be summarized or confined within any assumed unified approach or set of objectives.[48]

The relative 'invisibility' of women, as of other subordinate groups, in the conventional sources has led historians into greater inventiveness in their search for data. Roberts's work on the history of women and men provides one of the best recent examples of the use of a new type of source and methodology available only to historians of the recent past: oral history. She is sensibly critical of its limitations, claiming for it no superior authenticity over other sources, rather employing it as one source to be used alongside more conventional documentary material and with the same critical apparatus. The value of oral history, as she demonstrates, lies in its capacity to penetrate levels of experience not normally accessible in documentary sources, especially with reference to social groups who least often placed their experiences on written record.[49] In this case it enables her to explore the survival strategies of workers in greater depth than Levine was able to do with the more limited materials available for the earlier period.

Roberts, Levine and Medick share a recognition, which has been growing among historians, of the importance of studying the cultural changes which accompanied, and intersected with, economic change. This has been explored more fully for the early than for the later phases of industrialization, especially in relation to the role of the 'moral economy' of the pre-industrial worker in the emergence of industrialization. As Reid also points out, when workers in domestic industry or in 'pre-industrial' artisan workshops had a choice, they valued a modest income, sufficient for family necessities, and maximum leisure time over long and fixed hours of work or the opportunity to accumulate a surplus—the conventional characteristics of industrial capitalism. Work tended to be a direct response to the need for subsistence and was spread through the family according to need and to the capacity for work, rather than concentrated in regular long hours for one or two family members. As Reid describes, people would work long hours when they had to, relax when they did not, controlling, so far as they were able, their own work-lives and valuing the associated sense of independence. Work, leisure and family life were not consigned to the separate spheres of existence they were later to become.

This 'moral economy' should not be assumed to have been universal and should not be romanticized. In reality the difficulty of achieving subsistence severely and frequently limited independence and freedom of choice.[50] Experiences varied widely, but fell within a broad set of widely shared values. The result was a culture well suited to the needs of merchant capital, much less to those of factory-based industry. The gradual advance of mechanization, by a variety of paths,[51] necessitated a more regular workforce, a disciplined working day and week. This implied not simply a change in working habits but a fundamental cultural transformation: in attitudes to work, leisure, consumption, family life, and relations between worker and employer. Much recent social history, of which Reid's is an example, has been directed towards the study of this nineteenth-century cultural transformation, the distinct change in habits of life in most sections of society, the 'transformation of manners', the taming of the 'turbulent people' which is such a striking feature of the century,[52] though it has not always retained a clear perception of the object of study, collapsing rather into the study of leisure, or of the other associated processes, in and for themselves.

It is a difficult set of processes to study because its effects were various and because the associated transformation of the economy was relatively slow and uneven. Reid's study of 'Saint Monday'—one manifestation of the older moral economy—is a direct heir of Edward Thompson's pioneering essay 'Time, Work-Discipline and Industrial Capitalism' in the previous volume, in which Thompson, as so often, identified an important, neglected historical question. The greater empirical rigour with which Reid is able to examine one aspect of the emergence of time discipline enables him to draw a more nuanced picture of the process by which 'Saint Monday was eroded as much as it was demolished'. It did not, as Thompson suggests, die chiefly as a result of assault by employers and the march of the puritan ethic; rather, in more subtle ways, workers both chose, and were compelled to change, their ways of living through a complex of social and economic changes. Some skilled craft workers retained their independence and old habits by reason of the scarcity of their skills, which enabled them to exert some control over their hours of work. Others welcomed the transition from older, less disciplined work and leisure habits, impelled by religious and political motives—a drunken worker was of as little value to a religious or political movement as to an employer; discipline was essential for successful industrial and political movements. The habit of accumulation grew not simply because it was imposed upon the masses by an emerging capitalist ethic but as workers realized that it was indeed a means towards a more comfortable style of life; the desire for a better house and more comforts cannot simply be dismissed as 'embourgeoisement'; workers did not necessarily buy with them a package of 'middle-class values'. Also technological change, such as the growing availability of steam power to independent craftsmen, necessitated a more regular working week. In ways not yet fully understood, work discipline and a more 'respectable' style of life came to be equated with working-class independence, rather than seen as inimical to it.

This major cultural transformation is still far from being understood, but it has not been greatly illuminated by the use of categories borrowed, sometimes with excessive crudeness, from sociology, such as simplified notions of class or class conflict, or concepts such as 'embourgeoisement' or 'social control'.[53] Their use may oversimplify the processes involved, tend to interpret the change as a one-way imposition 'from above', underestimating the element of negotiation between the social groups involved, which was real, unequal though the sides generally were. Reid emphasizes that different groups of workers responded differently for reasons only partially dependent upon their occupational position. Employers, clergy and politicians *were* anxious to control them, but could do so with only limited success, and they met resistance. Many of the changes resulted not from conscious controls but from the unpredicted outcomes of technological and other economic changes. Reid's analysis of one feature of social change demonstrates how an apparently limited study can raise and begin to answer major questions about the central historical problems of how power in its broadest sense—the power to change the whole way of life of individuals—was constructed and sustained in the nineteenth century, and about how this is to be approached.

An important part in the process of negotiation about power relationships was played by social protest, with which social historians have long been preoccupied. Williams's lyrical representation of the recent flowering of Welsh social and labour history,[54] which he has done much to stimulate, raises many issues relating to work of this kind, for England as for Wales, and indeed is subtly critical of many of the pieties afflicting it in the recent past. He points out that the widespread and unprecedented Welsh popular movements of the 1820s and 1830s, culminating in Chartism, united people across a great variety of occupations and ways of life; people living indeed simultaneously 'on quite different time scales', from hill shepherd to quarryman to tinplate worker, yet all capable of responding to the same political appeal. These were not, as they have sometimes been interpreted, simply movements of factory proletarians or of declining occupational groups, responding to the impact of emerging industrialism. Hence Williams challenges any simple picture of Welsh social structure, commenting on the 'fluidity and class incoherence' of the membership of protest movements, and any simple correspondence between economic experience and political thought and action. Indeed he insists that 'it is necessary not to see modes of production advancing in pre-ordained column of route', carrying with it predictable packages of political beliefs. Rather, inhabitants of different economic time scales could all respond to one set of democratic ideals, born of the eighteenth century and crystallized among American artisans. Williams identifies what united them as a struggle for control over their lives, in a society which was eroding independence in a variety of ways: through economic change, and changes in legal and political institutions which diminished traditional channels for the assertion of popular rights. He describes, as Edward Thompson has done for England, how a common awareness of the erosion of independence and a common solution—popular democracy—were built through non-economic cultural links, through for example religious associations, which brought people together initially for non-political purposes but which could lead to recognition of common grievances.

This raises the question of whether what was 'made' by the 1830s, for Wales as for England, was a 'working class' in any useful sense, or a radical movement best characterized in some other way; perhaps in the terms suggested by Stedman Jones in his reassessment of Chartism: as a democratic movement prepared to embrace all of the 'people', including large and small employers, against the minority of wielders of political power, which only reluctantly and of necessity became a movement of independent craftsmen and wage earners, with minimal ideological commitment to such social exclusiveness.[55] This is the more important because Williams points out how obscure are the links between participants in this turbulent early radicalism and the sober non-conformist, Liberal, Welsh workers of the later nineteenth century. Whatever was 'made' in the earlier period was later broken, by processes the obscurity of which he recognizes (though Reid's contribution suggests what some of them might have been and Stedman Jones carries the discussion considerably further, giving particular prominence to the changing role of the State from the 1840s). Williams dismisses, however, explanations which have enjoyed a certain vogue in the past decade: the emergence of new agencies of control, such as police or schooling, or of new divisions among workers, in particular the emergence or creation of a 'labour aristocracy' of superior, less militant, workers.

Although he does not develop the latter points, Williams's contribution is symptomatic of growing current scepticism about simplified notions of Victorian social classification with which historians have operated in the past. For example, closer empirical scrutiny—to which both Reid's and Roberts's essays are contributions—is casting doubt on the existence of a clearly definable group of secure skilled workers with distinctive social and political characteristics, a 'labour aristocracy' capable of playing the moderating role once ascribed to it. Instead, the picture which is emerging is of a society more complex, more finely graded, with greater overlapping and shifting of living standards, cultural norms and political attitudes among more and less skilled workers, and others, than has been assumed.[56]

Williams also provides a particularly good example of the tradition, already referred to, of writing 'people's history' for a mass audience, aiming to politicize by informing working people of their past. Its most influential recent manifestation is History Workshop. At its worst, such work can be mere antiquarian celebration of the working-class past. At its best, as in the hands of Raphael Samuel, the inspiration behind History Workshop, it can yoke careful, empirical investigation with stimulating evocation of the reality of the past. In his study of rural labour in this volume Samuel reminds us how much we do not know, and how little such an apparently obvious source as the census can tell us, about the largest occupational group of the nineteenth century—agricultural workers—and about the variety of their activities.[57]

An important characteristic of the study of working-class history in the past decade has been a shift from an older tradition of studying the working class through its institutions—trade unions and political movements—and the biographies of labour leaders to a concern with the culture and experience of working people, organized and unorganized. In part this arose from dissatisfaction with the narrow focus of previous labour history and its consequent failure to generate satisfactory explanations of the existence and nature of such movements.[58] There was much to be dissatisfied with in this history, but not perhaps enough to account for the extent of its rejection. The work of Hobsbawm and Pelling, for example, *did* seek to locate working-class movements in the context of a broader understanding of working-class experience.[59] The failure to follow this lead has to be understood in terms of the particular preoccupations of the British Left in the early seventies, in particular the disillusionment with labour institutions which characterized it. The rejection of the history of organized movements went too far. They have had a certain historical importance, which needs to be understood; and there are signs, as McLean's contribution to this collection suggests, that the study of industrial relations and of working-class political movements is reviving. What it has gained from recent trends is a widening of focus; a willingness to place such studies in the context of workers' experience, including the (previously surprisingly neglected) study of work itself;[60] and, as already suggested, embodying greater scepticism about the previously assumed correspondence between trade union participation and political conviction.

Another weakness of the older labour history, which historians have been slower to rectify, was its failure to recognize that industrial relations had two sides: that not only workers but also employers need to be understood in order to understand strikes, trade unions and much else. More broadly in social history, the excessive concentration upon the working class has left the remainder of society either absent or presented as stereotyped wielders of power in stereotyped ways. This has been detrimental not only to the study of industrial relations but to the understanding of much, probably most, that went on in the past. At last historians show signs of serious study of those other than manual workers, as in this volume Crossick does for the lower middle class, Hay for employers, Rubinstein for the wealthy, and in the work of R. J. Morris, among others, on the middle class of the first half of the nineteenth century.[61]

Hay illustrates, as have others, that employers cannot be interpreted as a united social or political force, in the 1900s or before. They were acutely disunited on most political issues in ways not simply explicable by their relationship to market forces or with the labour force. They could influence *[margin handwritten notes: Hay (cont.) criticising of earlier studies of history of social policy prior which Hay's work breaks]*

government policy, as Hay illustrates from his discussion of social policy, but as just one of the many strands from which policy was woven. Hay's contribution is also a very good example of how in the past decade studies of the history of social policy have moved out of their previous confinement within administrative history and the whiggish concern for origins of the modern welfare state, analytically restricted to assumptions of progress and the essentially beneficent, redistributive, intent of welfare reforms. Here also, closer empirical study has revealed both the complexity of motive behind the making of policy—in which the furtherance of social stability and economic efficiency were at least as influential as the desire to alleviate poverty—and the ambiguities of its effects.[62] It has become clearer that such studies can illuminate attitudes to the State and the processes by which its role has expanded in modern times; suggest which individuals and groups influenced its actions; and explore the nature of its relationship with the individual. It is much more difficult for social historians of the twentieth century than of earlier periods to neglect the study of the role of the State, so central has it become to the regulation of social conditions, industrial relations and much else.

This raises a central question for historians, of precisely who did wield power, and how, in modern Britain. Plainly, from the accounts of Hay and others, if political power lay in the hands of any social group by the later nineteenth century it was not exclusively those of the industrial bourgeoisie. Rubinstein argues that a reason for this is that they were not as wealthy as has been assumed. He points out that historians of all persuasions have assumed that, in the most industrialized country in the world, industrialists must have been among the wealthiest and most powerful. He demonstrates that, on the contrary, the greatest wealth in nineteenth- and twentieth-century Britain was concentrated among landowners and London-based financiers rather than among northern industrialists, that there were few points of contact between holders of commercial and industrial wealth and that the financial and commercial rich had closer social ties with the political and landowning élite than did all but a minority of large industrialists.

A difficulty with Rubinstein's argument is the too-straightforward equation of wealth with power; in particular the precise power of the financiers of the City of London has been the subject of more myth and polemic than of substantial research. The importance of his work, however, lies in the questions it raises about the nature and composition of British élites, in suggesting that simplified conceptions of social structure are as unhelpful for the study of the upper classes as of the working class, as is any simple equation between economic role and political power.

One response to the discovery that the British State was not after all the executive committee of the employing class has been a revived fashion, especially among American historians, for stressing the continued social and political dominance of older landowning élites, to 1914 and beyond; that they succeeded in 'feudalizing' the new bourgeoisie, drawing them in to their own 'traditional' system of values, a parallel process to the assumed 'embourgeoisement' of workers.[63] Again, this usefully draws attention to the gradualness of change in the nineteenth century and to the problem of analysing the relationship between socially prominent groups. But just to turn an old simplification on its head risks introducing new distortions. Certainly in Britain, well into the twentieth century, members of ancient families remained prominent in the major centres of power (though fewer, and less prominent, the more closely they are investigated); but a landed aristocracy which had initiated the capitalization of agriculture and major infrastructural developments in the eighteenth century, and kept an acute eye on its investments thereafter, whilst running a government unquestionably supportive of a successful industrial economy, is not easily characterized as a repository of quasi-feudal values.[64] Again, too great stress upon apparent structural continuity may mask real change. If we are to understand the relative importance of landowners, financiers and other businessmen in relation to one another and to those below, these relationships need to be examined in greater detail and in less stereotyped ways. Though landowners remained powerful and prominent in 1914, they manifestly did not wield as much independent power as a century before. By 1914 a great hereditary landowner had more in common with a banker or steelmaster than with his *ancien régime* ancestor, though he had not merged with them into a clearly-identifiable ruling bloc. For the England of the later eighteenth century it may be reasonable to speak of a 'ruling class', in the sense that a clearly definable group of landowners wielded political, economic and social power. Everyone knew it, and of whom it was composed. In ways which remain to be explored, by the early twentieth century the landowners had become one of a constellation of highly influential élites. New élites had emerged which transcended the old and which cannot adequately be characterized as 'aristocratic' or 'bourgeois'.[65] Their relationships with one another, on what issues they agreed and disagreed and the relative significance of each, remain even less clear than our understanding of similar divisions within the working class and of their importance.

One of the strengths of social history in the past decade has been its willingness to pose and to begin to solve problems of this kind, which are as important for understanding political as social history. The starting-point for such questions has generally been the overwhelming preoccupation of British social historians with class and especially with the working class and its politics. The strong, and interestingly uniform, influence of functionalist sociology and of Marxism in this period has had the—by no means unavoidable—effect of encouraging much of this history to be written within a framework of rather rigid assumptions about the nature of social structure and its relationship with economic and political processes. The contributions to this volume suggest that such assumptions have not always been helpful and that they have come increasingly to be questioned. The picture of 'classes' which emerges from all of them is of groups which were acutely internally divided, vertically and horizontally. Other work has suggested the importance for society of other divisions: between religious allegiances, and between successive generations shaped by quite different formative experiences.[66] Similarly, the vertical ties of 'influence' between urban workers and employers, or between landowners, farmers and labourers, could create significantly variable political and cultural attitudes among people in the same occupational group.[67]

This raises the central question for historians of what 'class' actually means. Much social history has been written on the basis of the assumption that we know, and understand, the broad outlines of modern social structure. It looks increasingly as though we do not. Perhaps the time has come to abandon the terminology of class for a while, or at least to treat it with some scepticism, as at most an ideal type, reworked and developed to take account of a much wider and more subtle range of social formations; to stand back and interpret more dispassionately the actual experience of the nineteenth and twentieth centuries, out of which might come some greater under- standing of the meaning and uses of class. At some level of abstraction it had, and has, some meaning; the task is to discover what. Some time ago Edward Thompson berated sociologists for their static definition of class and pointed out that 'the crude notion of class attributed to Marx can be faulted without difficulty'. He went on: 'if we stop history at a given point, then there are no classes but simply a multitude of individuals with a multitude of experiences. But if we watch these men over an adequate period of social change, we observe patterns in their relationships, their ideas and institutions.'[68] For all Thompson's great influence upon recent social historiography there have been few attempts to explore whether this statement has a meaning which can be applied.

It could be objected that if the meaning of class is obscure to historians it was less so to contemporaries, who kept talking about class and class conflict; a variety of social groups created self-conscious institutions for the promo- tion of 'class' interests. But, as McLean's contribution suggests, contempo- rary perceptions of class conflict could be wrong, both on the Left and the Right, grounded in revolutionary optimism and anti-revolutionary fears rather than in understanding of actual social formations and attitudes. And the problem, as the work of Williams, Stedman Jones and Crossick demon- strates, is still precisely to understand the nature of institutions and move- ments assumed to be class based, rather than to proceed from the supposition that we know; to ask how, why and in what circumstances, individuals and groups demonstrably much divided in terms of their experiences come together to assert some sense of commonly held interest; how and why, for example, the deprived and subordinate, who *always* have potential cause for protest, only on rare occasions organize to do so.

In important respects, then, the map of social history is in the process of being redrawn. Central to the shift which is occurring, as the essays in this volume suggest, is a move away from 'class' as the central organizing concept for much historical work to an experiential dimension which is, within the limitations of current terminology, best defined as 'cultural'.[69] 'Culture' is a term which is in danger of being thrown around with the same imprecise abandon that 'class' has been, but if we remain alive to the dangers it will at least temporarily be useful. 'Class', for all the social implications it has acquired, is rooted in the assumption that social and political behaviour is in some sense determined by economic experience. The development of the concept by the classical economists was complemented by Marx's addition of the political dimension. However, in this century the growth of sociology, psychology and anthropology have increased our awareness of non-economic motivations for human behaviour. The search for a new framework for social analysis has been encouraged by awareness of the growing importance of the State-citizenship relationship in addition to the employer-employee relationship. Also important has been realization of recent changes in technology and in the structure of demand in Britain which have diminished the size of the manual workforce and have increased the size and heterogeneity of the middle class, a minority of them insignificant wielders of power, fewer still sizeable owners of capital. There has also been growing awareness of divisions in British society—notably those of race and gender—which are not readily reducible to class divisions. And historians have become more alive to the need to explain *absence* of class conflict and the capacity of subordinate groups for 'putting up with it' in the face of profound social differences.

Historical materialism was for a while able to incorporate these phenomena within concepts expressing, to a greater or lesser degree, interdependence between an economic 'base' and a 'superstructure', the outlines of which could be varied by non-economic influences without calling into question the presence of the base. The work of Gramsci aided this modulation, in particular by introducing the concept of 'hegemony', meaning literally 'leadership' or 'predominance', and emobodying a conception of the capacity of the ruling élite to impose its values upon society through cultural and political as well as economic institutions. This explanation of the tenacity of capitalist society has increasingly replaced rudimentary Leninism, because, for all its ambiguities, Gramsci's is not a crude conspiracy or control model. It allows a degree of autonomy to subordinate groups, for elements of negotiation, without abandoning awareness of the difference between the more and less powerful. Hence

Marxists as well as non-Marxists have been drawn further down the path opened by Edward Thompson, though not without disagreement.[70] They have moved towards paying closer attention to significant social phenomena which too rigid a class interpretation can overlook or underestimate, such as gender and religion or nationalism and regionalism. The emphasis on 'culture' is an acknowledgement that behaviour, political or otherwise, cannot be explained just by examining economic and political experiences but requires a wider understanding of experiences, ideas, language and relationships. It can lead, as Furet warns in respect of the fashion for the history of *mentalités*,[71] to absorption in trivia, to a collapse into descriptive narrative compilations of facts. This is a real danger of the current stress upon the complexities of social processes. But the complexities are real and one of the tasks of the historian is to make sense of them. The danger is avoidable if 'cultural' history retains a clear awareness of the central historical questions on which it bears. Cultural history, like social history, has been developed mainly in relation to subordinate cultures, although the work of Cannadine, F. M. L. Thompson and Wiener on landowners and that of R. J. Morris on the middle classes demonstrates its wider potential just as Morishima's work on Japan suggests how a cultural approach can enrich understanding of economic as well as of political and social change.[72]

Over the past two decades British social history has changed and developed in ways that we have tried, inadequately, to describe. In doing so it has opened up new approaches which historians in other countries have only recently begun to follow. There are, however, respects in which it has developed insufficiently. One of these is a certain, potentially dangerous, insularity. British historians have not been fully responsive to autonomous developments in social history in other countries. They have also been remarkably unconcerned to relate the British historical experience to those of other societies. For example Chartism, the industrial conflicts preceding and following the First World War, the development of the Welfare State, among others, have been perceived, even celebrated, as uniquely British experiences dissociated from similar contemporaneous developments elsewhere. Hence certain potential insights have been lost. It would be a pity if, as Britain itself becomes ever more marginal to world affairs, her historiography did so also.

NOTES

Pat Thane would like to thank Alastair Reid and the History Department seminar of the University of Essex for their comments on an earlier draft of her contribution to this Introduction.

1. The first volume was Flinn, M. W. and Smout, T. C. (eds.), *Essays in Social History* (Oxford, 1974).

2. Plumb's appraisal of the progress of social history first appeared in Arthur Marwick, *British Society Since 1945* (Harmondsworth, 1982), 8 – 9.

3. Wrightson, K., *English Society, 1580 – 1640* (London, 1982), 9.

4. Hobsbawm, E. J., 'From Social History to the History of Society', in Flinn and Smout, 1 – 22.

5. *Daedalus*, c (1971), 20 – 45.

6. Samuel, R., 'People's history', in Samuel (ed.), *Peoples' History and Socialist Theory* (London, 1981) xv – xxxix.

7. Above all in his *The Making of the English Working Class* (London, 1963).

8. 'Notre époque est volontiers portée vers une recherche de l'histoire totale, autrement dit vers une compréhension du passé appréhendé sous les différents aspects qu'a pu avoir, pour les hommes aux fonctions les plus diverses, la réalité vécue dans la complexité du temps qui passe.' Favier, J., 'Préface', in Lanhers, Y., *Archives du Château de Saint-Fargeau: Inventaire* (Paris, 1981), 7.

9. Furet, F., 'Beyond the Annales', *Journal of Modern History*, 1v (1983), 390.

10. Ibid., 394.

11. For example, David Braund's *Rome and the Friendly King* (London, 1983) incorporates political and military events into a model of the relationship between the Roman Empire and its client kings, in which the roles of the latter are rooted in the social conditions prevailing both on the periphery of the Empire and in Roman society itself.

12. Macfarlane, A., *The Origins of English Individualism: The Family, Property and Social Transition* (Oxford, 1978). For discussion of the themes of this book see White, S. D. and Vann, K. T., 'The Invention of English Individualism: Alan Macfarlane and the Modernization of Pre-Modern England', *Social History*, viii (1983), 345 – 63, and the review by Keith Wrightson in *History*, lxv (1980), 87.

13. Flinn and Smout, 5.

14. Briggs, A., *A Social History of England* (London, 1983), p. 8.

15. Furet, 405.

16. Jones, G. S., *Languages of Class: Studies in English Working-Class History, 1832 – 1982* (Cambridge, 1983), 3 – 4.

17. Hill, C., Hilton, R. H. and Hobsbawm, E. J., 'Origins and Early Years', *Past and Present*, c (1983), 3 – 13.

18. See, e.g. Elias, N., *The Court Society* (Oxford, 1983), 1 – 34.

19. For example, Anderson, M., *Family Structure in Nineteenth-Century Lancashire* (Cambridge, 1971).

20. Flinn and Smout, ix.

21. Davis, N. Z., 'Anthropology and History in the Nineteen-Eighties: The Possibilities of the Past', *Journal of Interdisciplinary History*, xii (1981 – 2), 274.

22. Davis, N. Z., 'The Rites of Violence: Religious Riot in Sixteenth-Century France', *Past and Present*, lix (1973), 51 – 91; 'The Sacred and the Body Social in Sixteenth-Century Lyon', *Past and Present*, xc (1981), 40 – 70.

23. Thomas, K., *Religion and the Decline of Magic* (London, 1971); Macfarlane, A., *Witchcraft in Tudor and Stuart England: A Regional and Comparative Study* (London, 1970).

24. See, e.g. Quadagno, J., *Aging in Early Industrial Society: Work, Family and Social Policy in Nineteenth-Century England* (London, 1982); Gittings, C., *Death,*

Burial and the Individual in Early Modern England (London, 1984); Gillis, J. R., *Youth and History: Tradition and Change in European Age Relations, 1770 – Present* (London, 1981).

25. See Below, p. 53.

26. Laslett, P. and Wall, R. (eds.), *Household and Family in Past Time* (Cambridge, 1972).

27. For example, those of Anderson and Macfarlane, cited above, and of L. Davidoff in this volume.

28. Parker, H. I., 'Concluding Remarks', *Social Research*, xlvii (1980), 589 – 90.

29. Thompson, 12 – 13.

30. Burnett, J., *Useful Toil* (London, 1974); Vincent, D., *Bread, Knowledge and Freedom: A Study of Nineteenth-Century Working-Class Autobiography* (London, 1981).

31. Judt, T., 'A Clown in Regal Purple: Social History and the Historian', *History Workshop*, vii (1979), 66 – 94; Eley, G. and Nield, K., 'Why Does Social History Ignore Politics?', *Social History*, v (1983), 249 – 71.

32. Flinn and Smout, 5.

33. For example, Brewer, J. and Styles, J. (eds.), *An Ungovernable People* (London, 1980); Wrightson, op. cit.

34. See below, p. 58.

35. See the recently published survey by John Stevenson, *British Society, 1914 – 45* (Harmondsworth, 1984).

36. For example, Obelkevitch, J., *Religion and Rural Society: South Lindsey, 1625 – 1875* (Oxford, 1970); McLeod, H., *Class and Religion in the Late Victorian City* (London, 1974).

37. See the bibliographical essay by Victor Bailey, 'Crime, Criminal Justice and Authority in England', *Bulletin of the Society for the Study of Labour History*, xl (1980), 36 – 46; and Bailey, V. (ed.), *Policing and Punishment in Nineteenth-Century Britain* (London, 1981).

38. See, e.g. Winter, J., 'Unemployment, Nutrition and Infant Mortality in Britain, 1920 – 1950', in Winter, J. (ed.), *The Working Class in Modern British History: Essays in Honour of Henry Pelling* (Cambridge, 1983); Webster, C., 'Healthy or Hungry Thirties?', *History Workshop Journal*, xiii (1982), 110 – 29.

39. Wrigley, E. A. and Schofield, R. S., *The Population History of England, 1541 – 1871* (London, 1981).

40. The intermediate character of much of the 'urban history' of the 1960s and 1970s is perceptively discussed by David Cannadine, 'Urban History in the United Kingdom: the "Dyos Phenomenon" and After', in Cannadine, D. and Reeder, D. (eds.), *Exploring the Urban Past: Essays in Urban History by H.J. Dyos* (Cambridge, 1981), 203 – 22.

41. See also McKendrick, N., 'Home Demand and Economic Growth: A New View of the Role of Women and Children in the Industrial Revolution', in McKendrick, N. (ed.), *Historical Perspectives. Studies in English Thought and Society: Essays in Honour of J. H. Plumb* (London, 1974).

42. Reid, A., 'Intelligent Artisans and Aristocrats of Labour: The Essays of Thomas Wright', in Winter, J.M. (ed.), *The Working Class in Modern British History: Essays in Honour of Henry Pelling* (Cambridge, 1983), 171 – 86.

43. Branca, P., *Silent Sisterhood* (London, 1975).

44. Hammerton, A. J., *Emigrant Gentlewomen* (London, 1979).

45. Prochaska, F., *Women and Philanthropy in Victorian England* (Oxford, 1981).

46. Harrison, B., *Separate Spheres: The Opposition to Women's Suffrage in Britain* (London, 1971).

47. Weeks, J., *Politics and Society: The Regulation of Sexuality Since 1800* (London, 1981).

48. Scott, J. W., 'Survey Article: Women in History, II: The Modern Period', *Past and Present*, 101 (1983), 141 – 57.

49. Thompson, P., *The Voice of the Past: Oral History* (Oxford, 1978).

50. Medick, H., 'Plebeian Culture in the Transition to Capitalism', in Samuel, R. and Jones, G. S. (eds.), *Culture, Ideology and Politics: Essays for Eric Hobsbawm* (London, 1982), 84 – 112.

51. Berg, M., Hudson, P., and Sonenscher, M. (ed.), *Manufacture in Town and Country Before the Factory* (Cambridge, 1983).

52. Storch, R. D. (ed.), *Popular Culture and Custom in Nineteenth-Century England* (London, 1982); Thompson, F. M. L., 'Social Control in Victorian Britain', *Economic History Review*, 2nd Ser. xxxiv (1981), 189 – 208.

53. For discussion see Donajgrodski, A., *Social Control in Nineteenth-Century Britain* (London, 1977); Jones, G. S., 'Class Expression Versus Social Control: A Critique of Recent Trends in the Social History of Leisure', in *Languages of Class,* op. cit.

54. See *inter alia* the other contributions to Smith, D. (ed.), *A People and a Proletariat: Essays in the History of Wales, 1780 – 1980,* from which the Williams essay is taken.

55. Jones, G. S., 'The Language of Chartism', in Epstein, J. and Thompson, D. (eds.), *The Chartist Experience* (London, 1982), 3 – 58; and also in 'Class Expression Versus Social Control', loc. cit.

56. Reid, 'Intelligent Artisans and Aristocrats of Labour', loc. cit.; Harrison, R. and Zeitlin, J. (eds.), *Divisions of Labour: Skilled Workers and Technological Changes in Nineteenth-Century Britain* (Brighton, 1985).

57. For some interesting comments on the limitations of the census as a source for occupational quantification, see Higgs, E., 'Domestic Servants and Households in Victorian England', *Social History*, viii (1983), 201 – 10.

58. Eley and Nield, loc. cit.

59. Hobsbawm, E. J., *Labouring Men* (London, 1964); Pelling, H., *Popular Politics and Society in Late Victorian Britain* (London, 1969).

60. Zeitlin, J., 'Craft Control and the Division of Labour: Engineers and Compositors in Britain, 1890 – 1930', *Cambridge Journal of Economics,* iii (1979), 263 – 74; Lazonick, W., 'Industrial Relations and Technical Change: The Case of the Self-Acting Mule', ibid., 231 – 62.

61. Morris, R. J., 'Voluntary Societies and British Urban Elites, 1780 – 1850', *Historical Journal,* xxvi (1983), 95 – 118.

62. See e.g. Harris, J., *Unemployment and Politics: A Study in English Social Policy, 1886 – 1914* (Oxford, 1972); *William Beveridge* (Oxford, 1972); Thane, P. (ed.), *Origins of British Social Policy* (London, 1972); *The Foundations of the Welfare State* (London, 1982).

63. Mayer, A., *The Persistence of the Old Regime* (London, 1981); Wiener, M. J., *English Culture and the Decline of the Industrial Spirit* (Cambridge, 1981).

64. Thompson, F. M. L., 'English Landed Society in the Nineteenth Century', in Thane, P., Crossick, G. and Floud, R. (eds.), *The Power of the Past: Essays for Eric Hobsbawm* (Cambridge, 1984), 195 – 214; Rubinstein, W. D., 'New Men of Wealth and the Purchase of Land in Nineteenth-Century England', *Past and Present,* xcii (1981), 125 – 47.

65. Cannadine, D., *Lords and Landlords: The Aristocracy and the Towns, 1774 – 1967* (Leicester, 1980) contains some interesting observations on this theme. See also Harris, J. and Thane, P., 'British and European Bankers, 1880 – 1914: An Aristocratic Bourgeoisie', in *The Power of the Past,* 215 – 34.

66. See Reid, A., loc. cit.

67. Moore, D. C., *The Politics of Deference* (Hassocks, 1976); Joyce, P., *Work, Society and Politics* (Hassocks, 1980).

68. Thompson, *The Making of the English Working Class,* 10 – 11.

69. See e.g. Storch, *Popular Culture and Custom;* Yeo, E. and S. (eds.), *Popular Culture and Class Conflict: Explorations in the History of Labour and Leisure* (Hassocks, 1981); Waites, D., Bennett, T. and Martin, G. (eds.), *Popular Culture: Past and Present* (London, 1982).

70. Jones, G. S., 'Introduction', in *Languages of Class,* 1 – 24; Nield, K., 'A Symptomatic Dispute? Notes on the relation between Marxian Theory and Historical Practice in Britain', *Social Research,* xlvii (1980), 479 – 506; Johnson, R., 'Thompson, Genovese and Socialist-humanist History', *History Workshop Journal,* vi (1978), 79 – 100, and the debate which followed in later issues.

71. Furet, loc. cit., 404 – 5.

72. Morishima, M., *Why Has Japan 'Succeeded'?: Western Technology and the Japanese Ethos* (Cambridge, 1982).

1

The Demographic Implications of Rural Industrialization: A Family Reconstitution Study of Shepshed, Leicestershire, 1600–1851*

DAVID LEVINE

In the debate about the growth of population during the first Industrial Revolution contending critics could be said to agree on one single point: that sustained growth began around 1750 and then continued unabated for more than a century afterwards. However, there has been a great deal of argument surrounding the causes of this radical demographic discontinuity. This disagreement revolves around the relative importance of a falling death rate and a rising birth rate—although it should be pointed out that no convincing evidence has ever been put forward to show that either the death rate fell or that the birth rate rose, let alone a description of the magnitude of these supposed changes. It could be said that so far almost as much heat as light has been generated by the contributors as they have attempted to buttress their contentions by referring to aggregated totals of births and deaths (or, to be more precise, baptisms and burials). Leaving aside the difficulties concerning the reliability of the various series of aggregated figures, the great problem with this method of inquiry has been that vital rates derived from aggregated totals do not distinguish between the various components of mortality and fertility. For instance, using an aggregative analysis we do not know if a rise in the birth rate was caused by higher fertility, a lower age at marriage, a higher incidence of marriage, lower parental mortality, higher infant mortality leading to shorter birth intervals, higher levels of illegitimacy, or any other cause or combination of causes. Another method of demographic analysis, family reconstitution, provides a solution to this problem of specifying the nature of population growth. Family reconstitution involves

* From *Social History*, 2 (1976), 177–96. Reprinted by permission of the author and the editors of *Social History*.

the re-creation of families ('demographic units of production') from the entries of baptisms, burials and marriages recorded in the parish register. But because this procedure is so time-consuming, we pay for our more exact information by having to focus our attention very narrowly. I have tried to get round this problem by *purposefully* selecting for examination a village at one end of the socio-economic spectrum in order to test the explanation which sees the acceleration of economic differentiation and social stratification as the critical factor undermining the pre-industrial demographic equilibrium.

The argument put forward in this essay is that economic change undermined the influence of traditional social controls which had maintained a homeostatic balance, a demographic equilibrium, in which one generation replaced its predecessor. In so far as economic independence had been a necessary pre-condition to marriage, the age at marriage was kept high because of the inelastic demand for labour in the pre-industrial economy. Members of the younger generation were expected to wait until their father's retirement or death before they assumed control over the family farm or workshop. For this reason peasants and artisans adopted a prudent approach to marriage. Older brides were often preferred because they not only had a shorter child-bearing period but their experience in farmwork and domestic duties were economic assets of some importance—these factors were of real significance among the poorer members of society. The transformation of peasants and artisans into agricultural and industrial proletarians resulted in the estrangement of growing sections of society from traditional controls which had previously been effective measures of maintaining an optimum population size. In this way the employment of proletarianized labour is of critical importance in understanding the demographic response to the first Industrial Revolution.

The social dislocation accompanying proletarianization occasioned a fall in the age at marriage—the linchpin of the pre-industrial demographic equilibrium—in two ways: traditional sanctions against early marriage were weakened and those groups who married early became proportionately more important while late-marrying groups became less important. In addition to extending the years of child-bearing, a fall in the age at marriage also shortened the interval between generations so that more children were born per unit of time. In this way a declining age at marriage produced a significant increase in the birth rate even in the absence of any change in fertility. It should be stressed, however, that proletarianization did not necessarily lead to a fall in the age at marriage, it only removed the disincentive to early marriage. The factor which led to earlier and more frequent marriages was the opportunity for employment offered by proto-industrial activity and capitalist farming. Arthur Young, the traveller and polemicist, remarked that 'It is employment that creates population: marriages are early and numerous in proportion to the amount of employment.'[1] This idea was commonplace among eighteenth-century social commentators; Young was joined in this belief by such unlikely bedfellows as Charles Davenant,[2] Adam Smith,[3] and Thomas Malthus,[4] who all saw the demand for labour as the most important variable in their contemporary demographic equation. In these new circumstances it was becoming ever more likely that the factors influencing the demand for labour were being determined outside the locale. This exogenous influence upon the village-level demand for labour was an important development because it was withdrawing large sections of the rural population from the relatively self-contained regional economy and was integrating them into a national or even world-wide division of labour. Thus, the well-being of rural proletarians could be determined by trade fluctuations or, more ominously, by the vagaries of international diplomacy and its logical extension, war. The demographic importance of this development is obvious—the decision to marry was being determined with reference to conditions beyond the betrothed couple's control and understanding.

The demographic profile of the proletarianized population was characterized by high rates of natural increase: early marriage and a long fertile period combined to produce a substantial rise in completed family size. This rise was of such a magnitude that it far outstripped the 'positive check' afforded by the higher levels of mortality that prevailed among the inhabitants of rural slums. Moreover, the high rates of natural increase had the further effect of altering the population's age-distribution by increasing the proportion below child-bearing age. A more broadly based age-pyramid meant that the size of the next cohort entering the marriage market was substantially larger than its predecessor. In this way population growth developed a self-sustaining impetus.

The causal arrows did not merely flow in one direction: economic activity transformed demographic conditions but, equally, there was a reciprocal movement in the other direction as population growth influenced the organization of production. Not only were the workers replacing themselves at a very rapid rate but any sustained period of prosperity occasioned both an increase in the number of marriages and an influx of new workers into the area. For these reasons labour costs were kept at a low level. As long as labour was both cheap and plentiful there was little incentive to undertake capital investments in order to raise productivity. Low wages meant that primitive techniques were most profitable while this low-level technology was labour-intensive so that cheap labour was of critical importance. In effect, these factors created the kind of vicious circle that has been called 'involution'.[5]

In this essay the interplay of economic and demographic change will be examined in the light of information gathered from the family reconstitution study of Shepshed, Leicestershire, between 1600 and 1851.[6] In the course of the eighteenth century Shepshed became the most intensively industrialized village in the county—the framework knitting industry was organized on a domestic system so that the whole family was integrated into the production processes. Shepshed was an unregulated freehold village on the edge of Charnwood Forest in which social control was very weak: there were five separate non-conformist congregations and the village was a centre of socio-political discontent, deeply involved in both Luddism and 'physical-force' Chartism.[7] Historians have argued that rural industrialization usually became important in areas where an impoverished population found it necessary to supplement its inadequate income.[8] The evidence derived from an analysis of surviving probate inventories lends support to such an argument in which the poverty of Shepshed's peasants was an important pre-condition to its subsequent industrialization.[9] An examination of later seventeenth-century probate inventories suggested that this population was poverty-stricken in comparison with the rural population in eastern Leicestershire, an area which remained steadfastly rural. Not only were the Shepshed peasants' estates small but much of their land was of an inferior quality: as much as half of the village acreage was in Charnwood Forest and was described as being 'rocky and stony, yielding fruit not without great labour and expences'.[10] The fact that so much land was quite unsuitable for intensive husbandry meant that the village population exerted substantial pressure on its fertile land. In the villages of Leicestershire there was a very strong correlation between the location of domestic industry and the pattern of landownership: all fifteen villages with over 240 knitting frames in 1844 were freehold townships while fifteen of the nineteen villages with between 121 and 240 knitting frames were also freeholders' villages.[11] In Shepshed the concentration of landed property was in an advanced state but the principal landowning family seemed to have been either unwilling or unable to exert rigid control over the village. The Phillips family had been of local importance in the village since 1683 when they bought the lordship of the manor of Shepshed. In the Land Tax returns for the period 1780–1832 they paid about half of the tax for Shepshed. Perhaps the village's proximity to the common lands of Charnwood Forest and the very large number of small landowners combined to frustrate any attempts to dominate parochial affairs. In the 1832 Land Tax there were 249 other landowners.[12] Many of these people owned tiny parcels of land less than an acre. Such tiny holdings, and the comparatively high landowner/family ratio (in 1831 there were 769 families of whom roughly one in three owned a piece of land) would seem to suggest that partible inheritance was the prevalent way in which land was passed from one generation to the next. Joan Thirsk has argued that a system of divided inheritance was an important feature of villages in which rural industries took root.[13]

In its first phase of development the framework knitting industry was essentially a London-based trade with a subsidiary centre of production in the East Midlands.[14] Production was confined to the manufacture of luxury goods, mainly embroidered silk stockings, which enabled a small group of London merchant-hosiers to dominate the industry by maintaining close contact with changing fashions. In 1663 this oligarchy secured a royal patent of incorporation empowering the Worshipful Company of Framework Knitters to exercise control over the whole industry. Through the use and abuse of their legally sanctioned powers the small group of London merchant-hosiers dominated the industry for the next sixty years. However, this power proved to be illusory. Even in the later seventeenth century hosiers were moving from London to the East Midlands in order to benefit from the lower labour costs and the relative freedom from the Company's interferences: in 1669 over 60 per cent of the frames were in London, by 1714 this figure had dropped to 31 per cent and in 1753 just 7 per cent of all knitting frames were in London. Moreover, the absolute number of frames in the capital had also declined from 2,500 in 1714 to 1,000 in 1753.

The movement away from London was undermining the Company's power and influence. With the advent of 'mass production' the provincial hosiers demanded a free hand in their dealings with labour but they were frustrated by the Company's restrictive apprenticeship regulations. Many of the provincial hosiers took matters into their own hands and disregarded the edicts of the London-based Company. In 1730 the Company acted against two Nottingham hosiers, Fellows and Cartwright, who were commanded to reduce their apprentices from forty-nine and twenty-three to three each. They refused to comply with this ruling and were fined £400 and £150. When they also refused to pay these fines the Company seized their property as indemnification. In response to this provocation, the Nottingham hosiers sought legal redress against the Company for trespass. Fellows and Cartwright won their suit and there were no longer any enforceable regulations controlling labour relations in the industry as the Company's authority was destroyed.

The expansion of the industry throughout western Leicestershire was very rapid and coincided with the transition from a journeyman's trade to one in which capitalist labour relations predominated and cheap labour was the critical factor. In Shepshed the framework knitting industry was first mentioned in 1655 when the burial of Thomas Trowell, 'silkstocking wever', was recorded in the parish register but the real commitment to industrialization did not come until the second quarter of the eighteenth century. In 1701 – 9 just 4 per cent of the entries in the parish register referred to framework knitters (or 'stockingers') but within twenty years, in the 1720s, this figure had jumped to 25 per cent. The expansion of the industry continued apace and by the early nineteenth century Shepshed was the most intensively industrialized village in Leicestershire—in 1812 there were more than 1,000 knitting frames for a population of just over 3,000.

For as long as the trade had been confined to the production of luxury articles, the semi-independent journeymen and even the wage-labourers had enjoyed a moderately high standard of living. After the 1730 trial the hosiers were liberated from the inhibiting regulations of the Company and they began freely to take on parish apprentices in order to lower their production costs. After the machine-operatives had been reduced to the status of dependent wage-labourers, their incomes were governed by the health of the industry. In an industry dependent on the vagaries of fashion, fluctuations in prosperity were quite usual but most depressions were short-lived. Only the years of the American Revolution, when the industry's best market was boycotting its goods, seem to have interrupted a long period of prosperity that ended in 1815.

In the years after the end of the Napoleonic Wars the hosiery trade was in a state of complete, unrelieved depression as a result of the stagnation of demand for knitted goods that was caused by changes in fashion and the increasing effectiveness of overseas competition. This situation was greatly exacerbated by the continuous rise in the number of people engaged in the industry. In these circumstances both wages and working conditions deteriorated and many abuses that had always been present became major sources of exploitation.

In 1845 a Royal Commission was appointed to inquire into the condition of the framework knitters and witnesses came forward to give personal testimony about their experiences.[15] Apart from their low wages and long, irregular working hours the framework knitters had several more specific grievances pertaining to their treatment by the employers. Abuses concerning frame rent, payments made weekly for the use of the employer's machine, were the most universal complaint. Journeymen framework knitters were further imposed upon by shop charges levied by the middlemen and small masters in whose workshops they were employed. Closely allied to frame rents and shop charges was another abuse which resulted from the employers' control over the labourers: the truck system of payments or payment in goods in lieu of money wages. The element of deceit involved in truck payments makes it difficult, if not impossible, to separate that system from other forms of fraud in the payment of wages.

Because wages were so low in the framework knitting industry it was very difficult for a family to survive on the husband's earnings alone. In very few of the proto-industrial workers' households was there just one wage-earner, in 50 per cent of their households there were three or more wage-earners. It was stated that 'Vast numbers of women and children are working side by side with men, often employed in the same description of frames, making the same fabrics, and at the same rate of wages; the only advantage over them which the man possesses being his superior strength, whereby he can undergo the fatigues of labour for longer hours than the weaker physical energies of women and children enable them to bear; and therefore he earns more money, but turning off more work.'[16] Because the children had to work long hours supplementing their fathers' inadequate wages it was uncommon for them to receive any real education. In the Shepshed marriage register for the years 1837 – 50 less than one framework knitter in three could sign his name, and the score for their brides was even worse. In contrast, the national levels of literacy were about 65 per cent for men and 50 per cent for women.[17] Overall, about one half of the framework knitters' wives were stated to have been employed at the time of the 1851 Census. A contemporary observer noted that the family paid dearly when the wife had to work: 'The cleanliness, providence and attention to cooking and mending, must inevitably be neglected when the mother and any daughters capable of working are compelled to toil for bread at a trade. . .' This was said to be so common that 'the female population must certainly be to some extent ignorant of the thrifty management of a household'.[18] Thus, the framework knitters were caught between the Scylla of absolute want and the Charybdis of secondary poverty.

This severe post – 1815 depression created a condition of 'industrial involution' which persisted until the second half of the nineteenth century, when the hosiery industry embarked on a period of technical advance as steam power was successfully applied to the process of mechanical knitting. The impulse to switch over to steam-powered production seems to have come from the increasingly strong competition that was directed against English products in overseas markets. Already, the Germans had become an important force in the American market and the threat of foreign encroachment on the home market was becoming clear. It was almost impossible for the English manufacturers to lower their wages bills by any significant amount and yet they were still being undercut by the Germans. This was because the German production was still being carried out as a supplement to cottagers' incomes, so that whatever these Saxon peasants received for their part-time activity was seen as a bonus. In this way the currents of international trade radically changed the cost advantage of English rural manufacturing: what had previously been low-cost production now, in the face of international competition, became *relatively* high-cost. In these circumstances the English manufacturers had no real alternative other than embarking on a capital-intensive programme of technological improvement in order to re-establish their competitive advantage. Of course this transformation did not occur overnight. Indeed, the country framework knitters held on to their 'independence' so that for as long as they were in competition with themselves, Saxon cottagers and the power-driven machinery they, like the hand-loom weavers of Lancashire and Yorkshire, remained the casualties of progress.

The changing employment opportunities offered by rural industry greatly influenced Shepshed's rate of population growth. During the first three-quarters of the seventeenth century there appears to have been no obvious trend in either the baptismal or the burial curve as their movements seem to have more or less cancelled each other out. After 1680, during the initial period of industrialization, there was a slow rise in the baptismal curve which, except for the later 1720s, was producing a small annual surplus. Then, after 1750, there appears to have been a radical demographic discontinuity. After the middle of the eighteenth century the baptismal curve was characterized by a wave-like movement with distinct peaks in 1771, 1790 and 1814 – 15, interrupted by equally distinct troughs in 1779 and 1799. After 1815 the baptismal curve reached a stable level around which it fluctuated until the end of the period under observation. When these oscillations in the baptismal curve are viewed in conjunction with the steadier upwards movement in the burial curve it would appear that in Shepshed it was changes in the birth rate which provided the dynamic impetus behind population growth.

In Fig. 1 we have plotted a nine-year, weighted moving average of baptisms, burials and marriages (× 4) occurring in Shepshed between 1600 and the middle of the nineteenth century. A weighted moving average was chosen in preference to a simple graphic representation of annual changes because it yields a clearer impression of overall long-run trends while still allowing for the effect of yearly fluctuations.

The pronounced oscillations in the post – 1750 baptismal curve are of obvious importance in explaining the village population's natural increase. In the seventeenth century Shepshed's population was between 550 and 600, in 1801 it had grown to 2,627, and in 1851 the village contained 3,724

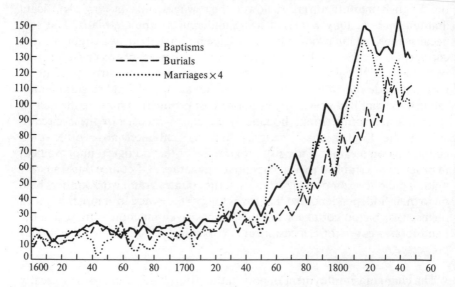

Fig. 1. *A nine-year weighted, moving average of babtisms, burials and marriages (× 4)*

inhabitants. Allowing for the fact that its response was not always immediate, and considering that no allowance has been made for variations in marital fertility, the baptismal curve's oscillations can be seen to have reflected changes in the frequency of marriage. These observed changes in the frequency of marriage can themselves be explained by referring to the changing fortunes in the framework knitting industry on which a growing section of the village population became dependent. To the extent that demographic behaviour was flexible, fluctuations in prosperity were critically important in determining the rate of population growth.

An aggregative analysis of population growth in Shepshed can show that a significant change occurred in the villagers' demographic behaviour during industrialization. The use of results derived from our family reconstitution study will enable us to see how these changes occurred on an individual level.[19]

In Table 1 we have presented figures describing the changes in the age at first marriage in Shepshed between 1600 and 1851. These figures are divided into four cohorts: 1600 – 99, the pre-industrial village; 1700 – 49, the transitional period; 1750 – 1824, full-scale industrial growth; and 1824 – 51, industrial involution.

The industrialization of Shepshed was accompanied by a very substantial deviation from the pre-industrial pattern of relatively later marriage for both men and women. By the second quarter of the nineteenth century both men and women were marrying almost five years earlier than their predecessors in the pre-industrial village. In terms of reproductive capacity, the implications of a five-year reduction in women's age at marriage were most important. The years which were being added to their married life were, from a physiological viewpoint, their most fecund.[20] In Table 2 we have presented figures describing the age-specific fertility rates derived from the reconstitution study.

Table 1. *Age at marriage*

	N	Mean	Standard deviation	Lower quartile	Median	Upper quartile	Inter-quartile range
Men							
1600–99	80	29.4	6.9	24.8	28.0	33.4	8.6
1700–49	119	28.5	6.3	24.0	27.5	31.4	7.4
1750–1824	500	24.0	5.0	21.0	23.3	27.0	6.0
1825–51	391	24.1	4.8	21.2	23.3	27.0	5.8
Women							
1600–99	121	28.1	5.9	23.6	26.8	31.2	7.5
1700–49	133	27.4	6.1	23.2	26.4	30.3	7.0
1750–1824	420	24.1	5.3	20.6	23.0	26.0	5.4
1825–51	479	22.6	4.6	20.1	22.1	24.7	4.6

David Levine

Table 2. *Age-specific fertility rates*

	Under 25		25–9		30–4		35–9		40–4		45–9	
1600–99	22/62	355	67/174	385	68/224	304	61/234	260	25/207	121	8/177	45
1700–49	44/111	395	81/220	368	94/316	297	72/282	255	25/241	112	120/212	52
1750–1824	254/568	447	263/765	344	245/778	315	160/624	256	65/482	135	10/482	32
1825–51	486/1129	430	396/1131	350	·272/892	303	132/898	235	38/312	122	2/120	17

In these calculations the numerator represents the total number of birth events, the denominator represents the total number of years that these women were 'at risk' in each age-group, and the product describes the age-specific fertility rate (per 1,000 years lived) for each age-group.

Fertility, like age at marriage, was roughly stable before the onset of full-scale industrial growth. This socio-economic discontinuity was accompanied by an unexplained rise in fertility which combined with the substantially lower age at marriage to produce the acceleration in the rate of population growth that is evident from the graphic representation of the baptismal curve in Fig. 1.

Evidence has been presented to show that in the course of industrialization there was both a large reduction in the age at marriage and significant variations in cohort rates of marital fertility in Shepshed. In order to determine the relative importance of these changes in terms of completed family size we have undertaken another set of calculations to create estimates of the Gross Rate of Reproduction attained by each cohort. We have created hypothetical families for each cohort on the assumption that these women married at the (mean) average age and that their fertility schedules conformed to the one displayed by the whole cohort to which they belonged. After revising these figures by taking parental mortality into account, we have then added illegitimate births, taken from the illegitimacy ratio of each cohort, so that our total of births per woman include pre-marital births.[21] The result of this set of calculations is presented in Table 3.

These figures show that there was a very pronounced change in the middle of the eighteenth century in fertility. Before 1750 the Gross Rate of Reproduction changed very little, but after the onset of full-scale industrialization the combination of earlier marriage, higher fertility and a higher ratio of illegitimate births led to a substantial rise in the number of births per woman.

The lower fertility rates in the later years of married life (particularly 35 – 9) observed for the 1825 – 51 cohort begs the question of whether this phenomenon was the result of a conscious attempt to limit fertility. In popu-

Table 3. *Gross rate of reproduction*

	1600–99	1700–49	1750–1824	1825–51
Age at marriage	28.1	27.4	24.1	22.6
Completed family size	4.38	4.54	5.86	6.16
Revised completed family size	3.62	3.88	5.21	5.29
Illegitimate births	0.04	0.06	0.32	0.39
GRR	3.66	3.94	5.53	5.68

lations practising family limitation the age-specific fertility curve tends to be concave to the upper side in the later years of married life.[22] Age-specific fertility rates for later age groups will be low in comparison to rates attained at the same age by a population not practising family limitation. This situation exists because women regulating their fertility cease having children once they reach the desired number. In such families, fertility is concentrated into the earlier years of marriage. If couples were restricting their fertility upon reaching a desired number of children, then those who married earlier would begin to do this at an age when others, who married later, would still be having children at regular intervals. In Table 4 we have compared this phenomenon within the 1750 – 1824 and 1825 – 51 cohorts. Comparison within cohorts should be even more revealing than comparisons between cohorts since such comparisons are less hindered by other intervening variables.

The evidence presented in Table 4 suggests that while family limitation was being practised by those married during the boom conditions of the later

Table 4. *Family limitation*

	30–4		35–9		40–4		45–9	
Part A. 1750–1824								
Married under 25	147/477	308	89/371	240	28/277	110	3/227	13
Married over 25	98/300	326	71/253	281	37/205	180	7/164	43
Young brides' fertility in relation to older brides'	0.94		0.85		0.56		0.30	
Part B. 1825–51								
Married under 25	182/641	284	72/367	196	17/173	98	1/35	28
Married over 25	90/257	350	60/195	308	21/139	151	1/85	12
Younger brides' fertility in relation to older brides'	0.81		0.64		0.65		2.3	

David Levine

eighteenth and early nineteenth centuries, it became even more prevalent among those married in the depressed conditions after 1825.

We have now seen how industrialization was accompanied by substantial variations in both nuptiality and fertility, how the 'prudential check' was being undermined. It now remains to discuss the changes in mortality, the 'positive check' to population growth.

Infant and child mortality rates for Shepshed are presented in Table 5. To illustrate the implications of these mortality rates in terms of life expectation at birth we have compared each cohort with the Ledermann Mortality Table to which it most closely corresponds.[23] A perusal of these figures indicates that whereas infant and child mortality was comparatively low before 1700 the onset of industrialization was accompanied by a deterioration in life expectation at birth. Furthermore, this deterioration appears to have been accentuated by the decline in living conditions that occurred during the period of industrial involution. The implications of these mortality rates can be seen in the fourth column which shows the number of children (per 1,000) reaching fifteen in each cohort. Children born after 1825 had a life expectation at birth that was seven years less than those born before 1825 and fully twelve years less than those born in the pre-industrial village.

Table 5. *Infant and child mortality*

| Cohort | Age | Reconstitution | | | | e^0 | Ledermann | |
		At risk	Dying	Rate per thousand	Survivors		Rate per thousand	Survivors
1600–99	0–	1,531	194	126	1,000	49.18,	126	1,000
	1–4	1,104	82	74	874	p. 115	80	873
	5–9	788	26	33	809		24	804
	10–14	577	9	16	782		15	785
					770			772
1700–49	0–	1,254	194	155	1,000	44.02,	158	1,000
	1–4	905	85	94	845	p. 90	96	842
	5–9	645	21	33	766		28	761
	10–14	493	6	12	741		17	740
					732			727
1750–1824	0–	4,046	639	158	1,000	44.02,	158	1,000
	1–4	2,977	281	94	842	p. 90	96	842
	5–9	1,953	65	33	763		28	761
	10–14	1,342	26	19	738		17	740
					724			727
1825–49	0–1	832	173	208	1,000	37.05,	207	1,000
	1–4	415	63	152	792	p. 135	162	793
	5–9	188	13	69	670		41	665
	10–14	64	1	16	624		26	638
					614			621

e^0 means life expectation at birth.

Unlike their children, the adults married in Shepshed do not seem to have suffered unduly from the small-scale urbanization of their village. The cohort married between 1750 and 1775 had a life expectation at twenty-five that was more than six years higher than did the cohort married before 1700 (over thirty-nine as opposed to less than thirty-three). The deterioration in health conditions in the industrial village that led to a dramatic rise in infant and child mortality did not leave the adult population unscathed. Those who married after 1775 had a lower expectation of life at twenty-five than did the previous cohort—by almost three years—and this decline was continued by the next cohort (married 1800–24). Still, more of those married after 1800 survived to forty-five than among the adult population married before 1750. Thus, in comparison with the drastic effect that Shepshed's urbanization had upon their children, the impact upon the adult villagers was slight.

The results derived from the reconstitution have shown us that, on the one hand, the industrialization of Shepshed was accompanied by a falling age at marriage, rising ratios of illegitimacy and variations in the levels of marital fertility. On the other hand, the urbanization of this village led to a dramatic fall in life expectation at birth but had less dire results in terms of adult's health. Now, I would like to examine the interaction of these demographic variables by estimating each cohort's Net Rate of Reproduction—the generational replacement rate, how many children from a 'typical' marriage would themselves survive to marry and have children. In Table 6 there are estimates of the different rates of generational replacement that were attained by the four cohorts between 1600 and 1851. In addition there are two further rows which describe the annual (compounded) rate of population growth suggested by the various Net Rates of Reproduction and the time period that would be required for the population to double under each regime. The methods by which these measurements have been derived are fully described in Appendix A.

The rate of population growth before the onset of full-scale industrialization was quite modest. The seventeenth-century population was producing a surplus of 10 per cent over and above the numbers needed to replace itself each generation. This suggested that a closed village population would double every 250 years. In the first half of the eighteenth century the Net Reproduction Rate was fractionally higher—the deterioration in infants' and childrens' health combined with the marginally lower fertility rates to

Table 6. *Net rates of reproduction*

	1600–99	1700–49	1750–1824	1825–51
Net rate of reproduction	1.10	1.12	1.74	1.57
Annual (compounded) rate of growth	0.28%	0.35%	1.74%	1.51%
Population doubles every ? years	250.0	200.6	40.1	46.4

produce a depressive effect on the rate of growth that was cancelled out by the somewhat longer child-bearing period and the shorter interval between generations. The figures in Table 6 show the disequilibrating effects of the interaction of a lower age at marriage and higher fertility (both illegitimate and marital) after 1750. At the same time the relative stability in infant and child mortality acted in conjunction with improvements in adults' health with the result that not only were families left unbroken by death for a longer period of time but a larger number of children survived and married. These changes, acting together, radically transformed the population's rate of generational replacement from a state of relative stability to one of very rapid growth.

The moderation of this state of affairs during the period of industrial involution in the second quarter of the nineteenth century resulted from the impact of higher mortality and deliberate fertility restriction which counteracted this cohort's lower age at marriage and the shorter interval between generations. The result was a decline in the rate of population growth from 1.74 per cent per annum to 1.51 per cent. Still, one should not lose sight of the significant fact that even during the period of involution the rate of natural increase was more than three times as great as it had been before the onset of full-scale industrialization.

It is apparent from the preceding discussion that the second quarter of the nineteenth century is of particular interest in that the villagers were confronted with drastically changed circumstances for which their newly acquired demographic profile was most unsuitable. The framework knitting industry, on which about two-thirds of the population was dependent, had entered a state of severe depression after 1815. Real wages had fallen by about 40 per cent. Emigration was a very popular response to these conditions and many young people left their native village to seek better prospects elsewhere. A simple index of this phenomenon is provided by the number of marriages celebrated in the village. In both absolute and relative terms 1815 – 16 marked the high point of the marriage curve (see Fig. 1). Since the village population would have contained an increasingly large number of children of marital age as a result of the broadening base of the age-pyramid in conditions of very rapid growth, and since the proportion of marriages involving partners who were residents of Shepshed went up, it would seem likely that there was considerable emigration among those of marital age. Moreover, movement appears to have been largely one-way: in comparison with the agricultural areas of the county the framework knitting villages had far higher rates of stability (i.e. proportion, over twenty, born in Shepshed) at the time of the 1851 Census. This was because there was substantial emigration from industrial villages, like Shepshed, but there was little immigration. The non-natives (i.e. proportion, over twenty, born elsewhere) were almost all from neighbouring industrial villages.[24] Those who stayed in

Shepshed were ill-equipped to reduce the number of children they would bring into the world. Evidence derived from the family reconstitution study has demonstrated that women married after 1825 were deliberately restricting their fertility as they grew older. But, as we have already seen, this action was insufficient to produce a significant decline in the rate of natural increase although, in conjunction with higher mortality, it did moderate the explosive effects of an even lower age at marriage and shorter interval between generations.

By the time of the 1851 Census it was apparent that the framework knitters had further responded to their adverse economic circumstances by making adjustments in their household structure.[25] Far from having the irrational behaviour that contemporaries ascribed to them, these industrial workers appear to have been quite aware of the disastrous consequences that would occur if a family was dependent upon just one wage-earner—in only 18 per cent of their households was this the case. In contrast to the agricultural labourers and the village's craftsmen and artisans, the framework knitters not only had the largest proportion of working wives but their children were also most likely to have been working from an early age. It was quite common for two, three, four, five or even more household members to have been employed in some branch of the hosiery trade. Their propensity to live with relatives and lodgers was another way in which the number of co-resident wage-earners was increased. Co-residence, two or more nuclear family units sharing the same household, was significantly higher among the framework knitters. Among these industrial proletarians more than one household in eight headed by a married man contained another co-resident family but among the non-industrial villagers such sharing was unusual—just one in twenty such complex households existed. The framework knitters' preference for living in large domestic units was part of their conscious effort to protect themselves from the precarious economic conditions.

By dint of emigration, fertility restriction, child labour and co-residence these industrial labourers created a system that enabled them to survive in a situation of industrial involution. But survival merely intensified the pressures. The effects of living in a demographic hothouse was that the framework knitters were both educationally and physically stunted by this experience. Whether they were able to overcome the anomie and hopelessness that resulted from their grinding poverty is another question, but the strength of Luddism, Chartism and non-conformity among the villagers of Shepshed suggests that they were not altogether passive sufferers.

This essay has been a demonstration of the argument that population growth during the first Industrial Revolution was both dependent upon and caused by contemporaneous changes in the social and economic structure of English society. A discussion of population growth in England during the period when it was being transformed into the 'workshop of the world' must be firmly set in an historical perspective. In pre-industrial society the demand for labour was inelastic and vacancies usually emerged with the death or retirement of an older member of the community. This form of succession or replacement was particularly prevalent in a society dominated by peasants and village artisans. Since marriage was conditional upon economic independence, the stagnancy of the pre-industrial economy created conditions that led to late marriage. This customary restraint to population growth was broken down by a series of economic changes which transformed peasants and artisans into agricultural and industrial proletarians. We have seen that in Shepshed the availability of industrial employment had important implications for the age at marriage. When employment became available to all who were willing to sell their labour, it was no longer possible to maintain the equilibrating mechanism of postponed marriage because men (and women) could reach their maximum earning capacity at an early age so that there was no longer any reason to defer marriage.

As the results derived from the reconstitution study of Shepshed have shown, the demand for labour acted as a powerful disequilibrating factor in the demographic equation. While proletarianization seems to be a necessary stage in the breakdown of the pre-industrial demographic balance, the transformation of peasants and artisans into wage-labourers did not, *by itself*, necessarily lead to population growth. It is at this point that village-level studies of demographic change must be linked into the development of the national economy. The critical link in this chain was the way in which pressures from the outside world were mediated through their influence upon the local demand for labour.

APPENDIX A. CALCULATING A NET RATE OF REPRODUCTION[26]

It should be made quite clear at the outset that these figures are estimates. They have been derived by making a number of assumptions, some of which are quite 'heroic'. Nevertheless, it seems to me that it is worthwhile trying to develop some method of analysing the total effect of the different demographic variables that are derived from a family reconstitution study.

I will explain the method by which I have derived these Net Rates of Reproduction with reference to the 1600 – 99 cohort. At the end of the Appendix, Table 8 will set forth the results of this procedure for the four cohorts that are discussed in this study.

The first priority was to create an approximation of the Gross Rate of Reproduction—the average number of births per woman. For this hypothetical seventeenth-century family I assumed that the wife married at the (mean) average age, 28.1, and had a fertility experience that corresponded to that of the whole cohort. The mean was chosen in preference to the median because it is an arithmetic rather than an ordinal measurement. The mean describes the mid-point of the area of the distribution rather than the mid-point of the cumulative frequency. This difference is important because of the skewed distribution of marriage ages. The completed family size was derived as follows:

Age	Years married	Age-specific fertility rate	Children
25−29	1.9	385	0.73
30−34	5.0	304	1.52
35−39	5.0	260	1.30
40−44	5.0	121	0.60
45−49	5.0	45	0.23
			4.38

The Gross Rate of Reproduction, 4.38, is based on the assumption that both the husband and wife lived long enough for the whole of the wife's fertile period to be completed. Therefore, it needs to be revised by taking adult mortality into account. This proved to be quite a complex affair. It was impossible to make any allowance for re-marriage because the available data describing the length of widowhood and widowerhood was inadequate. But, on the other hand, we have no real idea of the number of marriages that were broken for personal or socio-economic reasons. For our present purposes we have had to assume that the incidence of re-marriage was more or less balanced by the effects of marital breakdown. Bearing these caveats in mind, we began to assess the effect of parental mortality on fertility by making the assumption that the mortality experience of the husband and his wife was identical. Our age-specific mortality figures relate to the combined experience of both men and women—it was decided that the creation of mortality rates with the least susceptibility to chance fluctuations was a higher priority than the assessment of differential effects of male and female mortality. Moreover, we also assumed that the husband and wife were exactly the same age at marriage—in this case the wife's age. Given that this seventeenth-century marriage was intact at 28.1, the average age at marriage, we have been able to determine the pace with which death took its toll. For the 1.9 years remaining in the 25 − 29 age-group the mortality rate was 25 per 1,000 (0.025). Since the husband's likelihood of dying was assumed to have been independent of his wife's and vice versa, the probability that their marriage would have been broken by the death of at least one of them was the product of each individual's chance of dying: $0.975 \times 0.975 = 0.951$. Thus, of every 1,000 marriages intact at 28.1 there would be 951 surviving at the end of the 25 – 29 age-period. We further assumed that these deaths were evenly distributed during the 1.9 years that this hypothetical couple was 'at risk' in the 25 – 29 age-group, so that we are interested in the mid-point marital survival. This was easily derived as we merely added the number of intact marriages at the beginning of the age-group to the number surviving until the end and then divided this sum in two. Having established the mid-point frequency of marriages which, for each age-group, were unbroken by the death of at least one spouse, we have now to determine the implications of this set of survival rates in terms of the number of children born to each married woman.

The revised figure for legitimate marital fertility, after taking parental mortality into account, is 3.62.[27] Next we used the illegitimacy ratio of the seventeenth-century cohort, 1.2 per cent, to determine how many illegitimate births occurred per woman. The logic behind this procedure was that the relationship between the frequency of legitimate births and the completed family size should be proportional to the relationship between the frequency of both legitimate and illegitimate births and all births per woman. So, the total number of births—both legitimate and illegitimate—was derived as follows:

$$(0.988/3.62) = (1.000/x) \quad (x = 3.66).$$

The 'typical' seventeenth-century woman had a total of 3.66 births: 0.04 before marriage and a further 3.62 afterwards.

How many of these 3.66 children themselves survived to the average age at marriage, 28.1? By referring to the Ledermann Mortality Table to which this

Table 7

Age	Surviving marriages	Age-specific death rate	Survival rate, one partner	Survival rate, both partners
25–29	1.000	0.025	0.975	0.951
30–34	0.951	0.051	0.949	0.901
35–39	0.856	0.081	0.919	0.844
40–44	0.722	0.108	0.892	0.796
45–49	0.574	0.101	0.899	0.808

Age	Surviving marriages	Mid-point marital survival		Potential fertility		Legitimate children
25–29	0.951	0.975	×	0.73	=	0.71
30–34	0.856	0.903	×	1.52	=	1.37
35–39	0.722	0.789	×	1.30	=	1.03
40–44	0.574	0.648	×	0.60	=	0.39
45–49	0.464	0.519	×	0.23	=	0.12
						3.62

cohort's infant and child mortality most closely conformed it was found that 714 per 1,000 survived to 28.1. Therefore the number of children per family surviving to the average age at marriage was $3.66 \times 0.714 = 2.62$.

Of these 2.62 surviving children per family how many actually married? Demographers have observed that in populations marrying early marriage is practically universal but in populations where the average age at marriage is late, such as in pre-industrial England, a relatively high proportion of the population never marry at all. Bearing this in mind, the incidence of marriage has been calculated on the assumption that marriage was universal at an average age of 20.0 but that for every year later that it occurred there were 2 per cent who never married (of both men and women).[28] In seventeenth-century Shepshed, therefore, an average age at marriage of 28.1 suggests that its incidence was 83.8 per cent. Of the 2.62 children surviving to the average age at marriage in our hypothetical family there were $2.62 \times 0.838 = 2.20$ who married.

If there were no difference in the sex ratio of the marrying children then the Net Rate of Reproduction would have been: $2.20 \div 2 = 1.10$. We divide the number of children marrying in two because we are interested in a *net* replacement rate.

The seventeenth-century villagers were increasing by 10 per cent per generation. What did this rate of generational replacement mean in terms of an annual average rate of population growth? We can find an answer to this question by using the compound interest formula: $A = P(1+i)^n$. In our case A means the size of the population at the end of a generation while P is the initial size of the population, i is the rate of growth, and n is the length of a generation. We already know that the size of the initial population is 1,000 and that the size of that population after one generation is 1,100 but what we do not yet know is the length of a generation. To do this we started with the assumption that the length of a generation was equivalent to the mean age of child-bearing. Given that the woman married at 28.1 and had 3.62 children during her marriage, how long would it take for her to have 1.81 children, the mean point of her child-bearing? A mean age at child-bearing was chosen in preference to a median one because of the long 'tail' on the distribution of fertility. By 30 the woman had given birth to 0.71 children. Assuming that within each age-group births were distributed evenly the mean age at child-bearing was 33.6. This figure was derived by discovering the period of time that this woman would require to produce a further 1.10 children (1.10 plus 0.71, born before 30, equals 1.81). An age-specific fertility rate of 304 per 1,000 means an annual average of 0.304 births. To produce 1.10 children at a rate of 0.304 per year requires 3.6 years. Thus, the length of a generation, defined as the mean age at child-bearing, was 33.6 years. Armed with this extra bit of information it is a relatively easy matter to determine the annual compound rate of growth, 0.28 per cent, and also the period in which a

Table 8. *The Net Rate of Reproduction*

	1600–99	1700–49	1750–1824	1825–51
GRR	4.38	4.54	5.86	6.16
Revised GRR	3.66	3.94	5.53	5.68
Child survival rate	0.714	0.668	0.686	0.583
Surviving children	2.62	2.63	3.79	3.31
Incidence of marriage	0.838	0.852	0.918	0.948
Children marrying	2.20	2.24	3.48	3.14
NRR	1.10	1.12	1.74	1.57
Generation	33.6	33.4	31.8	30.1
Annual rate of growth	0.28%	0.35%	1.74%	1.51%
Population doubles every ? years	250.0	200.6	40.1	46.4

population with a Net Rate of Reproduction of 1.10 would double, 250 years.

It should be pointed out once more that no special claims are being made for the accuracy of this method of analysis. But it seems to me that it is a valuable way of measuring the overall combined effect of the different demographic variables. Moreover, it enables us to isolate each variable and test its contribution to the sum of the parts. In this way we can gain some insight into the relative importance of changes in the various components of the demographic equation.

In Table 8 a composite presentation is set forth in which all the salient bits and pieces of information for the four cohorts are included.

NOTES

1. Young went on to say: 'Provide new employment and new hands will inevitably follow' (*A Six Months Tour Through the North of England,* iv (1770), 561, 565.

2. *An Essay upon the Probable Method of making a People Gainers with Ballance of Trade* (1690), 34 – 5.

3. *The Wealth of Nations* (New York, 1937), 80.

4. 'A summary view of the principle of population', reprinted in D. V. Glass (ed.), *Introduction to Malthus* (1953), 159.

5. Clifford Geertz, *Agricultural Involution: The Processes of Ecological Change to Indonesia* (Berkeley and Los Angeles, 1963).

6. I have attempted to keep footnotes and other detailed analyses to a minimum in this paper. This information is fully set out in my Ph.D. dissertation, which compares the experience of Shepshed with that of Bottesford, a landlord-dominated agricultural village in eastern Leicestershire. 'The Demographic Implications of Rural Industrialization, a Family Reconstitution Study of Two Leicestershire Villages, 1600 – 1851' (Cambridge Ph.D., 1975). The full versions of these analyses together with examinations of the interplay of economic change and demographic behaviour in two other villages (Colyton, Devon, and Terling, Essex) will be the subject of my forthcoming book, *Economic Opportunity and Family Formation.*

7. Malcolm Thomis, *The Luddites* (Newton Abbot, 1970), 178, 182; A. T. Patterson, *Radical Leicester* (Leicester, 1954), 59.

8. Joan Thirsk, 'Industries in the countryside', in F. J. Fisher (ed.), *Essays in the Economic and Social History of Tudor and Stuart England* (Cambridge, 1961); E. L. Jones, 'The agricultural origins of industry', *Past and Present,* xl (July 1968).

9. This issue was the subject of my M. A. thesis, 'The agricultural origins of industry in Leicestershire' (University of British Columbia M. A., 1970).

10. Quoted by G. E. Fussell, 'Four centuries of Leicestershire farming' in W. G. Hoskins (ed.), *Studies in Leicestershire Agrarian History* (Leicester, 1948), 158.

11. Dennis Mills, 'Landownership and Rural Population, with Special reference to Leicestershire in the Mid – 19th Century' (Leicester Ph.D., 1963), 272.

12. Leicestershire Record Office, Quarter Sessions, 62/269/1 – 55.

13. Thirsk, op. cit.

14. The discussion of the history of the framework knitting industry is based on the following three works: F. A. Wells, *The British Hosiery and Knitwear Industry* (1935); J. D. Chambers, 'The Worshipful Company of Framework Knitters', *Economica,* xxvii (November, 1929); and S. D. Chapman, 'The genesis of the British hosiery industry, 1600 – 1750', *Textile History,* iii (December 1972).

15. B. P. P., *Report of the Commissioners Appointed to Inquire into the Condition of the Frame-work Knitters,* 1845, xv, 15.

16. Ibid., 101.

17. R. S. Schofield, 'Dimensions of illiteracy 1750 – 1850', *Explorations in Economic History,* x (Summer 1973).

18. W. Lee, *Report to the General Board of Health on a Preliminary Inquiry into the Sewerage, Drainage and Supply of Water and the Sanitary Conditions of the Inhabitants of the Parish of Loughborough* (1849), 18 – 19.

19. For a discussion of the comprehensiveness of parochial registration in Shepshed and the influence of non-conformity on the Anglican system, see my forthcoming article in *Population Studies,* 'The reliability of parochial registration and the representativeness of family reconstitution'.

20. F. Lorimer, *Culture and Human Fertility* (Unesco, 1954), 51 – 4.

21. For the four cohorts the illegitimacy ratios were as follows: 1600 – 99, 1.2 per cent; 1700 – 49, 1.5 per cent; 1750 – 1824, 5.8 per cent; 1825 – 51, 6.8 per cent. The way in which these ratios have been used to arrive at a figure of illegitimate births per woman is explained in Appendix A.

22. For a discussion of this subject see E. A. Wrigley, 'Family limitation in pre-industrial England', *Economic History Review,* xix, 1 (April 1966).

23. Sully Ledermann, *Nouvelles Tables—Types de Mortalité* (Paris, 1969). These life tables were chosen in preference to the Princeton 'regional' model life tables because they have been based on a more heterogeneous sample of sources and they allow for a wider range of variation.

24. This subject is discussed in chapter 3 of my Ph.D. dissertation (op. cit.).

25. This issue is the focus of chapter 4 of my Ph.D. dissertation (op. cit.).

26. Whatever errors or deficiencies there are in this way of analysing reconstituted results are solely my own responsibility. They would, however, have been far more serious were it not for the advice and encouragement of Roger Schofield, Tony Wrigley, Ron Lee and John Knodel.

27. It should be pointed out that for the thirty-three first marriages for this cohort for which evidence was derived on completed family size (i.e. marriages in which the

wife survived her fertile period or in which the death of the wife was recorded before the end) the mean average was 3.90.

28. Support for this set of assumptions was forthcoming from a comparison of the 1825 – 51 reconstituted cohort with the enumerated population at the time of the 1851 Census. Of the 85 women aged 45 – 49 at the time of the 1851 Census 95.3 per cent were either married or widowed. The reconstituted results suggest an age at marriage for the 1825 – 51 cohort of 22.6 and according to my assumptions this would mean that its incidence was 94.8 per cent.

2

The Proto-Industrial Family Economy:
The Structural Function of Household
and Family During the Transition
from Peasant Society to
Industrial Capitalism*1

HANS MEDICK

I. PRELIMINARY REMARKS

The history of household and family can no longer be regarded as the stepchild of historical research. At least within the spheres of Anglo-American and French research, it has almost reached the point of becoming an established branch of an expanding academic industry.[2] In West Germany and Austria a take-off in this direction also seems to be imminent.[3] However, the present state of investigation reveals certain specific deficiencies, whose removal cannot be guaranteed simply by proceeding further in the direction of current research trends.

The direction and extent of research into the history of the family has been heavily influenced by the work of P. Laslett.[4] This holds true not only for the favourable reception which Laslett's approach has experienced, for even his critics[5] are in many respects indebted to him. So far, progress has followed two main paths of development.

(1) In the theoretical area, there has emerged an historically oriented critique of the traditional social-scientific axioms concerning household and family.

(2) In the methodological and technical area, there has been the deliberative accumulation of quantifiable data.

The important new insights that have been gained by following these two paths should nevertheless not obscure the fact that the claim presented by

* From *Social History*, 3 (1976), 291 – 316. Reprinted by permission of the author and the editors of *Social History*.

Laslett that the new direction of research should be above all 'social structural history',[6] oriented toward entire societies, examining the essential 'structural function of the family in the pre-industrial world',[7] remains fundamentally unfulfilled. In the course of Laslett's empirical work, theoretical criticism and methodological innovation did not achieve a positive reciprocal relationship that would have made his research praxis fruitful in other systematic endeavours, and so have helped build a substantial model and theory yielding new insights into the 'structural function of the family', and its transformation in the transition from traditional agrarian society to industrial capitalism. Unfortunately, with Laslett, theory formation and empirical investigation drifted apart as research progressed. After a promising, if not unproblematical start in Laslett's first book, *The World We Have Lost,* systematic and theoretical interests on the one hand and the practice of research on the other, began increasingly to impede and hinder one another.

To be sure, the old hypothesis of the evolution from the large, extended, multi-generational household of the pre-industrial age to the nuclear family of the industrial age has been convincingly refuted by Laslett.[8] However, Laslett's historical rejection of this traditional myth of social-scientific evolutionary theory did not lead him to the construction of a substantial theory which would have allowed a more precise location of household and family as functional elements and social-structural factors in the genesis of industrial capitalism. Laslett's 'Null Hypothesis' which has been tested cross-culturally and over time, but seems to apply above all to England, shows the nuclear family already to be the dominant household type before the industrial revolution. This hypothesis destroys the assumption that there is an historical covariance between industrialization and the formation of nuclear family structures.[9] His proof that this constellation of a dominant nuclear family household type was relatively constant, not only before, but also during and after the industrial revolution, has called into question important assumptions of industrialization and modernization theory. These assumptions, like those of Parsonian structural-functionalist theory, originated in the premise of a symmetrical convergence or passive adaptation in which changes in family structure relate to the social and economic trans-formation of society.[10] Laslett's findings reveal household and family as a relatively resilient and enduring structural element within the genesis of industrial capitalism.[11] It is here that Laslett's systematic achievement, frequently overlooked by his critics, is to be seen, but he himself draws no systematic conclusion from these findings. For the categorical framework of his research offers no basis for a dialectical theory which would do justice to what E. Bloch referred to as *'gleichzeitige Ungleichzeitigkeit'* (synchronous anachronism),[12] which designates household and family as bearers of residual traditional structures in relation to those larger social and economic transformations characterizing the process of capitalist industrialization. It is only within this context that the structural function of household and family in the transition from traditional agrarian society to industrial capitalism can adequately be assessed.

Any concrete undertaking along these lines would have to be a modest one. For the time being, it would be unreasonable to pursue a research strategy which would try to offer an alternative to the older universalistic approaches of the evolutionary theory or to the current Anglo-American concepts of modernization and industrialization.[13] Rather, efforts to understand the dialectical nature of household and family during this fundamental transition to industrialism should aim at the formation of a model or theory based on a research terrain of manageable size, specified by status and region, for it is primarily in this way that an empirically-oriented historian can offer fruitful theoretical hypotheses. If, through the choice of his methodology and research techniques, the historian peremptorily eliminates the opportunity to pursue this dialectical question, the result will be unfortunate not only for his own research, but also for the desired critical dialogue between historians and social scientists, especially in the area of the sociology of the family.[14] For if the historian of the family leaves the formulation of conceptual questions to the social scientist, he conforms, whether he likes it or not, to the outmoded division of labour between history and the social sciences which traditionally limits the historian to the role of the 'supplier of data', and grants to the social scientist the role of 'producer of categories'.[15] Moreover, the historian also unwittingly helps to perpetuate the persistence of old approaches and questions behind his own back, even when he acts, as does Laslett, as their critic.

It is as a consequence of this lack of integration between conceptualization and empirical research that there may be seen in Laslett (but not only him) a trend of research that lays too much stress upon the isolated small group.[16] This trend may be defined by its proponents as 'micro-social history' but due to its inherent assumptions it cannot be carried out as 'functional micro-social history' within the framework of macro-historical questions and problems. In certain respects this orientation is indeed a necessary point of departure for historical research into the family. It is suited to a research situation in which the empirical 'unknowns' still outweigh the 'knowns' on the map of our knowledge. But where these tendencies harden themselves into a methodological and theoretical stance which proceeds on the assumption of a strict separation of empirical, antecedent data accumulation on the one hand, and the successive framing of materially substantiated hypotheses on the other,[17] not only will one fail to 'minimize the unanticipated theoretical consequences of methodology',[18] but there will also emerge serious disadvantages for the conduct of concrete historical research. These disadvantages result precisely from a situation in which the unreflected

categorical assumptions establish themselves as a seemingly timeless framework of research and guide the work of the historian in the wrong direction.

The problems with this approach manifest themselves in the case of
Laslett's 'formal and restricted concept of structure'[19] of household and
family, a concept which restricts itself all too easily to kin relations and
generational succession as decisive structural criteria, to which is then added
co-residence as the only delimiting criterion identifying the household unit. It
is indeed doubtful whether the employment of this structural concept of
household and family makes it possible at all to render significant findings in
the sense that 'social-structural history' demands. In the interest of too
rigorous a claim for quantification, Laslett the methodologist sacrifices *a
priori* and categorically the historical 'meaning' of those phenomena to be
measured and compared in favour of a universal scale of comparison and
measurement. If Laslett's structural criteria are used in isolation, without
considering the necessary 'contextual identifications'[20] which must be
derived from the changing socio-historical conditions under which the family
produces, reproduces and consumes, and if those structural criteria by way of
definitions of 'nuclear family', 'extended family' and 'multiple family'
become the sole basis for comparison and measurement, then the danger
arises of computing the incomputable. It is true that the industrial proletarian
grandmother may have lived in an 'extended family' as did the peasant grandmother, but this apparent uniformity by no means indicates an identity of
household structures. The 'extended family' of the proletariat primarily
functioned as a private institution to redistribute the poverty of the nuclear
family by way of the kinship system. The extended family of the peasant, on
the other hand, served as an instrument for the conservation of property and
the caring for the older members of the family.[21]

However, it is not only that comparison and measurement are blunted by
Laslett's 'restricted concept of structure'. The structurally relevant 'basic
processes'[22] of household and family, as they appear in production, reproduction and consumption, cannot be grasped using Laslett's structural
criteria; neither can the function of this familial unit within the larger socio-
economic context of the entire society. The categorical preconceptions and
restricted methodological perspectives reduce the relevance of Laslett's
approach towards the social history of the family in a decisive way.

It is in view of this lack of empirical differentiation and the narrow
theoretical scope of such a 'restricted concept' of household and family that
it becomes necessary to develop different concepts, models and definitions
based on a research area of middle range: small enough to enable deep
analysis, yet large and typical enough to form the basis for generalization.
These models and definitions should serve to analyse the changing
function of household and family in the social context of production,
reproduction, as well as power relationships, and in addition to deter-

mine the repercussions of social and economic changes on family structure.

In the following pages I hope to make such a preliminary attempt with a limited but significant historical example.

II. FUNCTIONAL INTERRELATIONSHIPS AND THE REGULATING SYSTEM OF THE PROTO-INDUSTRIAL FAMILY ECONOMY

The model whose main characteristics are sketched hereafter, and which has been more fully described in another context,[23] attempts to outline the function of household and family during a critical phase in the transition of certain types of agrarian societies to the industrial system. This phase was characterized by the emergence, expansion and final decline of rural industries. The main period of this 'protean stage of industrial development',[24] 'industrialization before the factory system'[25] or 'proto-industrialization',[26] as it has come to be called, may be dated from the sixteenth to the early nineteenth century.

The development of proto-industrialization indeed varied according to region and craft. But amidst all these differences it exhibited—apart from special developments in the mining and metallurgic trades—a common structural foundation. This consisted in the close association that existed between household production based on the family economy on the one hand, and the capitalist organization of trade, putting-out and marketing of the products on the other. Whether the home-industrial weaver, knitter, nailer or scythemaker entered the market as buyer and seller himself and so worked within the 'Kaufsystem', or whether he was organized in the 'putting-out system', he was always directly or indirectly dependent upon merchant capital.

The functional interrelationship between family economy and merchant capital, and the peculiarly stable and at the same time flexible character of this configuration, constituted a comprehensive set of social relations of production, giving to the historical process of proto-industrialization the traits of a socio-economic system.

The historical significance of this specific association of proto-industrial family economy and merchant capital emerges if one considers the social and economic conditions in which proto-industrialization originated. On a macro-historical level proto-industrialization appeared as the combined outcome of the destabilization and decomposition of traditional European peasant societies. Demographic growth and socioeconomic polarization of the rural population led, above all in the high middle ages and in the sixteenth and eighteenth centuries, to the emergence of a numerous, underemployed class of small peasants or landless rural dwellers. This process formed an essential pre-condition for the penetration of industrial production into the countryside. Declining marginal returns in the small peasant or sub-peasant economies left only one alternative open to the rural dwellers: the part-time or full-time transition from land-intensive agrarian production to labour-intensive craft production. From this viewpoint proto-industrialization could be called a special case of 'economic development with unlimited supplies of labour'.[27]

The transition of this underemployed rural labour force to the mass production of handicrafts could only materialize under the impact of a second essential factor: the emergence of a world market, extending beyond the confines of Europe, dominated by merchant capital. It was thus less the internal demand than the expanding demand from foreign markets which developed with the 'new colonialism' of the seventeenth century,[28] which brought about industrial mass production in the countryside. In view of the low elasticity of supply of the town economy confined within the guild system, merchant capital was forced to fall back on to the potential of the rural labour force, and to transfer craft production to an increasing degree to the countryside.

The emergence, rise and final agony of rural-handicraft industry cannot, however, be explained within this macro-historical framework alone. The macro-historical perspective needs to be supplemented by a micro-historical viewpoint. For proto-industry was domestic industry. It was closely tied to the inner dynamic which household and family of the rural artisans generated within a context increasingly determined by market and monetary relationships and by the capitalistic organization of trade, putting-out and marketing.

As was the case with the peasant economy, the rural-industrial production process rested to a large extent on the household economy of small producers. Proto-industrial and peasant households did not, however, share only the common characteristic of a mere form of production. Beyond this common form both shared the functional and organizational unity of production, generative reproduction and consumption within the social formation of the 'ganze Haus'.[29]

To be sure, this unity lost its autarky as a self-subsisting economy within the 'ganze Haus' of the rural artisan. With the loss of their agrarian base, production and consumption increasingly became factors dependent on the market. But nevertheless, the family economy and 'ganze Haus' remained an effective socio-structural force even after their original agrarian base had largely disappeared. Indeed it was the inertia of the traditional family economy as a self-regulating unity of labour, consumption and reproduction which determined the central functional role of the household within the process and systemic pattern of proto-industrialization.

The structural and functional link between proto-industrialization and household and family can most clearly be explained by the characteristic logic of the pre-capitalist family economy. This was first analysed empirically at the beginning of the twentieth century by A. V. Chayanov and initially presented in his 'Theorie der Familienwirtschaft im Landbau'.[30] The heuristic fertility of Chayanov's analysis, originally concerned with the patterns of peasant society, can be seen clearly in its application to its proto-industrialized variant: for Chayanov the central feature of the characteristic economic logic of the family economy was that its productive activity was not governed by the objective of accumulating a monetary surplus or a net profit. 'The family economy could not maximize what it could not measure.'[31] The object of its productive labour, rather, was to bring into equilibrium, into a 'labour-consumer balance',[32] the basic necessities of economic, social and cultural subsistence on the one side, and the expenditure of labour by the family on the other. Consequently, the family economy tried to maximize the gross product, not the net profit. It entered into exchange relationships as a producer of use values, even under circumstances in which its products necessarily became commodities whose exchange values were objectively determined by money relationships and merchant capital.

If, for example, the returns of the family economy fell, it increased its expenditure of work, even beyond the amount which is customary in an economic system depending on developed capitalist wage-labour. In developed capitalist systems the interest of capital in exploiting the labour force is regulated and at the same time limited by the necessity to reproduce that labour force permanently. For the family economy, by contrast, the work effort, regardless of the amount of labour expended, virtually presents itself as an invariable overhead cost because of the lack of alternative possibilities for employing its labour force. It implies 'zero opportunity costs' as long as the family subsistence is not guaranteed and the possibility of marginal returns to labour exists. This holds true even when the economic returns would yield a deficit in the framework of a net profit calculation which would be based on comparable income scales for wage labour. The net return calculated on this basis would appear to fall below the family's cost of production.[33] If, on the contrary, the returns of the family economy rise, for example because of more favourable economic conditions, the family economy has no need to increase its expenditure of work, rather it converts these additional returns into consumption and leisure; and a backward-sloping supply-of-labour curve sets in.

Thus although the behaviour of the family economy is influenced by the external conditions of production, it is not entirely determined by them. Rather, it depends in the main on the balance between production and consumption within the family. This labour-consumer balance does not originate, however, merely in the subjective preferences of the family members. Its logic is determined by socio-structural factors. It rests on the structural and functional nexus of the 'ganze Haus' as a self-regulating socio-economic formation, which organizes and combines production, consumption and reproduction through the common labour relations of the family members. Although this self-regulating system of the family economy was originally adapted to the needs of a peasant – artisan subsistence economy, it did not lose its effectiveness in the transition to proto-industrialization. On the contrary, the logic of family economic production became effective above all because of the inclination of the poor, landless producers to fall back on 'self-exploitation'[34] in the production of craft goods, if this was necessary to ensure customary family subsistence and economic self-sufficiency.

This dynamic had a macro-economic effect in reference to the emergence, the progress and also the internal contradictions of the proto-industrial system, above all in that the mechanism of self-exploitation by the family enabled the merchant or putting-out capitalist to realize a specific 'differential profit'.

Competition enables the capitalists to subtract from the price of labour what the family produces in its own garden and small plots.[35]

The 'differential profit' realized in this way surpassed both the profits that could be gained from the social relations of production in the guild system, and the profits that could be derived from comparable wage-labour relations in manufactures. The following hypothesis therefore seems justified: the primary social relation of production in the transition from traditional peasant society to industrial capitalism was established not in manufactures, but in the characteristic nexus of small and sub-peasant family economy and merchant capital. Manufactures in any event only fulfilled the role of a supplementary system of production. In the proto-industrial phase, as Karl A. Wittfogel suggested, 'a famishing Lilliputian cottage industry choked off large industry',[36] preventing its emergence as a dominant form of production.

If one considers the producing family of the rural—industrial lower classes from this viewpoint, it appears as the essential agent in the growth of emergent capitalism. The family functioned *objectively* as an internal engine of growth in the process of proto-industrial expansion precisely because *subjectively* it remained tied to the norms and rules of behaviour of the traditional familial subsistence economy. From this perspective the dominant impulse in the genesis of capitalism was not so much the 'Protestant Ethic' and the labour discipline subjectively inherent in this ethic, simultaneously enforced by capitalist wage-labour. Rather, the dominant impulse seems to have been the 'infinitely tenacious resistance. . .of pre-capitalist labour',[37] anchored in the family economy, which M. Weber completely pushed to the edge of his consciousness.[38] The origin of modern capitalism is not in any case to be separated from the specific function, which the 'ganze Haus' of the small peasant household carried out in the final, critical phase of its development which was at the same time the period of its demise. This insight into the symbiotic relationship of family economy and merchant capital possibly points beyond its own specific case. It illustrates the essential function which the preservation of pre-capitalist enclaves has had and still has for the evolution and stabilization of capitalist societies.[39] The example points at the same time, however, to possible contradictions and results of such functional relations of evolutionary and devolutionary processes. The proto-industrial system in any case contained within its structural foundation the essential seeds of its own destruction. In an advanced stage of proto-industrial expansion, this structural foundation became one of the negatively determining causes for the transition to industrial capitalism or led proto-industrialization into its *cul de sac*, i.e. into de-industrialization or 're-pastoralization' (F. Crouzet). This contradiction was anchored to the regulating system of the family mode of production as an effect opposed to productivity and surplus. It brought into operation the reverse side of the 'labour-consumer balance' of the family mode of production because it affected the replacement of productive labour effort through consumption and leisure, through feasting, playing and drinking in exactly those situations of potential growth in which the capitalist putter-out could have obtained maximum profits. It was this contradiction which in the long run could not be squared with the dynamic of reproduction and expansion inherent in the proto-industrialized system. So it led either beyond itself to industrial capitalism or retreated backward from proto-industrialization into de-industrialization.

III. HOUSEHOLD FORMATION AND FAMILY STRUCTURE AS ELEMENTS OF THE PROCESS OF PRODUCTION AND REPRODUCTION

The nuclear family without servants was the predominant type of household in rural cottage industry.[40] This scarcely distinguished the proto-industrial household from other rural groups during the period of the disintegration of peasant society. It was, rather, typical of the overwhelming portion of the sub-peasant and land-poor class. Nevertheless, if one controls for social class it is clear that the average household size of the rural cottage workers was significantly higher than that of farm workers.[41] Previous analyses have shown that the decisive factor determining larger household size was the larger number of co-residing children.[42] This did not result from a higher level of legitimate fertility among cottage workers' families nor was a reduced level of infant mortality a factor.[43] The higher average number of children is rather to be traced to the earlier age of marriage and possibly to an altered pattern of age-specific mobility in proto-industrial regions. R. Schofield, D. Levine and L. Berkner[44] have demonstrated in any case that the traditional status of servanthood as an age-specific precursor to adulthood amongst peasant populations largely lost its significance among the rural cottage workers. Children of rural cottage workers remained longer in their parents' house yet also married earlier than the members of peasant or sub-peasant classes. 'A family has a better bottom than formerly: residence is more assured and families are more numerous as increase of industry keeps them more together.'[45] Work within their family of origin by the children of weavers, spinners and knitters frequently took the place of work as servants in another household. But this alternative was not a result of free choice. Child labour, which both in its intensity and duration went far beyond that of the corresponding labour of farm peasant households, was in fact a vital necessity for the rural cottage workers' families.[46]

The extent to which the material existence of the proto-industrial family depended on child labour as the 'capital of the poor man' becomes clear in those cases in which children made no direct contribution to the 'working income' of the family. In those cases where they left home, children frequently were 'hired out' as already trained workers or they remained bound to the family by having to make regular payments to it.[47]

The longer residence of young people in their parents' house and the relatively low age at marriage resulted in a higher average household size among rural artisans. However, family structure did not follow the pattern of the larger peasant stem-families. That is, the more compelling integration of the child into the family work force, its longer period of socialization in the parents' home, and its early marriage did not bring about a closer connection between the generations in the sense of providing a stimulus to form large, three-generational households. On the contrary, the increasing dissolution of the agrarian basis and the transition to a proto-industrial mode of production under market conditions rendered ineffective the very causes which governed household and family formation among traditional peasants.

Among peasant populations the necessary connection of household formation to resources which were scarce and which could be acquired only by inheritance formed the decisive structural determinant. It enforced restrictive marriage patterns[48] as well as the co-residence of the generations in the 'ganze Haus'.[49] The iron 'chain of reproduction and inheritance'[50] at the same time functioned as a system of 'reproduction and patriarchal domination'. By controlling access to land as the only complete source of subsistence, the older generation controlled not only the pre-conditions of family formation on the part of the younger generation, but through inheritance it also controlled the structural connection of the family beyond the individual family cycle.[51]

Household formation and family structure among cottage workers, on the other hand, grew out of fundamentally different pre-conditions. Inherited property as the 'tangible' determinant of household formation and family structure receded in the face of the overwhelming importance of the family as a unit of labour. The foundation and continuing existence of the family as a unit of production and consumption was no longer necessarily tied to the transmission of property through inheritance. It was replaced by the possibility of founding a family primarily as a unit of labour. This not only reduced parents' control over the marital relations of the young, but it also loosened at the same time the structural connection of the generations, in so far as it had been guaranteed by property inheritance and patriarchal domination. It is true that parents were dependent on the labour of their children to an increasing extent, but they possessed no sanctions against adolescent children who wanted to leave the house and found a new nuclear family unit. Marriage and family formation slipped beyond the grasp of patriarchal domination; they were no longer 'tangibly' determined by property relationships, but they did not lose their 'material' foundation in the process of production.[52]

The 'beggars' marriages' between partners without any considerable dowry or inheritance, between 'people who can join together two spinning wheels but not beds',[53] were frequently criticized by contemporaries, and constitute evidence for the new conditions shaping household and family. They were based on an increasing exploitation (*Verwertung*) of the *total* family labour force. As Martine Segalen has demonstrated, the extra-ordinarily high rate of socio-professional endogamy among weavers[54] in developed proto-industrial regions shows that household formation of rural artisans depended decisively on the highest possible work capacity of *both* marriage partners. The practical ability of the woman to work as an artisan before marriage determined her value as a marriage partner even more than her background as indicated, for example, by her father's occupation, property or social status.[55] 'The better the weaving maids can weave, the better able they are to find a husband.'[56] The new objective conditions of exploiting family labour in rural cottage industry required the choice of marriage partners who possessed technical skills; in this way, these objective factors allowed, subjectively, a more individualized selection of partners. Moreover, the same conditions demanded the formation of a new family economy as early as possible in the life cycle of young men and women.[57] Maximum income opportunities were based on the maximum work capacity of *both* marriage partners and this reached its optimum at a comparatively early age.

This not only eliminated the restrictive conditions which had limited the formation of new households within the family cycle and the succession of generations among full peasants. The rural industrial family mode of production created new pre-conditions of household formation which were determined by market conditions on the one hand and by the poverty of the rural producers on the other. These conditions inscribed not only the process of family formation among the rural industrial class, but they were also the chief factor determining family structure because they governed the entire life-cycle of the family.[58]

The constitution of the family economy primarily as a unit of work had specific demographic consequences as well. The pressure for the maximal utilization of the family work force not only required an early age at marriage and the teamwork of man and wife, it also favoured a form of reproductive behaviour which, by 'producing' a maximal number of child labourers, raised the productive capacity of the family and thereby its survival possibilities beyond that critical threshold of poverty on the margins of which the family often began its existence. Therefore it may be said that the demo-graphic-economic paradox of the proto-industrial system[59] appears above all as a consequence of a mode of production based on the family economy. 'Women's earnings set a premium on early marriage, while the employment available for children encouraged large families and increased the supply of labour out of all proportion to the demand of the trade.'[60] The imbalance between a fluctuating process of economic growth and a relatively constant process of demographic expansion, typical of proto-industrialization, had its basis in a prime factor of the social relations of production: the paradox, that those whose material conditions of inherited possessions rendered them least capable of rearing large numbers of children nevertheless produced them, may only be explained by looking at the specific conditions of exploitation under which the entire family labour force was placed in proto-industry.[61] The drive toward marriage and intensive reproduction came about—within certain boundaries—more or less independently of the conjuncturally deter-mined demand for labour; even under worsening economic conditions, a retreat to a restrictive, traditional marriage pattern characteristic of peasants and a corresponding mode of reproductive behaviour offered no viable alternative to the rural artisans. The adult proto-industrial worker was not able to exist as an individual; especially under worsening 'material conditions of production', he had to depend to a growing extent upon the 'co-operation' of his entire family. 'No single-handed man can live; he must have a whole family at work, because a single-handed man is so badly paid he can scarce provide the necessaries of life. . .As soon as they [the children] are big enough to handle an awl, they are obliged to come downstairs and work.' (A domestic-industrial shoemaker from Northampton.)[62]

This pattern of reproduction of industrial workers, affecting household structure, family size, and relations of work, was not only an exogenous variable dependent on 'external conditions of reproduction'; it also acted as an endogenous variable shaping the family life-cycle from within. Functional and structural configurations of the working family were influenced by the reproductive process above all in so far as it regulated the 'dependency ratio' in its various phases through the family cycle. The ratio between workers and

consumers that existed at the founding stage of the family was endangered by
the reproduction process before it was again brought into balance. Before
children could contribute to the household economy, they both hindered its
productive capacity and increased its consumption. Successive births reduced
the mother's ability to participate in family labour and thereby narrowed the
margin of subsistence for both parents. It was precisely this temporal dis-
junction between production and reproduction within the proto-industrial
family which trapped it between the Scylla of 'primary misery' (arising from
the conditions of the proto-industrial system) and the Charybdis of
'secondary poverty' (brought on by the family life-cycle).

In bad times the longest working day does not suffice; the weavers who have between
two and four dependent children fall heavily into debt and must regularly resort to
poor relief. Only when two or three children sit at the loom can debts be repaid and
savings made. If the brothers and sisters remain within the family and conduct an
orderly economy, this offers a period when savings are possible. It is obvious how
important it is to the parents to make their children work as early as possible, for they
will not remain with them for long; the sons often marry at 22 – 23, the daughters at
18 – 19, both leave their parents and deliver them and their younger brothers and
sisters into destitution. *With the birth of children, the parents become poor; with their
maturation, they become rich; and with their marriage, they fall back into misery.*[63]

This dilemma of the family cycle was accentuated in its extreme above all
under bad conjunctural conditions. Nevertheless, rural industrial producers
were exposed to the ambivalent effects of the reproductive process not only
under marginal conditions of income. The independent, intrafamilial
dynamic of 'demographic differentiation' (A. V. Chayanov) was exhibited
precisely in those cases of small and medium-sized peasant households which
were not yet in a permanent proto-industrial situation. In this case, the
pressure of the reproductive process could turn peasants into temporary rural
artisans. This temporary transition of small and medium-sized peasant
households into rural industrial production occurred above all in those
critical phases of their family life-cycle in which their subsistence could not be
assured on the basis of agrarian production alone.[64]

The structural character of the dilemma to which the rural artisans were
exposed under their marginal conditions of existence shows up above all in
the constitution of extended households. The formation of extended families
may here be seen as an effort to counterbalance both the 'primary misery'
caused by the social relations of production and the 'secondary poverty'
generated by the family cycle in the absence of developed forms of trade-
union organization and the impossiblity of an effective wage struggle.

Complex household forms extending beyond the nuclear family occurred
occasionally among propertied proto-industrial producers. According to the
type of production, the stage of production and conditions of ownership,
households with servants and apprentices were to be found more or less

frequently. These households were sometimes those of traditional rural craftsmen[65] or of small entrepreneurs who owned landed property and at the same time were engaged in the production and distribution of industrial goods.[66] A third important group were the proto-industrial 'Kulaks'.[67] The lines of demarcation between these extended household forms and another special type of rural work and settlement unit were blurred; in this special type, sub-peasant, satellite households of industrial producers were grouped as temporary lessees around a full peasant homestead, supplying its seasonal demand for labour and thus simultaneously serving as a kind of proto-industrial buttress to an agrarian organization of work.[68]

These household and settlement patterns should be considered as specific variants or mutations of the substantial farmer's or craftsman's family and they must be distinguished from the main type of extended family to be found among the landless or land-poor proto-industrial producers.

This main type recruited its members above all from the closer circle of relatives or from a reservoir of non-related paying or working inmates.[69] Thus it displayed a structure formally parallel to the extended household of the full peasant classes. Nevertheless, the two types differed fundamentally in their material, legal and institutional determinants. The extended family among the rural industrial workers was formed as a result of growing pauperization, increasing population pressure, of limited and congested living conditions and not least by the secondary poverty engendered by the family life-cycle. The classical stem-family, on the contrary, was formed essentially to conserve peasant family property.

Viewed from a comparative perspective, the extended family of the rural artisans was much more the forerunner of the corresponding proletarian household configuration than a variation of the peasant stem-family.[70] It did not function as an instrument of conservation of property, of well-being and of care for the aged, as was the case with the full peasant household, but as a private means to redistribute the poverty of the nuclear family chiefly by way of the family-and-kinship system. Such a situation of need could either arise temporarily during a critical stage of the family cycle or it could become a permanent condition of existence for the proto-industrial family as was the case in its final stage during the period of so-called de-industrialization.

The sparse data which have been made available so far indicate that already during the expansionary period of rural industry during the eighteenth century, the classical, three-generational, stem-family pattern, consisting of grandparents, parents and children, did not occur to a significant extent.[71] There does appear, however, a force within the family-and-kinship system integrating it in another direction. Nuclear family households which contained widows, unmarried sisters or brothers, nieces and nephews of the married couple did turn up fairly frequently.

The conditions under which married couples co-resided in other households or left them again point towards the causes of forming such extended families: married couples who lived in another household—whether it was as relatives or as immates—left it as often as the birth of children began the process of 'demographic differentiation'.[72] Also within their familial subsystem the ratio of labour and consumption worsened. With more mouths to feed, the causes no longer existed which originally had made possible co-residence of this family in its 'host's' house. For the host, his 'guests' counted above all as labourers or paying inmates, which reduced the burdens and economic risks of his own family.

Extended household formations among rural artisans therefore aimed primarily at balancing an unfavourable ratio of labourers and consumers. Thus the reversion to the kinship system or the recruiting of contributing inmates created a partial substitute for those functions which had been fulfilled within the traditional household by servants. Extended households seem to have been produced by primary misery and secondary poverty.

The structural conditions and consequences of the specific connection of production and reproduction by which the proto-industrial family was formed, are only incompletely revealed, however, by the changes in the composition of the domestic group. Marginal conditions of existence substantially restricted the chances of engineering the survival of the family within this context. The proto-industrial family was by no means as free as the peasant household in its decisions as to recruiting additional members for its labour force. The adaptation of the household to early marriage and high fertility required by proto-industrialization entailed above all a change in the organization of work within the nuclear family unit itself. The range and penetration of this 'inner structural change',[73] taking place within the organization of work, became manifest in the transformation of the division of labour between the sexes, in the configuration of roles within the family and in its social character.

This 'inner structural change' cannot be sufficiently understood if it is conceived as a process of 'structural differentiation' and 'role segmentation' or as a mere prelude to the disintegration of the 'ganze Haus'.[74] The history of the proto-industrial family economy formed a part of the long post-history of peasant society to the same extent that it formed a part of the pre-history of industrial capitalism. In this *gleichzeitige Ungleichzeitigkeit* its main historical significance is to be seen. In any case its historical significance, even if conceived from the perspective of the history of a status-specific family type, cannot be reduced to that of an initial stage in the secular 'loss of function' of the family,[75] which is so often myopically considered to be an immediate consequence of urbanization and industrialization and formally defined as the 'differentiation of occupational roles from the context of the kinship structure'.[76] The proto-industrial family economy, it is true, was drawn into a progressive process of social division of labour. On the level of the family unit, this led to a loss of individual functions of production and thereby to the specialization of the productive unit as a whole; as a structural unit of work, however, the family economy during proto-industrialization was very cohesive indeed. In this respect it by no means underwent a process of disintegration. On the contrary, the necessity to work together under adverse conditions entailed a higher degree of functional integration and thereby also of structural cohesion than was necessary in the peasant family. 'In case of emergency, one man may be recruited out of two or three peasant families to protect the Fatherland without doing injury to agricultural production. This is hardly possible with families weaving woollen cloth. Their manufactures are like a machine consisting of many wheels which may not be touched.'[77]

Even when the internal organization of family labour underwent substantial change during the proto-industrialization period, and even when change in the existential basis of work affected the role configurations and the role relations of family members outside the immediate work process, still the framework of the 'ganze Haus' remained. The restrictive conditions under which the family economy had to ensure its survival in fact necessitated a 'maximum. . .of familial cooperation'.[78] This had to be achieved by optimally redistributing and balancing the scarce labour resources of the individual family members. Under certain market conditions and within certain branches of production this imperative could go so far as to erase the traditional division of labour between the sexes and the age groups. The domestic production process of the rural industrial workers was thus characterized by a more flexible allocation of the role responsibilities of family members than was the case for the peasant (including even the small peasant and the sub-peasant classes). Especially lacking was that separation of work between men and women which was common, though not rigidly adhered to in peasant households, whereby as a rule the men worked out of doors in the fields, while the women were occupied with household tasks (including the practice of household crafts for the personal needs of the family, the cultivation of the gardens, milking the cows, care of the livestock and the marketing of the surplus produce of the household).[79] Even when this sex-specific division of labour was largely erased, as it was among those small peasants or sub-peasants who were still overwhelmingly occupied with agricultural production, the man nevertheless remained, whether as a day-labourer, migrant-labourer or cottager, generally excluded from domestic cottage production. The sphere of woman's labour on the other hand extended its reach within this class and became increasingly important. Whether the wife became active as a spinner engaging in production of commodities for the market or whether she increased the marginal returns from petty agrarian production by intensive cultivation or by tending the livestock on the commons, often it was only her activity that assured the vital margin of the family economy's subsistence.[80] 'A woman cannot get her living honestly with spinning on the distaff, but it stoppeth a gap.'[81]

The proto-industrial household continued this sub-peasant pattern and at the same time changed it by making the man, so to speak, return to the household. At least in the textile trades he moved into a work situation that had been traditionally established by women though he did not give up his labour outside the house, at least as long as the partial agrarian basis remained intact.[82] In this historical sense it seems justified to describe women as the 'vanguard of peasant household industries'.[83] This holds true especially in those places where household industry was carried on in conjunction with a partial agrarian basis. Generally, however, the proto-industrial situation was characterized by a rather strong degree of assimilation between the production functions of men and women. Women in the roles of cutlers and nailers[84] as well as organizers of the marketing of the industrial products[85] were as common as men were in the roles of spinners.[86] Occasionally this adaptation of familial work organization to the conditions of survival went beyond the disappearance of the traditional separation of labour between the sexes. It could lead to its reversal: where the necessities of production compelled women to neglect household 'duties',[88] this 'loss of function' could be compensated for by the men assuming traditional women's roles. Behaviour which to contemporary observers from the middle and upper strata of society all too quickly appeared as a reversal of the 'natural order', posed no particular role problem to weavers or to specialized households of spinners. It was here that 'men. . .cook, sweep and milk the cows, in order never to disturb the good, diligent wife in her work'.[89]

The distribution of family labour across the lines separating the labour between the sexes and age groups did not only determine the behaviour of family members in the sphere of production. Social behaviour and especially consumption and sexual activities were also influenced by the respective forms of co-operation between men and women and their outward constraints. As 'role functions' they were not separate from the process of production and reproduction, although in their symbolic, socio-cultural meaning they were more than mere extensions of that process.

Although precise investigations are lacking, there are indications that role behaviour of the sexes in consumption among the rural artisans was by no means constantly tied to a division of labour in which men would function as privileged consumers 'symbolising the role of breadwinner' (N. J. Smelser), and were thus entrusted with status consumption in public, whereas women would be restricted to householding, to caring and preparing for the necessities of life.[90] It is precisely in status consumption that an egalitarian role of both sexes came to be symbolized. This happened within the boundaries of the house as well as in the wider community. In the 'plebeian public' of the rural artisans both sexes frequently articulated their needs by drinking and smoking in common.[91] Their communality manifested itself not only by passive consumption, it showed itself also in the active defence of traditional norms of subsistence.[92] During food riots and actions against unbearable price rises, women by no means withdrew from the public eye. Very often it was the women who were 'more disposed to be mutinous;. . .in all public tumults they are foremost in violence and ferocity'.[93]

Even in immediate sexual encounters, the new conditions of production led to a changing social texture. Property constraints and patriarchal controls were loosened and, as we have noted, largely replaced by the need to select marriage partners on the basis of their productive capacity. Nevertheless, these new criteria permitted more latitude, more individualization and personalization in the selection of partners and thereby produced a gradual 'transformation of the world of erotic feelings'.[94] Erotic expression, however, was not confined to a separate sphere, distinct from the work process, but was bound in a specific way to household production itself.[95] 'Where people of both sexes are always together, in the warmth of the same room, and where they. . .carry out work that occupies their head and heart so little', they spend their time in idle intercourse 'which is commonly concerned with lust and lasciviousness, with fraud and theft' and those who have 'the dirtiest ideas imagine themselves to be and are held by the others as heroes'.[96]

It was not only at the symbolic level that the enlarged significance of sexuality in the everyday life of the rural industrial workers changed the position of the sexes and age groups. It led both to a lowering of the age of sexual activity[97] and to increasing similarities in the sexual activity and behaviour patterns of men and women. The 'immorality' and 'shameless freedom of the sexes' which middle-class observers noted about the rural artisans in contrast to peasant behaviour[98] was primarily a criticism also of sex-specific role behaviour. Observed through the behavioural biases of the upper class, this similitude of the behaviour patterns of men and women certainly appeared as an unbalanced relationship:

Among these classes of men, the male sex is the reserved one and the women the ones who are on the make. . .The common maid understands the art of coquetry in its various forms just as well as the mature woman; she discloses her breasts without shame and certain other enticing parts of her body half way because she knows that is more alluring than all the way. If the young man still resists, she helps weaken him with liquor and if he doesn't respond to her invitation to her bed, she joins him in his. The usual plot of a romantic novel is thus reversed.[99]

This quotation unwittingly contains an important grain of historical truth pointing beyond its own specific content and once more illuminating the general problems with which historians of the family are confronted. Their critical praxis will indeed have to be informed by an understanding of those experiences which, according to the disapproving contemporary observer, formed part of the everyday life of the rural artisans. Quite apart from any reorientation of 'perspectives' this demands a much more fundamental change in the basic position of family history. The historian of the family must, in his conceptual approach, in the material questions which he asks and in the source material which he scrutinizes, try to 'reverse the usual plot of a romantic novel' as it too often has been retold by historians and sociologists of the family, even today.[100] Ruling-class perspectives not only determined the way contemporary observers perceived rural artisans; they persisted in the explicit or implicit middle-class bias which still seems enshrined in the conceptual approach and even methodological perspectives of much that is written in the contemporary history and sociology of the family. In this way, social scientists, be they sociologists or historians of the family, become what Walter Benjamin referred to as 'adherents of historicism', against whom he recommended a form of 'cautious' historical materialism that could well serve as an agenda for future family history: 'The adherents of historicism actually empathize. . .with the victor. And all rulers are the heirs of those who conquered before them. Hence, empathy with the victor invariably benefits the rulers. Historical materialists know what that means. Whoever has emerged victorious participates to this day in the triumphal procession in which the present rulers step over those who are lying prostrate. According to traditional practice the spoils are carried along in the procession. They are called cultural treasures, and a historical materialist views them with cautious detachment. . .A historical materialist. . .dissociates himself from . . .(them) as far as possible. He regards it as his task to brush history against the grain.'[101]

NOTES

1. This essay originated from a survey of the literature and source materials on rural industrialization which I undertook preparatory to regional field research in Germany. It represents some of my conclusions after completing the initial stage of a larger research project I began with two of my Göttingen colleagues, P. Kriedte and J. Schlumbohm. A first draft, presented to the spring conference of the *Arbeitskreis für Moderne Sozialgeschichte* at Bad Homburg in 1975, was published in the proceedings of this conference: W. Conze (ed.), *Die Familie im Übergang von der entfalteten Agrargesellschaft zum Industriesystem* (Stuttgart, 1976). A longer version was published as chapter 2 of: P. Kriedte, H. Medick, J. Schlumbohm with contributions by F. Mendels and H. Kisch, *Industrialisierung vor der Industrialisierung: Gewerbliche Warenproduktion auf dem Land in der Formationsperiode des Kapitalismus* (Göttingen, 1977), translated as *Industrialization before Industrialization: Rural Industry in the Genesis of Capitalism* (Cambridge, 1981). The English version of this essay was made possible by the generous and constructive help I received from Robert Berdahl, Wilf Holloway, David Levine and Roger Schofield.

2. The achievements and infrastructure of this field of research have been discussed in a factual survey by T. K. Hareven, 'Die Familie in historischer Perspektive. Laufende Arbeiten in England und den Vereinigten Staaten', *Geschichte und Gesellschaft,* 1(1975), 370 – 86. For research in French history see 'Famille et Société', *Annales, E. S. C.,* xxvii (1972). For Western Europe as a whole see L. K. Berkner, 'Recent research on the history of the family in Western Europe', *Journal of Marriage and the Family,* xxxv (1973). An interesting overview and critical analysis of current research trends and recent literature was presented by Christopher Lasch in *The New York Review of Books:* 'The family and history', no. 18 (13 Nov. 1975), 33 – 8; 'The emotions of family life', no. 19 (27 Nov. 1975), 39 – 42; 'What the doctor ordered', no. 20 (11 Dec. 1975), 50 – 4.

3. See the special number of the new journal *Geschichte und Gesellschaft* devoted to this subject: 'Historische Familienforschung und Demographie', 1 (1975), no. 2/3.

4. See, especially, *The World We Have Lost* (2nd edn. 1971). See, also, his contributions to the volume *Household and Family in Past Time* (Cambridge, 1972) which he co-edited with Richard Wall: 'Introduction: the history of the family', 1 – 73, and 'Mean household size in England since the sixteenth century', 125 – 58. On this subject Laslett has also co-authored an essay with E. A. Hammel, 'Comparing household structure over time and between cultures', *Comparative Studies in Society and History,* xvi (1974), 73 – 109.

5. *Household and Family in Past Time* attracted a great deal of critical attention. Among the most far-reaching reviews the following stand out: E. P. Thompson (anon.), 'Under the rooftree', *The Times Literary Supplement,* no. 3713 (4 May 1973), 485 – 7; L. K. Berkner, 'The use and misuse of census data for the historical analysis of family structure', *Journal of Interdisciplinary History,* iv (1975), 721 – 38; H. Rosenbaum, 'Zur neueren Entwicklung der historischen Familienforschung', *Geschichte und Gesellschaft, 1 (1975), 210 – 25;* M. Mitterauer, 'Familiengröße – Familientypen – Familienzyklus. Probleme quantitativer Auswertung von österreichischem Quellenmaterial', *Geschichte und Gesellschaft,* 1(1975), 226 – 55; and T. K. Hareven, *History and Theory,* xiv (1975), 242 – 51.

6. Laslett, *The World We Have Lost,* 241 – 53.

7. Ibid, 20.

8. Already in Laslett, *The World We have Lost,* 93 ff., 248 f., and *passim*; explicitly in Laslett, 'Introduction', 4 ff., 45ff.

9. Laslett, 'Mean household size', 125 – 58; the same position was already taken before Laslett with reference to a special West European type of lower-class family as an essential pre-condition of industrialization by W. J. Goode, *World Revolution and Family Patterns* (1963), 10 ff.

10. On the correspondence of modernization and industrialization with the formation of the nuclear family unit in relative isolation from the kinship system cf. T. Parsons, 'The social structure of the family', in R. N. Anshen (ed.), *The Family: Its Functions and Destiny* (New York, 1959), 241 – 74; N. Smelser, 'The modernization of social relations', in M. Weiner (ed.), *Modernization: The Dynamics of Growth* (New York, 1966).

11. Cf. esp. Laslett, *The World We Have Lost,* 265, fn. 22.

12. E. Bloch, *Erbschaft dieser Zeit* (Frankfurt, 1973 [1935]), 104 ff: 'Ungleichzeitigkeit und die Pflicht zu ihrer Dialektik'.

13. H. U. Wehler's pragmatic proposal (cf. his *Modernisierungstheorie und Geschichte*) (Göttingen, 1975), esp. 47 ff.) to use the 'potential' of current modernization theories by furnishing them with a 'historically concrete framework' (ibid., 47) which according to the author seems to lie in their increasingly being 'tied to occidental history' (ibid., 50) does not escape from those weaknesses which Wehler criticizes himself: their euro- and ethnocentric prejudice and their unilinear historical perspective; cf. Lasch, 'The family and history', 36 ff.

14. Interesting suggestions for positive mutual co-operation between historians and social scientists in developing a historical theory of the family are made by K. Hausen, 'Familie als Gegenstand historischer Sozialwissenschaft. Bemerkungen zu einer Forschungsstrategie', in: *Geschichte und Gesellschaft,* 1 (1975), 171 – 209.

15. Thus ran (without being fundamentally contradicted by the historians present at this occasion) the arguments of the sociologist F. Neidhardt in a contribution to the autumn session 1975 of the *Arbeitskreis für Moderne Sozialgeschichte* which he entitled: 'Fragen eines Familiensoziologen an die Historiker' ('questions of a family sociologist to the historians').

16. Cf. the individual contributions to the volume *Household and Family in Past Time* with the notable exception of the important essay by the anthropologist J. Goody, 'The evolution of the family', ibid., 103 – 24, to which E. P. Thompson in his review of the whole volume rightly referred as a 'time-bomb ticking inside Mr Laslett's own covers' (Thompson, 'Under the rooftree', 486).

17. Cf. Laslett, 'Introduction', 24; Laslett and Hammel, 'Comparing household structure', 75.

18. Laslett and Hammel, 'Comparing household structure', 76.

19. H. Rosenbaum, 'Zur neueren Entwicklung', 216 ff., here 217; cf. the similar criticism by M. Mitterauer, 'Familiengröße – Familientyp – Familienzyklus', 226 ff.

20. Thompson, 'Under the rooftree', 486; cf. the substantive treatment of this problem in Thompson's important review-essay 'Anthropology and the discipline of historical context', *Midland History* (Spring 1972), 41 – 55: 'The discipline of history is, above all, the discipline of context; each fact can be given *meaning* [my emphasis] only within an ensemble of other meanings' (ibid. 45).

21. See on this below pp. 31 ff.

22. D. Groh, 'Basisprozesse und Organisationsproblem. Skizze eines sozialgeschichtlichen Forschungsprojekts', *Festschrift für W. Conze zum 65. Geburtstag* (Stuttgart, 1976).

23. Cf. the relevant parts written by me in the study quoted above in fn. 1, esp. chapters 2.2 to 2.6.

24. E. Hobsbawm, 'The crisis of the seventeenth century' (1954) in T. Aston (ed.), *Crisis in Europe, 1560 – 1660* (1965), 38.

25. C. and R. Tilly, 'Agenda for European Economic History in the 1970s', *Journal of Economic History,* xxxi (1971), 186; cf. the same authors' more extended version, 'Emerging problems in the modern economic history of Western Europe' (mimeograph, 1971).

26. F. Mendels, 'Proto-industrialization: the first phase of the industrialization process', *Journal of Economic History,* xxxii (1972), 241 – 61.

27. W. A. Lewis, 'Economic development with unlimited supplies of labour', *Manchester School of Economic and Social Studies,* xxii (1954), 139 – 91.

28. Hobsbawm, 'The crisis of the seventeenth century', 21 ff., 50 ff.

29. O. Brunner, 'Das "Ganze Haus" und die alteuropäische Ökonomik' (1958), in id., *Neue Wege der Verfassungs- und Sozialgeschichte* (2nd edn. Göttingen, 1968), 103 – 27.

30. A. V. Chayanov, *Die Lehre von der bäuerlichen Wirtschaft. Versuch einer Theorie der Familienwirtschaft im Landbau* (Berlin, 1923), esp. 25 – 41; a revised and augmented English edition, translated from the first Russian edition (Moscow, 1925) appeared under the title 'Peasant farm organization', in A. V. Chayanov, *The Theory of Peasant Economy,* edited by D. Thorner, B. Kerblay and R. E. F. Smith (Homewood/Ill., 1966), 29 – 269, esp. 70 – 89; cf. the same author's 'Zur Frage einer Theorie der nichtkapitalistischen Wirtschaftssysteme', *Archiv für Sozialwissenschaft und Sozialpolitik,* li (1924), 577 – 613; English translation under the title 'On the theory of non-capitalist economic systems', in Chayanov, *The Theory,* 1 – 29; excellent introductions to Chayanov's work are given by D. Thorner, 'Chayanov's concept of peasant economy', in Chayanov, *The Theory,* xi – xiv, and B. Kerblay, 'A. V. Chayanov, life, career, works', ibid. xxv – lxxv; an interesting aspect of Chayanov's model which does not amount, however, to a 'reformulation' of his theory is pointed out by J. R. Millar, 'A reformulation of A. V. Chayanov's theory of the peasant economy', *Economic Development and Cultural Change,* xviii (1969), 219 – 29; critical inquiry into the results of Chayanov's field research: M. Harrison, 'Chayanov and the economics of the Russian peasantry', *Journal of Peasant Studies,* ii (1975), 389 – 417; after 1945 O. Brunner was the first West-German historian to recognize the pioneer character of Chayanov's works without, however, making intensive use of them: cf. Brunner, *Adeliges Landleben und Europäischer Geist. Leben und Werk Wolf Helmhards von Hohberg 1612 – 1688* (Salzburg, 1949), 359; Brunner, 'Das "Ganze Haus"', 107; Brunner, 'J. J. Bechers Entwurf einer Oeconomia ruralis et domestica', in *Sitzungsberichte der Phil. Hist. Klasse der Österreichischen Akademie der Wissenschaften,* 226, 3 (Vienna 1949), 85 – 91. M. M. Postan's and J. Z. Titow's reference to the German edition of Chayanov's *Peasant Farm Organization,* in Postan and Titow, 'Heriots and prices on Winchester manors' (1959), reprinted in: M. M. Postan, *Essays on Medieval Agriculture and General Problems of the Medieval Economy* (Cambridge, 1973), 174 fn. 35, seems to be based on a misunderstanding of Chayanov's intentions; this is overlooked in the interesting if somewhat sceptical remarks on Chayanov by R. H. Hilton, *The English Peasantry in the Later Middle Ages* (Oxford, 1975), 6.

31. J. R. Millar, paraphrasing Chayanov, in id., 'A reformulation', 228.

32. Thorner, 'Chayanov's concept', xv ff.

33. Chayanov, 'Peasant farm organization', 86 ff.

34. Chayanov, ibid., 70 ff.; on craft-good production of the peasant household, ibid., 107 ff.

35. F. Engels, preface to the 2nd edition 'Zur Wohnungsfrage' (1887), in Marx-Engels *Werke,* vol. xxi (Berlin, 1962), 331 f.

36. K. A. Wittfogel, *Wirtschaft und Gesellschaft Chinas* (Leipzig, 1931), 670.

37. M. Weber, *Die protestantische Ethik und der Geist des Kapitalismus.* Part I, Ch. 2: 'Der "Geist" des Kapitalismus', in M. Weber, *Die protestantische Ethik,* vol. 1, ed. by J. Winckelmann (Munich, 1969, 7th edn.), 50.

38. Weber's grandfather on his father's side, Karl August Weber, was a linen

merchant at Bielefeld, the urban centre of the north-west German linen-producing area of Minden-Ravensberg. He was one of the shareholders of 'Weber, Laer und Niermann', which, as a leading merchant house of the region, helped to spread the 'fame of Bielefeld linen' [Marianne Weber, *Max Weber. Ein Lebensbild* (Heidelberg, 1950), 29]; Max Weber's precise, but strangely nostalgic remarks on the reciprocal relationship which existed during the proto-industrial phase between a pre-capitalist mentality on the part of the producer and the rentier mentality of the putter-out, who followed a 'standesgemäße Lebensführung' rather than a 'capitalist ethic' (Max Weber, *Protestantische Ethik,* 55 ff.), may be traced back to his early personal experiences in his grandfather's house at the time of proto-industrial decline (cf. Marianne Weber, *Max Weber. Ein Lebensbild,* 30).

39. This is shown by the interesting discussion on women's domestic labour, which refers to another historical context but is nevertheless comparable to the problems discussed in this essay, if one sees 'housewife labour' in historical terms, as a residual element of the family mode of production: W. Seccombe, 'The housewife and her labour under capitalism', *New Left Review,* lxxxiii (1974), 3 – 24, esp. 8 ff.; J. Gardiner, 'Women's domestic labour', ibid. lxxxix (1975), 47 – 58, esp. 53 ff.; M. Coulson, Br. Magaŝ, H. Wainwright, 'The housewife and her labour under capitalism. A critique', ibid, 59 – 71; W. Seccombe, 'Domestic labour—reply to critics', *New Left Review,* xciv (1975), 85 – 96; L. Müller, 'Kinderaufzucht im Kapitalismus—wertlose Arbeit: über die Folgen der Nichtbewertung der Arbeit der Mütter für das Bewußtsein der Frauen als Lohnarbeiterinnen', *Probleme des Klassenkampfs,* xxii (1976), 13 – 65. Important new insights are contained in C. Meillassoux, *Femmes, greniers et capitaux* (Paris, 1975), esp. 139 ff.

40. Among the few quantitative and status-specific investigations of household sizes and family structures for regions or locations of rural industry the following are to be mentioned: L. K. Berkner, 'Family, Social Structure and Rural Industry: A Comparative Study of the Waldviertel and the Pays de Caux in the 18th Century' (Ph.D. Harvard University, 1973), 294 – 346, esp. 307 – 9 and the tables on pp. 310, 329, 347 ff.; D. Levine, 'The Demographic Implications of Rural Industrialization. A Family Reconstitution Study of Two Leicestershire Villages 1600 – 1851' (Ph.D. University of Cambridge, 1974), 66 – 97; cf. the references in: M. Mitterauer, 'Zur Familienstruktur in ländlichen Gebieten Österreichs', in: H. Helczmanovszki (ed.), *Beiträge zur Bevölkerungs- und Sozialgeschichte Österreichs* (Vienna, 1973), 168 – 222, here 181, 190 f.; M. Mitterauer, 'Vorindustrielle Familienformen. Zur Funktionsentlastung des "ganzen Hauses" im 17. und 18. Jahrhundert', in F. Engel-Janosi *et al.* (eds.), *Fürst, Bürger, Mensch: Untersuchungen zur politischen und soziokulturellen Wandlungsprozessen im vorrevolutionären Europa* (Vienna, 1975). 133, 157, 160 ff.; also the references in Rudolf Braun's pioneering study: *Industrialisierung und Volksleben. Veränderungen der Lebensformen unter Einwirkung der verlagsindustriellen Heimarbeit in einem ländlichen Industriegebiet (Zürcher Oberland) vor 1800* (Winterthur, 1960), 89, 162 ff.

41. Levine, *Demographic Implications,* 74 ff.; the same situation is indicated by a comparison of the findings in R. Wall, 'Mean household-size in England from printed sources', in P. Laslett and R. Wall (eds.), *Household and Family in Past Time* (Cambridge, 1972), 159 – 203, where the mean household sizes for settlements in the heavily proto-industrialized area of Lancashire (esp. the region round Manchester) are

decisively larger than those for agrarian regions (ibid., 178 f. and 180 f.); cf. also E. J. Walter, *Zur Soziologie der alten Eidgenossenschaft. Eine Analyse der Sozial- und Berufsstruktur von der Reformation bis zur Französischen Revolution* (Berne, 1966), 78 – 82.

42. Levine, *Demographic Implications,* 69.

43. Ibid., 129 f.

44. R. Schofield, 'Age specific mobility in an eighteenth-century rural English parish', in *Annales de Démographie historique* (1970), 261 – 74; Levine, 'Demographic Implications', 72; Berkner, 'Social Structure', 200, 323 – 47, esp. 331 ff.

45. Charles O'Hara, *Account of Sligo 1760* (referring to changes in family structure following the transition of the small and sub-peasant population of North-West Ireland to linen weaving), as quoted by W. H. Crawford, *Economy and Society in South Ulster in the Eighteenth Century,* in *Clayton Record* (1973), 253 f.

46. I. Pinchbeck, *Women Workers and the Industrial Revolution 1750 – 1850* (2nd ed. London, 1969), 122, 160, 168, 179, 232 ff., 272 ff.; E. P. Thompson, *The Making of the English Working Class* (Harmondsworth, 1970), 366 ff.; A. Thun, *Die Industrie am Niederrhein und ihre Arbeiter* (2 vols. Leipzig, 1879), i. 109, 150; Braun, *Industrialisierung und Volksleben,* 24 ff., 183, 192 ff.

47. See the precise description in Braun, *Industrialisierung und Volksleben,* 83 ff.; cf. also J. N. von Schwerz, *Beschreibung der Landwirtschaft in Westfalen und Rheinpreußen* (2 vols, Stuttgart, 1836), i. 111; Pinchbeck, *Women Workers,* 273, 278, 279.

48. J. Hajinal, 'European marriage patterns in perspective', in: D. V. Glass and D. E. C. Eversley (eds.), *Population in History: Essays in Historical Demography* (London, 1965), 101 – 46; J. D. Chambers, *Population, Economy and Society in Pre-Industrial England* (London, 1972), 34 – 50; Braun, *Industrialisierung und Volksleben,* 60 f., 155 ff.; G. Mackenroth, *Bevölkerungslehre* (Berlin, 1953), 421 ff.

49. On the connection of inheritance, peasant property and family structure as governed by the developmental cycle of domestic groups see the exemplary study by L. K. Berkner, 'The stem family and the developmental cycle of the peasant household: an eighteenth-century Austrian example', *American Historical Review,* lxxvii (1972), 398 – 417; Mitterauer, 'Zur Familienstruktur', 197 ff.; id., 'Familiengröße – Familientypen – Familienzyklus', 243 ff.; id., 'Vorindustrielle Familienformen', 134 ff.; cf. also M. Anderson, *Family Structure in Nineteenth-Century Lancashire* (Cambridge, 1971), 79 ff.

50. C. and R. Tilly, 'Agenda for European economic history', 189.

51. Berkner, 'Stem family', 400 ff.; Anderson, *Family Structure,* 81 ff.; M. Segalen, *Nuptialité et alliance. Le choix du conjoint dans une commune de l'Eure* (Paris, 1971), 99 ff.

52. The transitional character of the marriage behaviour of rural industrial producers standing between the behaviour of peasants, determined by property relationships and that of the modern individualistic 'companionate marriage' is rightly stressed by M. Segalen, *Nuptialité, 106;* R. Braun lays too much emphasis on 'sublimation' and 'intimization' as characteristics of rural-industrial marriage customs: cf. Braun, *Industrialisierung und Volksleben,* 64 ff.; an even more one-sided interpretation from the point of view of a unilinear concept of 'modernization' and 'emancipation' is to be found in E. Shorter, 'Female emancipation, birth control, and

fertility in European history', *American Historical Review,* lxxviii (1973), 614 ff.; E. Shorter, *The Making of the Modern Family* (New York, 1975), 255 – 68.

53. J. Hirzel, *Rede über den physischen, ökonomischen und sittlich religiösen Zustand der östlichen Berggemeinden des Kanton Zürich, Synodialrede 1816* (Zurich, 1816), 16, as quoted by Braun, *Industrialisierung und Volksleben,* 66.

54. Segalen, *Nuptialité,* 75 ff.

55. Segalen, *Nuptialité,* 99 ff.

56. J. N. v. Schwerz, *Beschreibung der Landwirtschaft,* vol. 1, 111.

57. Cf. Levine, *Demographic Implications,* 104 – 16; Chambers, *Population, Economy and Society,* 49 ff.; J. D. Chambers, *The Vale of Trent, 1670 – 1800: A Regional Study of Economic Change* (*Economic History Review,* Supplement 3, Cambridge, 1958), 51 – 3; W. Troeltsch, *Die Calwer Zeughandlungskompanie und ihre Arbeiter. Studien zur Gewerbe- und Sozialgeschichte Altwürttembergs* (Jena, 1897), 405; Braun, *Industrialisierung und Volksleben,* 59 – 80.

58. For a systematic discussion of the relationships between household-cycle and family structures see M. Fortes, 'Introduction' to J. Goody (ed.), *The Developmental Cycle in Domestic Groups* (Cambridge, 1958), 1 – 14; the same essay reprinted as 'The developmental cycle in domestic groups', in J. Goody (ed.), *Kinship* (Harmondsworth, 1971), 85 – 98; a critique of the Laslett—Fortes approach has been applied to the analysis of peasant households by Berkner, 'Stem family', 405 ff.; cf. Mitterauer, 'Familiengröße – Familientypen – Familienzyklus', 243 ff.

59. Systematic analyses of demo-economic relationships during the proto-industrialization phase have been attempted in: F. Mendels, 'Proto-industrialization', 249 – 53; for a brilliant condensation of his arguments cf. F. Mendels, 'Industrialization and population pressure in eighteenth-century Flanders', *Journal of Economic History,* xxxi (1971), 269 – 71; important 'systemic' interpretations have been given by two members of the 'Cambridge Group for the History of Population and Social Structure': E.A. Wrigley, *Population and History* (1969), 136 ff.; idem, 'The process of modernization and the industrial revolution in England', *Journal of Interdisciplinary History,* iii (1972/3), 150 – 3; R. Schofield, 'The relationship between demographic structure and environment in pre-industrial Western Europe' in W. Conze (ed.), *Sozialgeschichte der Familie in der Neuzeit Europas: Neue Forschungen* (Industrielle Welt, 21; Stuttgart, 1976), 147 – 60; a most important field study is D. Levine, *Demographic Implications, passim;* a critical assessment of F. Mendels' approach has been undertaken by G. Hohorst, 'Bevölkerungsentwicklung und Wirtschaftswachstum in Preußen 1816 – 1914' (Ph.D. in Economics, University of Münster, 1974), esp. 122 ff.; cf. idem, 'Bevölkerungsentwicklung und Wirtschaftwachstum als historischer Entwicklungsprozeß demo-ökonomischer Systeme', in R. Mackensen and H. Weber (eds.), *Dynamik der Bevölkerungsentwicklung. Strukturen und Bedingungen* (Munich, 1973), 91 – 118.

60. Pinchbeck, *Women Workers,* 179.

61. This aspect has been stressed in the unduly neglected work of S. Coontz, *Population Theories and the Economic Interpretation* (1957), ch. vii, 145 ff.

62. 'Statement of a working man', in *Meliora,* ed. by Ingestre (London, 1952), 226 f., as quoted by J. Foster, *Class Struggle and the Industrial Revolution. Early Industrial Capitalism in Three English Towns* (1974), 94.

63. Thun, *Die Industrie am Niederrhein,* i. 150; cf. the interesting statistical

information for linen and cotton-weavers' families in the Saxonian district of Oberlausitz for the year 1832 given by F. Schmidt, *Untersuchungen über Bevölkerung, Arbeitslohn und Pauperismus in ihrem gegenseitigen Zusammenhang* (Leipzig, 1836), 296 ff., esp. 298; cf. D. Bythell, *The Handloom Weavers* (Cambridge, 1969), 136; Pinchbeck, *Women Workers,* 179.

64. E. R. R. Green, 'The cotton hand-loom weavers in the north-east of Ireland', *Ulster Journal of Archaeology,* vii (1944), 30 – 41; S. Bucher, *Bevölkerung und Wirtschaft des Amtes Entlebuch im 18. Jahrhundert* (Lucerne, 1974), 228 (table), 229; cf. the remarks on the age-specific participation of women in the industrial production process, in: Levine, *Demographic Implications,* 47; cf. J. Knodel and V. Prachuabmoh, *The Fertility of Thai Women. Results of the First Rural and Urban Rounds of the Longitudinal Study of Social, Demographic and Economic Change in Thailand* (Institute of Population Studies, Chulalongkorn University, Bangkok 1973),49.

65. On the conditions in the lower Rhine small metalware trades (at Remscheid) see Thun, *Die Industrie am Niederrhein,* ii. 148 ff., 150 f.; v. Schwerz, *Beschreibung der Landwirtschaft,* i. 110 f. (weavers of fine linen fabric in the district of Ravensberg). One of the effects which 'home-industrial' production had on the guild-organization of certain trades in the countryside seems to have been that children to an increasing degree remained in the household of their parents as apprentices, which led to a gradual disappearance of the traditional tramping habits of the artisan; cf. Troeltsch, *Calwer Zeughandlungskompagnie,* 208 ff.; Berkner, *Family Social Structure,* 200; caused by the qualitative conditions of work, the craft pattern of 'extended households' with apprentices and servants was especially marked in the finishing stage of the textile trades.

66. A good example of this household-type is furnished by the 'clothiers' in the West Riding of Yorkshire, cf. H. Heaton, *The Yorkshire Woollen and Worsted Industries* (Oxford, 1920), 295 f.; E. Lipson, *The Economic History of England,* ii (1931), 69 ff.

67. H. Kisch, 'The textile industries in Silesia and the Rhineland: a comparative study in industrialization', in P. Kriedte, H. Medick, J. Schlumbohm (eds.), *Industrialization before Industrialization: Rural Industry in the Genesis of Capitalism* (Cambridge, 1981), 178 – 200, for this household-type as it existed in the linen industry of North-West Germany, where the full-peasant households of 'Kolonen' and 'Meier' had weaving and spinning male and female servants—cf. the description by v. Schwerz, *Beschreibung der Landwirtschaft,* i. 128; parallels can be found in the peasant 'manufacturers' of the Northern Irish linen trades, cf. A. Young, *A Tour of Ireland* (2 vols, London, 1780), i. 149 f.—for the entrepreneurial functions of this social group cf. C. Gill, *The Rise of the Irish Linen Industry* (Oxford, 1925), 145 ff.; for home-industrial 'Kulak-manufactures' cf. Wittfogel, *Wirtschaft und Gesellschaft Chinas,* 652 f.

68. This 'Heuerlingssytem' was very common in the north-west German linen-producing areas; cf. H. Ripenhausen, *Die Entwicklung der bäuerlichen Kulturlandschaft in Ravensberg* (Mat. Nat. Diss. Göttingen, 1936), 107 ff.; H. Wrasman, 'Das Heuerlingswesen im Fürstentum Osnabrück', *Mitteilungen des Vereins für Geschichte und Landeskunde von Osnabrück,* xlii (1919), 53 – 171; ibid., xliv (1921), 1 – 154; parallels may be found in the linen-producing areas of Northern

Ireland (cf. Crawford, 'Economy and society in south Ulster', 253) and in the 'masure' system of the Pays de Caux in upper Normandy as described by Berkner, *Family, Social Structure,* 238 ff.

69. For the data base of the following remarks on the 'extended family' but not necessarily for its interpretation cf. Levine, *Demographic Implications,* 66 – 97 and Berkner, *Family, Social Structure,* 294-346.

70. Cf. especially Foster, *Class Struggle,* 91 ff. and Anderson, *Family Structure,* 79 ff., 111 ff.

71. Levine, *Demographic Implications,* 85 ff., esp. 93, and Berkner, *Family, Social Structure,* 296 ff., esp. 298, 307 ff.

72. In confirmation of M. Anderson's thesis this has been stressed by Levine, *Demographic Implications,* 93 ff.; Anderson, *Family Structure,* 48 ff.; cf. Foster, *Class Struggle,* 91 ff., especially tables on pp. 98, 99; contrary to Anderson's assumptions (id., *Family Structure,* 166 f.) the views of Anderson and Foster possibly contradict each other only on the surface; their contradictions seem in any case to be founded less on different empirical findings than on divergent perspectives of interpretation; while Foster places his emphasis on the 'cycle of poverty' and the critical life phases of the 'host family' and tries to understand its extension beyond the nuclear family through the formation of complex households and the falling back on to the kinship system ('sharing', 'huddling') as an effort to solve the problem of 'secondary poverty' of the working-class family, Anderson fixes his attention primarily on the co-residing 'guest family' and its point of departure from the host family (Anderson, 48 ff., esp. table 14); what seems to be necessary is a combination of both perspectives. It is interesting to note in this connection that a status-specific interpretation of Anderson's own data shows for the case of the group of 'lower factory, labourer, and handloom weaver' (ibid., 51, table 14)—in clear distinction from other social groups such as 'higher factory and artisan'—a tendency to extend their families by 'sharing' in exactly those critical phases of the life-cycle of the family, which are characterized by a high rate of dependent children.

73. Braun, *Industrialisierung und Volksleben,* 83.

74. This is the problematical thesis of the works of N. J. Smelser, which is in need of a historical critique. Within the strait-jacket of structural-functionalist theory ('empty theoretical boxes', 'filling the boxes', 'refilling the boxes') Smelser all too quickly assumes a convergence of family economy and *industrial* capitalism and sees this tendency on its way already during the proto-industrialization phase: N. J. Smelser, *Social Change and the Industrial Revolution: An Application of Theory to the Lancashire Cotton Industry 1770 – 1840* (1959), esp. 50 – 60, 129 – 43, 158 – 79, 180 – 212; *idem,* 'Sociological history: The industrial revolution and the British working-class family', in: M. W. Flinn, T. C. Smout (eds.), *Essays in Social History* (Oxford, 1974), 23 – 38; for a critique of Smelser's hypothesis of a successful process of 'adaptation' by the family work-force to conditions of factory-industry in the initial phase of machine spinning: M. M. Edwards and R. Lloyd-Jones, 'N. J. Smelser and the cotton factory family: a reassessment', in: *Textile History and Economic History. Essays in Honour of J. de Lacy Mann,* ed. by N. B. Harte and K. G. Ponting (Manchester, 1973), 304 – 19.

75. T. Parsons, 'The American family: its relations to personality and the social structure', in: id. and R. F. Bales, *Family, Socialization and Interaction Process* (1956), 3 – 33, here p. 16.

76. T. Parsons, 'Das Problem des Strukturwandels: eine theoretische Skizze' ('An outline of the social system. IV, the problem of structural change'), in W. Zapf (ed.), *Theorien des sozialen Wandels* (3rd edn. Cologne – Berlin, 1971), 35 – 74, here p. 48: in the context quoted here Parsons explicitly refers to Smelser's study on the cotton industry.

77. J. P. Süßmilch, *Die göttliche Ordnung in den Veränderungen des menschlichen Geschlechts, aus der Geburt, dem Tode und der Fortplanzung desselben erwiesen* (2 vols, Berlin, 3rd edn. 1765), ii. 67.

78. Hausen, 'Familie als Gegenstand historischer Sozialwissenschaft', 200.

79. Pinchbeck, *Women Workers,* 7 ff.; J. Scott and L. Tilly, 'Women's work and the family in nineteenth-century Europe', *Comparative Studies in Society and History,* xvii (1975), 36 – 64, here 43 ff., esp. 44 ff. n. 26; R. H. Hilton, 'Women in the village', in id., *The English Peasantry in the Later Middle Ages* (Oxford, 1975), 95 – 110; cf. H. Schmidlin, *Arbeit und Stellung der Frau in der Landgutswirtschaft der Hausväter* (Phil. Diss. Jena, 1940, published at Heidelberg 1941) which on the whole is confusing but contains some useful individual observations and interesting contemporary illustrations.

80. Pinchbeck, *Women Workers,* 19 ff.; cf.—without sufficient attention to status-specific differences—E. Richards, 'Women in the British economy since about 1700: an interpretation', *History,* lix (1974), 342 ff.; on the essential marginal returns from women's work see Pinchbeck, *Women Workers,* 20 f.; for a later phase cf. the interesting findings of J. Kitteringham, 'Country work girls in nineteenth-century England', in R. Samuel (ed.), *Village Life and Labour* (History Workshop Series, 1975), 113 ff.

81. J. Fitzherbert, *The Book of Husbandry* (1534) ed. by W. W. Skeat (1882), 96, as quoted by Lipson, *Economic History,* ii. 50.

82. On the division of labour in rural-industrial households, cf. Pinchbeck, *Women Workers*, 111 ff. (cotton industry); ibid. 129 ff. (spinning); ibid. 157 ff. (weaving); ibid. 202 ff. (smaller domestic industries); ibid. 270 ff. (small metal trades); Lipson, *Economic History,* ii. 50 f. (wool industry); even in the textile trades the division of labour within the household showed no uniformity; it varied according to the branch of production, its developmental stage and its market conditions; it frequently deviated from the 'classical' pattern (as described for instance in Smelser, *Social Change,* 54 f., 183) in which the man was weaving, the wife was spinning, and the children were occupied with subsidiary activities such as the preparation of materials for the production process; cf. the variants mentioned in Braun, *Industrialisierung und Volksleben,* 210; Thun, *Die Industrie am Niederrhein,* i. 108 f., 148; an important form of domestic division of labour—resulting from the combination of a partial agrarian subsistence base with industrial production—has been precisely observed by C. H. Bitter: 'If one enters the cottages of those rural dwellers, who do not hold larger pieces of land and who have to gain their basic subsistence by spinning, one often finds the whole family sitting at the spinning wheel. It does not seldom happen, that grandmother, mother and grandchild are occupied with spinning, whereas the father and his grown-up son work in the field or do other jobs around the house, such as to prepare the meals, clean turnips or peel potatoes, if and as long as they have any. In the weavers' cottages the father is busy with preparing the yarn if he has not gone out to buy yarn or sell the linen that has been produced, or if

he does not cultivate the plot of land together with his grown-up son. The mother is occupied about the hearth or tends the animals. The elder daughters sit at the loom and the younger children, still going to school, in their spare time have to wind yarn on to bobbins', C. H. Bitter, 'Bericht über den Notstand in der Senne zwischen Bielefeld und Paderborn' (1853), in *64. Jahresbericht des Historischen Vereins für die Graftschaft Ravensberg* 1964/5 (Bielefeld, 1966), 22; cf. the corresponding general remarks in Pinchbeck, *Women Workers,* 159.

83. Wittfogel, *Wirtschaft und Gesellschaft Chinas,* 656.

84. Pinchbeck, *Women Workers,* 270 ff.; W. H. B. Court, *The Rise of the Midland Industries 1600 – 1838* (2nd edn. Oxford, 1953), 100 f.; M. B. Rowlands, *Masters and Men in the West Midland Metalware Trades Before the Industrial Revolution* (Manchester, 1975), 160 f.

85. C. L. Ziegler, 'Nachricht von der Verfertigung der Spitzen im Erzgebirge', in Joh. Beckmann (ed.), *Beyträge zur Ökonomie, Technologie, Polizey und Cameralwissenschaft,* i. (Göttingen, 1779), 108 – 14, here pp. 110 f.; Scott and Tilly, 'Women's work', 47; Thun, *Industrie am Niederrhein,* ii. 154 (small metalware trades of the Lower Rhine area).

86. Süßmilch, *Die Göttliche Ordnung* (1765), ii. 47 (cotton spinners); Bitter, 'Bericht', 27 (men as spinners of coarse, women as spinners of fine linen yarn); v. Schwerz, *Beschreibung der Landwirtschaft,* i. 128 f. (manufacture of 'Löwendlinnen' (a coarse quality of linen) under conditions of seasonal agrarian employment of males by temporary cottager-leasers ('Heuerlinge') in the region of Tecklenburg: 'weaving here is the main occupation of women. Spinning on the other hand is carried out by men as well and it seems strange that they spin the finest yarn whereas women and children spin the coarser qualities' (ibid., 128 f.).

87. See the numerous instances mentioned by Ziegler, 'Nachricht', esp. 108 f., 114.

88. Braun, *Industrialisierung und Volksleben,* 97, 175, 195 f.; E. Sax, *Die Thüringische Hausindustrie,* iii (Jena, 1888), 58 n. 2.

89. J. N. v. Schwerz, *Beschreibung der Landwirtschaft,* i. 111.

90. Thus the assumption in Smelser, *Social Change,* 161 f., 342 ff., esp. 345.

91. Cf. Anon. (G. W. Consbruch), *Medicinische Ephemeriden, nebst einer medicinischen Topographie der Graftschaft Ravensberg* (Chemnitz, 1793), 44 f.; Pinchbeck, *Women Workers,* 237; interesting source material is quoted in H. Strehler, 'Beiträge zur Kulturgeschichte der Zürcher Landschaft. Kirche und Schule im 17. und 18. Jahrhundert' (Phil. Diss. Zürich, 1934), 37: 'women and men. . .frequently smoke on their way to church and the sacrilegious sort of people even do so during the sermon'.

92. Cf. E. P. Thompson, 'The moral economy of the English crowd in the eighteenth century', *Past and Present,* 1 (1971), 115 ff.; on the status-specific recruitment of these protests cf. ibid., 108 and esp. E. P. Thompson's review of J. W. Shelton, *English Hunger and Industrial Disorders: a Study of Regional Conflict during the First Decade of George III's Reign* (1973), *Economic History Review,* xxvii (1974), 483.

93. R. Southey, *Letters from England* (1807) (1814), ii. 47, as quoted by Thompson, 'Moral economy', 116.

94. Braun, *Industrialisierung und Volksleben,* 68.

95. It appears to be one of the central weaknesses in E. Shorter's arguments about changes in the sexual behaviour patterns and family life of the working classes since the second half of the eighteenth century (cf. Shorter, *The Making of the Modern Family,* 255 ff.; id., *Female Emancipation,* 614 ff.) that he traces them back to the abstract effects which an emerging capitalist market had through 'market mentality' or to the impact which wage labour relationships were exerting on women through the 'liberating' influence of individual incomes. Shorter does not sufficiently locate those changes in the concrete conditions of production and reproduction, which—even under the impact of emerging capitalist markets—continued to be determined by the family mode of production. These conditions exerted their formative influence not only amongst the 'rural artisans' but continued to do so amongst the industrial working class until far into the nineteenth and twentieth centuries; cf. the interesting remarks by L. Tilly and J. Scott, 'Women's work and the family in nineteenth-century Europe', *Comparative Studies in Society and History,* xvii (1975), pp. 36 – 75, here 55 ff.

96. J. Schulthess, *Beherzigung des vor der Zürcher Synode gehaltenen Vortrags* (Zurich, 1818), 54, as quoted by Braun, *Industrialisierung und Volksleben,* 131.

97. Braun, *Industrialisierung und Volksleben,* 68 ff., 119 ff., esp. p. 123.

98. J. M. Schwager, 'Über den Ravensberger Bauer', *Westfälisches Magazin zur Geographie, Historie und Statistik,* ii (1786), no. 5, 49 – 74, here 56 f.; cf. Anon. [G. W. Consbruch], *Medicinische Ephemeriden,* 44 f.; Braun, *Industrialisierung und Volksleben,* 65 ff.

99. Schwager, 'Über den Ravensberger Bauer', 56 f.

100. An example of this form of a mistaken but none the less interesting identification of the subject is contained in Shorter, *The Making of the Modern Family.*

101. W. Benjamin, *'Geschichtsphilosophische Thesen "Über den Begriff der Geschichte" ' (1940),* Thesis VII, in W. Benjamin, *Zur Kritik der Gewalt und andere Aufsätze,* ed. by H. Marcuse (Frankfurt, 1965), 82 f.; English translation by Hannah Arendt, in W. Benjamin, *Illuminations: Essays and Reflections,* ed. by H. Arendt (New York, 1968), 258 f.

3

Locating a Welsh Working Class:
The Frontier Years*

GWYN A. WILLIAMS

The chapel stands on the slope, square and uncompromising in the manner of Welsh Dissent, but with gracefully rounded windows and an unexpectedly Palladian aspect. Above it, on the tops, a big sky suddenly opens up on a breathtaking sweep of hill country running north to Mynydd Bach. There in the 1820s, men and women of Cardiganshire fought their 'Rhyfel y Sais Bach' (War of the Little Englishman) with their Turf Act and their huntsman's horn, their 'ceffyl pren' (wooden horse) secret society and their six hundred men in women's clothes, so many premature Children of Rebecca, under Dai Jones the blacksmith, to drive out an enclosing English gentleman, his soldiers and his hired goons, even as their cousins were similarly engaged, in similar style, as Children of the 'Tarw Scotch, gelyn pob dychryndod' (Scotch Bull, enemy of all fear) among the Scotch Cattle of Monmouthshire's militant and ingenious colliers. North, too, lies Tregaron, a black gnarled knuckle of a drovers' town in a crook of the moors; Henry Richard's town, the Apostle of Peace, first Welsh Nonconformist radical MP to be elected on working-class votes and working-class issues, when the men of Merthyr got their vote in 1868.

Look east; across the river down there is Llanybyther, famous for its horse fairs. In the nineteenth century it specialized in pit ponies for the Valleys over across the Black Mountain. And to the south and west curves the Teifi, threading its way from bleak uplands to the summer lushness of a coracle-haunted mouth, peopled with gentry mansions and the craggy chapels of radicalism—and peopled in the nineteenth century with woollen mills churning out flannel shirts for the Valleys' miners. The whole region in the nineteenth century was locked into the industrial world of the south-east, in its migrant workers, its chapel fraternities and its kindred networks, as the gravestones in its churchyards testify.

* From G. A. Williams, *The Welsh in their History* (London, 1982), 16–46. Reprinted by permission of the author and Croom Helm Ltd. [The article first appeared in D. Smith, ed., *A People and a Proletariat: Essays in the History of Wales 1780–1980* (London, 1980), 16–46.]

Not far from this hill Daniel Rowland used to hurl thousands into those public ecstasies which earned Welsh Methodists the nickname of Holy Rollers and Jumpers. On this rock, however, he made no impression whatsoever. For this is *The Black Spot* of Calvinist demonology, the original Unitarian hub in Wales; this is Rhydowen, a mother church of Welsh Unitarianism, founded in 1726 in a heretic secession from the Carmarthen Academy. It was the Unitarians of Wales who were the motor force in the creation of the first Welsh democracy, the first Welsh populist nation, the first Welsh Jacobinism, the first Welsh working-class movement. It is a tradition which, in our own day, re-engaged its radicalism and experienced its most significant mutation.

For this chapel is Gwilym Marles's. It was built in 1834, the year in which two Unitarians over in Merthyr produced Wales's first working-class newspaper, *The Worker/Y Gweithiwr,* in the service of Robert Owen's syndicalist movement. Gwilym Marles took time off from becoming Dylan Thomas's great-uncle to fight a great battle against landlords. He was thrown out of his chapel and radical Wales built him a new one. This old one has become a museum. You'll see something familiar yet incongruous in one of the windows: a bust of Lenin.

A bust of Lenin alongside the pulpit is unusual, even for a chapel of Welsh radical Dissent. It was presented by a Unitarian from Aberystwyth who, rumour has it, is buried in the Kremlin Wall. For this was the final persona (to date) of Welsh Unitarianism's extraordinarily adaptable yet intransigent organic intelligentsia, personified in the Welsh-language poet, an Independent of 'unitarian' temper and Communist veteran T. E. Nicholas, 'Niclas Glais'; a dentist, he used to preach the Five Year Plan to his victims as he pulled their teeth: Suffering, like Freedom, is Indivisible.

The history of the Welsh working class in the frontier years seems familiar; the familiarity is false. Long neglected by a Welsh historiography created by the new 'nation' of a 'Nonconformist people' to which it was alien, it was marginal to the customarily ethnocentric historiography of the English, even the Labour English. The first recapture was by an act of will in the generation of militancy around the turn of the nineteenth and twentieth centuries, the enterprise of such as Ness Edwards. The work of academics in our own time has built a formidable structure, impressive in its scholarship and its sympathy, with David Williams and Edward Thompson as twin if opposite architectural supporters; recently there has been a shift into a deeper historical autonomy. We have our *Llafur,* our societies, our workshops, our miners' library. But we inch our way across continents of ignorance. And the people whom we try to serve as people's remembrancers, are a people without memory. Even 'traditions' have been manufactured late and imperfectly; not until the 1970s did Merthyr raise a plaque to its 1831 martyr Dic Penderyn (but not to the leader Lewsyn yr Heliwr) or Gwent celebrate the March on Newport of 1839.

We do not have many answers yet; indeed the first struggle is to find the right questions. The first need is to rid ourselves of the illusion that these frontier years from the 1780s to the 1850s are an historical region whose contours and parameters at least have been mapped. Maps we do not have; maps are what we need to draw.

PERSPECTIVES

Some truths remain truths even if they are familiar. If the nascent Welsh working class in the early nineteenth century had a vanguard, it was without doubt the colliers of Monmouthshire who started it, in the most consistent and most effective tradition of proletarian militancy in early industrial Wales. And it was Merthyr the iron town which produced the first working-class martyr, the first working-class press, the first serious political movement, the first red flag.

Other truths remain truths even if they are unfamiliar or perhaps ideologically awkward. The first revolt against capitalism in Wales broke out in Merioneth and Montgomeryshire, in rural west and north; the first Welsh trade union known to have affiliated to a national British movement was formed in Newtown; the first Working Men's Association in Wales emerged in Carmarthen. In the 1790s, it is possible to detect a species of 'radical triangle' in Wales, with its points in Montgomeryshire's Llanbryn-mair — Llanidloes — Newtown (with southern Merioneth as a spiritual annexe until Britain blew its radical brains out across the Atlantic), the southern Valleys and that complex in south Cardiganshire/north Carmarthen-shire/north Pembrokeshire which was the human matrix of so many working-class movements. That triangle appears and reappears in the years which follow, to find some kind of appropriate symbolic climax in Hugh Williams the Chartist leader *and* grey eminence of Rebecca, with his patriotic songs and his tricolour, linking in his person the textile workers of mid-Wales, the urban and rural sansculotterie of Carmarthen and its hinterland and the ironworkers and miners of the Valleys.

The first obstacles to confront are the related notions of isolation, backwardness and 'primitive rebels'.

Running across mid-Wales in the late eighteenth century, from Machynlleth to the English border, was the flannel country, a scattered industry of farm-based weavers and spinners focused on the mini-factories of the fulling mill and dependent on the 'Shrewsbury Drapers'. When industrial capitalism drove into the region on the backs of 'Welsh drapers' from Liverpool and Lancashire, the whole district was thrust into a crisis of 'modernization'; the emergence of shoestring native entrepreneurs, the first

Gwyn A. Williams

factories in Llanidloes and Newtown, a massive growth in pauperization as small commodity producers were turned into proletarians. The response was a distinctive and millenarian migration to the United States, highly Jacobin in temper, and the emergence of a rooted radicalism which was ultimately to debouch into Chartism. It would be ludicrous to talk of isolation, backwardness and primitive rebels in the Llanidloes-Newtown Montgomeryshire which was the stamping ground of Henry Hetherington, the *Poor Man's Guardian* himself, of Charles Jones and Thomas Powell and their kin. But it would be no less ludicrous to apply such terms to that rural Llanbrynmair to the west which became virtually a factory-parish in its own right, even if its inhabitants did speak Welsh. There, over the winter of 1795 – 96, great crowds assembled in defiance of the civil power, men made Jacobin speeches. Llanbrynmair, home of one of the most distinctive of Madoc migrations, was the home of the man who fathered the first native-born governor of the state of Ohio in the United States. Customary descriptions of the weavers of Montgomeryshire talk of 'part-time' work by farmers. In fact, the cloth trade was the vital margin between survival and desperate poverty; the first migrations in 1793 were stopped at Liverpool under the law against the migration of *artisans;* the leader, Ezekiel Hughes, had been apprenticed to a clock maker; their first concern in their Welsh liberty settlement of Beula in the United States was to create a rural industry, with which they had been familiar at home. This was a population of worker-peasants with its own breed of tough, literate and effective organic intellectuals. Desperate they may have been; isolated, backward and primitive rebels they were not.

Even more striking is the *web* cloth country of Merioneth, a belt of unremitting mountain poverty running along the Berwyn mountains to Corwen and north and west to the armpit of Llŷn. Over the winter whole families from this intensely poor and intensely Welsh people would meet to knit *en masse,* cheered on by the harpists, poets and singers who turned the district into a heartland of Welsh popular culture as it was later to be of popular preachers and craggy polemicists over Biblical texts. Peasants with primitive technique in a harsh environment, no doubt. But their production, which could sell 20,000 pairs of stockings at £18,000 a year in Bala and Llanrwst, was directed entirely at Charleston in the United States, the West Indies and the Gulf of Mexico, through the busy little port of Barmouth. There was a panic over American Independence in Dolgellau in 1775, and it was when Barmouth was closed in the French Wars, as the Welsh drapers moved in, that Merioneth suffered its crisis, with Jacobin toasts in the pubs of Bala, mass riots against the militia, calls for a 'government of the poor' and its own Madoc migration to the Land of the Free.

Much the same was true of the south-west, of the similar stocking trade concentration around Tregaron and Llandovery, of the hard-pressed artisans and smallholders of Cardiganshire encroaching without cease on the two-thirds of its stubborn soil owned by the Crown, of the deeply *American* temper of its southern district with its neighbours in upland Carmarthenshire and Pembrokeshire. This was the region most intimately in contact with America, the source of some of the earliest migrations. Here, the Baptist trans-Atlantic international, focused on Pennsylvania and Rhode Island College, with its own small fleet of four or five favoured vessels, its endless flow of Jacobin letters between Wales's unofficial consul in the United States, Samuel Jones of Philadelphia, and his brethren back home, found a firm and fecund anchorage. The American dimension is central, of course; it turned relatively affluent and literate Glamorgan, for example, with its coteries of craftsmen, artisans, small merchants and workshop owners, patriots Welsh and universal and Jacobins, into one of the nurseries of the democratic ideology in an age of Atlantic Revolution. But, once more, to apply such terms as backwardness and primitivism to such a region would be ludicrous; Joseph Priestley could bring pious divines in deepest Cardiganshire to the point of fist fights; the Unitarian hub was here, 'buried' in Welsh Wales. It was the Baptist Association of the south-west which committed itself to produce French translations of the Puritan and millenarian Canne Bible and to produce them *en masse* to serve Morgan John Rhys's crusade for Protestant liberty among the sans-culottes of Paris.

Even in the more familiar world of the ironworkers and miners of Glamorgan and Gwent, the primitive-rebel approach has been grotesquely overworked. Certainly God never meant men and women to live at those valley heads, but from the 1790s, the whole area was ribbed with canals and tramways; along one of the latter the first steam locomotive in the world ran in 1804. Before 1790 the 'primitive' frontier village of Merthyr could boast a bookseller taking weekly consignments from London; I repeat, *weekly*. Lewsyn yr Heliwr himself, charismatic hero of the Merthyr Rising of 1831, was the son of a butcher in the marginal mountain parish of Penderyn; he was literate in English, so literate in fact that on the convict ship *John* he was employed in teaching his English fellow prisoners to read and write their own language. The discourse of English radicalism, in its most advanced form, was commonplace in Merthyr and Monmouthshire by the 1790s; *Infidelity* was a periodic mushroom growth. It was not ignorance or isolation or primitiveness or the Welsh language which made the response of these men to sophisticated practice and ideology so apparently sporadic and discontinuous; it was their predicament, which was in fact that of American workers during their years of frenetic and revolutionizing industrialization.

That much of Welsh hill farming was primitive and at subsistence level, that communications were poor (at least before 1790 in the south-east), that many Welshmen were 'traditional' (as many were continuously mobile), that the Welsh language was an insulating factor (which I do not believe for a moment, having lived with it and in it through an English-speaking adolescence) have become truisms. A truism may be true, but it is necessary not to submit to useful simplification, even in a good cause; it is necessary not to see modes of production advance in a pre-ordained column-of-route. One minor but symptomatic fact: Volney's *Ruins of Empires* (1791) which became, as an exercise in revolutionary fantasy or science-fiction, a standard text of working-class intellectuals for three generations was available in Welsh in 1793, just after the first English version and earlier than the first popularly effective version in English.

Two factors need to register in the mind: firstly, the autonomy of the 'superstructural', to quote the vernacular—'primitive' structures are quite frequently exposed to quite unprimitive ideologies and secondly the coexistence of modes of production.

The only way for a serious historian of the working class, for a Marxist historian, a people's remembrancer, to approach the early history of a Welsh 'working class', is firstly for him/her to shed all notions of backwardness-isolation-primitive rebels (however august their apostolic descent), to shed all notions of a linear progression in orthodoxy (and comprehensibility) and secondly, to accept, in its full reality (and analytical horror) the idea that modes of production coexist, that people can simultaneously live in different time-scales. Time is not indivisible. At one moment in the early nineteenth century, a man in Merthyr could be living within the world of a highly-skilled worker in an integrated firm, probably the largest and most advanced of its kind on earth, while another man, tramping after sheep in some cloud-capped and barren valley, could be living in a world whose *mores* were fixed by the medieval, kindred and 'tribal' laws of Hywel Dda. More disconcerting is the thought that these men might well have been brothers.

MODES OF PRODUCTION

The industrialization of Wales was imperial from birth and it hit a country which, almost uniquely in Britain, still had 'peasants'.

The Wales of the *ancien régime,* no less than the Wales of the Alternative Society, was a product of the creation of Great Britain with its Atlantic dimensions. The historic British nation formed in the eighteenth century around the armature of Anglo-Scottish union, merchant capitalism and liberal oligarchy. Wales, subjected to the jurisprudence of capitalism from the days of the Tudors, was formed in the process. There was a massive shrinkage in the political nation, power in parliamentary terms shrivelling up into a handful of magnate families, often Scottish in origin and devoid of any Welsh content, just as the Church in Wales became the fief of broad-bottomed and Whig bishops en route to higher things (one of them was accused by his clergy of being an atheist); Wales's own judicial system, the

Great Sessions, could be abolished in 1830 without an eyebrow raised. The multitudinous lesser gentry of Wales, product of its kindred social structure and critical to any distinct identity, was decimated, lost its foothold in public life, dwindled into a merely local and poverty-stricken prestige; men of long pedigree and short purse, they cultivated an alternative system of values, lending some power to Dissent, the new Methodism and the Welsh cultural revival. Challenging them were the multiplying professional and artisan groups which gained power from the rapid sweep of British Atlantic and mercantile empire. A peasant society living on the edge of subsistence characterized most of upland and pastoral Wales, but it was a society which also lived by the drove-herds of cattle seasonally tramping into England, bringing back currency and breeding banks, accompanied by the great droves of equally skinny people tramping no less purposefully into England to be fattened. And into and through this 'peasant' society throbbed the thrusts of merchant capitalism. Before 1800, the copper and brass industries of Britain were located, 90 per cent of them, around Swansea with its dependent mines in Anglesey under that Thomas Williams who clawed out a world monopoly. Tin-plate differentiated itself in the same period, located in Monmouthshire and around Swansea, almost totally directed to export, once more a British monopoly. By 1800, no less, the new iron industry with its coal dependency was accounting for 40 per cent of British pig-iron production and was also geared almost wholly to export. Even Merioneth fed the Gulf of Mexico; the production of Montgomeryshire, through Blackwell Hall in London, went out to Europe and the Americas. The great thrust of British capitalist breakthrough during the Revolutionary and Napoleonic Wars was pivoted on Atlantic slave power. The British export sector in copper, brass, iron, tin-plate, plebeian cloth, was in Wales; the new Welsh economy was built on the backs of the blacks.

In consequence a plurality of modes of production coexisted within a country measuring scarcely 200 miles from end to end, to generate a bewildering complexity of popular response. Each mode of production produced its own working population; each working population had to live with others and with a rural population of peasants and worker-peasants in complicated interaction. It was the thrust of the iron industry, above all, after the adoption of the vital puddling process, the 'Welsh method' from the 1790s, which most closely approximated to Marx's model of an endlessly innovative, revolutionizing, expanding process of self-generated contradiction.

The overall consequences are familiar but no less staggering. Over little more than two generations, the population of Wales nearly tripled; from 1841, most of it was sucked into the frenetically industrializing and increasingly English-speaking south-east. The Welsh, by the thousand, broke away from Establishment. Dissent, with the novel Methodism, may have accounted for perhaps 15 per cent of the population by 1800; by 1851, Dissent's predominance was so overwhelming that Anglicanism became a kind of historical joke. Together with Methodism, driven into Nonconformity by official repression in 1811, Dissent outnumbered the Establishment by seven or even ten to one in some places and averaged a five-to-one hegemony. The sects of Dissent threatened to become as much of a 'national church' as Catholicism had become to the Irish. From mid-century onwards, only the Nonconformist Welsh (maybe about half the Welsh on the ground) are historically visible. The rest, before the 1890s, are un-persons.

It is in this context that one has to locate the emergence of a Welsh 'working class'. During the 1830s, its presence is *visible* and *audible*; from the conjuncture of 1829 – 34, the Monmouthshire colliers' strike of 1830 with its remarkably sophisticated system of control, the Merthyr Rising of 1831, the penetration of the Lancashire colliers' union and the National Association for the Protection of Labour, the enrolment of the locked-out workers of Merthyr in the National Union of the Working Classes in November 1831; from that climacteric moment, through the revived but now quasi-political Scotch Cattle of the early 1830s, the upsurge of the Owenite movement with the first Welsh working-class journal in 1834, the massive and decisive intervention of the Merthyr working class in the election of 1835, the crystallization in Chartism which united Carmarthen, Llanidloes and the Valleys, the abortive national uprising whose trigger was the march on Newport, the generation-long experience of Chartism which became virtually a sub-culture within British society, Welsh working-class consciousness, sometimes in revolutionary form, is an unavoidable *presence* in the history of Wales.

The 'disappearance' of that consciousness in the years after 1842, at least in the autonomous form which characterized it from 1829 onwards, no less than its formation in the preceding years, remain, in our virtually total ignorance of the things that matter, major priorities for the people's remembrancers of Wales.

Clearly the work situation was one determinant. The striking feature of the new working populations was, on the one hand, the high proportion of skilled men among them and on the other, their fluidity and class incoherence. Copper had the lowest proportion of skilled workers, maybe 15 per cent; tin-plate, however, with a skilled proportion of around 25 per cent was as stable as copper. The communities they created around the social and intellectual capital of Swansea had some of the worker-peasant characteristics of the northern slate quarries: there was no serious conflict in the copper industry throughout the period. To the east, however, the iron industry, 30 – 40 per cent of whose workers were skilled men, experienced continuous technical innovation and a roller-coaster growth; the collieries dependent on the ironworks shared some of their characteristics, while those of the sale-coal trade of Monmouthshire, run by under-capitalized Welsh entrepreneurs in cut-throat competition, witnessed some of the fiercest and most sophisticated struggles of the frontier years, led often by the skilled men who formed 20 – 25 per cent of the workforce.

Most works were a mosaic of sub-contractors, ranging from the master-craftsmen of tin-plate, through co-operative contracts with 'gentlemen puddlers' to the cutter commanding his team, with the *butty* or *doggy,* in effect a minor sub-capitalist of working-class origin, a distinctive figure—and an ambiguous one, now a staunch defender of the rights of property, now a spokesman for 'responsible' if militant protest. All over the coalfield, workers were mobile, flitting from job to job, following the shifts of an unpredictable iron-coal complex. The inflow from west Wales, at first seasonal, was continuous; the Irish started to flood in during the 1830s, when the huddled clusters of houses, chapels and pubs clinging to the valley sides went through their major ecological disaster; as many as 10,000 people could move through Merthyr in a year; men would tramp twenty miles to watch a foot-race; there were many Klondyke settlements alongside the model housing of the ironmasters and the indescribable tangles of cottages thrown up by middle-class speculators. The accident rate was high and, from the 1830s, became murderous; the infantile death rate was catastrophic; three-quarters of those who died were under five and average life expectancy at birth in the 1830s was about twenty. The 'natural' death rate, however, was lower than that of country towns and the housing was superior to that of the west. Friendly societies were as numerous as the pubs which housed them and the chapels which confronted them. Wages were high if fluctuating, though sectional unemployment was rife and, in the Monmouthshire sale-coal areas, general unemployment was epidemic. Some of the more skilled trades had regular training systems and most had some kind of rough and ready approximation to apprenticeship, but with the continuous inflow and permanent insecurity, with the townships collapsing under the challenges, with no-go areas like Merthyr's *China* coexisting with a black economy of penny capitalists and drifters, permanent organization proved extraordinarily difficult.

In the process, distinctive communities with distinctive patterns of action and response mushroomed. Most striking were the sale-coal villages of the lower valleys of Monmouthshire. Bleak, barren places, lacking even the amenities of a Merthyr, they were largely one-class settlements. Considered only half-human by their employers and the middle class, often quasi-permanently trapped in debt by the truck system, racked by the merciless competition of shoestring firms and by periodic bouts of miserable unemployment, this people, distinguished from each other often only by the presence or absence of window-sashes in their houses, proved the most militant and also the most capable of sustained and sophisticated struggle.

More mixed in origin than most coalfield townships, they developed out of a very Welsh and semi-rural popular culture, highly organized and effective resistance movements and unions. From these villages came the hard core of the physical force Chartists; it was at Blackwood that the Newport insurrection was planned. By the 1830s these embattled men and women had created a vivid, living working-class culture, at once intransigent and cultivated, and had made themselves into a proletarian vanguard.

The ironworks settlements to the north, clustering around their capital of Merthyr, were more varied and richer in texture, with resident masters and a fashionable 'society', with a more complex (and wealthy) middle class. Skilled men like the puddlers were organizing themselves early and *ad hoc* combinations of ironstone miners and colliers were frequent, with marginal, semi-artisanal groups like the hauliers playing a distinctive role. Artisan crafts were themselves strong and, above all, there was a persistent tradition of multi-class Jacobin democracy, very visible in Merthyr, but present throughout northern Monmouthshire. It was from the late 1830s and the 1840s that the *mores* of the colliers began to rise within this iron-dominated complex, as the valleys of Aberdare and the lower Rhonddas were opened up and Monmouthshire men moved west.

In that same period, driven on by its technical development, iron and its related trades were also shifting west to disturb the more settled pattern of the anthracite coalfield and to impose a more uniform style on the whole region from Pontypool to Llanelly. Beyond the latter lay a south-west Wales in quasi-permanent crisis and in continuous adjustment into a catchment zone for the south-east. Hit harder by the population explosion than most regions, Cardiganshire was the most disturbed county in Wales, a county of land hunger, inching self-improvement, smallholder resistance movements and seasonal migration, the Galicia of Wales. The Dissent of the region, heavily colonized by the newer Methodism, was moving out of the defensive and negative withdrawal of the west into militancy as the whole region slithered into an occult malaise and a permanent disaffection from an Anglican magistracy. It was this which tipped the already and traditionally turbulent town of Carmarthen with its press, its myriad small trades in crisis, its tribes of bloody-minded artisans, its brisk Bristol Channel commerce, over the edge into a kind of secession from public order. The endless faction feuds of Blues and Reds in Carmarthen took on a sharper tone, as its hinterland was riven by that tension between Dissent and the Church in which a populist 'nation' was shaping itself behind a language and religious line which was also a class line. There was a rooted populist radicalism in Carmarthen, fed by its neighbour villages, which could make it a 'sans-culotte' sort of place. In a sense, it served as a staging post between the south-west and the industrial complex; Chartism in Wales was appropriately born there.

Hugh Williams certainly found it a fairly easy jump from the textile towns of mid-Wales, with their small but alert and highly self-conscious factory population among a countryside scarcely less industrial in character. It was a tougher jump up into the north, where the relationships between the subculture of the quarry men of the north-west and the ironworks, collieries and mixed industry of north-eastern Denbighshire and Flintshire resembled those between Swansea and Merthyr at first. It was out of the Denbighshire of the 1790s, from 'remote' Cerrig-y-Drudion that Jac Glan y Gors, the Welsh Tom Paine, came; the north-eastern coalfield was the first seriously to respond to the millenarian unionism of 1830. The industrialization of the north, however, ran into stasis, the population drain was continuous and Methodist-dominated Dissent a defensive reaction before the 1840s. With some brief exceptions, working-class radicalism in the north, before the great struggles of the late nineteenth century, was a matter of scattered groups and even individuals, though the quarrymen were already shaping that distinctive commonwealth of theirs which in later years would turn a lockout into a three-year civil war and a major crisis of community and tradition.

Each group, in its own particular environment, within its own pattern of authority and resistance, had to find its own way to cope with class incoherence and fluidity, to seek modes of thought and action within whatever traditions they brought with them from the sparse and bitter villages or artisan towns, whatever practices and skills they had learned from earlier struggles in industry, whatever they could marshal from their native cultures and the cultures to which they were continuously and often dramatically exposed.

What is clear, from a necessarily cursory and ill-formed survey of their actions from the 1790s to the 1840s is a pattern of episodic but frequent (sometimes annual) organization to resist wage reductions and defend a traditional standard, occasional eruptions from what was, evidently, the familiar world of the 'moral economy' and a steady and ever richer elaboration of more permanent fellowship, whether in pub, craft, club, chapel or eisteddfod. There is quite evidently some qualitative change in the 1820s and at the critical conjuncture of 1830 a veritable 'explosion' of self-consciousness. Three factors seem general and influential: debt as the forcing-house and negative definition of a working class; a shift from consumer to producer awareness and, concurrent with the latter, a shift from protest to control as the objective. Indeed, control, of their workplace, their trade, their industry, their communities, moves centre-stage in working-class and popular action in the crisis of 1830. This drive for control, which was also a drive for dignity, found a more secure and a more permanent anchorage in a political outlook than earlier consumer protest had done. Indeed working-class consciousness in recognizable form emerges in the Valleys of South Wales with abrupt and explosive force around 1830 precisely because a popular thrust for control, in the teeth of a debt crisis among a population which had elaborated a dense network of partly-occult institutions, essentially cultural in character, coincided with an equally sudden incursion of a political culture at the crisis of the Reform Bill.

Politics had been present, in some form or other, throughout; politics was in fact central. A radical and populist political culture, providing a possible frame of reference, already existed: it was there, to their hand.

For the birth of democracy had preceded their own.

CULTURES AND IDEOLOGIES

The ideology of democracy is pre-industrial (a truth whose implications we do not seem to have thought through). The Chartist programme was first published in 1780, in the reform campaign of the American crisis. The Anglo-American character of British Jacobinism, of which Thomas Paine is an appropriate symbol, was even more marked in Wales, one of the sectors of Britain in the most direct contact with America. In the last years of the eighteenth century, the first Welsh democracy and the first modern Welsh 'nation' were born of the conjuncture.

One of its strongholds was Glamorgan, with its big Vale villages full of a bilingual artisanry and a patriot lower-middle class, its Cowbridge Book Society, its Dissenting network linking it to the tough-minded chapels of the hill country, with its own Academy and its access to Bristol colleges. Such men as Lewis Hopkin, craftsman extraordinary, his house full of books, Welsh, English, Latin, French, grammars of the Welsh bards and the latest number of the *Spectator;* John Bradford of Betws near Bridgend, traditional nursery of Glamorgan's Welsh poets, a Deist fuller and dyer, William Edward who built the bridge at Pontypridd, Edward Ifan of Aberdare, apprentice in wood and verse to Hopkin and on tramp like most of them before he settled as Unitarian minister, created a lively, open but frustrated society living in the interstices of gentry politics like some kind of diffused Philadelphia. They nurtured the political culture of Morgan John Rhys of Llanfabon, a Baptist Jacobin who travelled to France to preach Protestant liberty, brought out the first political periodical in the Welsh language in 1793 and founded a Welsh liberty settlement in America, and of Iolo Morganwg, Edward Williams, the tramping stonemason of the Vale, a fantastic and maimed genius who invented the Gorsedd of Bards as Jacobin, Unitarian and Masonic inheritors of a Druid tradition turned into something akin to Rousseau's Natural Religion, and gave the newly-awakening Welsh a half-approximation to a national and radical ideology. Out of this world came two of the major British radicals of European and American reputation: Richard Price, the political Dissenter whose sermons on the French Revolution provoked Edmund Burke into his *Reflections* and who was invited by

Congress to serve as financial adviser to the new United States and David Williams the Deist who may have supplied Robespierre with his Cult of the Supreme Being.

These people worked closely with the London-Welsh in their new and radical society of the Gwyneddigion, staffed largely from modernizing Denbighshire, by such as Owen Jones, William Owen, David Samwell and the rest who tried to revive the eisteddfod as a kind of national academy and to re-engage an interrupted tradition. In alliance with Iolo Morganwg, these men, with some radicals of the Old Dissent, shuffled together into a loosely united organic intelligentsia in the 1790s with a journal and a campaign to create (in their own words, to 'revive') a Welsh nation conceived in liberty.

They made heavy weather of it, in the teeth of population explosion, wartime pressure-cooker industrialization, government repression, loyalist witch-hunts, and Methodist advance. They used the revived Madoc myth to break through this wall and make contact with the disaffected working populations of west and north, whose migrations to the United States were charged with a millenarian passion, but their combative little 'nation' foundered on the rocks not only of the old regime but of the alternative society battling its way into existence.

For the real organic intelligentsia of the populist Welsh were the preacher-journalists of Dissent. It is from the 1790s that Methodism, closely followed by Dissent, surges forward in west and north, to disrupt Old Dissent itself. There was a profound difference in quality. In 1823, when Thomas Clarkson went on an anti-slavery mission to Wales, he found Dissenters of west and north, there mainly Methodists, almost an underground of withdrawn, inward-looking and defensive dissidence; the gentry would not sit with them on committees, subjected them to endless petty persecution and exclusion. John Elias himself, the Methodist leader who towered over many Welsh minds like a pope, did not dare meet Clarkson at home; they had to slink off to Chester. In the more varied society of east and south, Dissenters, among whom Baptists and Independents were more prominent, moved with far greater ease and sharper radicalism.

This distinction between 'quietists' and 'politicians' which, under the drive of evangelicalism, with its sensuous hymns and mass participation, actually ran *through* the Old Dissent itself, persisted. The first major press of Welsh Dissent, from *Seren Gomer* onwards, moved in an Independent-Baptist milieu to generate the radical *Diwygiwr* of Llanelly in the 1830s and to supply Chartism with many of its spokesmen, but a great body of Nonconformist opinion, particularly the Methodist, was a dead weight of apolitical quietism, often indistinguishable from a bilious Toryism.

As the chapels moved to embrace more and more of the working population of the industrial areas, the consequences were complex. The sweeping advance of Methodism and a 'methodized' Dissent into north and west could perhaps be interpreted in terms of the currently fashionable 'psychic compensation'; I cannot say. It was clearly a response to the disruption of traditional society. For a couple of generations, it locked its people away in a defensive bunker, a passive self-definition against hegemonic society. But there was a trend, a minority but powerful trend running in the opposite direction, driving men out with God's Sword to build a new Jerusalem. The Unitarian cause, minority but trenchant and highly influential, grew stronger right through into the 1830s; trends called 'unitarian' within Independency and Baptistry bucked the dominant evangelical drive. The Baptists were split wide open around 1800 as Independent chapels fell to Unitarians. There is a clear regional divergence; it is in Glamorgan-Monmouth and in mid-Wales that the minority Dissenting radicalism found some kind of permanent home, fed by the productive powerhouses on the Teifi and in Carmarthen. They produced a freethinking, Deist, Infidel wing of outriders and ran into congruence with the patriot Jacobinism of bohemians and unbiblical radicals.

After the great storms of the revolutionary decade, the migrations, the repression, the rampant evangelicalism, a new political tradition was rooted in Wales, in clusters of Unitarians, radical Baptists and Independents, Deists, Welsh revivalists scattered over the face of the south-west, mid-Wales and, most visible of all, in Merthyr and Monmouthshire. Merthyr village became a stronghold of Jacobinism, its freeholders 'sturdy old Republicans', with their Cyfarthfa Philosophical Society, their radical and, in 1831, free-thinking and Deist eisteddfodau, their *Patriot* pubs and political societies of Welsh-patriot *Cymreigyddion;* Zephaniah Williams over in Nant-y-Glo and Blaina, with his Humanist Society and political clubs, sprang from the same root and all across the Valleys, there was a scatter of such men, some flamboyant like William Price, many, earnest moles of democracy who were often the backbone of working-class movements and ended their lives as Liberal municipal reformers.

The relationship between these people and the nascent working-class movements was complex, as the single, unified tradition of democracy splintered in the early nineteenth century under the pulverizing hammer of class formation which ground society apart like some clumsy cast-iron mechanism. Petty bourgeois many without doubt were, in social status and outlook, but it is not in fact possible to draw a clear line; there were working-class and artisan Unitarians and freethinkers. Much the same is true of the chapels, at least of the Old Dissent. Not until the mass Temperance movement of the late 1830s do the chapels in the Valleys play that unambiguously social-control role which English working-class historians unhesitatingly allot to them. It is quite possible that class structures and the ideologies which went with them created a quite different pattern in Wales; certainly the Welsh elementary schoolteacher of later generations did *not* play the role customarily assigned to him in England; very often he displaced the minister and challenged the miners' agent as a popular leader. Something of that populist order seems to have held good, at least in the Valleys, in the textile townships of mid-Wales and in parts of Cardiganshire, Carmarthenshire and Pembrokeshire. Many chapels were exclusive, battling for grace and respectability out of the sinful world of the 'roughs', but many were not and most chapels in the Valleys were strongly working-class from their foundation. It was the heavy commitment of Baptist and Independent spokesmen to the Welsh Chartist movement which was one of its distinguishing features. Certainly the cultural world of the chapels with their big and busy Sunday schools, their training in music and poetry, offered not only a home to the displaced but an arena for their talent. A rival to the pub world, the chapel world in the early generations in fact interacted with it. Not until the massive restabilization of the middle years of the century and the impact of Temperance, does the more familiar dichotomy register clearly.

What is striking is that the radicalism of what one can call, loosely, the 'unitarian' connexion found an entry into working-class life through its popular culture. Ultimately derived from old Catholic Wales and settled by the eighteenth century into a form of 'folkloric' and customary adaptation to a hard life, this was rich and complex, with its 'cwrw bach' (little beer; self-help mutual loan and community celebrations rather like the American 'shower') its 'ceffyl pren' (cock-horse) extra-legal village discipline, its passion for games, for betting, for sometimes almost incredibly arduous foot-races, its admiration for physical prowess and pugilism, its folk-heroes like the red-haired giant Shoni Sguborfawr, champion of Wales (so he claimed), Emperor of China, army spy among the Scotch Cattle, mercenary hero of Rebecca and Australian convict dead of drink; or like Lewsyn yr Heliwr, the huntsman leader of the Merthyr Rising, a local Emiliano Zapata. Equally passionate, however, was the commitment of many of them to the standard-bearers of a culture ultimately derived from the old and dead bardic order, the harpists, the singers of the complex verse 'penillion', the ballad singers. Shoni Sguborfawr's boon companion in his Rebecca phase, after all, was Dai'r Cantwr, Dai the Singer, a hedge-poet. Dic Dywyll, Dic Dark, a blind ballad singer from north Wales, was the Voice of the People in the Merthyr of 1831; selling his song sheets on a Saturday night, he could make more money in a week than a furnace manager. It was in 1831 that Dic Dywyll won an eisteddfod prize—and the eisteddfod was that of the Merthyr Free Enquirers, the Zetetics who had been organized by Richard Carlile around his journal the *Republican*.

This amorphous and vivid world of the popular culture could find some organized outlet not only in eisteddfodau but in the choirs and verse festivals of the chapels, with their combative working-class conductors and teachers. Characteristically two of the recognized centres of this new kind of popular excellence in Wales were Merthyr and Llanidloes. It was the Unitarians who launched the secular eisteddfodau which blossomed from the 1820s in Merthyr and Monmouthshire to find a focus in Abergavenny, home of that dreaded figure in modern Welsh folklore, the eisteddfod adjudicator (it still produces them; Raymond Williams was born nearby.) And it is characteristic that it was out of this world that the first Chartist leaders in Wales came: Morgan Williams, a master-weaver of rooted local stock (there were harpists in his family), Unitarian like the brothers John, sons of a Unitarian minister. At the height of the rebellion of 1831, Matthew John walked alone up to the fortress of Penydarren House to present the rebels' terms and to make clear his hourly expectation of national insurrection. Most striking of all was John Thomas (Ieuan Ddu), a Unitarian from Carmarthen who was the greatest music teacher in south Wales (he is said to have introduced Handel's Messiah into Wales); a Zetetic friend of Zephaniah Williams, he launched his Zetetic eisteddfodau in 1831 and with Morgan Williams, edited Wales's first working-class newspaper, *The Worker/Y Gweithiwr;* he was responsible for the Welsh section: a eulogy of the Tolpuddle Martyrs. Men like these were among the first generation of Chartist leaders; they served their apprenticeship in the crisis of 1830. Those of Merthyr are *visible* because they were concentrated and because their activities have been documented. But they were everywhere in the Valleys, around Llanidloes and Newtown, in Carmarthen and the southwest. Zephaniah Williams in Monmouthshire, William Price in Pontypridd were highly distinctive individuals, but it would be a fundamental error to consider them unrepresentative; they had hosts of brothers, far less visible, but identifiable from their actions and occasional side-comments.

It seems to have been through this cultural milieu, under the dramatic pressures of industrial capitalism (much as the Scotch Cattle grew out of the 'ceffyl pren' world) that the new working class achieved an identity and committed itself to democracy.

Such an outcome, of course, was not inevitable.

FORMS OF ACTION

In considering working-class and popular action between the 1790s and the 1840s it is difficult to avoid some sense of a linear and almost inevitable progression towards Chartism. Even if one tries to break free of this teleological prison and to analyse particular and concrete conjunctures, the end-product seems much the same.

The 1790s clearly belong to Edward Thompson's moral economy of the crowd: mass actions in north Wales against the militia, the Navy Act, enclosures, grain prices; 'traditional' price actions all over Wales during the dreadful years of 1795 – 96 and 1800 – 1801; and in those latter years a natural justice insurrection at Merthyr, with the troops in and two men hanged. Even then, however, a political thread of Jacobin democracy runs through everything, weaving in and out of the crowd actions. It is present in the slogans of Swansea colliers in 1793, in the speeches during the great Denbigh riot of 1795, in the crowd protests in Merioneth and Llanbrynmair; it is present above all in the emigrants who voted with their feet and in their free Wales in America drank toasts to the brave sans-culottes and voted for Thomas Jefferson. It finds some kind of institutional base in the Merthyr and Monmouthshire of the 1800s. Moreover, as an epilogue to the Merthyr grain action of 1800 – 1801, a broadsheet found locally locks at least a militant minority into the nation-wide insurrectionary conspiracies of that year which were to debouch into the abortive Despard affair. How far this represents any interaction between Jacobin villagers and proletarian and populist rebels it is difficult to say; the Jacobins had re-emerged in the petitioning campaigns of 1800. By 1806 the local ones were organized into a Philosophical Society even as friendly societies, often the cover for trade unions and gun clubs, mushroomed in the pubs of that same radical quarter of Merthyr on the lip of what became *China*.

Even more mysterious is what was clearly a decisive conjuncture in 1810 – 13; in a country so heavily dependent on Atlantic trade, the crisis which precipated the American War of 1812 in the middle of the Napoleonic blockade was bound to be severe. Yet we know practically nothing about it. What we do know seems significant. These were the years when puddlers formed trade unions and took a Luddite oath, in which tradition places the origin of the Scotch Cattle of Monmouthshire, certainly Luddite in their impenetrable secrecy. The garrison at Brecon was established at the same time. One senses a proletarian rebellion in virtually total autonomy, made manifest by the remarkable south Wales strike of 1816, perhaps the most massive movement on the coalfield throughout the nineteenth century (and trenchantly reconstructed by David Jones). That strike, against the vicious wage reductions of the post-war slump, was an intensely active and sustained movement, ranging back and forth across Monmouthshire and the Merthyr complex, using traditional forms like the marching gangs and attacks on works and masters' houses but also evidently characterized by a high degree of organization and an apparent independence of any other social grouping. In the aftermath, once more, a leaflet unmistakably linking at least some militants to national insurrectionary movements, such as the Pentrich Rising hints at. How far was this totally independent? Speeches by Hunt and Cobbett came down in Welsh translation immediately afterwards and from 1811 there had been a harsh government crackdown on itinerant preachers (driving Welsh Methodism to seek the protection of the Toleration Act) which radicalized Dissent. The anti-war campaign of the Ricardo-influenced bourgeoisie certainly mobilized radicals and the Merthyr Jacobins made their first organized entry into parliamentary reform in 1815. We just do not know. What *is* clear, however, is that working-class and popular protest on the whole seems to have taken a familiar form, essentially a defensive protest, expressing a consumer mentality, including that of wage-earners as consumers.

There is a qualitative change in the 1820s, mysterious in Merthyr—which nevertheless seems to have shared in the 'silent insurrection' of those years, to judge from responses after 1829 and suggestions of a leftward lurch in the eisteddfod world (there was also a Mechanics Institute at Dowlais by 1829)—most vivid in Monmouthshire. It is at this point that the Monmouth-shire colliers take the initiative, wrest it from the skilled iron-men. The colliers' strike of 1822 was a highly sophisticated exercise and running alongside the mass actions, often violent, always highly intelligent, of the troubles of the 1820s are the Scotch Cattle. A highly effective underground movement, with its own Scotch Law and code of honour, its regular rhythmic practice of warning notes, summons by horn, midnight meetings, intimi-datory visits by a Herd (from a different valley) under its Bull to blacklegs, profiteers, aliens, offenders against community, this was rooted in the colliery villages which were to be strongholds of the physical force Chartists, but subjected much of the ironworks belt to its moral authority. The 'primitiveness' of this movement (again brilliantly analysed by David Jones) has been grossly overstated. It was in fact a sophisticated, well-ordered exercise in solidarity (necessarily terrorist in the circumstances of Monmouthshire). It looks like a wholly proletarian exercise moreover and noticeable is the stress on *control*. This, however, is no less apparent, strikingly so, in the great strikes of 1830 when the colliers, trying to impose production quotas on shifty and arrogant employers, were in fact elaborating a complicated mechanism in defence of their trades, their communities and their standard of living, and moreover did not hesitate to call in a local surgeon to help them. By 1832 the Bull's warning notes were carrying the slogan *Reform*.

This rising significance of ideas of workers' control, running into congruence with the explosion of self-consciously *working-class* politics in the early stages of the crucial Reform crisis, is also visible in Merthyr, where of course the outcome was dramatic. The slump of 1829 generated a severe debt crisis. The new stipendiary's court together with the local debtors' court co-operated to hold the working class together during the slump. Inevitably this imprisoned much of the working class in debt (Merthyr at one time ran out of funds for poor relief) and thrust the shopocracy into crisis. Distraints for debt and a campaign against petty criminals subjected a whole sector of the population to misery and repression, began to mark off a 'working class' negatively defined *against* the rest of the population at the very moment when the great tide of radical and working-class propaganda of 1830 came flooding into a Merthyr, whose Unitarian radicals were organizing political unions, preaching them to workers, striking for local power in alliance with William Crawshay, a radical ironmaster who did not hesitate to deploy his own men in the cause.

The trigger was the arrival of delegates from the new colliers' union affiliated to the National Association for the Protection of Labour. The latter had made its first penetration into Wales at Newtown; the colliers' union swept north-eastern Wales over the winter of 1830–31, provoking riots and a millenarian response. The coming of the delegates to the great working-class Reform meeting in Merthyr at the annual Waun Fair (last of three such held by independent working-class initiative) precipitated an explosion, in which Owenite unions were engulfed in a classical (but highly organized) natural justice action against the shopocracy, led by Lewsyn yr Heliwr; a direct attack on soldiers marched in from Brecon, again led by Lewsyn, with the loss of two dozen dead and seventy wounded, was itself followed by a communal insurrection which held the town for four days, defeated regulars and yeomanry twice, mobilized (too late) a force of 12,000–20,000 from Monmouthshire and was beaten only after anything from 800 to 1,000 troops had converged on the town and after sustained efforts by masters, using some of the town radicals, to divide and disorganize the rebels. Melbourne played the whole incident cool; a dozen or so scapegoats were punished; Lewsyn was reprieved and only Richard Lewis went to the gallows, as Dic Penderyn, to become (and to remain) the first martyr of the Welsh working class.

More significant in many ways than the Rising itself (and generally ignored by historians) was the massive union campaign and the ghastly, hard-fought lockout which followed, as dour and grim as anything in the black history of the coalfield. In this lockout, the men of Dowlais and Plymouth works acted as a conscious vanguard for the whole working class of south Wales. Support came from as far away as Maesteg; at the last moment, as the Plymouth men were caving in, men marched to try to stiffen them, not only from Cyfarthfa but from Nant-y-Glo. In this struggle, when the men were left isolated, even by Unitarian Jacobins and radical Baptists, the emphasis was wholly on working-class independence and, as among the Monmouthshire colliers, on *control*. By the November when the men were finally beaten, they were rallying to the simultaneous meeting called for by the National Union of the Working Classes (NUWC) in London and committing themselves to the radical, self-consciously working-class wing of the movement at the crisis point—the people Francis Place and the Birmingham crew were organizing to defeat. In this cause moreover, the Merthyr men sent delegates to Carmarthen.

The movement was patchy. Of course it was. Dowlais was often out of step with Cyfarthfa; there was great difficulty in co-ordinating with Monmouthshire and such difficulties often led to recrimination and disunity. The men of the Swansea and Neath valleys acted independently. The kind of pheno- menon is normal and customary in working-class action; it reflects some rooted realities; Merthyr was never a stronghold of the Scotch Cattle, for example, probably because of its more complex mix of trades and much more visible democratic organizations. But what is really significant is that in both Merthyr and Monmouthshire, as men's minds concentrated on the idea of control (central to the new colliers' union) in a context of almost millenarian political crisis, what can only be called a working-class consciousness emerged. It was defeated, as the N.U.W.C. and their kin were defeated in the nation. It had to live in a South Wales where there were garrisons in the five major towns and in which the middle class had been armed against them. That consciousness could not immediately act in independence; it had to operate under other people's hegemony.

But its existence was real enough. Patchy and incompletely autonomous though it was (the Merthyr men of 1831 were committed to Free Trade, for example), it persisted and billowed up in strong waves of feeling and action through the 1830s; in the massive Owenite union movement of 1834, when its first newspaper appeared; in the last great movement of the Scotch Cattle in support, in the intervention in the Merthyr election of 1835 and the power which buttressed the Unitarians as they took over Merthyr from 1836, above all, of course in the unforgettable experience of Chartism, that Chartism which yoked Scotch Cattle and Unitarians, the eisteddfod world and *China,* which united the Valleys with the not-so-very-different world of Llanidloes, Newtown and their villages (where the differences are really those of scale and concentration) and the distinctly more sans-culotte milieux of Carmarthen and its villages; that Chartism which was so much more than the march on Newport, significant though *that* is, the Chartism with its coveys of girls in white dresses and green flags, its men marching blue uniformed into the churches, its ritual and colour and ceremony, its endless debating clubs and hidden arms clubs, its Chartist caves and Chartist churches, its massive and all-pervading working-class culture, which lived on in South Wales long after the climacteric moment of 1838 – 42 and the upsurge of 1848, which so registered on the minds of Marx and Engels and which indulged in its last ghost campaign as its former militants moved on to councils and library committees and sat on the platforms of Nonconformist radicals (including Henry Richard).

The strength and reality of working-class consciousness in the 1830s and early 1840s is best measured by the response of its enemies. Official and respectable reaction to the Merthyr Rising, at the height of the Reform Bill crisis of course, had been hesitant, unsure, careful. Ironmasters were divided over the unions; the Home Secretary of an alarmed government, recognizing it eight years later as 'the nearest thing to a fight' they had ever had, trod very carefully indeed. As soon as the Act passed and the great wave of anti-working class legislation began to surge through the Commons, as soon as necessary if rather rowdy allies had become Destructives, all that changes. In 1834 the masters presented a uniform face of brass to the unions and broke them without mercy; troops, police, spies, propaganda, the pulpits were turned massively against the Scotch Cattle to stamp them into the ground. After the Newport march, the Cabinet were hell-bent on hanging Frost, Williams and Jones and were stopped only by a liberal Chief Justice, while the working-class people of the Valleys were drenched in the respectable spittle of ferocious class hatred. Not until the later 1840s, with the education commissions and others coming down to 'solve' the problems of Wales, did that virulent tone slacken.

But by that time, of course, Chartist militants were already on their long march into the radical wing of Liberalism.

MEMORY

The realignment and the absorption of much working-class enterprise into a liberal consensus, the 'disappearance' of militancy, of autonomy, are, of course, as familiar in Wales as in Britain as a whole. They remain unexplained, peculiarly so in Wales.

Some of the central features are symptoms rather than causes. There is the creation of county constabularies and the battle for *China;* the Temperance movement with its great choirs which wrenched the eisteddfod out of the pub; the preoccupation with education and the renewed Nonconformist drive against the Anglican counter-attack, the increasing mobilization of working-class leadership by Dissent. Can there be a more structural explanation along the lines advocated, in varying terms, by Lenin, Eric Hobsbawm and John Foster, the articulation of a labour aristocracy in a new imperialism? Certainly, from the 1850s, there was another pulse of growth which made South Wales into yet more of an Atlantic economy, in the world-wide and massive railway empire of its iron industry; coal begins its thrust into world power. Sub-contracting dies out rapidly. But, to put it bluntly, we do not yet know enough to be able to give even a tentative answer.

What is clear is that with the rise of South Wales into an imperial metropolis of British world hegemony, the Dissent of rural Wales moves over to the offensive. From 1843 dates the first aggressive Nonconformist press of rural west and north, reaction against resurgent Anglicanism and the bilious anti-Welsh racism of an education report of 1847 whipped a species of Welsh nationalism to life. Since it took the form of a 'Nonconformist people', there were here the makings of a powerful synthesis, as the leadership of working-class self-help movements in the industrial areas also moved into the orbit of Dissenting populism. Such a synthesis in fact occurred. It is visible as early as the 1840s in the Aberdare Valley to which initiative in the south had been shifting; it registers dramatically in the shock election of Henry Richard at Merthyr in 1868. The seeds had been germinating earlier of course. Popular and working-class radicalism through the frontier years had been a dialectic between attitudes and actions which later commentators could and did label 'middle class' and 'working class'; in its later phases the Chartist movement itself seems to have acted as a force for integration. By the late nineteenth century, the Nonconformist people had become the hegemonic power in Welsh popular life; the un-persons were not to acquire historical existence, and then a Socialist one, until the 1890s.

The most striking consequence for a historian is that, in this process, the Welsh working class lost its memory.

Industrial capitalism seems to destroy the popular memory; perhaps it needs to. The circumstances of its rise in Wales, its cultural expression in the pseudo-nation of Welsh Dissent, were even more inimical to working-class memory and therefore of identity. When the history of Wales came to be written, it was the new organic intellectuals of that pseudo-nation who wrote it, spitting the Anglican gentry out of it. Within it, the Welsh working class figured as 'hearers' in a Nonconformist service or as incomprehensible hooligans outside. On no people do the corpses of the dead generations weigh with quite so peculiar and particular a heaviness as on the working class of Wales. It is time to remove them.

We have one, rather melancholy, consolation. There is evidence that *some* memory of the frontier years *did* survive into the later years of the century. Characteristically it was a martyr, not a leader, they chose to remember. My great-grandmother, Sarah Herbert, came from a Tredegar family of long radical tradition. A pillar of the chapel in Dowlais, she was the sister of a Chartist. She was an indefatigable worker for Henry Richard and on behalf of the 'working classes' of the Nonconformist people. But she was prepared to spend the not inconsiderable sum of 4d to see what was alleged to be Dic Penderyn's ear on display in Dowlais market. Some kind of Dic Penderyn was alive, then, in people's memory. What those people chose to remember from the frontier years was the condition which Dic himself had denounced in his last cry from the scaffold: *injustice.*

BIBLIOGRAPHICAL NOTE

I assume that you've just read the essay to which this note is an appendage. If you want to follow up this early period and you're a newcomer to the history of Wales, the first thing to do is to read the essays in this volume. Then get back to the 1920s and the organic intellectuals of the Welsh working class. Read Ness Edwards, *The Industrial Revolution in South Wales,* brought out by the Labour Publishing Company in 1924 complete with foreword by A. J. Cook and a bibliography which includes *The Times (Bloody Old)*.

The first serious history of Wales, serious in the sense that it (a) took cognisance of the Welsh as they actually existed on the ground, rather than in an instrumental ideology which bordered on theology, i.e. took cognisance of a 'proletariat' as well as a 'people' and (b) was theoretically aware at a high level of intensity, worked to a 'problematic' without losing its grip on the essential *human* character of its discipline, employed the empirical method without succumbing to empiricism, was produced in the 1920s *by* organic intellectuals of the Welsh working class. Classic examples themselves of that Gramscian Hero, they dedicated themselves to the no less Gramscian objective of achieving the *historical autonomy* of their class.

Inevitably at that stage they were obsessed with their own experience, in industrial south Wales; only recently, of course, have 'peasants' ceased to be 'sacks of potatoes' in Marxist thinking. Their enterprise did not outlast the 1920s. Nearly two generations later, however, it has been re-engaged, characteristically by a generation of academics whose family roots lie deep in the same seam (soil sounds too folkish). It was such people as these who launched *Llafur,* the Welsh Labour History Society, which now has some 1,200 subscribers, which successfully assimilates academics and workers and whose journal, published annually, were it more charged with theoretical awareness, could be identified, albeit through the refraction of two generations' dark-glass experience, as the (or perhaps an) inheritor in apostolic succession of those maimed but creative militants of the Central Labour College and the Plebs League.

In between lies Dagon's Country, black as night, people by one ambivalent giant and a clutch of industrious and unduly defensive apprentices. But this is no place for an essay in historiography. Begin with our onlie true begetters in the twenties.

You can savour something of their calibre (and their sweat) in the *Position Paper* which the Ruskin History Workshop Students Collective presented to History Workshop 13 (Oxford, 1979). They raided the archives of Hywel Francis and the South Wales Miners Library (50 Sketty Road, Swansea) to print the syllabuses, notes and other material of D. J. Williams, Glyn Evans and George Thomas from the C.L.C. of the 1920s. Their project was stunning in its sweep, its rigour, its ambition, with a literally ferocious concentration on *totality,* conceptual precision, theory of knowledge and *process.* Not until our own day, as our bookshelves and journals have slithered into that acid-bath of clinical scholasticism which leaves the consumer feeling he has just got drunk on vinegar, have we met people quite so obsessed with 'epistemology' and 'conceptual rupture'. The 1920s brew is more accessible and congenial. Admittedly, their syllabus left little scope for *particularity;* this was *inserted* by an act of will or tribal loyalty. Their enterprise bore all the stigmata of its time and place. We are uncomfortably aware that some of these militants were to tread that road, so faithfully followed by the labour movement from its birth, onward and upward into the huge absorbent sponge of the bourgeois hegemony in its peculiarly succubus-like, voracious and glutinous British form. Nevertheless, 'The point was', said George Thomas (and he had *and has* a point) 'we had the bourgeois textbooks of course but we knew how to handle them. . .It was this drilling in Marxism really that put us on our feet, also Marxist philosophy, they did a lot with Dietzgen in those days, Joseph Dietzgen, *The Science of Understanding,* as an introduction to dialectical materialism. So when I left the Labour College I was equipped, I knew what I was doing and why I was doing it. . .'

And, nevertheless, after a syllabus almost blinding in its totality and its methodological and epistemological obsessions, George went on to focus on the history of Dic Penderyn, the first Welsh working-class martyr. And D. J. Williams, in a course of lectures in 1926, after a Long March from the General Strike and Modern Capitalism through a breathtaking vista of medieval heresies, Marxism, Problems of Knowledge, the British Working Class Movement, and Economics, closes with. . .'No. 11. Early Industrial Development in Gwaun-cae-Gurwen. . .'

Out of this world comes Ness Edwards's *Industrial Revolution in South Wales* (sample his own histories of the Miners, too and Mark Starr's *A Worker Looks at History*). Faults it has in plenty and conceptual ruptures by the dozen, no doubt, but there had been nothing like it before and there was to be nothing like it for more than a generation. It is a remarkable achievement, not least in his pioneer use not only of Blue Books and the press but of what became the celebrated Home Office 52 series. We should dig it up like the Republicans of 1830 dug up Tom Paine.

We have no political economy yet in Wales but there are some very useful 'economic-history' introductions, notably A. H. John, *The Industrial Development of South Wales* (Cardiff, 1950), A. H. Dodd, *The Industrial Revolution in North Wales* (Cardiff, reprint 1971) and J. Geraint Jenkins, *The Welsh Woollen Industry* (Cardiff, 1969). If you have, or can learn, Welsh, there are brilliant essays by the man who taught David Williams how to walk a country like an historian and was himself the 'organic intellectual' of a whole people, R. T. Jenkins, *Hanes Cymru yn y Ddeunawfed Ganrif* and *yn y Bedwaredd Ganrif ar Bymtheg* (Wales in the eighteenth and first half of nineteenth centuries) (Cardiff, reprints, 1972).

But the only real place to 'begin' is David J. V. Jones, *Before Rebecca: Popular Protest in Wales 1793 – 1835* (Allen Lane, London, 1973). David Williams, of course, is step-father to the lot of us. He is a small universe in himself. But if we are to boldly go where no man has gone before, it's necessary to get our parameters right. David Williams did an almost incredible job in mapping out the territory; his list of writings is longer than De Gaulle's nose. You can find it in the special number of the *Welsh History*

Review (1967) devoted to his work. His masterpiece, of course, is his *Rebecca Riots* (Cardiff, 1955) which is a *total* achievement (Art Schoyen, Harney's biographer, exploded into ecstasy over it. . .'A gem. . .a gem. . .a gem.' and rightly so). David Williams came from Narberth, of course, where they demolished the workhouse. On industrial Wales his work is technically strong, informative and a starting point. *John Frost* (Cardiff, 1939; reprint, Evelyn Adams and Mackay, London, 1969) was written *in a single year* and he followed up with his essay on Chartism in Wales in *Chartist Studies,* ed. Asa Briggs (London, 1959). These badly need to be corrected and followed through in David J. V. Jones, *Chartism and the Chartists* (London, 1975), his article in the special Welsh Labour History number of the *Welsh History Review,* vi (1973), the work of Angela John, 'The Chartist Endurance: Industrial South Wales 1840 – 68', *Morgannwg* (journal of Glamorgan History Society) xv (1971) and her MA (Wales) thesis on the theme, and the work in progress of Brian Davies.

On industrial militants, David Williams's sympathy faltered; his favourite adjective for them was 'unsavoury'; his comments on two of them in Gwent Chartism, *Jones the Watchmaker* and *Mad Edwards the Baker* would fill an anthology of feline malice. But his heart was in the right place and he tolerated the vagaries of the young. So David Jones managed to break through to his thesis and his fine book *Before Rebecca.* This has quite literally opened up a world. Particularly effective are the essays on the South Wales strike of 1816, on riotous Carmarthen and on the Scotch Cattle. This last is quite brilliant—compare it with the 1920s essay of E. J. Jones reprinted in *Industrial South Wales 1750 – 1914*, ed. W. Minchinton (Cass, London, 1969) and even more revealing, with the section on the Cattle in Eric Wyn Evans's technically sound *The Miners of South Wales* (Cardiff, 1961).

So, as a quick (well, relatively quick but essentially painless) initiation into the half-explored years of the emergence of a 'working class' in Wales, start with this book, go back to Ness Edwards, brief yourselves in A. H. John and A. H. Dodd and Geraint Jenkins and then get down seriously to David Jones, *Before Rebecca*. Read his chapters 1 and 2 first, together with chapter 5 on Carmarthen. Then switch to my *The Search for Beulah Land: the Welsh and the Atlantic Revolution* (Croom Helm, London, 1980); for further human material, chapters 5, 6, and 7 of my *Madoc, the Making of a Myth* (Eyre Methuen, London, 1980). Go back to David Jones, *Before Rebecca,* for his chapters 3, 4 and 6 and follow up with my *The Merthyr Rising* (Croom Helm, London, 1978). Then go for David Williams, *The Rebecca Riots.* Stop for breath before you tackle Chartism as I've suggested above. To look ahead, read Ieuan Gwynedd Jones's essay in this book and trace his many articles in Welsh journals. To get some sense of movement over time in one, quite important area, sample *Merthyr Politics: the Making of a Working-Class Tradition,* ed. Glanmor Williams (Cardiff, 1966)—a series of lectures organized by the W.E.A., you remember, the Other Lot whose heart was better placed than their collective head.

Keep your eyes on the *Welsh History Review,* of course, and see if you can work through the Byzantine labyrinth of the *Bibliography of the History of Wales* (Cardiff, 1962, supplements in the *Bulletin of the Board of Celtic Studies).* After 18 years, I still can't.

Above all, of course, after a reassimilation of Ness Edwards and Mark Starr and the History Workshop Position Paper of 1979, read *Llafur.* Read it constantly. In fact, you'd better subscribe to it; you don't know what you're missing.

4

Village Labour*

RAPHAEL SAMUEL

The village labourer of the nineteenth century remains a curiously anonymous figure, in spite of the attention given to agriculture, Speenhamland, and Captain Swing. We know a certain amount about his movements (though the years from 1830 to 1872 remain uncharted territory), but very little about his life. We do not know whether he was man, woman or child, though often it is assumed that he was the first (yet 143,000 women farm servants and agricultural labourers are recorded in the census of 1851); nor where he lived (whether in 'closed' or 'open' villages, by a green or on the waste); nor what he worked at during the different seasons of the year. Drainage is discussed as a factor in agricultural 'improvement' or in relation to the Corn Laws (some £12 million of public money was borrowed for it under Peel's Land Drainage Act of 1846, with the aid of which between two and three million acres of land were drained),[1] but not as a source of work. There is a whole spectrum of occupations which historians (following the census enumerators) have overlooked, either because they were too local to show up prominently in national statistics, like coprolite digging in Cambridgeshire and Bedfordshire,[2] or because they were too short-lived to rank as occupations at all. (Perhaps this is why the well-diggers are statistically invisible; the job was often taken on as an autumn or winter standby, and unless rock was encountered would be over in a matter of weeks.) Industrial occupations in the countryside, such as lime burning, brick-making, or quarrying, are ignored. So too is the whole range of country navvying jobs which kept the out-of-work farm labourer employed—sand getting and gravel drawing, for instance, clay digging, wood-cutting and copse work, and such locally important occupations as river cutting and dyking in the Fens. (At Cholderton, in Wiltshire, the Rev. T. Mozley recalled of the 1830s, there was a 'regular craft' who made pond-making for the local sheep keepers their chief resource.)[3] We know very little about the alternative

 * From R. Samuel, *Village Life and Labour* (London, 1975), 1 – 26. Reprinted by permission of the author and Routledge & Kegan Paul PLC.

sources of employment open to the labourer; the census enumerators very largely ignore them. 'Field labour' covers all.

The notion of occupation in the countryside is one that needs to be complicated and refined. Many of those who worked in the harvest fields had other jobs besides. Three-quarters of the farm labourers of Monmouthshire, according to a report of 1892, engaged in wood-cutting, quarrying and mine-work. 'With respect to many of them, it is difficult to determine whether they may be styled wood-cutters and quarrymen, coming to the land for hoeing, harvesting, and sundry piece-work, or whether they are in the main agricultural labourers, going to the woods, quarries and mines in the winter months.'[4] In Suffolk, George Ewart Evans tells us, there was a whole class of farm labourers who, when they were turned off after the harvest, went to spend the winter in the 'maltings' at Burton upon Trent.[5] Others from the same parts went off to Lowestoft and Yarmouth, where the herring season lasted from Michaelmas to December. 'By far the greater part of them are farm labourers,' wrote a *Morning Chronicle* commissioner in 1850 of the herring crews at Yarmouth. 'Immediately after the harvest they start off in search of employment at Yarmouth, and various other small ports on the coast of Norfolk. . . . When mishaps . . . take place, the children or widow of the lost man receive the full share of the earnings which would have been paid . . . had he been alive.'[6] The Norfolk Broadsman pursued a more local cycle of work:

When mowing the marsh-hay is over, after the hay is poled and stacked, he turns his attention to the gladdon, which had already begun to show the yellow leaf. He is now seen daily in his huge marsh-boat, with his meak, cutting and sheaving the long leaves, which he sells at a good profit. As the winter draws on he dries and packs his eel-nets, locks his cabin door, and those haunts know him no more until the following summer. Now, at even-tide, you will see him in his boat with dog and gun, hidden in a clump of reed, waiting for the flight of duck and plover; there he will sit patiently until the darkness sends him home, generally with a bird or two for his supper. When the first ice covers the Broad he is up betimes, and with his whole family, in an old hulk, you will see him busy breaking and gathering the thin ice, which he afterwards sells to the Yarmouth smacksmen. A little later he is to be seen, in tall marsh-boots, standing in the icy water, and cutting the reed with which he makes his fences and thatches his roof. In early spring he devotes himself to babbing for eels. If a very zealous naturalist, he will also be taking eggs for the dealers.[7]

Occupational boundaries in the nineteenth-century countryside were comparatively fluid. They had to be, where so much employment was by the job rather than by the regular working week, and where work was difficult to get. In the country building-trade jobs were chronically short-lived, and there was a great deal of movement from one class of work to another. The country craftsman or mechanic was a man with two or three strings to his bow. The thatcher might turn hay trusser for the summer season,[8] the hurdle maker to repairing carts and wagons,[9] the stonemason, when out of work, to jobbing carpentry.[10] A Wiltshire thatcher whom Alfred Williams writes about at Liddington turned his hand to making sheep-cages when there was no thatching to be done; he also built cottages of wattle and daub, or chalk stone, letting them out to poor labourers at 1s. a week, or selling them off.[11] Joseph Arch, the farm workers' leader in 1872, carved out a modest independence for himself through jobbing.

Finding, two or three years after his marriage, that he could not, as a regular farm labourer, support his wife and family—for by that time he had two children, a boy and a girl—he determined to try his fortune as a jobbing labourer. Taking with him some necessary tools, he therefore left home and sought piece-work in various localities. He began by gravel-digging; from that went to wood-cutting. Then he got some draining work to do, having, it is said, whilst occupied in this work, to stand sometimes for as much as twelve and thirteen hours a day up to his ankles in water. After this he took to hedge-cutting, and became so proficient in this kind of work that he got to be much in request by the farmers in the districts around.[12]

As well as being what he called an 'experienced' agricultural labourer ('master of my work in all its branches'), Arch also took jobs as a country mechanic, being employed by one of his friends as a carpenter 'when he got very busy coffin-making, or putting on roofing, or making church work. . . . Then my skill at hurdle-making and gate-hanging would come in handy . . . Being a good all-round man I was never at a loss for a job.'[13]

   Another neglected area for investigation concerns the cottage economy, and the unofficial sources of income on which a labouring family (to keep off the parish or the workhouse) had often to rely. Poaching, for instance may be discussed in relation to the game laws, or else as a colourful page from the past, but there is no attempt to relate it to the seasonal cycle of plenty and want (the rabbiting season began in September or October), to the local lie of the land (there were more rabbits in wooded than in open country), or to the range of totting and foraging activities of which it formed a part. Gleaning, so far as I know, has yet to be the subject of an article in a learned journal, though village autobiographies—and police court reports—are full of the kind of evidence on which a discussion might be launched. Nor has anyone thought it worth paying research attention to the cottager's pig, though (as Flora Thompson shows in *Lark Rise*)[14] there was a whole nexus of economic and cultural relationships which formed around it. Land, too, could be a source of secondary incomes. The whole question of proletarian landholding in the countryside cries out for investigation (it might lead to quite substantial redrawing of the map of British farming); so does the equally neglected question of common rights (heaths and commons did not disappear from the countryside with the advent of enclosure, though their size was drastically curtailed: in the open villages east of Oxford there was a whole class of cow-keepers still profiting by them in the 1860s).

In the absence of satisfactory statistics historians have often neglected the question of family earnings (difficult or even impossible to quantify) and instead have argued from wage rates—such as those published in the Parliamentary Blue Books—to judgments about the standard of life. The published figures, as Wilson Fox pointed out long ago, 'probably relate to the men in fairly regular work attached to the staff of the larger farms'.[15] Moreover, they cannot tell us much about net earnings. Wage rates may be useful as a barometer for secular trends, but they can tell us little about the kinds of vicissitude which a labouring family experienced from one week to the next. Farm labour books, such as those used by David Morgan,[16] make possible a more realistic account: they deal with net earnings rather than average rates, and show that even for the regularly employed farm servant there could be quite sharp variations in earnings according to the job in hand (a great deal of nineteenth-century farm work was given out on 'piece' or 'task' work, even to the annually hired). They cannot tell us much, however, about what happened between periods of employment, or about the economy of the household group. One crucial variable, especially in the earlier nineteenth century, when wood was still more generally used than coal, concerns accessibility or otherwise to fuel, a major item in the household budget to those who could not get it free. (Cobbett believed the labouring family of the woodland districts comfortable on this count alone, and compared them with the 'poor creatures' he had seen about Bedwin and Cricklade, 'where I saw the girls carrying home bean and wheat stubble for fuel', and with those at Salisbury where firing was so scarce that poor families had to take it in turns to boil kettles for their tea.)[17] Another concerns the availability or otherwise of winter work (the comparative well-being of labouring families in the hop growing district of Kent seems to have been due to the fact that the cycle of employment for both men and women began in the autumn rather than the spring).[18] Then again there is the question of family size and of the existence or otherwise of independent sources of income. These are not questions which this book claims in any way to have resolved, but perhaps it will help to point to their importance.

Woodland villages had an economy all of their own, and experienced a kind of inverted seasonality of employment. Their two native harvests—fern cutting and bark stripping—occurred in the autumn and the spring, and there was a good deal of winter employment in the woods. Bark stripping, which began in March and lasted for about six weeks (it provided 'flaw' for the tanners) was a major harvest, drawing extra hands from afar as well as providing employment for woodlanders themselves. As in corn harvesting the work was undertaken sometimes by men, sometimes by family groups, sometimes by travelling gangs.[19] 'Faggoting the lop' was done by men, while women and children did the 'hatching' (cleaning the bark of moss).[20] 'A good "woman hand" may earn 8*d*. a day; a child (doing the work badly) perhaps

3d. . . . .'[21] In summer wage-paid employment in the woodlands was liable to give out. Farms in such vicinities were characteristically small (they would have originated in squatters' intakes on the wastes) and those who wanted work had to travel—as far away as 'the market gardens near London, and even to a small extent to the fruit districts of Kent' in the case of the very migratory inhabitants of Pamber and Tadley, two adjoining villages on the Hampshire – Berkshire border.[22] The crofters of Ashdown Forest, Sussex, moved within a nearer vicinity, since there were hop gardens nearby and a local demand for harvest labour. They settled back on the forest in October, mowing bracken and selling it to local farmers at a rate of 8*s.* the waggon load; cutting turf for sale was another of their autumn trades, while the gypsies among them hawked clothes pegs in the neighbouring towns and villages.[23] (Earl De La Warr, lord of the Manor of Duddleswell, carried on a long war against these depredations, but in spite of decisions favourable to him at the local magistrates court—and eventually in the High Court—he does not seem to have been able to put a stop to them, until the trades died away of themselves.)[24]

The forest villager, though a labourer, was often a landholder as well, and sometimes a cottage manufacturer besides. At Nomansland, Wiltshire, a very proletarian village on the northerly edge of the New Forest, most of the cottagers had 'ground', some having thirty to forty poles, others as much as three acres. 'The men who have two or three acres of land cannot take regular work as labourers', the Agricultural Employment Commissioners were told in 1868. 'They grow chiefly vegetables and roots for the cows; they are better off than men who have regular employment.'[25] On the New Forest, pasture rights were even more important than holding land. They enabled the labourer to raise himself by degrees to the status of a peasant proprietor, chiefly by keeping cows or ponies, or fattening pigs. Eyre has left some fine examples in his paper of 1883:

Z. is the son of a stable-helper and labourer who earned 10s. per week, and lived in a lifehold cottage (quit rent 2*s.* 6*d.* yearly) on the edge of a common excellent for milch cows, and connected with the Forest. As a boy he worked for a carrier for some years at 3*s.* and 5*s.* per week and, at 20 years of age, while living at home, set up as a carrier, with two ponies and a van purchased with a windfall of 40*l.* that fell to his parents. The carrier's business not paying was sold at a loss of 10*l.*; a mare was reserved and turned out upon the Forest, and 2 cows were bought for 20*l.* The father died; the widow maintains herself by a cow and pig kept almost entirely upon the common. Z. began to rent a cottage and $2\frac{1}{2}$ acres of land at a very high rent, and married. At 25, he keeps 3 cows which produce about 40*l.* per annum in butter, maintaining themselves almost entirely upon the common in summer, and in winter living on the produce of his plot and land, supplemented by about a ton of hay (say 4*l.* 10*s.* 0*d.*) and about 5*l.* worth of food. He sells 2 calves yearly, keeps 2 sows, and sells 18 to 20 piglings (6 weeks old). He calculates that he clears about 12s. to 13s. per week, though burdened by a very heavy rent paid to a small freeholder. He is prepared to take a 'little place' of 5 to 6 acres.

Y. is a labourer aged 52, earning 12s. a week (including occasionally skilled task-work). His 10 children have all turned out well and helpful. Rents a cottage, garden, and plot, about $1\frac{1}{4}$ acre. On his marriage, he bought a calf for 10s. on credit, and paid for her when a milch cow by sale of her milk, rearing her on the common, and in winter by the hay grown at home, say 1 ton, supplemented by an out-of-pocket cost of about 30s. The annual stocking of his garden does not cost 20s. Made 4 lbs. of butter a week, and sold it to a dealer at his gate for an average price of 1s. 2d. per lb. Sold a calf; bought a sow, and sold upwards of 15 pigs yearly at 25l. Owns a mare and 2 good colts, and is about to take a little farm of $12\frac{1}{2}$ acres; his son, aged 26, is able to retain the old home, and inherit his father's improvements.

X. is a woodman and farm labourer, a first rate workman. By working early and late, especially at hurdle-making, and in the barking or 'rinding season', he saved 100l. before he married, though living in a parish 'without chances', i.e., where there were no commons. With great difficulty, he was able to keep his savings and the interest intact, while his family increased and grew up. He then took a woodman's and underkeeper's place on the edge of the Forest, but was unable to add to his fund, though his hard-working wife earned as much by taking in washing as he earned abroad. At 45, his family being nearly independent, he hired a 2 acre field and house plot of about $\frac{3}{4}$ of an acre, and bought a cow and kept pigs. Sold the first calf for 4l. before winter, and being accidentally able to earn 10l. during the 2 years following bought a second cow for 14l., and took a small place of $5\frac{1}{2}$ acres, and increased his pigs. Has since taken a grass farm of 35 acres by means of his original capital. In 3 years, he has a dairy of 10 cows, a horse and foal, 2 sows, and makes about 16l. per annum profit by breeding and selling pigs.[26]

The English countryside in the early and middle years of the nineteenth century—in many places down to the 1870s—was more densely peopled than at any other time before or since. This was partly due to the rise in population, general from the 1760s, steepest of all in the years from 1780 to 1821, partly to the extension of agricultural and industrial employment, and partly to changes in the pattern of settlement. The demographic explosion of the later eighteenth and early nineteenth century was almost as marked in the countryside as in the towns. In Cambridgeshire, for instance—'a purely agri-cultural country, no manufactures being carried on', according to the county report of 1846[27]—the population rose between 1801 and 1851 at slightly more than the national rate.[28] In Lincolnshire, where 'large increases' in popu-lation became marked from about 1770, the population of many rural townships doubled between 1801 and 1851.[29] In Suffolk in the same period the population increased by some 86 per cent.[30] The causes of this increase—whether falling death rates, rising fertility, or changes in the economy—are a matter for scholarship and dispute, but the consequences are not in doubt: by the 1830s, when the Poor Law commissioners set about trying to reduce it, the 'super-abundance of labourers'[31] was as much a feature of the English countryside as shortage of population had been a century before.

One result of this 'superabundance' of labour was the decline of living in. In the eighteenth century labour had been a scarce resource. The typical farm servant—a young, unmarried man or woman—was boarded and lodged by the farmer until able to set up in an occupancy or tenancy of their own, whether as farmer, farmer's wife, or cottager. Living-in survived strongly into the nineteenth century in pasture districts, where there was constant work for stockman and dairy maid; and in sparsely populated counties like Westmorland, something like the old system of informal farming apprenticeships prevailed.[32] But in much of the country radical changes were taking place in the relationship of the farmer to those he employed: 'servants in husbandry' were becoming 'hands'.[33]

On the large arable farms of east and southern England, living-in servants were replaced by outside labourers and hands, and this labour force came to be divided into two, with a nucleus of 'regulars'—ploughmen, stockmen, and shepherds, and labourers hired by the year—and a wider periphery of men, women and children, employed by the day, the week, the month, or the task. This extra labour force was decisive at harvest time,[34] but it was by no means only then that farmers had to call on it. Hoeing and singling, for instance, was very often undertaken by the task. In Norfolk and Lincoln these jobs would be done by the travelling gangs of juveniles whom Jennie Kitteringham writes about.[35] On the leviathan farms of Salisbury Plain, Caird reported in 1851:

the turnip crop is hoed by men at task-work—strangers who migrate into the district every season, and work late and early, that they may earn good wages. They are paid from 7s. to 8s. an acre, besides beer, and expert hands can make 3s. to 4s. a day at this rate, beginning work, of their own accord, at three o'clock in the morning, resting during the mid-day heat, and after resuming their labour in the afternoon, continuing till eight o'clock in the evening.[36]

Strangers were also an important element on the grass lands of Middlesex, though for rather different reasons. Here the land, 'celebrated for the quality of its hay',[37] was divided up into numerous farms, rented by dairymen or small tenant farmers. The number of agricultural labourers was comparatively speaking low (three labourers to every farmer at the time of the Census of 1831). At Perivale, when Henry Tremenheere visited it in 1842 – 3, there were no resident labourers at all, though there were five farms in the parish 'the largest of which comprises 179 acres'.[38] At haymaking time the deficiency of hands was made up for by a large mobilization of itinerants; Cobbett wrote in 1822 that it was the 'first haul' of the Irish 'and other perambulating labourers';[39] and the situation was very much the same when

Clutterbuck made his report on the agriculture of Middlesex in 1869, though according to him the Irish element, 'which at one time bore a large proportion to the whole casual supply' was 'nearly extinguished':

The mowing is for the most part performed . . . by strangers who come in companies from the counties of Bucks, Berks and Oxford, and other places. Mowing . . . is . . . undertaken by the acre, the price varying very much with the state of the weather, the supply of labour, the condition of the crop, and such like variable incidents. The haymakers, like the hop-pickers of Kent and Surrey, are often strangers from various quarters seeking casual, and, for a time, well paid employment.[40.]

Among the mowers would have been the six or eight men who went up each year from Filkins in Oxfordshire. '. . . When the haymaking was done, they worked their way back by doing hoeing for market gardeners . . . by the time they got to Wantage, the harvesting was ready.'[41] In the orchards and market gardens of Middlesex, seasonal disparities in employment were pronounced. 'They afford occupation during the winter months to three persons per acre', wrote Henry Tremenheere of the garden grounds at Ealing, 'and in the summer at least five more; and in some of the gardens during the fruit season the whole amount of industry called into activity, including market people, basket women, dealers, and hawkers cannot be estimated at less than 30 persons per acre.'[42]

Women played a large part in the new labour force, as day labourers employed on the roughest, if not the heaviest, classes of work. Women and girls predominated for instance in the stone-picking gangs of East Anglia and the fens, 'a form of organized labour which have chiefly sprung up within the last twenty-five years' according to an account published in 1864.[43] They went out stone-picking after the land had been ploughed and harrowed. Later on, when the crops began to grow, they were employed as human weed-killers, 'charlocking' or picking twitch and thistles, and they returned to this work at the end of the year with the autumn ploughings. Another winter job done by women, in Norfolk at least, was cleaning turnips and beet for cattle. 'They would come home up to there knees in mud and whet, and then they would have the household work to do, washing cooking mending, and all the other Jobs which came along wen there is a big famley to do for.'[44] The cycle of women's work at Bramley, in Hampshire, was recalled by William Clift, writing in 1897 about his childhood fifty or sixty years before.[45] It began on 14 February with bean setting. 'The price paid was 3*d*. or 4*d*. per gallon; so that supposing a woman had two children to help her she might add 12*s*., or 13*s*. to her husband's earnings in a week. Good and quick setters could earn more.' The next job women were called on to perform was the hoeing of wheat—'this was begun about the middle of April, and carried on until haymaking'. At haymaking they were employed at tedding and raking out ('each woman had to find a rake and prong of her own'); finally came 'a full month's work' at harvest. The women at Bramley were the wives of regularly employed farm labourers, but they also did jobs for outsiders.

Some families used to ask their employers to let them go out to where corn ripened sooner than her (say at Chichester, or some such forward place); there they would get a fortnight's harvest work before our corn was ready. And after harvesting our corn, they would also ask for another fortnight to go into more backward counties (say, Wiltshire or elsewhere) and get another two or three weeks' work.

The proportion of women engaged in agriculture varied sharply from place to place, depending partly on local tradition (an important force in mid-Victorian years, when field work was attacked as unwomanly), partly on the alternative forms of employment available. (In Lancashire, Caird reported in 1851, farmers had to pay out men for singling turnips, because the women took up employment in the mills.)[46] In the East Riding 'very few women' worked regularly in the fields except in the extreme south-west.[47] On the large farms of Norfolk, when Caird visited it in 1851, the proportion of women to men among the regular field labourers was 6.25 to 51.4.[48] Much market-garden work was done by women; in Middlesex, Tremenheere reported, the number of women employed in it throughout the year was 'in the proportion of two to one'.[49] Fruit picking was very largely undertaken by women and girls, except in the case of apples, which ripened later, when harvest work was over and men were hungry for jobs.[50]

The kind of tasks which women undertook also varied, even as one Suffolk writer remarked depending on the habits of 'narrow localities'.[51] Turnip pulling, for instance, was regarded as 'men's work' in the neighbourhood of Dartford, Kent,[52] but Hardy's Tess and her friend Marian worked long hours at it in the wintry fields of Flintcombe Ash.[53] In many places men and women worked in tandem at potato lifting, the men doing the pulling, the women gathering up, but women might do it alone.

The rise of population produced a shift in the balance of numbers from the landlord-dominated 'closed' village to the more plebeian 'open' villages rising on their flank. In the closed village—Nuneham Courtenay near Oxford is a fine example, with its model cottages symmetrically arranged—building was undertaken by the landlord himself and numbers restricted, so far as possible, to a nucleus of regular staff—'the shepherd, carter, blacksmith, and a few other superior farmworkers'.[54] Responsibility for their workers, let alone for their dependents, was to be avoided as far as possible. In some cases cottages were deliberately pulled down for fear of creating settlements under the Poor Law, the great engine of clearance, until Union Chargeability in 1865. An extreme case is that of Colwick, Nottinghamshire, a parish which in the 1830s was owned in its entirety by a Mr Masters. It contained 1,250 acres of land, 'but except for the porter's lodge and one cottage occupied by a servant . . . there was not another small house . . .' (Masters drew his labour from Nottingham and from the nearby open villages of Sneiton and Carlton).[55] Dr. Hunter in his report to the medical officer of the Privy Council on the state of rural housing in 1864, gives many examples of parishes where numbers had been deliberately reduced. At Preston, Northants, a parish of 1,470 acres, there were only fourteen houses 'of which only 4 were . . . cottages'.[56] At Horton, nearby, with 2,790 acres, there were only fifteen houses 'the number of inhabitants having sunk from 79 in 1831 to 31 in 1861'. 'Of the few cottages now standing only two are available for mere labourers, the cowman, shepherd, and gamekeeper having everywhere to be served first.'[57]

In the open village, by contrast, cottage ownership was diffused, and new ones could be built as speculations without meeting any impediments from above. Where demand was brisk the number of inhabitants could grow fast. By the middle of the nineteenth century the open village had become the great source of farmers' labour in arable parts of the country. The open village was typically much more populous than the closed. (Denis Mills suggests a population range of from 300 to 500 inhabitants in the case of the open village, compared with 50 to 300 in the closed,[58] but the averages would need to take account of the open hamlets and village 'ends', and the clumps of squatters' cotts on the common or straggling by roadside wastes.) A symbiotic relationship developed between the two, the overflow of population in the one making up for the deficiency of labour in the other.[59] The relationship has been interestingly mapped out for East Yorkshire by June Sheppard, using the manuscript census returns of 1851 for the number of hands employed at individual farms, and comparing it with the resident populations of agricultural labourers.[60]

Open villages (the term first comes into general use in the 1830s: I do not think it is used by Cobbett in *Rural Rides*) are often said to have originated in old freeholders' villages. But in fact some of them were new settlements of the late eighteenth and early nineteenth centuries, by-products of the pressure of population on the land, of urban growth (which led to the formation of extra-parochial clumps of cottages)[61] and of the movement to enclosure (Arthur Young in his *Inquiry into Wastes,* 1801, has a list of some of these).[62] A striking example is Flora Thompson's North Oxfordshire village of Lark Rise, 'the spot God made with the left overs when He'd finished creating the rest of the earth'.[63] Its real name was Juniper Hill and originally it had stood on an open heath. About 1820 it had only six houses;[64] by 1853, when it was subject to the Cottisford Enclosure, forty working men held cottages there, and 'looked upon interference with their "territorial possession" as a measure to be resisted'. When the authorities, at Bicester petty sessions, issued writs for ejectment it was thought that the occupants would resist. In the event a compromise was reached: the occupants were stripped of their land, but given fourteen-year leases at 5s. a year for their residences and gardens[65] (thirty years later most of these cottages had fallen into the hands of Bicester tradesmen and the rent payment of 1*s.* or 2*s.* a week was the 'first charge' on the labourer's weekly wage of 10*s.*).[66]

These new squatters' villages were decidedly shabby in appearance and it is not surprising that in the minds of the rich and respectable they had a bad name. Headington Quarry, for instance, appeared to Edward Elton, the perpetual curate of Wheatley, 'a strange collection of cottages in pits' when he made a visit there in 1861.[67] Lark Rise, in the 1880s, 'consisted of about thirty cottages and an inn, not built in rows, but dotted anywhere within a more or less circular group. A deeply rutted cart track surrounded the whole, and separated houses or groups of houses were connected by a network of pathways.'[68] Another new nineteenth- or late eighteenth-century squatters' village, Bourne, on the edge of Farnham, Surrey, is described by George Sturt its biographer, as 'abnormal':

As you look down upon the valley from its high sides, hardly anywhere are there to be seen three cottages in a row, but all about the steep slopes the little mean dwelling-places are scattered in disorder. So it extends east and west for perhaps a mile and a half—a surprisingly populous hollow now, wanting in restfulness to the eyes, and much disfigured by shabby detail.[69].

Open villages were often found on the doorstep of the towns, inhabited by plebeian independents (like pig jobbers, horse and cart men, milk sellers and so on) and by a class of half-rural labourers who looked both to town and country for their livelihood. At Kinson, Dorset, which Dr. Hunter visited in 1865, many of the men were employed in building work at Bournemouth (some came home only weekly, staying in lodgings while away).[70] At Potter Newton, two miles outside Leeds, the labouring population in 1858 was 'mainly employed in agriculture and the getting of stone'.[71] At Radford, Warwickshire, some of the men went into Leamington for work, others did field work round Offchurch. The women of the village were mostly employed in the fields, but supplemented this by taking in washing from Leamington.[72] The inhabitants of Mixen Lane, Casterbridge, which Hardy describes as the 'Adullam' of the surrounding villages, were separated from the town only by a bridge, but their orientation, Hardy tells us, was primarily towards the country:

Mixen Lane . . . was the hiding-place of those who were in distress, and in debt, and in trouble of every kind. Farm-labourers and other peasants, who combined a little poaching with their farming, and a little brawling . . . with their poaching, found themselves sooner or later in Mixen Lane. Rural mechanics too idle to mechanize, rural servants too rebellious to serve, drifted or were forced into Mixen Lane.[73]

'Improvement' in the countryside was absolutely dependent on numbers. The agricultural revolution of the eighteenth and early nineteenth centuries had nothing to do with machinery, but demanded instead a prodigious number of hands. Cheap labour rather than invention was the fulcrum of economic growth. The 'New Husbandry' brought a much intenser level of farming, with heavier yields and the elimination of fallow. Green crops—the pivot of the Norfolk system—were labour intensive to a degree. Turnips in particular 'the soul of the best husbandry',[74] 'the grand base of the present system',[75] demanded an almost gardenly care. 'Upon no one crop is so large an outlay made, either in manure or labour. . . .'[76] 'Every operation connected with it requires great nicety', wrote John Grey of Dilston. The soil had to be in such a state of pulverization 'as to fall from the plough like meal',[77] with ploughings, harrowings, rollings, pickings, and liberal dressings of manure before it was ready for the seed. Once the crop had begun to appear the earth had to be continually prodded and poked. 'The more irons are among the turnips . . . the better' was a common farmers' saying, 'even if there are no weeds to overcome, the turning back and forward of the soil, and the free admission of air, have a great effect in promoting the health and growth of the plants'.[78] The first hoeing began as soon as the leaf appeared. Then, two or three weeks after, came a second hoeing and the setting out of the individual plant 'each hoer having a boy or girl following him to part and pull up any he may have left . . . to see . . . that they are not left too thick'.[79] A third hoeing might be necessary if the weather proved unusually warm and moist: 'the weeds may get so fast ahead as to render a third hand-hoeing necessary, and neither this, nor the further expense of getting women and children to weed out wild mustard, charlock, ketlock, or any other rubbish which may afterwards spring up should ever be grudged.'[80] Hoeing time—like haymaking and harvest—was an occasion when extra labour was taken on. In Monmouthshire, as on Salisbury Plain, it was the occasion for a local migration. 'In the months of July and August small gangs of people from Herefordshire, accompanied by dirty and ragged children, come to this parish for turnip hoeing', runs a report from Llantillo Crosseney in 1870.[81]

The extension of arable cultivation into heath, fen and upland pasture, another feature of the 'New Husbandry', also involved heavy demands on labour. The black lands of the Fens, for instance, required a great expenditure of toil. To start with there was dyking, and ditching, and claying to bind the peaty soil.[82] In Cambridgeshire this was a winter job for the out-of-work farm labourer, 'heaving the heavy clay from the sides and the bottom to be spread out later on the land'; they went out into the Fens with thick, lace-up boots reaching halfway to the knees, and pieces of sackcloth wrapped round their legs for additional protection.[83] The newly reclaimed land was difficult to keep clean on account of the luxuriant growth of weeds. 'The black land is . . . peculiarly infested with twitch', wrote John Algernon Clarke in 1852; 'great and incessant labour is required in eradicating its long matted fibres, which spread so deeply and rapidly in this light soil.'[84] The 'heavy twisted crops'[85] also called for a great expenditure of labour, and this is one of the districts to which the travelling Irish harvesters were still coming in 1911, long after they had disappeared from most of Eastern England. 'The crops could hardly be got in without such extraneous assistance, for the modern reaper and binder often fails to deal with them', wrote A. D. Hall in his *Pilgrimage of British Farming*.[86] Hand weeding was also still very much in evidence, according to an account from Wicken Fen in 1902: 'women do work a good deal in the fields at Wicken and in the neighbourhood, where they get a shilling or more a day for hoeing and weeding which they prefer to washing or charing'.[87]

The availability of cheap labour was one of the reasons why the advent of machinery in the countryside was so long delayed. Another was the force of village opinion in face of the chronic scarcities of work. According to Henry Tremenheere, this is why almost no machinery was in use in Middlesex. The only machine of 'comparatively modern construction' which he noted was a winnowing machine at Norwood. 'There is a strong prejudice in this district against the use of all modern inventions for facilitating or abridging labour, and the dislike to so many admirable machines, now much used in husbandry, originates in a conscientious though mistaken solicitude for the welfare of the labouring classes.'[88] Clutterbuck had very much the same to say of Middlesex twenty years later, in 1869:

Mowing by machinery is not so often practised as might be expected: some persons keep a machine, rather 'in terrorem', to secure themselves against the difficulty of unreasonable demands, as to price, and wages, in time of pressure, than from preference for this method of cutting the grass crop; some will own that they are unwilling to risk a collision with their regular staff of labourers who look with an evil eye on that which they consider (however unjustly) an interference with the rights of labour.[89]

On the large farms of Oxfordshire, Caird reported in 1851, thrashing machines were employed on the wheat crop, but barley was still thrashed with the flail, 'both to give employment to the labourers, and because the machines in use cut the grain too short, and thus injure it for the maltster'.[90] At High Easter, Essex, most of the barley was still forty years after Captain Swing thrashed by hand. 'Certain men went into the barns after harvest; and many were thus employed until late in the spring . . . on a farm growing forty or fifty acres of barley, two men would be at this work.'[91]

In harvest work the chief change in early Victorian years, the replacing of the sickle by the scythe, was taking place within a hand technology, though reaping machines, it seems, had been in operation since the 1820s. Not until the 1860s did the reaper come into widespread use, and a scatter of machine-breaking incidents (more will no doubt be turned up by research) suggests 'the foolish prejudice against the introduction of machinery'[92] may still have been at work. J. S. Fletcher, writing in 1914 from Yorkshire, had a 'very clear recollection' of the breaking up of the first self-binding reaper introduced into his village, 'and of the savage determination of the labourers to deal out similar treatment to any successor'.[93] Steam ploughs also faced resistance, as David Morgan shows.[94] (A ploughing machine appears to have been selected 'as an especial object of malice' by a group of Kent labourers on strike in 1878, and it was in attempting to discover the perpetrators of the mischief done to it that Arthur Gillow, the owner, was murdered.)[95] We know as yet very little about the state of rural opinion after the crushing of Captain Swing. A rare glimpse is provided in the manuscript autobiography of Charles Slater, a farm labourer at Barley, Royston (Herts.), which has come into the possession of R. A. Salaman. The writer recalls an argument, some time in the 1870s, about the comparative merits of hand labour and the machine in hay-making:

... I heard an argument on the way to make the best hay some did not believe in machines one man said explaining. You first of all take two horses out of the stable with their stomachs full yolk them to the machines and then the horses dropings about the hay next you take a horse rake and drag it all up together put it in a stack and it get heated with a nasty smell and you have to starve you cattle to eat it and if you wanted to sell it it wont make more than one pound per ton. The hay that has been cut with the scythe and as not been trample about and shaken up nicely and has had a nice heat on it will make five pound per ton. That the hay for the stock. They will do as well again on that as they will do on hay cut with the machines, youll see what machinery will do. spoil all your stuf. starve all your cattle. ruin your land. And farmers will lose all their money, everywhere men out of work workhouses full of starving people. And England ruined. And all through some fool inventing machinery . . . why they ought to pass a law to have all those machines collected up and took out to sea some miles and droped into the sea.[96]

The rural population began to decline in the 1860s, but the balance of numbers and employment was slow to shift. At Lark Rise in the 1880s, despite the coming of machinery, labour (Flora Thompson tells us) was still 'lavishly used':

Boys leaving school were taken on at the farm as a matter of course, and no time-expired soldier or settler on marriage was ever refused a job. As the farmer said, he could always do with an extra hand, for labour was cheap and the land was well tilled up to the last inch.[97]

But not everything was the same. The young women of Lark Rise were now going into service,[98] not into the field. The children were at the village school, and subject not to gang-masters but to the Revised Code of Her Majesty's Inspectors.[99] The men all worked for one employer—in the neighbouring village of Fordlow, a 'closed' village with a thin population a mile and a half away. Flora Thompson tells us that their incomes were the same 'to a penny'.[100]

The general tendency of the later nineteenth-century years was towards a smaller rural population, and a more stable labour force consisting almost exclusively of adult males. The pattern of settlement reflected this, with the spread of tied cottages, on the one hand, and the destruction of squatters' cotts on the other, a work to which the newly formed rural sanitary authorities addressed themselves with vigour (at Headington Quarry they also made war on the cottagers' pigs). Land under cultivation contracted with the onset of the great depression, in 1879, and it was the labour-intensive wheat lands which suffered most. The progress of machinery helped farmers to dispense with the need for extra hands, though whether as cause or consequence is not clear. Steam ploughing reduced the amount of labour in tillage; chemical fertilizers abridged the time that had to be spent on manure; the reaper and binder took the place of women's and children's hands. These changes however were long drawn out and uneven: the horse, as George Ewart Evans reminds us in his splendid books, retained its hegemony in many places down to 1914;[101] in Headington Quarry the freelance labourer did not disappear until the coming of the motor works at Cowley.

NOTES

1. E. H. Whetham, 'Sectoral advance in English agriculture, 1850 – 80', *Agricultural History Review,* 16, 1968, p. 46.

2. The industry produced a remarkable boom in mid-Victorian Cambridgeshire, for which see Revd. Edward Conybeare, *A History of Cambridgeshire,* London, 1897, pp. 259, 268; H. C. Darby, 'The nineteenth century' in *Victoria County History, Cambridge and the Isle of Ely,* London, 1948, vol. 2, pp. 119 – 20. There is an account of mission work among the coprolite diggers at Eversden in Lilian Birt, *The Children's Home Finder,* London, 1913. 'The coprolite-diggers earn 17s. or 18s. a week, and at harvest time desert the diggings for the farm. They are in fact, agricultural labourers; but the work is much harder than that of the ordinary farm hand . . . and farm hands who have tried the work often go back to their old occupation at 13s. a week.' Frederic Clifford, *The Agricultural Lock-Out of 1874,* London, 1875, pp. 46 – 7.

3. Rev. T. Mozley, *Reminiscence, chiefly of Towns, Villages and Schools,* London, 1885, vol. 2, p. 306.

4. Parliamentary Papers (hereafter P.P.) 1893 – 4 (C. 6894 – IV) xxxv, Royal Commission on Labour, B – IV, 28.

5. George Ewart Evans, *Where Beards Wag All,* London, 1970, pp. 235 – 76.

6. *Morning Chronicle,* 1 February 1850, Labour and the Poor: Rural Districts, xviii.

7. P. H. Emerson and W. C. Goodall, *Life and Landscape on the Norfolk Broads,* London, 1886, p. 14.

8. Raphael Samuel, Headington Quarry Transcripts, 1969 – 70, Ward.

9. Bodleian Library, MS. Top. Oxon., d. 475, History of Filkins, fol. 93.

10. See 'Quarry roughs', p. 195.

11. Owen Alfred Williams, *Villages of the White Horse,* London, 1913, pp. 135 – 6.

12. Francis G. Heath, *Joseph Arch, a Brief Biography,* London, 1874, pp. 6 – 7.

13. *The Life of Joseph Arch by Himself,* London, 1898, pp. 62 – 3.

14. Flora Thompson, *Lark Rise to Candleford,* World's Classics ed., 1971, pp. 9 – 13.

15. A. Wilson Fox, 'Agricultural wages in England and Wales during the last half century', *Journal of the Royal Statistical Society,* 66, 1903, reprinted in W. E. Minchinton (ed.), *Essays in Agrarian History,* Newton Abbot, 1968, vol. 2, p. 145.

16. D. H. Morgan, 'The place of harvesters in nineteenth-century village life', in R. Samuel (ed.), *Village Life and Labour,* London, 1975, pp. 27 – 72.

17. William Cobbett, *Rural Rides,* Everyman's Library, 1922, vol. 1, pp. 29, 58 – 9; Cobbett returns to the theme in a number of places, cf. ibid., pp. 220, 240, 294, 302.

18. Sir Charles Whitehead, *Retrospections,* Maidstone, 1913, p. 23. For some examples, Kent County Record Office, The loose farm account book, 1846 – 53, cf. also A. D. Hall, *A Pilgrimage of British Farming,* London, 1914, p. 54.

19. Frederick Jones, 'The oak and tan-flawing industry in Sussex', *Sussex County Magazine,* 11, 1928, pp. 176 – 8.

20. F. G. Heath, *The English Peasantry,* London, 1874, p. 183.

21. P. P. 1868 – 9 (4202) xiii, *2nd Report of the Commissioners on the Employment of Children, Young Persons and Women in Agriculture,* Appendix pt II, p. 121.

22. P. P. 1893 – 4 (C. 6894 – I) xxv, Royal Commission of Labour, *The Agricultural Labourer,* B – IV, 57. The village had been largely settled by gypsies, led by a man named Reuben Hicks. There is an interesting account of it in Florence A.G. Davidson, *The History of Tadley,* Basingstoke, 1913.

23. Henry Wolff, *Sussex Industries,* Lewes, 1883, pp. 151 – 3 (to be found in Brighton Reference Library).

24. S. J. Marsh, *Ashdown Forest,* privately printed, 1935; East Sussex Record Office, Add. MSS., 3780 – 4104; Sussex Archaeological Society, RF/2/C, interviews of W. A. Raper with old foresters.

25. P. P. 1868 – 9 (4202) xiii, Appendix pt II, p. 240. There is a splendid account of the origin, character and economy of this village in H. M. Livens, *Nomansland, A Village History,* Salisbury, 1910.

26. G. E. Briscoe Eyre, *The New Forest, its Common Rights and Cottage Stock-Keepers,* Lyndhurst, 1883, pp. 54 – 5.

27. Samuel Jonas, 'Farming of Cambridgeshire', *Journal of the Royal Agricultural Society of England,* 7, 1846, p. 35.

28. Darby, op. cit., p. 121.

29. D. R. Mills, 'The development of rural settlement around Lincoln', in D. R. Mills (ed.), *English Rural Communities,* London, 1973, pp. 87 – 8, 91.

30. John G. Glyde, *Suffolk in the Nineteenth Century,* London, 1856. p. 360.

31. J. A. Clarke, 'On the farming of Lincolnshire', *Journal of the Royal Agricultural Society of England,* 12, 1851, p. 405.

32. C. Stella Davies, *The Agricultural History of Cheshire, 1750 – 1850,* Chetham Society, series 3, vol. 10, Manchester, 1960, pp. 83, 91; Frank W. Garnett, *Westmorland Agriculture, 1800 – 1900,* Kendal, 1912, p. 90.

33. There is an accessible tabulation of the ratio of 'indoor' to 'outdoor' farm servants in J. P. D. Dunbabin, 'The incidence and organisation of agricultural trades

unionism', *Agricultural History Review,* 16, 1968, pp. 123 – 4.

34. Morgan, op. cit.

35. Jennie Kitteringham, 'Country work girls in nineteenth-century England', in Samuel (ed.), op. cit., pp. 73 – 133.

36. James Caird, *English Agriculture in 1850 – 51,* London, 1852, p. 82. These 'strangers' may have come from North Wiltshire, a region of pasture farming and decayed manufactures where there was a chronic labour glut. Caird says that they came in force for the wheat harvest on Salisbury Plain (ibid.).

37. *British Husbandry,* London, 1834, vol. 1, p. 489.

38. Henry Tremenheere, 'Husbandry and education in five Middlesex parishes', *Journal of the Royal Statistical Society,* 6, 1843, p. 124.

39. Cobbett, op. cit., vol. 1, p. 84.

40. J. Clutterbuck, *On the Farming of Middlesex,* London, 1869, p. 12.

41. Bodleian Library, MS. Top. Oxon., d. 475, History of Filkins, fol. 95^r.

42. Tremenheere, op. cit., p. 125.

43. Rev. Thomas Hutton, 'Agricultural gangs', *Transactions of the National Association for the Promotion of Social Science,* 1864. p. 650. In fact the system was older than that and was extensively documented by the Children's Employment Commission in 1843. Joan Thirsk dates it in Lincolnshire from about the 1820s; see Joan Thirsk, *English Peasant Farming,* London, 1957, p. 268. Marx wrote of the gang system, 'For the farmer there is no more ingenious method of keeping his labourers well below the normal level, and yet of always having an extra hand ready for extra work, of extracting the greatest possible amount of labour with the least possible amount of money . . . The cleanly weeded land, and the uncleanly human weeds, of Lincolnshire, are pole and counter-pole of capitalistic production', Karl Marx, *Capital,* London, 1949, vol. 1, pp. 717 – 18.

44. Lilias Rider Haggard (ed.), *I. Walked by Night, Being the Life and History of the King of the Norfolk Poachers,* London, 1951, p. 93.

45. William Clift, *Reminiscences of William Clift of Bramley,* Aldershot, 1897, pp. 61 – 5.

46. Caird, op. cit., p. 284. 'This makes the manual labour on the turnip-crop nearly double the cost in Lancashire, compared with other countries.'

47. June A. Sheppard, 'East Yorkshire's agricultural labour force in the mid-nineteenth century', *Agricultural History Review,* 9, 1961, p. 44.

48. Caird. op. cit., p. 175.

49. Tremenheere, op. cit., p. 125.

50. Charles Whitehead, *Fruit Growing in Kent,* London, 1881, p. 9; Charles Whitehead, *Profitable Fruit-Farming, an essay,* London, 1884, p. 88.

51. Glyde, op. cit., p. 364.

52. Trinity College, Cambridge, MS. Diaries of A. J. Munby, xvii, 3 January 1863.

53. Thomas Hardy, *Tess of the D'Urbervilles,* ch. 43.

54. Flora Thompson, *Lark Rise to Candleford,* World's Classics ed., 1971, p. 37.

55. J. D. Chambers, 'Nottingham in the early 19th century', *Transactions of the Thoroton Society,* 46, 1942, p. 29.

56. P.P. 1865 (3484) xxvi, *7th Report of the Medical Officer of the Privy Council,* Appendix 6, *Inquiry on the State of the Dwellings of Rural Labourers,* by Dr. Hunter, p. 243.

57. Ibid.

58. Denis Mills, 'English villages in the 18th and 19th centuries: a sociological classification', *Amateur Historian,* 6, 1965, p. 276. There is a very clear demonstration of the different rate of growth in closed and open villages in Alan Rogers (ed.), *Stability and Change, Some Aspects of North and South Ranceley in the Nineteenth Century,* Nottingham, 1969. For another recent discussion of the subject, B. A. Holderness, ' "Open" and "close" parishes in England in the eighteenth and nineteenth centuries', *Agricultural History Review,* 20, 1972.

59. Lincolnshire farmers provided their open village labourers with donkeys, Caird tells us, in order that they should not wear themselves out on the six or seven mile journey to work, op. cit., p. 197.

60. Sheppard, op. cit., p. 52.

61. Among them Summertown, Oxford, 'A Place which is but of yesterday', founded by James Lambourn, an itinerant horse dealer in 1820. There is a very good account of the village in 1832 in Bodleian Library, MS. Top. Oxon., e. 240.

62. Arthur Young, *Inquiry into Wastes,* London, 1801.

63. Thompson, op. cit., p. 279.

64. Ibid., pp. 73 – 4.

65. *Oxford Chronicle,* 20 August 1853, p. 8, col. 2.

66. Thompson, op. cit., p. 6.

67. W. O. Hassall (ed.), *Wheatley Records,* Diary of Rev. Edward Elton, 12 April 1861.

68. Thompson, op. cit., pp. 1 – 2.

69. George Bourne (Sturt), *Change in the Village,* London, 1959, pp. 2 – 3.

70. Dr Hunter's Report, p. 178.

71. Robert Baker, 'On the industrial and sanitary economy . . . of Leeds', *Journal of the Royal Statistical Society,* 11, 1858, p. 429.

72. Dr Hunter's Report, p. 277.

73. Thomas Hardy, *The Mayor of Casterbridge,* Macmillan ed., 1964, pp. 254 – 5.

74. *British Husbandry,* III, 1840, p. 29.

75. William Marshall, *The Rural Economy of Norfolk,* 1787, 1, p. 256. For a general discussion of the labour intensive character of the 'New Husbandry', David Grigg, *The Agricultural Revolution in South Lincolnshire,* Cambridge, 1966, pp. 3 – 4, 40 – 1, 48, 58; Joan Thirsk speaks of the 'unprecedented demand for farm workers' when the Lincolnshire uplands were ploughed up (op. cit., pp. 267 – 8).

76. R. N. Bacon, *Report on the Agriculture of Norfolk,* London, 1844, p. 214.

77. John Grey of Dilston, 'A view of the present state of agriculture in Northumberland', *Journal of the Royal Agricultural Society of England,* 11, 1841, p. 165.

78. Ibid., p. 168.

79. Jonas, op. cit., p. 43.

80. *British Husbandry,* 11, 1837, p. 340.

81. P.P. 1870 (c. 70) xiii, *3rd Report of the Commissioners on the Employment of Children, Young Persons and Women in Agriculture,* Appendix pt II, p. 9.

82. John Algernon Clarke, 'On the great level of the Fens', *Journal of the Royal Agricultural Society of England,* 8, 1847, pp. 92, 101, 119.

83. Arthur R. Randell, *Sixty Years a Fenman,* London, 1966, p. 6.

84. John Algernon Clarke, *Fen Sketches,* London, 1852, p. 256.

85. Hall, op. cit., p. 75.

86. Ibid.

87. M. Knowles, *History of Wicken,* London, 1902, pp. 8, 11.

88. Tremenheere, op. cit., p. 122.

89. Clutterbuck, op. cit., p. 12.

90. Caird, op. cit., p. 21; Cf. also Clare Sewell Read, 'Farming of Oxfordshire', *Journal of the Royal Agricultural Society of England,* 15, 1855, p. 247.

91. Isaac Mead, *The Life Story of an Essex Lad Written by Himself,* Chelmsford, 1923, p. 32.

92. The statement is that of a judge at the Berkshire Lent Assizes, 1853, summing up in a rick burning case 'out of revenge, it was supposed, because a reaping-machine had been introduced into the parish'. Two men were sentenced to transportation for fifteen years, and four to ten years. *Oxford Chronicle,* 5 March 1853, p. 3, col. 2. 'Several cases of incendiarism' were reported from Devon in November of the same year, in two instances being perpetrated on farmers with thrashing machines on their premises. 'It seemed likely that the offenders belonged to that misguided class of men who think that machinery for agricultural purposes injures the labourer and diminishes wages,' *The Times,* 29 November 1853, p. 7, col. 6.

93. Joseph Smith Fletcher, *The Making of Modern Yorkshire,* London, 1918, p. 176.

94. Op. cit.

95. 'Strikes and machinery', *Ironmonger,* 14, December 1878, p. 1390. When double furrowed ploughs were introduced into the Yorkshire Wolds in 1872 'in several instances' the labourers and yearly servants refused to work them and were prosecuted under the Master and Servant Act. The plough 'worked by a man and three horses' effected the saving of a man and horsekeeper. *Labour News,* 18, May 1872, p. 3, col. 2.

96. MS. Reminiscences of Charles Slater of Barley, 11, 45 – 7. The writer is very grateful to Mr Salaman for letting him see a copy of this valuable MS.

97. Thompson, op. cit., p. 41.

98. Ibid., ch. 10, 'Daughters of the Hamlet'.

99. For the visit of one of them to Lark Rise, ibid., ch. 12 'Her Majesty's Inspector'.

100. Ibid., p. 39.

101. See especially George Ewart Evans, *The Horse in the Furrow,* London, 1967.

5

The Decline of Saint Monday
1766–1876*

DOUGLAS A. REID

It is axiomatic that the long-neglected historical study of leisure must proceed from a firm understanding of work. In recent years a more appropriate amount of academic attention has been paid to the dimensions and experiences of leisure time,[1] yet it remains true that the insights derived from the study of work have not been systematically used to enhance the study of leisure.[2] The imposition of work-discipline has been treated from the points of view of religious ideology,[3] of the supply of labour,[4] as a problem for managers,[5] in its relation to consciousness of time,[6] and, most recently, to drink.[7] These approaches have not been brought together to illuminate each other, nor has the question been taken much beyond the early stages of the growth of industrial capitalism. This article seeks to advance these studies by explicating the history of the custom of Saint Monday within one important locality and within the dual perspective of work and leisure.

I

Birmingham, like other eighteenth-century industrial centres, exhibited patterns of economic traditionalism alongside outstanding technical progress. As a matrix of small workshops the town formed a conducive environment for the survival of immemorial work-rhythms.[8] The surrounding agricultural area—including commons and small-holdings —must have sustained the independence of many workers.[9] The water-milling of metals was central to the town's prosperity but seasonal variations in the supply of water tended to reinforce uneven patterns of application to work.[10] Though the 'hardware village' rose to become 'the great Toy Shop of

* From *Past and Present*, 71 (1976), 76 – 101. World Copyright: The Past and Present Society, Corpus Christi College, Oxford, . . . England. This article is reprinted with the permission of the Society and the author from *Past and Present: a Journal of historical studies*, No. 71 (May 1976).

Europe'[11] the demands of the clock were yet often subordinated to the desire for sociability:

... the industry of the people was considered extraordinary; their peculiarity of life remarkable. They lived like the inhabitants of Spain, or after the custom of the Orientals. Three or four o'clock in the morning found them at work. At noon they rested; many enjoyed their siesta; others spent their time in the workshops eating and drinking, these places being often turned into taprooms and the apprentices into pot boys; others again enjoyed themselves at marbles or in the skittle alley. Three or four hours were thus devoted to 'play'; and then came work again till eight or nine, and sometimes ten, the whole year through.[12]

Within this context there arose the renowned custom of Saint Monday:

When in due course, SAINT MONDAY wakes the day,
Off to a *Purl-house* straight they haste away;
Or, at a *Gin-shop,* ruin's beaten road,
Offer libations to the tippling God:
And, whilst the gen'rous liquor damps their clay,
Form various plans for saunt'ring out the day.
.   .   .   .
Perhaps at work they transitory peep,
But *vice* and *lathe* are soon consigned to sleep:
The shop is left untenanted awhile,
And a cessation is proclaimed from toil.[13]

There is evidence that Saint Monday in Sheffield lasted longer as a workshop-based observance,[14] and the earlier dissociation of the two in Birmingham probably reflected the earlier emergence of a stratum of disapproving masters. But the situation was never clear-cut:

... people of all ranks, at times, obey
The festive orgies of this jocund day.

It is probable that some putting-out of work was done on Mondays as 'reckoning-time' was late on Saturday, and this too would encourage a day out of work.[15]

The prime supporters of Saint Monday were the better paid. High piece-rates could provide good wages for skilled men, but they more often elected to take a moderate wage and extensive leisure.[16] Tuesdays, and even Wednesdays, were sometimes their holidays.[17] For such 'playing away' followed not merely from weekend drinking but from deeply held traditional attitudes towards a potential surplus of wages: 'the mean . . . [are] regulated by the expense of their families, and their necessities; it is very well known that they will not go further than necessity prompts them, many of them'.[18] Even 'the lowest class' of workmen who received 'the second rate wages' would try to observe the custom.[19] As late as 1842 'the master' stated 'that they often have great difficulty in getting their men to work on Mondays, unless by that time they have expended the earnings of the previous week'.[20] In these circumstances the pawnshop was the unavoidable resort.

Teiz'd with the head-ache, the mechanic groupe,
On *Tuesday morning,* seek the greasy shop;
And if *dead horse* be not yet clear'd away,
But hangs on hand—how heavy wears the day!—
Their pockets empty, and their cupboards too,
Their wardrobe goes (not knowing what to do,
By hunger urg'd, and deeply sunk in hope,)
To where grim Ruin keeps a retail shop;
Till all life's necessaries oft are gone
To pledge for food—at *FULLER'S two-to-one.*[21]

And the hardest work was undertaken on the emptiest stomachs on Friday nights.

Of course Monday observance was also affected by the state of trade, 'the lowest class' being most vulnerable in times of depression. In 1822, however, when 'the revival of trade . . . diffused cheerfulness and contentment' among 'the great body' of artisans its concomitant was 'idleness and dissipation' on 'each succeeding Monday'.[22] Cyclical economic depression proved to be no inducement to the development of financial prudence and to the exercise of forethought in the family economy.

A sweeping survey of the recreations to which Saint Monday was patron in the eighteenth and early nineteenth centuries reveals the ale-house as the primary venue, and drink, bar-games, and entertainment of various sorts as the primary pastimes. Out of doors the most prominent sports were pugilism and animal fights. The poem *Saint Monday* was dedicated to '*Sir* Benjamin Faulkner—Puissant Pugilist!':

Accept my panegyric,—tis your due;
For you, the most of all I ever knew,
Have honour'd great ST. MONDAY'S noisy cause;
And gain'd the mobs unbounded, loud applause.

Up until the late 1830s 'dog-fights used to be got up every Monday', a degenerate pugilism survived, and 'there used to be some cock-fighting carried on almost every Monday afternoon in public-houses in and around the town'. Only Friendly Society meetings and summer theatricals relieved this somewhat limited recreational scene.[23] It nevertheless encouraged a care for personal appearance: 'This industrious race are distinguished by a black beard on Saturday night, and a white shirt on Monday morning'.[24]

Not surprisingly, entrepreneurs found Saint Monday (and all it represented in irregularity and insobriety) an irksome, not to say, a ruinous characteristic of the labour force. Before the year 1766 Samuel Garbett transferred his chemical works to Preston Pans in Scotland; partly for technical reasons but partly because the Birmingham workers evidently did not have the same 'obedient turn of the Scotch'.[25] The troubles which Boulton and Watt went through with skilled workmen who were drunk when needed are well known.[26] At Soho Manufactory in 1773 Boulton and Fothergill nearly suffered bankruptcy partly as a consequence of the difficulty of supervising the large numbers of the workforce.[27] Boulton's problems were but those of numerous aspiring small men 'writ large'. Many must have experienced the frustration that Archibald Kenrick felt about the irregular work of his six men and one apprentice:

Some plan must be laid down and strictly adhered to to prevent the inconvenience of loss of time in the workmen; a present evil must be preferred to obviate a constant one . . . I told them in the afternoon that I would not have any loss of time, that if they neglected my business they might go to those who would put up with it.[28]

Necessity, however, compelled him to adjust to the situation; the costs and processes of supervision were as yet uneconomic to such men, the resistance too widespread. Julius Hardy, joint-owner of a small button-making business, apparently found it politic to ignore it if his men played away; on the other hand he came down strongly on the apprentices. His diary entry for Thursday, 22 January 1789, reads:

This evening Edward Lingard's misconduct in going to the Public House in the afternoon for drink, contrary to my inclination and notwithstanding I had forbidden him from it only yesterday—this, I say, and meeting him on his way back, induced me hastily to strike him. With which my middle finger was so stunned as to give me much pain.

On another occasion, Hardy 'caused Joseph Langstone an apprentice to be secured in the dungeon for neglect of service', with the wish that it 'may reform his conduct on his return'.[29] Nevertheless, such examples did not deter future apprentices from worshipping at Saint Monday's shrines.[30]

II

Thus, in 1840, Monday was 'generally kept as a holiday by a great portion of the working classes', and when a correspondent alleged that the workers had 'not an hour to spare for education without a sacrifice' he was greeted with incredulity.

This . . . is so far from being the case, that I only wonder how an inhabitant of Birmingham could have asserted such a thing in a public journal. You must certainly, sir, have been greatly misled . . . Do you not know it to be a notorious fact, that the Birmingham mechanic will not in general, if ever, work more than five days a week? Does he not too frequently spend the Monday in the ale-house, greatly diminishing his hard-earned wages; and, indeed, when trade flourishes, and labour is abundant, it is not an uncommon occurrence to find him but four days only at his customary employment. There is not a manufacturer in this important town, but will affirm my statement to be strictly correct.[31]

Even by 1864 it was reported that 'In Birmingham . . . an enormous amount of time is lost, not only by want of punctuality in coming to work in the morning and beginning again after meals, but still more by the general observance of "Saint Monday" '.[32] The popularity of the festival appeared to be undiminished.

Moreover, as the old framework of leisure time had survived into the mid-nineteenth century so recreations had been adapted to suit the times by the working people.[33] The first recorded cheap railway excursion from Birmingham was in the summer of 1841. An examination of the pattern of excursions after five years development provides clear evidence of the way in which the new pursuit had been integrated into the customary framework of working-class leisure..Of twenty-two excursions in 1846 only six of them did not leave on a Monday. The significant feature of these trips was that they were mostly organized or sponsored by the organizations of the working class—the Friendly Societies. The Manchester Unity, the Wolverhampton Unity, the Druids, the Foresters, and the London and Independent, as 'affiliated orders', were attractive to the better paid working men, precisely the social stratum most capable of keeping Saint Monday.[34]

A similar process is illustrated by attendances at the Mechanics' Institute fund-raising exhibition of 1840 – 1. It was an 'intellectual treat' said the *Journal*:

Comprising three hundred thousand specimens, in ancient and modern paintings, sculpture and carvings; interesting philosophical apparatus; collections in natural history, (including 300 cases of rare and beautiful birds). Antiquities and Curiosities, including a fine specimen of an Egyptian Mummy. The chair in which Charles I sat during his trial, and on the morning of his execution . . . Interesting documents connected with the French Revolution . . . Models of the Guillotine, the Tuileries . . . Illustrations of British Manufactures and Models of Engines and Machinery . . .

At 6*d*. a head the exhibition was incorporated into the recreational life of many working people. On the second Monday in February 1840 'the rooms were visited by about 2,500 persons'. In May 1841, nothing was wanted 'excepting a few days of settled sunshine, to fill the rooms every day in the week, as completely as they always are on Monday'.[35]

Hence, by this period, Saint Monday was patron to quite unexceptionable relaxations. Cricket and archery had been introduced to a set of 120 'steel toy' workers by their employer on the firm's annual outing, and soon Saint Monday was again being utilized to indulge changed recreations:

the men possess bats, wickets and balls, bows and arrows and targets in common; In summer . . . [they] turn out to play two or three times a week, and often sacrifice a Monday afternoon to the exercise of these sports, which, at all events, is better than drinking away the Monday.[36]

In 1845 there was a notable addition to the town's recreational facilities when the Edgbaston Botanical Gardens were opened to the 'working classes' at 1*d*. a head on Mondays: 'on . . . which day their habits lead them more than any other to seek for amusement'.[37] It was an experiment to see 'whether the working classes would avail themselves of their advantages';[38] the increasingly enthusiastic response is indicated by the following Table.*

Year	'Monday perambulators'
1847	7,445
1848	11,116
1849	22,353
1850	28,463
1851	41,639
1852	31,725
1853	45,509

* Figures compiled from the *Annual Reports* of the Birmingham Horticultural Society for 1847 – 53. I am grateful to the Birmingham Botanical and Horticultural Society Ltd. for permission to inspect and quote from these and other reports.

To an observer in 1851 the gardens 'were literally swarming with a well-dressed, happy and decorous body of the working classes. All appeared to be luxuriating in the glories of the objects presented'. The consequence in 1853 was that 'if the summer had not come to an end the lawn certainly should'.[39]

By mid-century Saint Monday was well on the way to being internally transformed. A symbolic moment occurred in 1852 when the Magistrates were astonished to discover that not one case requiring summary jurisdiction had arisen 'from Monday morning till Tuesday afternoon . . . White gloves were presented to the gentlemen on the occasion'.[40] Friendly Societies had held their 'club-feasts' on Mondays in the 1780s, but their descendants of the 1840s were never reported as allowing 'the social glass' to make their members 'mad with liquor' until 'Loud Tumult' and 'Uproar' characterized the meetings.[41] By the 1840s the Birmingham Order of Friendly Sisters, the Wolverhampton Unity and others were holding galas and fêtes in Birmingham's Vauxhall Gardens, at which thousands peaceably enjoyed their Monday evenings.[42] The traditional Monday holiday was also utilized for the great Chartist rallies. The famous Holloway Head meeting of 6 August 1838 had been organized on a Monday, and in 1839 the Convention was welcomed on the same spot, on the same day. John Fussell's speech to the latter noted a trend in politics but also a change in the uses of Saint Monday:

He was proud to say that without any display of music, or those other incentives which usually collected them together, they had congregated in their immense masses, to give a glorious reception to the delegates who were endeavouring to work out their salvation.[43]

At the Theatre Royal every Monday saw a 'heaped-up gallery' crammed with proletarian life.[44]

Here, if anywhere, was surely progress. Yet despite all this there was a notable contrast between the Reports of the Children's Employment Commissioners of 1843 and of 1864. In the former, Saint Monday was mentioned only a few times in passing—it had been an accepted fact of life—but in 1864 it was widely noted and thoroughly condemned.[45] The fundamental reason for this contrast was the application of steam-power to hardware production. Only in the mid-nineteenth century did Birmingham significantly emulate the cotton industry in its use of steam, and only then did Saint Monday become truly vulnerable. In Birmingham in 1800 applied steam-power amounted to only 127 h.p.; in Manchester in the same year there was perhaps ten times as much. But thereafter steam-engine power in Birmingham increase in a geometric ratio: 2,700 h.p. in 1835, 5,400 h.p. in 1851, 11,272 h.p. in 1870.[46]

The capitalist wished for the most efficient employment of his investment. The worker wished to defend his way of life. This elemental conflict was epitomized in the events related by Charles Iles, a hook-and-eye manufacturer.

When we started a steam engine, I told the people that it would be necessary to begin at a fixed hour, instead of the irregularity which had been usual. The men objected very much, and said it could not be done, and only gave in when I said it was of such importance to me, that if they would not agree to it I would not keep them. Even then, some of those holding the best situations, and who thought they were the most valuable, left, though they were glad enough to return when they had been out of work some time.[47]

In 1835 four thousand males and thirteen hundred females were employed in the working of steam power in Birmingham; by 1849 between eight and ten thousand people were so employed. They all had to come to terms with the logic of the situation as defined by the masters: 'In all places using steam machinery and many hands there will of necessity be a certain regularity'.[48]

Of course this issue had been raised earlier in the century, and employers —like G. F. Muntz, owner of steam-powered metal-rolling mills—had begun then to operate a tight régime, as his answers to the following questions show:

What do you mean by full employment; how many days a week are they [Birmingham workers] employed now?
It depends upon the nature of the work.
What do you call a full week's work?
Working all the week.

Do they do it now?
Some of them do.
Do they work Mondays and Saturdays?
My men do always.[49]

No doubt Muntz used the conventional sanction of fines, as did Ryland and Company, screw-manufacturers, to deter 'late attendance' in their largely female workforce.[50] But the significant feature of the mid-century period was the swiftness with which steam power was now being extended throughout the town. In consequence, there was a rapid reduction of opportunities of alternative employment for the contumacious. In 1835 there were 169 engines in Birmingham; by 1870 there were 814.

A further inducement to employers to achieve a disciplined workforce was the investment in large plant which might be associated with the installation of steam power. Thus in the gold- and silver-chain trade 'roomy and substansial buildings' were constructed in 1853 to house the four hundred workers of Messrs Goode and Bolland.[51] In some other trades large factories were developed for different technical reasons. Elkingtons's electroplating business had grown to one thousand workers by 1864; the railway rolling-stock trade had developed from nothing (in 1838) to over three thousand workers in 1864. The latter was concentrated at Saltley, and, of the four firms there, the largest employed between twelve and thirteen hundred boys and men, 'chiefly' on 'carpentry and smith's work; with painting'. They had been drawn from Birmingham workshops, but the manager could state: 'Monday probably does not make a difference of 30 out of the whole number. We set our faces against any irregularity; and any one persisting in it would be discharged'. Furthermore—and this may well apply to the large businesses being founded in Smethwick and King's Norton at this time—'Being a mile or so out of Birmingham, we are more free from the force of custom in this respect'.[52]

At first glance then it would appear that the threat of unemployment was sufficient to achieve the required work-discipline. Such an analysis would seriously over-simplify the transition in social behaviour which took place in this period, for Saint Monday was eroded as much as it was demolished.

The chief agent of erosion was the Saturday half-holiday movement. There had been a statutory Saturday half-holiday in textile mills from 1850, and historians have tended to assume that the holiday was extended elsewhere by a kind of inevitable social osmosis.[53] But Birmingham's history demonstrates that an area had to generate its own dynamic, and only this proposition will explain the differing dates at which the half-day was instituted: in Manchester in 1843, in Sheffield in the 1840s, in St Helens in 1857, in Nottingham around 1861, in Barrow-in-Furness only in the late 1860s.[54]

In Birmingham, John Frearson—hook-and-eye manufacturer and 'general machinist' of Gas Street—was first to close down his works at

1.00 p.m. on Saturdays.[55] This example was followed by John Henderson of the London Iron-works, Smethwick.

Having already conceded to the men an hour and a half on the Saturday, by allowing them to leave at four o'clock, he found that if they gave up the dinner hour, and left at two, there would be nominally only an hour sacrificed, and virtually only half an hour; but when he came to take everything into consideration, he came to the conclusion that it was no sacrifice at all.

He saw no conflict between philanthropy and sound business sense.

He believed that everything which was done to induce the working classes to be more steady, to promote temperance amongst them, to spread education amongst them, to give them the means of lawful recreation, must be eventually of advantage to the employer.[56]

A campaign was generated by press reports and agitation by working men who wrote to thank their employers and thereby publicize the reform. It quickly became apparent that these spokesmen rejected the traditional pattern of work and leisure. To John Frearson's workers Saint Monday was an 'evil practice'. They looked to the Saturday half-holiday to stop it, for 'How serious must be the loss to the employer and how ruinous to the happiness and welfare of the working man and his family'.[57] 'A working man' wrote to recommend his fellows to abstain from Saint Monday every week as that would be the best argument in favour of the half-holiday.[58] Thus already the suggestion of a rationalization of hours had arisen—from a most unexpected quarter. It was a short step from this to the manipulation of the half-day by manufacturers so as to shift the leisure emphasis from Monday to Saturday; from irregular unapproved 'playing away' to recognized and much-lauded Saturday afternoon holidays.

The movement became organized under the aegis of Reverend G. S. Bull—Oastler's old colleague. A committee was formed, although its working class members were rather overwhelmed by the Reverends on the one hand, and the Hendersons, Wrights, and Winfields—all large manufacturers—on the other. Town Hall meetings passed resolutions which stressed 'the comfort, improvement and elevation of the Industrious Classes' consequent upon the holiday, and especially congratulated

. . . the *females* who are so relieved, because they are thus enabled to attend to many important duties, social and domestic, which must otherwise have been neglected or else so postponed as to hinder a due preparation for the approaching Sabbath day, and also because the comfort of the domestic circle, to husbands, wives and children is thereby greatly enhanced.[59]

Subsequently, two large railway carriage firms and the Eagle Foundry, Winfield's the brass and Osler's the glass firms announced their grant of a Saturday half-holiday. By June 1853, between ten and twelve thousand workers from 'thirty of the largest manufactories in the town and neighbourhood' were emancipated from Saturday afternoon toil;[60] such a figure must have closely corresponded with the numbers of those who were employed in the working of steam power in the town by this time. Advocacy of reduced hours by large employers was a striking phenomenon. Several manufacturers had consciously sought or else acted upon reports from their Manchester and Glasgow counterparts.[61] It appeared that an age of enlightened labour policies was at hand. Yet employers could not help being aware that the prosperity of the early 1850s made them liable to labour discontent.[62] Neither could it have escaped notice that large firms might consolidate their position if small traders were induced to cut back their output in a period of booming trade.[63]

By 1854 the clergy had withdrawn, and the leadership of the campaign had passed over to the dominant figures in local politics. Councillor J. W. Cutler spoke from the chair: 'He believed it was not only the duty, but the interest of the employer to contribute to the comforts, enjoyments and intellectual development of the employed'. Councillor Joseph Allday proposed the 'moral and social advantages which might accrue' from a general adoption of the holiday, and a committee 'representing the mercantile and carrying interests' was formed. A deputation to the merchants and factors of the town was 'to urge them to the adoption of a unanimous course of action'.[64]

By 1864 it had become clear that the Saturday half-holiday had been used as a sprat to catch a mackerel; a Saturday reduction of three hours (usually) in return for a Monday's labour of ten or eleven hours. Some employers implied that the sequence was accidental. Charles Iles was one of these.

I have found it extremely . . . [beneficial] myself, for the men as well as for the young. Men will have some recreation, and it is very likely to be better by day than by night. It has diminished irregularity in the early part of the week, and the hands are more ready, if wanted, to work extra at other times.

But a coercive note crept in: 'Punctuality and discipline are very essential. I always insist on my wishes being carried out. There is no intermediate stage between this and disorder'. He concluded: 'Formerly the workpeople were apt to come in at all times, but the half-holiday enables me still more strongly to insist on regularity, and say, "No, you have had your Saturday, and must be regular now" '.[65] However employees like Josiah Metcalfe, twenty years a button worker, were in no doubt that the half-holiday was a *quid pro quo*: 'A great many used not to come on Mondays at all; but they are more regular now, since the employers have given a half-holiday on Saturday and insisted that in return the people should not be so irregular on Monday'.[66] This appears even more plausible when it is realized that, in most cases, workers achieved no net gain in leisure hours through the granting of the half-holiday. In the Children's Employment Commission Report of 1864 ten firms mentioned giving a Saturday half-holiday. Only three of these enlarged their employees' total weekly leisure: one by three hours, the second by two, the third suffered 'a slight loss of working time'.[67] Two other firms re-arranged the working hours without affecting the total.[68] Four firms actually gained time from their employees.[69] The most glaring case was that of tinplate manufacturer, Mr Thomas Beckett, an enlightened capitalist, who believed:

the great means for bringing about a general improvement in the condition of the working classes, are—healthy comfortable work-places, proper rules and discipline in their work, and a half-holiday on Saturday, with any additional helps such as reading rooms and libraries.

These measures, he thought, would bring the working classes 'as near to perfection as is likely to be obtained'. Acting on the second part of his programme, Beckett cut two hours off Saturday's work, but then added half-an-hour to each weekday, and reduced both the tea break and dinner time by ten minutes each, so that altogether his time-account gained two hours and twenty minutes. 'We have now . . . laid down our system as above, with printed rules for the work-people, showing them the rules and discipline which must be observed, and which are strictly enforced'.[70] So the half-day concession may be more correctly described as a rearrangement of working hours. In this context it seems unlikely that employers remained unaware of the bargaining counter placed in their hands by the Saturday campaign.

Nor did these possibilities go unnoticed elsewhere. At Nottingham the half-holiday had been granted 'instead of certain irregular holidays at the races, fair, etc. It answers better for business'.[71] No doubt proximity to textile mills was a factor behind the institution of the half-day in Lancashire metal trades, West Riding engineering, and Belfast and Bradford textile warehouses by the 1860s,[72] but what history lay behind each particular case? The interconnection of mechanization and half-holidays was unmistakeable in the boot factories of provincial England, and in the large mechanically-aided potteries.[73] The employers were re-fighting the battles of Wedgwood and Arkwright in an altered and fundamentally favourable era.

Despite this, some employers continued to adopt courses of action which—had they been adopted generally—could have caused great social tension. At least two Birmingham employers resorted to lock-outs, saying 'If you will not come on Monday, you shall not on Tuesday'.[74] Elkingtons, the electroplaters, adopted another tactic. The manager confessed:

It is a pity that females should work in factories at all, as it interferes with their proper life, the domestic. They are, however, very useful. . . Indeed we have employed them upon a branch of work which was formerly done by men, because the latter were so much more difficult to keep steady at their work.[75]

III

Saint Monday survived into the second half of the nineteenth century (and sometimes into the twentieth) where there obtained several specific work situations. Wherever unmechanized small workshop production remained then Saint Monday might accompany it: in Birmingham, in the gun trade, in pearl-button making, and among tool-makers; in Leicester workshops; among Scottish handloom weavers and Whitby jet-ornament makers; among woodworkers and tailors everywhere.[76] On the other hand, certain heavier trades were noted for playing away at the beginning of the week, sometimes despite the presence of steam engines or other substantial capital investment: in Birmingham, wire-workers and heavy steel-toy workers; elsewhere, in Sheffield's metal trades, in South Wales ironworks, in Black Country iron, glass and sheet-metal works, in the Potteries, in brickfields and in the mines.[77] It appears that the unanimity of the men in upholding the customary ways was sufficient to overcome the opposition of the owners. Though steam-engines operated tilt-hammers and drew wire in the aforementioned Birmingham trades they did not dominate the productive process. In Sheffield and in the mines the owners made the best of the situation by using Monday as a repair day.[78]

In all work contexts the skilled men were the most capable of observing Saint Monday. Brass-casters might earn 30*s.* to 40*s.* a week, and the custom with many of them was neatly summed up by the boy who helped one brass candlestick maker: 'The caster very seldom comes to work on Monday; not four times a year perhaps'. Even those who did go seldom arrived by 10.00 a.m. and left by five in the evening.[79] Elkingtons had abolished irregularity by utilizing women, but one or two of their workers continued to be absent on Mondays—the explanation offered was that they were 'superior workmen'.[80] In a toolmaker's workshop a small master complained of irregularities in time-keeping but bore them nonetheless 'in order to keep his men' for they were 'skilled workers, and not to be replaced by the first comer'.[81] The essence of the skilled worker's position was his indispensability to the employer, and his payment at piece rates. A gun-furniture manufacturer averred:

In gun work they are very irregular, as they work so much for themselves at home, and even when they work in factories the men work chiefly by the piece, and come when they please. We have scarcely any control over them in this respect.[82]

Inasmuch as the observance of Saint Monday by the élite of the working class represented a confirmation of their status then the potential for a successful defence or extension of Monday playing time for the majority was diminished. Nevertheless, examples of unskilled Saint Mondays may be found where mechanization had not yet replaced the custom of the trade. An employer in the glass- and emery-paper trade complained: 'We can get the lads on Monday but not the women and the girls who are more giddy'.[83] For wives and mothers such 'giddyness' was in fact very sensible if their wage only supplemented the family income and they needed the Monday to perform domestic tasks. In a button 'factory' little work was done on Mondays 'as the women reckon to make enough on the other five days'. Mary Anne Field, a press-woman there, appreciated lax time-discipline: 'Coming late in the morning suits me best, because of getting the children's breakfast'.[84] On Mondays, Mrs Field and other Birmingham working women doubtless did as Elizabeth Pritchard, a Black Country woman: 'Don't work much on Monday, don't play, but do washing and fetch coals'.[85]

A generational cycle helped perpetuate Saint Monday. Daniel Thompson, aged eight, was already at work in a brass foundry shop—except, that is, on Mondays: 'Don't work on Mondays, nor does father, at least its a long time since. But Mondays you don't work'.[86] Young working boys soon caught the attitude, for—as in spoon-making—

As the boys work under the men they are liable to the same irregularities; thus if they do not work on Monday or Tuesday, which is generally the case, whether their trade is good or bad, the boys are idle and playing about the streets.[87]

The young were subject to great temptations, as in the pearl-button trade where masters drinking with their men was said to be 'very bad and brings up the boys to the habit'.[88] Again, the frantic working at the end of the week to make up for lost time was harmful to the children: 'It was as common as possible to work all night on Fridays'.[89]

Astonishingly, cultural attitudes which had sustained the Saint Monday of the eighteenth century survived in some measure into the 1860s and beyond. It seemed that the 'inward notation of time' of heavy steel-toy workers of the 1860s was still oriented to the task (or to leisure) rather more than to the clock. These piece-workers would come 'what time they please; perhaps in summer they will come at 5 and leave by dinnertime'. On Mondays very few went at all.[90] Nor is the evidence confined to one trade. As late as the 1870s,

It was no uncommon thing to see batches of workmen standing at street corners with dirty aprons all hours of the day and the public house well patronised . . . Instead of working during the day they resorted to their small workshop after hours.[91]

Even in the last decades of the century wage incentives had not begun to take effect with some toolmakers: 'as soon as they feel they have a few shillings in their pockets they leave off work'.[92]

These groups of skilled workers must obviously have contained a fair proportion of the 'natural leaders' of the working class. Yet it has already been noted that working men prominent in the half-holiday campaign were the first to suggest giving up Saint Monday.[93] How is this crucial split within the natural leadership of the working class to be explained? By what means was an important section of the working class brought to accept time-discipline as a fair and admissible basis for work?

IV

E. P. Thompson has rightly stressed the role of Puritanism and its 'marriage of convenience' with industrial capitalism in the conversion of men to new valuations of time.[94] Yet men had to wish to be converted and unless they did evangelism was not bound to succeed. In 1790 a Birmingham button manufacturer invited 'such of my workmen to meet at my house as choose, to hear some edifying portion read, an hymn sung, and prayers'. Significantly, the readings were mostly from Richard Baxter's works, beginning with ' "Saints' Everlasting Rest", where he recommends our reproving the ungodly and inviting them to return to Christ'.[95] Five men came on a Tuesday evening, but a fortnight later Hardy unwisely brought the day forward one. There had been an initial period of 'curiousity', but Hardy realized that Monday, 'being a sort of "holiday" so called', had affected the numbers. A fortnight after he blamed further decline on a 'Foot-Ale' being drunk for a fresh workman. From the height of nine, out of his thirty-strong workforce, the attendance dropped to two, and that was the last of his proselytizing.[96] However, the Hardys of Birmingham were soon to be reinforced by those 'steam-engines of the moral world'—the schools. Michael Frost has found evidence that there was indeed an important emphasis on 'habits of industry' in the schools of the area in the early nineteenth century.[97] By mid-century 'time-thrift' had been inculcated into several generations of children—most notably, the children of artisans.[98] Employers marked the correlation between schooling and working habits:

The best educated are the most valuable workmen; they are generally more attentive to their business, do not so much neglect it in the beginning of the week; and take more pride in it . . . the more ignorant on the contrary, will neglect their work in the beginning of the week, with the notion that by overworking towards the end, they will make up the lost time.[99]

On the one hand, 'time-thrift'; on the other, political moderation. After Chartism, politically-active working men were almost totally integrated into the system of justification and explanation surrounding the local capitalist industrial structure. Some of the reasons for this have been explored by Briggs and Tholfsen,[100] but another point must be added here which is directly related to both time-discipline and the lack of any political opposition to the employers.[101] It is that the sub-letting of steam power was an important factor in the disciplining in regularity of many of the potential leaders of working men. Birmingham's equivalent to the handloom

weaver—the independent worker in metals—often imposed time-discipline
on himself:

. . . the mere working man, who has saved a trifling sum, is enabled by renting a *room*
and *power,* in some extensive rolling mill or other considerable establishment, to
pursue on a small scale, an occupation, which would otherwise be out of his reach.[102]

'Independence' was in fact qualified by the necessity of attending on the
steam-engine's motion, in marked contrast to the experience of earlier
Birmingham artisans who had needed only hammer, file, vice, or perhaps a
foot lathe. For one family the transition in working modes took place in the
1820s. George Jacob Holyoake's mother was 'an entirely self-acting,
managing mistress' of a horn button workshop attached to their house; she
simultaneously made time to raise her family. But young George was
entrusted with some newly-invented machinery 'for turning buttons' and
required to attend on the 'steam-power' which his father hired for him 'at
the Baskerville Mill'.[103] In the early 1860s a Children's Employment
Commissioner gave an example of such a mill: 'a nest of small shops on
different floors, in which steam power is let off from an adjoining gun and
sword factory, and used for various purposes'. Of the seven tenants, three
were silver and electroplate polishers, and there was a pearl-shell grinder, a
glass cutter, a razor grinder and a tube drawer. The hours worked by these
men were dependent on the steam power of the mill. They commenced work
at 7.00 a.m. and—beginning on Monday—the daily closing hours were 6.00
p.m., 7.00 p.m., 8.00 p.m., 9.00 p.m., 7.00 p.m., and 2.00 p.m.[104] Clearly the
millowner had made a token obeisance to Saint Monday but taken good care
to recoup that hour and the Saturday half-day. In this way 'independent'
workers came voluntarily to associate themselves with the time-discipline of
the earliest factory workers.

Underlying these changes there lay the perhaps even more fundamental
alteration in the economic horizons of the majority. Consumer demand, or
acquisitiveness *vis-à-vis* subsistence wage earning, was becoming the pattern
of popular economic aspiration.[105] The development of the building society
movement in Birmingham by the 1790s indicated in bricks and mortar that
some exceptional artisans had greatly raised their economic sights.[106] Once
this evolution took place then foresight became a popular economic virtue
and regularity of wages became an important consideration. The process of
transition must have been greatly retarded by the cyclical unemployment of
the years 1790–1850, but became established once the relatively sunny
uplands of the 1850s and 1860s were reached. In those years regular wages
necessitated regularity of attendance, but employers who insisted on such
regularity acted as magnetic poles for men who had come to accept economic
progress. At the very least, they might be attracted by the promise of stability
in such firms and the diminished threat of unemployment. At the Midland

Railway Carriage and Wagon Company in 1864, 'piece-workers engage boys subject to [managerial] . . . approval. The youngest are mostly brought in by parents or relatives . . : as it is considered a privilege to the boys, affording them the opportunity of becoming regular workmen'.[107] Such attitudes help to explain the complete absence of Saint Monday in the trade which, next to guns, was most suited for it, namely jewellery, with its highly paid artisans inhabiting hundreds of small workshops.[108] 'Staid, quiet, respectable', the jewellery trade had developed extremely rapidly in the 1850s and 1860s and was probably the trade with the most stable employment prospects in the town. By contrast, the gun trade was subject to 'extreme fluctuations in . . . demand', and gun men were reckoned 'a good deal like sailors; the transition from a life of hardship and privation to a short reign of plenty induces a recklessness which is fatal to good economy'.[109]

Stating the problem in terms of a rift between artisans instead of employing the model of a unitary labour aristocracy may also aid the analysis by directing attention to a dialectic of social alternatives. Low economic horizons seemed to make less and less sense in an age when railway excursions and cheaper newspapers opened up the wonders of the British Isles and the world. Each year the rift between the supporters and the abjurers of Saint Monday was intensified. Each year the devotees of Saint Monday grew less and less reasonable in their persistent refusal to acknowledge progress. The more that leading artisans rejected Saint Monday, the more the unfortunate adherents of the Saint came to light. The less that Saint Monday was a central working class tradition, the more it became associated in fact as well as in imagination with that part of the class who bore 'the taint of Bohemianism';[110] that area where social delinquency appeared to be caused by moral deterioration, where Saint Monday was less a positive custom, more an expression of heedless resignation. An attitude notoriously held by casual labourers and by members of declining trades: sword-makers, Willenhall locksmiths, Black Country nailers.[111] An attitude prevalent perhaps among garret masters in the pearl button trade, who were,

for the most part men who are not 'in society', and one inducement for some of them to set up for themselves in this way is the liberty it enables them to take of playing at cards in beershops, and drinking and smoking away the Monday and Tuesday, which they cannot have in a regular shop.[112]

Moreover such attitudes directly aroused the enmity of trade society men, because, in the peculiar circumstances of industrial relations in small workshop trades, the garret master—who might undercut the standard prices—was seen by the skilled worker as his greatest enemy.[113] In these circumstances the distinctive recognition of 'Saint Monday' gave way to the pejorative term 'shackling day'.[114] More widely, being 'shackled' or befuddled by drink came to be seen as a poor basis for the organization of labour.[115]

Thus a blend of economic pressures and the potent image of progress combined to create a division within the natural leadership of the working class and ensured the eventual triumph of those who rejected Saint Monday. In the moral atmosphere of Victorian England it therefore became easy to see Saint Monday as an 'evil practice' and be blind to the internal transformation of the festival. Even so sympathetic an observer as Thomas Wright thought it 'fairly questionable' whether Saint Monday was beneficial to 'the Great Unwashed'. He remarked on the widespread Monday patronage of excursion trains, of pleasure gardens, of public parks, of 'running grounds', and he observed the family nature of much of this leisure, yet in the final analysis he allowed the combative Saint Monday of the Black Country, and the 'lushingtons' and the 'loafers' to tip the scales of his argument.[116] Similarly, the Secretary of the Scissors' Grinders Union observed that 'half the men in Sheffield kept Saint Monday by their own folly'. It was only as an afterthought that he did justice to the situation: 'those people who keep Saint Monday we must not put them all down as getting drunk. I take it for granted that some of them are going out of town . . . tripping . . . Sheffielders are noted for going to other places on Monday'.[117] In 1853, it was an unnoticed irony that excursions were the chosen means of the Birmingham Saturday Half-holiday Committee in their efforts to provide suitable activities to fill the new leisure.[118]

V

The tenor of middle-class opinion was expressed by the comment of *Aris's Gazette* that ' "St Monday" is not an institution which meets with our general approval'.[119] Saint Monday posed a cultural problem which went to the heart of the ruling order. A London journalist acknowledged that the opening of the Edgbaston Botanical Gardens on Mondays fulfilled a crying need, but, nonetheless, it

encourages the working classes in the bad habit of keeping 'Saint Monday' . . . They are already well enough disposed to do so, and to waste a day that should be devoted to honest labour. They need no further inducement of this or any other kind.[120]

The ideology of 'honest labour', of the 'rational' use of time, of moral conformity to the steam engine's constant regularity had no intellectual opponent at this time. Knowledge of the agreeable and harmless activities which had replaced most of the brutality and much of the drinking was repressed, even by radical working men. A gulf was opened up between Saint Monday and their proffered alternative—'rational amusements'. In 1846 they sponsored threepenny Saturday-evening miscellaneous concerts at the

People's Hall, which failed to attract support. The disappointed reformers diagnosed the cause to be that 'the working classes did not appreciate even such a cheap and rational amusement as that'. They could not conceive Saint Monday as an admissible alternative. 'Rational amusements' were seen to be morally superior, partly because they refreshed the mind vis-à-vis sensual pleasure, partly because they accorded with the perceived dominant economic and social directions. They contrasted with the non-intellectuality of the pub; they were in the cultural forms approved by the leaders of 'Culture'. Since the application of power represented progress and moral improvement was also progress, amusements which were an adjunct to both were especially desirable to reformers whose 'great object' was 'the educational, moral and political improvement of the people".[121] The idealism embodied in the concept of 'improvement' and its counterpart 'progress' incorporated but transcended the ideology of the rational use of time.[122]

By 1853 the Saturday half-holiday movement was already beginning to affect the pattern of mass leisure. In 1840 and 1841 there were only nine Saturday performances at the Birmingham Theatre Royal, but in October 1853 a theatre Saturday was said to be 'the commercially busiest night of the week'.[123] Two major landmarks were yet to be passed before the main recreational accent shifted to Saturday. The 1867 Factory Act brought Birmingham into line with the textile districts by instituting a mandatory Saturday half-holiday for women; by 1876 'the bulk of . . . factories under the 1867 Act'—'especially those where women are employed'—closed at 1.00 or 2.00 p.m. on Saturdays.[124] The second stage was the great wave of reductions in working hours achieved by the 'Nine Hours Movement' of the prosperous years 1871 – 2.[125] The Newcastle engineers' strike of 1871 assumed the nature of a test case, and, following its success, employers throughout the country reacted similarly to the Birmingham Tangye Brothers: 'when whirlwinds were about, it was better to ride and direct them, than to be overwhelmed by them'.[126] The fifty-four hour week was granted virtually before the men had a chance to organize a campaign; and this pattern of concession was followed in other major trades, such as guns, tin-plate, railway rolling-stock, and screws.[127] Since a 1.00 p.m. Saturday finish was an integral part of the fifty-four hour week, the reductions in hours were significant in confirming and extending the Saturday half-holiday in those trades (by-passed by the 1867 Act) with a preponderance of male workers. Thus for most large groups of industrial workers (but not bakery or railway workers[128]) the process begun in 1853 was complete. By 1873, 'It [was] . . . needless to say that on Saturday nights the "gallery gods" muster in strong force at the theatres',[129] and the ground had been prepared for the growth of Association Football.[130]

Clearly, these trends detracted from the vigour of Saint Monday. At the

Birmingham Botanical Gardens between 1854 and 1857 the annual average of Monday attendances was 40,450; by 1869–73 the average was down to 20,600 (and much of the latter was composed of attendances on one or two particular Mondays—the precursor of the 1871 Bank Holidays).[131] Nor had the workshops escaped the legislative broom, for the 1867 Workshops Act instituted a Saturday half-holiday for their juvenile workers and restricted their daily labour to six and a half hours.[132] In the 1860s there had been fifteen to sixteen thousand children and young persons employed in Birmingham, and when, eventually, their labour was curtailed piece-workers were deprived of the young helpers whose labour—if mechanical – was often essential.[133] It therefore became too expensive to take Monday off if the work could not be made up at the end of the week. Meanwhile, in many of Birmingham's 'large concerns' work-discipline seemed to be evolving into 'a sort of military discipline' wielded by a type of employer 'hard, proud, fond of power, and a tyrant'.[134] That the 1876 Factory and Workshop Commission noticed the custom only once signifies something of the impact of these developments on Saint Monday.[135] Only its ghost lingered on.[136]

It may be concluded that the eradication of Saint Monday did real harm to the actual and potential quality of working-class life. Half a day was given in exchange for a whole one; in submitting to the norms of industrial capitalism the notion of a proper balance between work and leisure was lost. But to the half-holiday campaigners in Birmingham Town Hall in 1853 there was no question that they were right. Whether through idealism or interest, or an imponderable mixture,

There were present that evening employers and employed, masters and workmen, Ministers and people, those who had obtained and those who had granted the holiday, all rejoicing together in the possession of a mutual benefit, and the watchword of the assembly was 'progress'.[137]

ACKNOWLEDGEMENTS

Earlier versions of this paper have benefited from being read to the Social History Seminar at Birmingham University and to the Society for the Study of Labour History Conference at Sussex University in Autumn 1975. In addition I should like to thank Dorothy and Edward Thompson for their advice and encouragement.

NOTES

1. Brian Harrison, 'Religion and Recreation in Nineteenth-Century England', *Past and Present,* no. 38 (Dec. 1967); J. A. R. Pimlott, *Recreations* (London, 1968); R. W. Malcolmson, *Popular Recreations in English Society 1700–1850* (Cambridge, 1973); J. H. Plumb, *The Commercialisation of Leisure in Eighteenth-Century*

England (University of Reading, 1975); Conference Report, 'The Working Class and Leisure', *Bulletin of the Society for the Study of Labour History*, 32 (1976).

2. Except by Keith Thomas, 'Work and Leisure in Pre-Industrial Society', *Past and Present,* no. 29 (Dec. 1964); cf. Conference Report, 'Work and Leisure in Industrial Society', ibid., no. 30 (Apr. 1965).

3. Christopher Hill, *Society and Puritanism in Pre-Revolutionary England* (London, 1969 edn.), pp. 121 – 3, 142 – 9.

4. D. C. Coleman, 'Labour in the English Economy of the Seventeenth Century', in E. M. Carus-Wilson (ed.), *Essays in Economic History* (London, 1962), ii, pp. 300 – 4; T. S. Ashton and Joseph Sykes, *The Coal Industry of the Eighteenth Century* (Manchester, 1929); pp. 168 – 70; T. S. Ashton, *An Economic History of England: The Eighteenth Century* (London, 1955), pp. 201 – 35.

5. Neil McKendrick, 'Josiah Wedgwood and Factory Discipline', *Hist. Jl.*, ·iv (1961); Sidney Pollard, 'Factory Discipline in the Industrial Revolution', *Econ. Hist. Rev.*, 2nd ser., xvi (1963 – 4); id., *The Genesis of Modern Management* (London, 1965), pp. 160 – 208.

6. E. P. Thompson, 'Time, Work-Discipline, and Industrial Capitalism', *Past and Present,* no. 38 (Dec. 1967), esp. pp. 72 – 6 for Saint Monday.

7. W. R. Lambert, 'Drink and Work-discipline in Industrial South Wales, c. 1800 – 1870', *Welsh Hist. Rev.*, vii (1975).

8. *Birmingham and its Regional Setting, A Scientific Survey* (British Association, Birmingham, 1950; Wakefield, 1970 edn.), pp. 144 – 58; Victoria County History (hereafter V.C.H.), *A History of the County of Warwick,* vii, W. B. Stephens (ed.), *The City of Birmingham,* (London, 1964), pp. 81 – 101; on work-rhythms see Thompson, op. cit., pp. 60 – 1, 70 – 2.

9. W.H.B. Court, *The Rise of the Midland Industries, 1600 – 1838* (Oxford, 1938), p. 42; V.C.H., op. cit., p. 248; William Hutton, *An History of Birmingham* (Birmingham, 1781), p. 5; M. A. Bienefeld, *Working Hours in British Industry. An Economic History* (London, 1972), p. 18.

10. V.C.H., op. cit., pp. 253, 81 – 2. See also, S. Timmins, *The Resources, Products and Industrial History of Birmingham and the Midland Hardware District* (London, 1866), pp. 241 – 3; John Lord, *Capital and Steam-power, 1750 – 1800,* 2nd edn. (London, 1966), pp. 94 – 5; Court, op. cit., pp. 34, 241, 251.

11. J. A. Langford, *A Century of Birmingham Life,* 2 vols. (Birmingham, 1868), i, pp. xxxii, 282.

12. *Birmingham Journal* (hereafter B.J.), 26 Sept. 1855, 'Hints for a History of Birmingham'. The writer evidently drew on tradition: cf. Hutton, *An History of Birmingham* (Birmingham, 1795 edn.), pp. 90 – 1: 'I could not avoid remarking, that . . . the people of Birmingham . . . did not suffer others to sleep in their beds; for I was each morning, by three o'clock, saluted with a circle of hammers'. The diary of a partner in a buckle-making business several times recorded in 1787 that men arrived at work drunk, or left in the afternoon 'to spend the rest of the day drinking': R. A. Church, *Kenricks in Hardware. A Family Business 1791 – 1966* (Newton Abbot, 1969), p. 24.

13. George Davis, *Saint Monday; or, Scenes from Low-Life* (Birmingham, 1790), pp. 7 – 8.

14. *The Songs of Joseph Mather* (Sheffield, 1862), pp. 63 – 4, 88 – 9. Cf. M.

Dorothy George, *London Life in the Eighteenth Century* (Harmondsworth, 1966 edn.), p. 383.

15. Davis, op. cit., p. 7; cf. A. Temple Patterson, *Radical Leicester* (Leicester, 1954), pp. 42, 48 – 9.

16. *Minutes of evidence taken before the Committee of the Whole House . . . to consider of the several petitions . . . against the orders in Council,* P[arliamentary] P[apers], 1812 (210), iii, pp. 6, 35 – 6, 56. For wages see Ashton, *An Economic History of England,* p. 232.

17. *Minutes of evidence . . .,* pp. 35, 56 – 7. In 1792 John Byng visited Henry Clay's papier mâché manufactory on Tuesday, 3rd July, 'but the workmen were absent': *The Torrington Diaries,* ed. C. B. Andrews, 4 vols. (London, 1934 – 8), iii, p. 149, and cf. i, p. 49, Wednesday, 4 July 1781; *C[hildren's] E[mployment] C[ommission] (Trade and Manufactures), Appendix to the Second Report of the Commissioners,* pt. I, *Reports and Evidence from Sub-Commissioners,* P.P., 1843 [432], xv, p. f136; London, *Morning Chronicle,* 7 Oct. 1850; Timmins, op. cit., p. 479.

18. *Minutes of evidence . . .,* p. 35. Cf. Hutton, *An History of Birmingham* (1781 edn.), p. 69; 'if a man can support his family with three days labour, he will not work six'; and Pollard, 'Factory Discipline', p. 254.

19. *Minutes of evidence . . .,* pp. 28, 35; and see below, note 87.

20. *Local Reports on the Sanitary Condition of the Labouring Population of England,* P.P., 1842, H.L., xxvii, p. 216.

21. Davis, *Saint Monday,* p. 19; *'dead-horse'*: work left over from Saturday, to be finished before the new 'piece' could be begun; *'FULLER'S two-to-one'* was asterisked by Davis as 'a pawnbroker's shop'. Cf. Birmingham Ref. Lib., 256712, 'Ballads . . . printed in Birmingham c. 1820', p. 74: 'Fuddling Day, or Saint Monday'; this has been reprinted (from a Norwich source) in Roy Palmer, *A Touch on the Times* (Harmondsworth, 1974), p. 144.

22. *Aris's Birmingham Gazette* (hereafter *A.B.G.*), 8 Apr. 1822.

23. Davis, op. cit., pp. iv, 8 – 11; *Morning Chronicle,* 3 Mar. 1851. For Monday recreations in Spitalfields, see E. P. Thompson, *The Making of the English Working Class* (Harmondsworth, 1968), p. 157, and George, *London Life,* pp. 191 – 2, 200.

24. Hutton, *An History of Birmingham* (1975 edn.), p. 94.

25. E. Fitzmaurice, *Life of William, Earl of Shelburne,* 3 vols. (London, 1875 – 6), i, p. 404. This has also been quoted by Pollard, 'Factory Discipline', p. 255.

26. Lord, *Capital and Steam-power,* p. 196; H. W. Dickinson and Rhys Jenkins, *James Watt and the Steam Engine* (Oxford, 1927), pp. 267, 280 – 1; Erich Roll, *An Early Experiment in Industrial Organisation, being a History of the firm Boulton and Watt, 1775 – 1805* (London, 1930), pp. 61, 191.

27. Pollard, 'Factory Discipline', p. 264.

28. Church, *Kenricks in Hardware,* pp. 23 – 4.

29. Birmingham Ref. Lib., 'The Diary of Julius Hardy, Button-maker of Birmingham (1788 – 1793)', transcribed and annotated by A. M. Banks (1973): entry for 22 May 1789. That Hardy was not averse to using the Magistracy to correct other faults in his men is demonstrated by the diary entries for 16 May 1789 and 19 July 1790.

30. For example, *B. J.,* 30 July 1836; Birmingham, *The Philanthropist,* 1 Sept. 1836. Court cases against men (*vis-à-vis* apprentices) were conspicuous in their isolation, as that against a gun stocker who was charged with 'absenting himself from

the service of his master without leave', and was punished by a month's hard labour and a Magisterial homily about idleness: *A.B.G.,* 9 Dec. 1811. This is prima facie rather puzzling, especially in view of the use made of the 1823 Master and Servant Act in the Potteries in the 1850s: Thompson, 'Time, Work-Discipline, and Industrial Capitalism', p. 75, note 67; cf. another isolated example, from 1862, quoted by J. E. Williams, *The Derbyshire Miners* (London, 1962), p. 60. The explanation appears to lie partly in the wide prevalence of Birmingham Monday observance, partly in the earlier decline of annual hiring in the 'hardware village', and perhaps mainly in the indispensability of the skilled man. See, *Minutes of evidence . . .*, pp. 58, 108, and below, pp. 91 – 2. On the Master and Servant Act, see Daphne Simon, 'Master and Servant', in J. Saville (ed.), *Democracy and the Labour Movement* (London, 1954). Simon appears to have been misled by the category, 'Servants, Apprentices, or Masters, Offences relating to', in the *Judicial Statistics.* She states (p. 195) that Birmingham had 2,351 Master and Servant prosecutions in the years 1868 – 75, but according to the Birmingham Clerk to the Justices only *four* cases were heard in the town in 1868 – 75: *Labour Laws Commission, First Report of the Commissioners appointed to inquire into the working of the Master and Servant Act, 1867,* P.P., 1874 (C. 1094), xxiv, pp. 103 – 5.

31. *B.J.,* 15 Feb. 1840, 22 Dec. 1838.

32. *C.E.C., 1862, Third Report of the Commissioners,* P.P., 1864 [3414 – 1], xxii, p. 57.

33. The complex causes of the nineteenth century 'reformation of manners' among the common people lie beyond the scope of this paper; for a useful preliminary inquiry, see M. J. Quinlan, *Victorian Prelude: A History of English Manners 1700 – 1830* (New York, 1941, repr. London, 1965).

34. P. H. J. H. Gosden, *The Friendly Societies in England 1815 – 75* (Manchester, 1961), pp. 75 – 6. For excursion trains, see *B.J.,* 28 Mar. – 17 Oct. 1846; commercially organized trips had a similar price range, and also left mainly on Mondays.

35. *B.J.,* 15 Feb. and 7 Mar. 1840, 8 May 1841.

36. *Morning Chronicle,* 20 Jan. 1851.

37. Ibid., 3 Mar. 1851; *B.J.,* 19 Apr. 1845.

38. Ibid., 26 Nov. 1853.

39. Ibid., 26 July 1851, 24 Dec. 1853.

40. Ibid., 18 Sept. 1852.

41. Davis, *Saint Monday,* pp. 8 – 9.

42. For example, *B.J.,* 28 June and 5 July 1845, 20 July 1849.

43. Mark Hovell, *The Chartist Movement* (Manchester, 1918), p. 107; *B.J.,* 18 May 1839.

44. *B.J.,* 24 Jan. 1846.

45. *C.E.C., Second Report,* 1843, pp. f131, f133, f136, f145, f169. For 1864 see below, *passim.*

46. Birmingham Philosophical Institution, *The Report presented by the Committee of Managers . . . together with . . . a Statement of the Steam Power employed in Birmingham from 1780 to 1835* (Birmingham, 1836); *Birmingham Mercury,* 16 May 1891: Birmingham Ref. Lib., 286526, newspaper cuttings; Robert Rawlinson, *Report to the General Board of Health on . . . the Sanitary Condition . . . of . . . Birmingham* (London, 1849), p. 43; J. R. Immer, 'The development of

production methods in Birmingham, 1760 – 1851' (Univ. of Oxford D. Phil. thesis, 1954), p. 91. For Manchester see A. E. Musson and Eric Robinson, *Science and Technology in the Industrial Revolution* (Manchester, 1969), pp. 406, 423, 426. The contrast in 1838 is much less striking; Manchester and Salford used $9,924\frac{1}{2}$ h.p. by then: J. H. Clapham, *An Economic History of Modern Britain,* 3 vols. (Cambridge, 1926 – 38), i. pp. 442 – 3.

47. *C.E.C., 1862, Third Report,* p. 106.

48. Ibid., p. 112.

49. *Third Report from the Select Committee appointed to inquire into the State of Agriculture,* P.P., 1836 [465], viii, pt. ii, QQ. 16657 – 60. I am grateful to Mr Clive Behagg for drawing my attention to this reference.

50. *C. E. C., Second Report,* 1843, p. f155.

51. London, *The Leisure Hour,* no. 62, 3 Mar. 1853.

52. *C.E.C., 1862, Third Report,* pp. 122, 132; for new locations of industry, see V.C.H., *The City of Birmingham,* pp. 132 – 3. G. C. Allen, *The Industrial Development of Birmingham and the Black Country 1860 – 1927* (London, 1929), p. 113, expounds the view that, by 1860, 'there had been no "industrial revolution" in Birmingham and district. Its great economic development was marked by a vast increase in the number of producing units rather than by a growth in the size of the existing few, and the factory remained unrepresentative of the majority of the concerns producing finished goods'. This has been criticized—with some justice—by Immer, 'The development of production methods', pp. 294 – 6, who asserts that in 1851 Birmingham 'was a city of large industries'. It is partly a question of definitions, but attention must be drawn to the influence—far out of proportion to their numbers—which large manufacturing units could exert.

53. Clapham, *An Economic History of Modern Britain,* ii, pp. 448 – 50; Brian Harrison, *Drink and the Victorians* (London, 1971), p. 305; Bienefeld, *Working Hours in British Industry,* p. 94.

54. J. S. Hodgson, 'The movements for shorter hours, 1840 – 75' (Univ. of Oxford D. Phil. thesis, 1940), pp. 213 – 5; G.I.H. Lloyd, *The Cutlery Trades* (London, 1913), p. 181: Sidney Pollard, *A History of Labour in Sheffield* (Liverpool, 1959), pp. 61 – 2; T. C. Barker and J. R. Harris, *A Merseyside Town in the Industrial Revolution, St Helens 1750 – 1900* (Liverpool, 1954), pp. 417, 461; R. A. Church, *Economic and Social Change in a Midland Town, Victorian Nottingham 1815 – 1900* (London, 1966), p. 375; J. D. Marshall, *Furness and the Industrial Revolution* (Barrow-in-Furness, 1958), pp. 247, 315 – 6, 401.

55. *B.J.,* 24 May 1851.

56. Ibid., 11 June 1853.

57. Ibid., 24 May 1851.

58. Ibid., 15 Jan. 1853; see ibid., 13 Nov. and 25 Dec. 1852, 30 Apr. and 11 June 1853 for similar opinions.

59. Ibid., 11 June 1853. G. S. Bull, George Dawson, J. C. Miller (St Martins), G. M. Yorke (St Philips) were present *inter alia* at the Town Hall meetings. Miller voiced the mainstream of clerical opinion, that the Saturday afternoon leisure should be supported because from it 'a better spirit would arise in the heart, and a greater desire be evinced righteously to observe the Holy Sabbath': *B.J.,* 11 June 1853. For Miller's evangelism, see David E. H. Mole, 'John Cale Miller: a Victorian Rector of

Birmingham', *Jl. Eccles. Hist.*, xvii (1965). For the forceful and independent George Dawson, see E. P. Hennock, *Fit and Proper Persons. Ideal and Reality in Nineteenth-Century Urban Government* (London, 1973), pp. 63–77.

60. *B.J.*, 13 Nov., 11 and 25 Dec. 1852, 14 May and 11 June 1853; *A.B.G.*, 2 May 1853.

61. *B.J.*, 30 Apr. 1853; Richard Tangye, *The Rise of a Great Industry* (London, 1905 edn.), pp. 48–9; *C.E.C., 1862, Third Report*, p. 106.

62. *B.J.*, 30 Apr., 14 and 21 May, 4 June 1853, for wages' and hours' claims by shoemakers and various building trades. For the national context, see Bienefeld, *Working Hours*, pp. 84–6, 190.

63. Ibid., pp. 48, 78, 51; and the letter from W. A. Adams, Midland Works, Saltley, complaining of the advantage taken by Wright (the leading manufacturer of rolling-stock), in *B.J.*, 25 June 1853.

64. *B.J.*, 11 Mar. 1853. For Allday and Cutler, see Hennock, op. cit., p. 32. The deputation was apparently successful with regard to the button trade where a 10.00 p.m. Saturday finish gave way to an 'early' 5.00 p.m.: *C.E.C., 1862, Third Report*, p. 98.

65. Ibid., p. 106.

66. Ibid., p. 95.

67. Ibid., p. 80 (May and Co.—engineering), p. 132 (Metropolitan Railway Carriage and Waggon Co., Saltley—formerly Messrs Wright), p. 108 (Edelston and Williams—wire-drawing and pin-making).

68. Ibid., p. 110 (Nettlefold and Chamberlain—screws), pp. 122–4 (Elkingtons).

69. Ibid., pp. 84–5 (Beckett—tinplate), p. 91 (Cope—buttons), p. 126 (Schlesinger and Co.—glass-and emery-paper), p. 128 (Lander—spectacles).

70. However (in another context) Beckett mentioned the state of housing as 'a great drawback to any general improvement of the people'; also he had recently moved his works into 'spacious and ventilated buildings'. Ibid., pp. 84–5.

71. *C.E.C., 1862, First Report of the Commissioners*, P.P., 1863 [3170], xviii, p. 267 (I owe this reference to Church, *Economic and Social Change in a Midland Town*, p. 375). Other references to the Nottingham half-holiday are to be found on pp. 209, 217, 223, 237, 268–9, 282 of *C.E.C., 1862, First Report*.

72. *C.E.C., 1862, Third Report*, p. 180; *C.E.C., 1862, Fourth Report of the Commissioners*, P.P., 1865 [3584], xx, p. 59; *C.E.C., 1862, Fifth Report of the Commissioners*, P.P., 1866 [3678], xxiv, pp. 169, 173.

73. *C.E.C., 1862, First Report*, p. xxviii; *C.E.C., 1862, Fourth Report*, p. 124.

74. *C.E.C., 1862, Third Report*, pp. 57, 126.

75. Ibid., p. 123.

76. Ibid., pp. 101–2; *Birmingham Morning News*, 26 June 1871; Paul de Rousiers, *The Labour Question in Britain* (Paris, 1895; London, 1896 edn.), p. 6; *Report of the Commissioners appointed to inquire into the working of the Factory and Workshop Acts*, P.P, 1876 (C. 1443–1), xxx, pt. ii, Q. 7141; *C.E.C., 1862, Second Report of the Commissioners*, P.P., 1864 [3414], xxii, pp. 217, 228; *C.E.C., 1862, Fourth Report*, p. 127; *C.E.C., 1862, Fifth Report*, pp. 118, 196–7; Charles Booth, *Life and Labour of the People in London*, 17 vols. (London, 1902–3), 1st ser., iv, p. 202 (I am grateful to Dr Hugh McLeod for this last reference).

77. *C.E.C., 1862, Third Report*, pp. 79, 115; Pollard, *Labour in Sheffield*, p. 211;

Lambert, 'Drink and work-discipline', p. 306; *Report . . . into . . . Factory and Workshop Acts,* QQ.6064, 6851, 6911; E. Hopkins, 'Small Town Aristocrats of Labour and Their Standard of Living, 1840–1914', *Econ. Hist. Rev.,* 2nd ser., xxviii (1975), p. 233; *C.E.C., 1862, First Report,* p. xxvii; *C.E.C., 1862, Fifth Report,* p. 131; Rhodri Walters, 'Labour Productivity in the South Wales Steam-Coal Industry, 1870–1914', *Econ. Hist. Rev.,* 2nd ser., xxviii (1975), pp. 293–4; Williams, *Derbyshire Miners,* pp. 60, 274, 532–3, 791, 846, 848.

78. Thompson, 'Time, Work-Discipline and Industrial Capitalism', p. 74, note 65.

79. *Morning Chronicle,* 6 Jan. 1851; cf. *C.E.C., 1862, Third Report,* pp. 66, 68. Brass casting was so unhealthy that Saint Monday was almost a physical necessity. An employer noted: 'in our old casting shops we reckoned four days in the week as much as the men could stand'.

80. *Morning Chronicle,* 17 Feb. 1851.

81. Rousiers, op. cit., p. 6.

82. *C.E.C., 1862, Third Report,* p. 76.

83. Ibid., p. 126.

84. Ibid., pp. 98–9. The 'factories' of the button trade were not paced by the steam-engine but (as in gun work) consisted largely of centralized workshops.

85. Quoted by Ivy Pinchbeck, *Women Workers in the Industrial Revolution 1750–1850* (London, 1930), p. 280. Cf. *C.E.C., Second Report,* 1843, p. f133.

86. *C.E.C., 1862, Third Report,* pp. 64–5.

87. *C.E.C., Second Report,* 1843, p. f169.

88. *C.E.C., 1862, Third Report,* p. 101.

89. Ibid., p. 131, 115; *Birmingham Morning News,* 26 June 1871.

90. *C.E.C., 1862, Third Report,* p. 79.

91. *Birmingham Gazette and Express,* 19 Sept. 1907: Birmingham Ref. Lib., 217750, newspaper cuttings.

92. Rousiers, op. cit., p. 6.

93. See above, notes 57 and 58. Also cf. *B.J.,* 18 June 1853, letter from the pseudonymous 'L.W.A.' replying to a suggestion by 'A Workman' that the Saturday half-holiday should be a real extension of leisure, and not involve re-organization of hours in lieu: 'As one of the working class . . . I have ever been an ardent and strong advocate of the half-day . . . but . . . neither employers or employed ought to suffer in any pecuniary matter by its adoption. If masters are willing to concede this half-day . . . thanks should be given . . . we ought not to expect them to pay for that for which they will never get any return'.

94. Thompson, 'Time, Work-Discipline and Industrial Capitalism', pp. 83, 95.

95. Birmingham Ref. Lib., 'The Diary of Julius Hardy', 12 and 25 Jan., 8 and 22 Feb. 1790. On Baxter's influence, see Thompson, *The Making of the English Working Class,* p. 393.

96. Birmingham Ref. Lib., 'The Diary of Julius Hardy', 12, 19, 25 Jan., 1, 8, 15, 22 Feb., 1, 8, 15 Mar. 1790.

97. Michael Frost, 'Working Class Education in Birmingham, 1781–1851' (Univ. of Birmingham M.A. thesis, in progress). Cf. Thompson, 'Time, Work-Discipline and Industrial Capitalism', pp. 84–5, and also M. W. Flinn, 'Social Theory and the Industrial Revolution', in Tom Burns and S. B. Saul (eds.), *Social Theory and Economic Change* (London, 1967), pp. 9–34.

98. *C.E.C., Second Report,* 1843, pp. f129 – 30, f145, f168 – 9.

99. Ibid., p. f131, also pp. f126, f129 – 30, f132, f134, f146, f148, f168; cf. p. f145.

100. Asa Briggs, 'Social Structure and Politics in Birmingham and Lyons, 1825 – 1848', *British Jl. of Sociology,* i (1950); id., *Victorian Cities* (Harmondsworth, 1968), pp. 168 – 9; T. R. Tholfsen, 'The Artisan and the Culture of Early Victorian Birmingham', *Univ. of Birmingham Hist. Jl.,* iv (1953). Also see Hennock, *Fit and Proper Persons,* pp. 99 – 101.

101. It appears that such politically articulate opposition as there was to the exploitation associated with steam power disappeared with Chartism; cf. 'The Steam King' by Edward P. Mead of Birmingham which was published in the *Northern Star,* 11 Feb. 1843 (quoted by F. Engels, *The Condition of the Working Class in England* [London, 1969 edn.], pp. 213 – 4):

There is a King, and a ruthless King,
Not a King of the poet's dream;
But a tyrant fell, white slaves know well,
And that ruthless King is Steam.

.   .   .   .

Then down with the King, the Moloch King,
Ye working millions all;
O chain his hand, or our native land
Is destin'd by him to fall.

102. William Hawkes Smith, *Birmingham and its Vicinity as a Manufacturing and Commercial District* (Birmingham, 1836), pt. iii, p. 9. Cf. Jennifer Tann, *The Development of the Factory* (London, 1970), p. 27; Church, *Economic and Social Change in a Midland Town,* p. 85; John Prest, *The Industrial Revolution in Coventry* (Oxford, 1960), pp. 94 – 6, 101; Duncan Bythell, *The Handloom Weavers* (Cambridge, 1969), pp. 38 – 9, 43 – 4, 75, 116 – 7, 131 – 2, 259.

103. G. J. Holyoake, *Sixty Years of an Agitator's Life,* 2 vols. (London, 1892), i, pp. 11, 23.

104. *C.E.C., 1862, Third Report,* p. 129.

105. E. W. Gilboy, 'Demand as a Factor in the Industrial Revolution', in R. M. Hartwell (ed.), *The Causes of the Industrial Revolution in England* (London, 1967), pp. 121 – 38; D. E. C. Eversley, 'The Home Market and Economic Growth 1750 – 1780', in E. L. Jones and G. E. Mingay (eds.), *Land, Labour and Population in the Industrial Revolution* (London, 1967), pp. 206 – 59; Neil McKendrick, 'Home Demand and Economic Growth: A New View of the Role of Women and Children in the Industrial Revolution', in N. McKendrick (ed.), *Historical Perspectives. Studies in English Thought and Society in honour of J. H. Plumb* (London, 1974), pp. 152 – 210, esp. pp. 183 ff. Cf. V.C.H., *City of Birmingham,* pp. 91 – 3, 101 – 4.

106. S. D. Chapman and J. N. Bartlett, 'The contribution of Building Clubs and Freehold Land Society [sic] to Working-Class Housing in Birmingham', in S.D. Chapman (ed.), *The History of Working-Class Housing* (Newton Abbot, 1971), pp. 235 – 8.

107. *C.E.C., 1862, Third Report,* p. 132.

108. Timmins, *The Resources, Products and Industrial History of Birmingham and the Midland Hardware District,* pp. 452 – 62.

109. *Birmingham Morning News,* 3 July and 26 June 1871.

110. Ibid., 5 June 1871.

111. *Morning Chronicle,* 30 Dec. 1850; Timmins, op. cit., p. 88; Court, *Rise of Midland Industries,* pp. 198 – 211.

112. *Morning Chronicle,* 4 Nov. 1850; *C.E.C., 1862, Third Report,* pp. 101 – 2.

113. Alan Fox, 'Industrial Relations in Nineteenth-Century Birmingham', *Oxford Economic Papers,* new ser., vii (1955), pp. 63 and *passim.*

114. Cf. *Morning Chronicle,* 7 Oct. 1850; *Birmingham Morning News,* 17 July 1871.

115. Cf. 'An Old Potter' cited in Thompson, 'Time, Work-Discipline and Industrial Capitalism', p. 75, and W. Hamish Fraser, *Trade Unions and Society. The Struggle for Acceptance 1850 – 1880* (London, 1974), pp. 208 – 25, esp. pp. 214 – 6.

116. [T. Wright], *Some Habits and Customs of the Working Classes by a Journeyman Engineer* (London, 1867), pp. 108 – 30.

117. *Report . . . into . . . Factory and Workshop Acts,* QQ. 12, 144 – 6, also 12,081.

118. *B.J.,* 25 June 1853. Also see *Report from the Select Committee on Public Houses,* P.P., 1854 [367], xiv, Q. 261: 'Monday was the day on which working men went to . . . [Hampton Court] Palace', and Cf. QQ. 815 – 6, 3,117.

119. *A.B.G.,* 4 Apr. 1863.

120. *Morning Chronicle,* 14 Oct. 1850.

121. *B.J.,* 28 Mar. 1846. Temperance opinion, *per se,* must have helped to erode Saint Monday by striking at the main traditional custom of observance; a process apparently exemplified in the observation of 'an intelligent journeyman' in the cabinet brassfoundry trade that: 'if one of the workmen absents himself from work for drunkenness, he returns to the manufactory amidst the ridicule and hootings of his comrades' (*Morning Chronicle,* 6 Jan. 1851). However, this quotation deserves to be viewed sceptically (*pace* Harrison, *Drink and the Victorians,* p. 305) as it is by no means unlikely that the reporters went to the establishment of J. Bourn—the most prominent Cabinet Brassfounder in Birmingham—as an earlier investigator had done, who had been told: 'Has always been very careful in preventing drunkenness and encouraging regularity of conduct and work. As the workpeople know his feelings on these subjects, they conform to his wishes' (*C.E.C., Second Report,* 1843, p. f144). For Bourn as Birmingham's High Baïliff encouraging Temperance; see *B.J.,* 29 Mar. 1845. For brasscasting, see above, notes 79 and 86.

122. On 'progress', see J. F. C. Harrison, *Learning and Living 1790 – 1960* (London, 1961), pp. 39 – 40, 75; Fraser, *Trade Unions and Society, pp. 55 ff.*

123. *B.J.,* 29 Oct. 1853.

124. *Report . . . into . . . Factory and Workshop Acts,* P.P., 1876 (C. 1443), xxix, p. 59.

125. G. D. H. Cole and A. W. Filson, *British Working Class Movements. Select Documents 1789 – 1875* (London, 1967), pp. 597 – 9; Hodgson, 'Movements for shorter hours', pp. 395 – 6; Bienefeld, *Working Hours in British Industry,* pp. 106 – 8; E. Allen, J. E. Clarke, N. McCord and D. J. Rowe, *The North-East Engineers' Strikes of 1871* (Newcastle upon Tyne, 1971).

126. Tangye, *Rise of a Great Industry,* pp. 110 – 2.

127. See *Birmingham Daily Post,* 5 Aug. – 16 Dec. 1871, and, for very sympathetic coverage, national as well as local, George Dawson's *Birmingham Morning News,* 5

Aug. – 18 Nov. 1871. Also the retrospective survey in *Board of Trade, Report on Trades (Hours of Work),* P.P., 1890 (375), lxviii, pp. 24, 29 – 30, 32 – 4, 43.

128. Ibid., pp. 7, 46 – 7.

129. *Birmingham Daily Post,* 17 Feb. 1873; cf. [Wright], *Some Habits and Customs of Working Classes,* pp. 184 – 203.

130. D. D. Molyneux, 'The development of physical recreation in the Birmingham district, 1871 – 92' (Univ. of Birmingham M.A. thesis, 1957), pp. 26 – 30, 39 – 43. Cf. James Walvin, *The People's Game* (London, 1975), pp. 52 ff.

131. The figures have been rounded-off to the nearest fifty, and are compiled from the *Annual Reports* of the Birmingham Botanical and Horticultural Society.

132. *Report . . . into . . . Factory and Workshop Acts,* P.P., 1876 [C. 1443], xxix, pp. xii-xiii.

133. *C.E.C., 1862, Third Report,* pp. 52 – 3; cf. Allen, *Industrial Development of Birmingham and the Black Country,* pp. 176 – 7, 206 – 8, on the numbers of working children after 1870.

134. *Birmingham Morning News,* 14 Aug. 1871, and cf. 16 Aug. 1871.

135. *Report . . . into . . . Factory and Workshop Acts,* P.P., 1876 [C. 1443 – 1], xxx, pt. ii, Q. 5152; cf. Hodgson, 'Movements for shorter hours', pp. 45, 349 – 50.

136. Rousiers, *The Labour Question in Britain,* p. 6. For recalcitrance of workers who had been disciplined out of 'playing away' but not out of unpunctuality, see *C.E.C., 1862, Third Report,* pp. 110, 116, 126, 130; 'Rules for workmen in the employment of J. Wright and Sons, Saltley Works', c. 1880, typescript in Birmingham Ref. Lib. In 1907 an advocate for the brass trade employers tried to establish that 'short time' was made on Mondays for football: [Board of Trade], *Brass Trades Arbitration, 1907* (n.p., 1907), pp. 43, 49 – 52. Since the tail-end of the custom was intertwined with drink, the licensing restrictions of the First World War probably reduced any survivals even further: see Arthur Marwick, *The Deluge* (Harmondsworth, 1967), pp. 68 – 9, 71. The full Saturday holiday—or the five day week—was achieved generally only in the 1930s: see *The Times,* 3 Dec. 1936.

137. *A.B.G.,* 15 June 1853: speech of Henry Wright, rolling-stock manufacturer.

6

Mastered for Life:
Servant and Wife
in Victorian and Edwardian England*

LEONORE DAVIDOFF

During the first half of the nineteenth century, an increasing proportion of
the working population was employed as factory labour. Factories and
workshops were growing larger. At the same time the nature of farm labour
changed as the yearly hiring was gradually replaced by a more casual monthly
contract and young, unmarried farm servants no longer lived in their
employer's household. Integral to this fundamental change to a more limited
contract, was the long and sometimes savage conflict over the abolishing of
the Law of Master and Servant and its replacement by the Employer and
Workman Act of 1875.[1]

At about the same time, there began a very gradual shift in the conception
of the married woman's relationship to society (a process that is by no means
complete even now); a move to make marriage a contract, voidable like other
contracts involving two legal personalities.[2] This basic change, too, was
reflected in some of the legislation that made inroads into the ancient
common law concept of couveture: 'the husband and wife are one and the
husband is that one,' *Blackstone*.

Despite all the political and social ferment these changes generated, the
impassioned debates in Parliament and in the press, there were two groups
who, almost unnoticed, were hardly touched by the new order. Domestic
servants and working-class married women continued, up to the First World
War and beyond, in their pre-industrial, almost Biblical, subordination to
their masters and husbands. Regulation by Factory and Workshops Acts,
Trades Boards or investigations into sweated labour passed them by. Trade
Union organization proved to be unworkable for servants, unthinkable for

* From *Journal of Social History*, 7(4) (1974), 406–28. Reprinted by permission of the
author and the editors of *Journal of Social History*.

wives. Insurance schemes left them aside. Enfranchisement was not for them for they had neither domicile nor property of their own. Their legal definition and, in significant ways, their real situation was closer to the age-old common law doctrine of *potestas*: children, wives and servants are under the protection and wing of the Master.[3] He is the intermediary to the outside world; he embodies the governing principle within the household. It is no accident that such a relationship is called paternalistic, the basic elements of which are given in Max Weber's classical description of what social and political theorists have called patriarchal domination.

Under patriarchal domination the legitimacy of the master's orders is guaranteed by his personal subjection and only the fact and the limits of his power of control are derived from the 'norms' yet these norms are not enacted but sanctified by tradition. The fact that this concrete master is indeed their ruler is always uppermost in the minds of his subjects. The master wields his power without restraints, at his own discretion and above all, unencumbered by rules insofar as it is not limited by tradition or competing powers.[4]

This term can apply to general expectations for society as a whole, for certain groups within a society or for certain relationships only within a society built on quite other norms, e.g., our attitude towards children in contemporary society. *What* (the franchise, labour relations, etc.) is being studied will determine which one of these is stressed. Here I am concerned primarily with the interpersonal relations between master and servant, husband and wife. *By definition* the subordinate group within each pair had few other links to the wider society.

I

In this paper I would like to examine this relationship in detail, looking at both the conventional expectations embodied in law and expounded by dominant groups as well as the reactions to it by those in subordinate positions. What happened to this doctrine under pressure from an increasingly cash- and market-oriented economy, where home and work place had become physically separated?[5] What were the forces which led to its decline in service, and its attenuated survival in marriage?

In such a speculative essay, precise documentation is not possible, for necessarily the discussion covers a very long time-span. Much of the argument stems from sociological concern with the nature of authority, stratification, deference and similar abstract concepts. Nevertheless, it is important to make every effort to ground such abstractions in historical time and place. It is at this point that the problems of documenting personal interaction can lead to treacherously simple generalization. Domestic service and working-class marriage are exceptionally elusive areas of study as so much of their activity took place in private homes. Surviving written evidence is overwhelmingly from the superordinates' side and from the more articulate and powerful individuals within even that stratum.[6]

Bearing these problems in mind, the first question that must be asked is how the relationship operated on a day-to-day basis.[7] Secondly, there is the extensiveness of control through all areas of life for the subordinate. The existence of alternative loci of independence, including the *right* to be independent in any sphere, becomes crucial. For example, the assertion that, because even living-in servants had to sell their labour in the market place, if only once a year, their relationship to their master was not patriarchal,[8] neglects this dimension. The cash reward may be seen as an extension of bed and board[9] regarded by the servant as a form of enforced savings for young maids and youths before marriage. The existence of cash payment *in itself* does not mean escape from paternalistic control; it only creates possibilities for an alternative way of life. This point is supported by looking at the way the wife's earnings have continued to be seen as part of the family income. The effort to maintain the paternalistic relationship within marriage by denying an *individual* wage to the wife is a thread which runs through debates on family income from the Poor Law of 1834 (which resulted in some unions paying for children to be fostered by strangers rather than pay the mother direct out relief), to the present controversy over the payment of Family Allowance directly to the mother or in the form of tax rebates to the father.[10]

Finally, and perhaps most important of all, is the extent of control over the life-span of the subordinate. Again this can be seen as a matter of degree rather than as a polar opposition, a continuum of control. At one end the father has complete control over the child until one day, no matter what the struggle for independence involves, they both know that the subordinate will break free, if only through the death of the parent.[11] The servant is attached to the master for an unspecified time; often the master wished to believe that the attachment was permanent when in fact many people seem to have served only when they were young and single, causing a high turnover. The wife, on the other hand, knew it was forever. John Stuart Mill recognized the significance of this point when he said:

surely if a woman is denied any lot in life but that of being the personal body-servant of a despot, and is dependent for everything upon the chance of finding one who may be disposed to make a favourite of her instead of merely a drudge, it is a very cruel aggravation of her fate that she would be allowed to try this chance only once . . . since her all in life depends upon obtaining a good master she should be allowed to change again and again until she finds one.[12]

By looking at the context in which such relationships took place, asking basic ·sociological questions about the size and structure of the groups involved,[13] it should be possible to avoid some of the pitfalls of an extreme reductionist psychology.[14] What was the physical setting, how much of the individual's time was spent in this setting through the day, the week, the year? Were there alternative groups for subordinates to identify with and was this identification and interaction 'legitimate' within the system or did it have to be carried out covertly[15] (e.g., was time off given to servants as a right at stated times or did it have to be taken in snatches between tasks)? Could servants see whom they wished when off-duty or were their companions overlooked or even banned by the employer, (the 'no followers' rule)?

The intense privacy of the English middle-class household in individual dwellings often surrounded by gardens, in isolated settings or suburbs separated from working-class districts, made English domestic service exceptionally confining. This was in contrast, for example, to continental cities. There the custom was to have all the maids sleep together on the top floor of blocks of flats. When flats finally began to be built in London towards the end of the century this feature was deliberately omitted for fear of losing personal control over the servant.[16]

As the rest of the society changed, the service relationship, always fraught with potential difficulties, came under increasing pressure. In 1908, Simmel described this transitional stage as a breakdown in the 'objective idea' which occurs at either of the extremes of the service relation.

under the condition of full patriarchal subordination, where the house still has, so to speak, an absolute value which is served by the work of the housewife (though in a higher position) as well as by that of the servant; and then, under the condition of complete differentiation where service and reward are objectively pre-determined, and the personal attachment . . . has become extraneous to the relationship. The contemporary position of the servant who shares his master's house, particularly in the larger cities has lost the first of these two kinds of objectivity without having attained the second.[17]

That this is a transitional stage can only be revealed by hindsight. No unilinear development can be taken for granted. A political and economic regime pledged to permanent exploitative paternalism can seemingly continue the relationship indefinitely.[18]

In this context, the most important fact about our period is that the majority of girls moved from paternal control, in their parents' home, into service and then into their husband's home—thus experiencing a lifetime of personal subordination in private homes. This was in growing contrast to boys and to those girls who began to find other forms of work towards the end of the century.[19]

In the following discussion, I have no wish to strain the analogy between the situation of domestic servants, *both men and women,* and working-class married women. In certain respects, most crucially in the presence of dependent children but also in legitimate expectations for sexual relationships and affection, they differed. In other, sociologically decisive areas they were similar.

II

The image of a working woman in nineteenth-century England is that of the mill girl or possibly the milliner or seamstress. Yet it is well known that servants—in the early part of the century farm and later purely 'domestic' servants—made up by far the largest occupational group of working women, indeed the largest occupational group in the whole economy except for agricultural labourers. In 1881, servants of both sexes represented one person in every 22 of the population. In London the proportion was 1 in 15; in Bath 1 in 9, while in Lancashire it was only 1 in 30. However, the great majority of indoor residential servants was made up of girls and women.

Numerically they grew from 751,541 in 1851 to a peak of 1,386,167 in 1891 and never fell below one million until the late 1930s.[20] They were 34 percent of all women employed in 1891 and still 23 percent in 1930. A high proportion of female domestic servants was young: those under twenty were 39 percent of the total in 1860, 42 percent in 1880 and 31 percent in 1911. In 1881, 1 in 3.3 girls aged 15 to 20 was classified as a domestic servant (Census of Occupations, England and Wales). A minority remained as servants all their lives, some experienced 10 to 15 years of service and then married; some left after a short time. It is impossible to tell the exact proportions in each category.[21]

Whatever proportion remained as 'career' servants, a great number of working-class women must have gone through some experience of service at sometime in their lives, usually including the formative years of adolescence. At an early age, in the first half of the century as young as 9 or 10 years old, servants had left their childhood home where they had been entirely subordinated to the authority of their parents. From this household they were transferred to the household of their master, under his direct authority or that of his deputy, the mistress or upper servant. From there, in turn, the servant passed to her husband's home, where, theoretically at least, she remained under his protection and his rule.

Within this large group there was a very wide range of experience. At one extreme was found the better known form of service in a great house within a graduated hierarchy of servants, which could lead to a measure of autonomy, a high standard of living and a good deal of authority over others. At the other, and numerically more important extreme, was the less visible, less well known 'slavery' in the lower-middle-class suburban or artisan household or lodging house. Fenimore Cooper, on his arrival in Southampton in the 1830s was shocked at the treatment of the girl where he lodged 'worse off than an Asiatic slave'.[22] The same conditions were still observed in 1897 in a lodging house where the little maid 'believes she belongs body and soul to the missus'.[23]

Despite these vast differences, all service positions shared certain characteristics. The master was expected to provide total support: food, housing and a small cash wage.[24] The servant reciprocated by being entirely at the disposal of the master, to obey his personal authority including directions as to the way in which the work was to be performed. In her demeanour she was to exhibit deference to the higher position of the master and his deputies (mistress, guests; even children). The relationship was residential and located in a private home.[25]

The wages for domestic service did vary very widely from household to household (tables of wage rates in household manuals can give a spurious uniformity) and from area to area.[26] Such variation increased the 'pocket money' character of the cash income because it was a private negotiation between two individuals. In fact, female kin could be and were used as domestic servants without pay. Household service and kinship obligations overlapped to the extent that legally the payment of wages had to be explicitly stated in the contract, otherwise it could be assumed that service was being given voluntarily.[27]

At the beginning of the nineteenth century, ruling groups perpetuated an image of society built on a hierarchy of service. As King is to God, Lord is to King, so servant is to master. All had obligations to serve those above them, to show their loyalty and devotion through service.[28] More prosaically a servant might comfort herself that 'even gentlemen have to bow and scrape to the Royal Family'.[29]

Such an ideal of service to a common and visible goal must be based on a society of small units, limited to a well-defined locality. (Even the great estate households with all their staff, both indoor and outdoor, seldom numbered more than 100 persons.) Such an ideal carries most credibility when the majority of other households in the locality are based on the same principles: therefore it can be as applicable to a farm community as to a castle. In such a setting, an 'external and spiritual community of fate' (Weber), there were no alternatives to challenge the system and 'the elision of "is" in power to "ought" to be in power' is much easier to sustain.[30] Thus employers often favoured servants who had come directly from country districts over those who had had some experience of city life.

It was at about this time, however, that the domination of the older élite, whose wealth had been based on land holding, was being challenged in a fundamental way by groups whose claims to power rested on new wealth garnered from trade and industry as well as by radical forces within the lower class. A consequence of this challenge was the growing concern with stricter controls of admission into the social and political élite, including control over social and personal behaviour. Those with incomes which gave them a substantial surplus were able to take part in the elaborate rituals of 'Society' and sport which had become formalized as part of this control.[31]

At the same time, several other factors had combined to increase both the numbers and scale of servant-employing households. Manufacturers and shopkeepers began moving their households away from mill and counting house to set up separate establishments. The creation of new professions and the expansion of old, meant that more households were established in market towns as well as in the rapidly-growing cities, while the wealthier farmers banished work activities, particularly dairy work, from the house and immediately surrounding grounds.

These households were consumption units only. Even those homes where business affairs were carried on under the same roof kept both work activities and accounts separate from household affairs. The goals and activities of such households were dominated by the concern with social placement and social closure necessitating not only a great upsurge in display of material objects but elaborated rituals of etiquette. The surest way of proving social superiority was to surround oneself with 'deference givers', even specialized 'deference occupations'. As J. F. C. Harrison points out: 'the essence of middle-classness was the experience of relating to other classes or orders of society. With one group, domestic servants, the middle classes stood in a very special and intimate relationship: the one fact played an essential part in defining the identity of the other'.[32]

Domestic servants gave the 'prompt complete respectful and easy obedience' due to their superiors apart from, or even in spite of, the moral or temperamental qualities of the individual master. The superior was thus guaranteed at least a minimum of deference even if he was 'alone' in his own home, i.e., with only his servant or servants.[33] Furthermore the bestowing of deference can be elaborated to vast proportions through ritual. Such ritual can easily become an end in itself and does not necessarily imply a belief in or even awareness of the symbolic or mystical properties of those involved, either deference givers or receivers. When the elaboration of ritual becomes a whole ceremonial performance, such as the dinner party, the private ball or the houseparty, it takes on many features of a dramatic performance.[34]

In elaborated upper-class households, upper servants were crucial agents in the performance of these deference ceremonies. In order to be free to receive or give deference, to take part in activities which had symbolic importance or more prosaically to work for the surplus necessary as the basis for these activities, the master (and his family) had to be protected from the mundane pressures of life; the higher the position, the more protection was needed. Not only did servants protect the household from the external world—the kitchen staff dealt with working-class callers at the back door while the butler or parlourmaid dealt with the ritual of calls and card-leaving by social equals at the front door—but within the family, the master and mistress were protected by upper servants from lower servants and children. This protective function reached a point where the most intimate human relationships were mediated through servants in order to give maximum time for preparation and minimum unpleasantness in face-to-face contacts.[35]

Such rituals of deference could only be fully carried out in upper-class households with large specialized staffs. By and large, it is these households which have come to the notice of observers and form the basis of the stereotype of English domestic servants.[36] The typical middle-class family, on the other hand, aimed at having two or three servants,[37] only one of whom was concerned with personal service: answering the door, waiting at table, valeting the master or helping the mistress to dress. In yet less affluent families these functions had to be dispensed with or combined with 'rituals of order' in the material sphere, (cleaning, cooking and child care), tasks which in wealthy households were relegated to lower servants. The underlying rationale of these activities, however, was still the protection of superiors from defiling contact with the sordid, or disordered parts of life. A scanning of household manuals and magazines shows that these cleansing rituals took on heightened significance during this period of rapid social change.[38]

As we know, dirt is essentially disorder. It is matter out of place . . . uncleanness or dirt is that which must *not* be included if a pattern is to be maintained. In chasing dirt, cleaning and washing we are positively re-ordering our environment, making it conform to an idea, separating, tidying and ultimately purifying.[39]

The second factor increasing demand for servants in middle- and upper-class homes was the survival to maturity of increasing numbers of children.[40] More children meant potentially more disorder, for children were considered socially unplaced and therefore had to be kept in segregated parts of the house and fed at separate times. Young children, especially in large numbers, were also creatures of disorder in a material sense and therefore required more adults to keep them under control and to care for them. Generally, greater numbers of servants were needed to deal with the potentially disruptive and polluting fundamentals of life: birth, infancy illness, old age and death, as well as the key sphere of food preparation. Many millions spent their working lives in this unending struggle: fetching, boiling, steeping their hands in the purifying element of water.[41]

Those who were closest to defiling and arduous activities were, whenever possible, to be kept out of sight. In great houses their very existence was denied. Upper servants were themselves protected from such defiling activities by having lower servants to wait upon them. As more men were defined as upper servants, especially from the 1880s onwards, this meant that the heaviest as well as the dirtiest tasks could be given either to young girls and boys or charwomen, the two groups physically least fitted for them.[42] This does not mean that considerate men servants could not and did not help, for example, to carry coal and water, or to clean outside windows, but they could legitimately ignore this sort of work.

The Victorian preoccupation with rituals of order and cleanliness hardened the traditional division between labouring and other work. White, shapely hands free from dirt, burns or callouses were the *sine qua non* of gentility; any woman seen outside the house without gloves could not be a lady. Again and again attention is brought to the importance of *hands*. A. J. Munby, in his fascination with both sex and class differences, continually returns to the contrast between the delicate hands of the lady, encased in scented kid gloves and the 'brawny, brick red, coarse grained (work-hardened) hand, with its huge clumsy thumb' that belongs to the servant girl.[43]

The need to prove that the advantages of wealth and status were deserved and the disadvantaged were undeserving, their lowliness in some sense being their own 'fault', meant that this division between dirt and cleanliness, just as the division between wealth and poverty, was cast in moral terms of good and evil: 'Dirt is the natural emblem and consequence of vice. Cleanliness in house and dress and person is the proper type and visible sign of a virtuous mind and of a heart renewed by the Holy Spirit'.[44]

The symbolic power of cleansing and ordering rituals in warding off the dangers of social displacement was applied with intensity to those women and girls who had no family to place them or to those who had been labelled as having fallen outside legitimate society by having (or being suspected of having) sexual relations outside marriage. Whenever possible, they were 'placed' in institutional substitutes for homes: Homes for Orphans, Charity Homes, Homes for Fallen Women—or the Workhouse. Here they were considered to be safe from the dangers of public or street life. Within these institutions, anti-pollution rites combined with problems of discipline led to the use of intensive domestic work as control and as punishment: 'A laundry carefully worked is a capital place for moral training and moulding of the character where sins can be washed away'.[45] Almost without exception, the aim of all these institutions was to prepare the girl or woman for domestic service. For the only legitimate and respected (or respectable) alternative to living with one's own family was living as a servant with another family.

III

In any system of hierarchy expressed in rituals of deference, at a face-to-face level, there will be a continuing tension between identification with the superior (the giver of gifts and rewards) and social distance (protection of independence). How far the subordinate identifies with the goals of the system *and/or the personal superiors,* and by so doing accepts his or her inferior place within it, partly depends on the rewards—both psychic and material—he receives but also partly on how easy it is for him to find compensatory definitions of self-worth. Deliberate, narrow identification with the place of work, 'my kitchen', pride in the job no matter how menial, 'keeping my brass taps always shiny', or pride in the status and possessions of the employing family allowed servants a certain self-respect without total allegiance to or acceptance of the system.

Another device for maintaining dignity and a sense of worthiness was to magnify the dependence of the superior on the subordinate's skill, strength and emotionally supportive activity, a kind of subtle inversion of the relationship. Thus servants often emphasized the 'helplessness' of the gentry. A tweeny in service in the early twentieth century said, 'If it hadn't been for the working class, all the folk in Ryton would have been "hacky dorty", because it took the working class to keep them clean. The majority of people didn't know the right end of a duster'.[46]

These are responses limited to what was possible within the relationship. Strength to resist its encroachments could only come from external sources. Education, especially basic literacy, for servants was important as such a factor. But education, along with the acquisition of skills outside domestic work, posed a dilemma for the master; they made the servant more useful but at the same time potentially more independent. Particularly threatening to the employer was the possibility of the servant earning extra cash, especially from others.[47] Fears of losing control over servants lie behind the master's objections to both the practice of giving vails (gratuities) and board wages (payment in lieu of food) as such payments decreased the servant's dependence: 'by multiplying the hours during which they were free of supervision it increased their opportunities to live a life outside the family'.[48] Servants, on the other hand, deliberately stressed the 'modern' cash side of service partly because other working-class occupations were increasingly seen in this light and partly because by stressing their monetary attachment to the household they had a defence against the persuasive paternalism of service.

Especially when residence and being on call twenty-four hours a day were required, another important device for maintaining self-respect was to accept identification with the employers' household for a time, but then to leave for another situation, apparently without 'reason'. This is the restlessness of servants which was so resented by employers.

Which device was used depended on the particular situation of the servant, including background, age and sex. Accommodation within the relationship might be more characteristic of younger girls under the double discipline of service and femininity. In discussing the vexed question of time off an employer in the 1890s said: 'Men servants can get out for the best of all reasons, that they insist on it . . . As regards women servants, it is not a disadvantage for them, when they are young, to be under such control as admits of their having only a short time for going out. Restraint is always distasteful to the young and servants share the feelings of the daughter of the house, who would like more freedom in directions which custom deems perilous'.[49] But by the turn of the century, as new leisure time activities and the possibility of increased mobility by train, omnibus or bicycle increased the expectation of a more independent life for girls, the restraints of residential service became less and less tolerable.[50]

Under the constant pressure for autonomy by their subordinates it is not surprising that the qualities of the good servant extolled by masters were humility, lowliness, meekness and gentleness, fearfulness, respectfulness, loyalty and good temper. Many of these characteristics were equally part of the 'service' ethic whether it was in the armed services, church or public service. In the case of servants, however, they appeared in an exaggerated form, symbolized in behaviour such as walking out of the door backwards, maintaining absolute silence while performing their duties, never sitting down in the presence of their employers and never initiating an action or a speech.

When looked at in a slightly different light, these are also the despised qualities of the menial or lackey (both synonyms for servants as well as being derogatory terms in themselves). Such qualities were considered particularly degrading in men, in an era where 'manliness' was so important, and they often were counteracted by a strained haughtiness and dignity. The relationship I have been describing may, indeed, produce such virtues on the part of the subordinate but also it often results in slyness, evasiveness, a manipulative attitude and an 'uncanny' or 'intuitive' ability to see through the master's weaknesses.[51]

Were these qualities a 'mask' assumed while in the front regions when interacting with the master group, to be sloughed off in private? Or had many servants internalized a belief in their own unworthiness? We do not know. After all, human beings have an infinite capacity for living on many levels at once. As Simmel says in a general discussion of super and subordination: 'A highly complex interaction is hidden beneath the semblance of the pure superiority of the one element and a purely passive being-led by the other';[52] a dialogue between the superior constantly justifying the legitimacy of his rule, the subordinate constantly restating his self-worth, by seeking 'pockets of resistance'.[53]

Resistance could take other forms than flight or the escape into fantasy of servants' romantic literature. The traditional weapons such as sulking, mishearing, or semi-deliberate spoiling of materials, creating disorder, wasting time, deliberate 'impudence' or 'answering back' were developed to a high art by servants and recognized by both sides. An upper-class employer:

A housemaid, butler or cook had a unequalled power of taking it out on their master or mistress in subtle ways. Orders could be received with veiled sulks, and insinuations of trouble in the background.[54]

A cook:

Servants that feel they're being put upon can make it hard in the house in various ways like not rushing to answer bells, sullen dumb insolence and petty irritations to make up for what you're not getting.[55]

The organization of a front and back stage in larger middle- and upper-class homes gave more scope for such disruptive, individualized reactions including deliberate pollution of a very crude kind.[56]

By the mid-nineteenth century some of the latent hostility of servants focused on the sphere of personal behaviour which symbolized lowly position.[57] The daughter of a coachman recalls,

I was once told I had to curtsey and my father said, I'll curtsey you if you curtsey. It seemed it was a certain lady my father was coachman to and the gardener's children used to curtsey to them. And my father said, I'll do the curtseying but my child's not going to curtsey. And he said if I find you curtseying I'll give you a good thrashing. So I hadn't to curtsey.[58]

Such hostility reflected the forces which eventually were to undermine the whole fabric of hierarchy and deference. A similar etiology can be observed in the plantation system of the southern United States in the nineteenth century: the conflict between 'the patriarchialism of the plantation community, and the commercial and capitalistic exploitation demanded by the exigencies of the world market'.[59] In the case of households based on consumption—or the 'production' of social ritual—it was the exigencies of the *labour* market which undermined their rule.

The aversion to domestic service which resulted from the growth of alternative occupations and increasing working-class political awareness first affected men servants. It was they who led the campaign against the most personal and direct effect of subordination, i.e., physical punishment. Some took an ever increasing manipulative and cynical view of their occupation; some used the contacts they had made while in service as a way out of purely domestic posts, to become shopkeepers or run commercial services. These developments were spread over a long period with beginnings in the eighteenth century. Often there was not a complete break with service because more outdoor non-residential servants were used not only in stable and estate work, but also in the innumerable subsidiary service occupations which were an (as yet uninvestigated) feature of Victorian life. Livery stable employees, peripatetic clockwinders, couriers, private carriers, etc., all added to the amenities of middle-class life but were no longer under the close personal control of an individual master.

On the whole, employers seem to have accepted the declining use of men servants. It is difficult to find proof, but there are indications that it was not so much the increased cost of keeping men servants but the increased difficulty of controlling them within the house which led to the gradual substitution of girls for men in the 1870s and 1880s.

Girls and women did not make the transition to other occupations as easily. Socialization, the ideology which decreed that the 'natural' place for all women was a private home, and opportunity all conspired to keep them in service positions. Slowly, however, opportunities for alternative work were appearing[60] and, where available, servants were almost always more difficult to recruit.[61] The 400,000 who left service during World War I were only the most striking case of what was a continuing pattern.

The second force ultimately undermining the master/servant relationship was the concept of citizenship. Once it is admitted that all are equal members of the commonwealth, then the contract must be limited; outside it master and servant meet 'man to man as two British citizens'. Servants were one of the last groups to gain this citizenship either in the form of the franchise or citizen's rights in the form of insurance.[62]

In keeping with my original analogy, however, it is interesting that married women were the very last group of adults to participate fully in civil society; even now vestiges of their status as appendages to their husbands remain and are being debated in questions about pensions, National Insurance and married women's domicile. T. H. Marshall made this point in an aside whose importance even he underestimated: 'The story of civil rights in their formative period is one of the gradual additions of new rights to a status that already existed (i.e., freedman) and was held to appertain to all adult members of the community—or perhaps one should say to all male members, since the status of women or at least of married women, was in some important respects peculiar'.[63]

Middle- and upper-class households defiantly defended themselves against the encroachments of these disruptive forces but the private drives and the gates could not completely keep out the alien influences; for by surrounding themselves with 'deference givers' the stranger was already within their doors.[64] They did everything in their power to deny this was so, stressing the organic nature of the household by devices such as family worship. The danger lurking below the surface, however, was that without the power to enforce loyalty—the vigilant personal enforcement of deferential behaviour—divergence of interest would come to the surface and threaten the whole façade.

In 1826, as a very old and bedridden lady, the famous writer on moral affairs, Hannah Moore, was confined to an upper room alone in her home as her sisters died one by one. The large staff of servants, who had always hitherto been under the rule of the most practical of her sisters, now had such a gay life at her expense that she exceeded her income by £300 in one year and was powerless to stop it; a victim in her own house. At last her friends stepped in and carried her off to lodgings, fired the servants, lamenting that 'the poor old lady had to be made aware that these dishonest and vicious servants were making her appear to tolerate the sins she had testified against through life'.[65.]

IV

I have argued elsewhere that the isolation of working-class girls in middle-class homes during the course of their service put them at a disadvantage in the marriage market compared to their less restricted working contemporaries.[66] Under the strict regulations imposed on girls in service, courting had to be done in snatches of time: on their afternoon off, which early in the century could be only once a month, 'at the area steps' or with boys from home who they might see only once a year.

Once married, whatever the personal qualities and occupations of their husbands, they shared the basic precariousness of all working-class families dependent, at least theoretically, for support solely on the husband's wage, an expectation peculiar to this period of economic development.[67] Married women quickly became absorbed in the arduous battle of housekeeping where purifying rituals had to be carried out by one person in the restricted confines of a working-class home. The content of their work, as in service, was creating order in the house, preparing food and generally dealing with the detritus of personal life. As in service, also, these activities could fill up all the day and some of the night as well—there was no definite time off or time of one's own. Their material equipment was very often makeshift leftovers from middle-class households where 'rational' use of labour was the last consideration; just as working-class homes were often 'rooms' in converted middle- or upper-class houses.

By the latter part of the nineteenth century, the customary division of labour within the household laid most managerial responsibility for household organization as well as the majority of manual tasks upon the wife. Often she had little knowledge of her husband's work or he of hers. Unlike, therefore, an enterprise where the subordinate may defer to the *technical* expertise of the superior, her deference was to his paternalistic status; hers was a subordination of a more pervasive personal kind. Little attention, for example, has been paid to the use (or even more the threat) of physical coercion as a source of the husband's control.[68]

There was undoubtedly great satisfaction to the wife in the knowledge of her power to run the household and control the family's affairs, of her importance as the mainstay of family life. This knowledge, however, increased the pressures on her to protect her husband (and older children who were earning) from knowing how the household was managed to produce meals, clean clothes and rent, much less extras. Such protection from mundane matters paralleled that given by servants to the master or mistress. The husband was freed from 'bother' that he might engage in higher level affairs, (after his often monotonous and arduous work was done), be it the masculine culture of the pub, solitary hobbies like pigeon racing or above all, politics. The women themselves summed up their task of constant figuring and planning in such expressive phrases as: 'to contrive and consider', to 'make do and mend'. These decisions had to be made under emotional pressure from the competing demands of husband and children (and possibly elderly parents). Such constraints were compounded by the women's ill-health due to poverty, multiple pregnancies and self-neglect. The price paid was the narrowness of horizons, the closing in of the woman's world.[69]

In both service and marriage, master (mistress) or husband did not see what was happening. This unthinking blindness to what was going on within their own household was not usually the result of deliberate malice or even unkindness; rather *it was built into* the relationship. It was the essence of mastery that the lives of subordinates did not matter, that their concerns were, on the whole, of no interest or importance and were even faintly ridiculous. When the husband gave his wife money over and above the basic housekeeping allowance or other 'treats', or if he helped with heavy washing or took the children out on a Sunday, it was much in the same tradition as the 'kindly' squire and his lady who gave charitable extras to their retainers and villagers. Very close ties and great mutual affection often existed in such a situation but having either a good husband or 'a real bad 'un' was, in a sense, to be accepted as a stroke of fate in just the same way as the wife accepted the goal of family survival over her individual interests.

If, for any reason, the wife did not receive support and help from her husband, the only alternative recourse for her was to seek help from her family or from her neighbours whose own resources might be limited. But very little is really known about the support available to wives through the network of female neighbours and kin.[70] More attention should be given to the conventions of close-knit communities, such as 'rough music,' which were used to control excessive wife abuse or neglect. (See Weber's 'restraint on personal subjection through tradition', page 2.)[71]

The other source of independence I have described for servants, e.g. outside earnings, was vitiated, for the most part, in the case of wives. This was partly because the women's wages were so low and were counter-balanced both by problems of child care and loss of social status, and partly because all of what was earned almost invariably went into the family budget. If extra money was needed, one of the most frequently used sources was taking in lodgers. Although it solved the child care problems, it also created more overcrowding and more *work of the same kind* for the housewife while introducing a new, potentially disruptive set of personal relationships into the household.[72] The only possible exception to this pattern was where the wife was highly skilled in a trade which offered work near to where she lived (therefore *not* including many ex-domestic servants) or in textile districts where married women's work was accepted, with consequently higher earnings.[73] But behind the objective problem of low wages lay the basic dilemma of reconciling paternalistic relationships with a market economy nowhere better illustrated than in the legal ruling which required that a married woman who wanted to hire herself out to service must obtain the permission of her husband. An employer who did not gain this permission when hiring her could be sued for 'loss of services', in exactly the same way as an employer could be sued for enticing away a servant. In lay terms, a woman could not serve two masters.

The wife's isolation in a separate household and without colleagues or a work group to enforce expectations of 'fair play' or 'justice' of reward was an extension of the single servant's isolation.[74] Indeed, Marx's well-known metaphor describing the peasants of France is applicable to married women and servants alike.

The small-holding peasants form a vast mass, the members of which live in similar conditions but without entering into manifold relations with one another . . . in this way the great mass is formed by simple addition of homologous magnitudes such as potatoes in a sack form a sack of potatoes. The identity of their interests begets no community, no national bond and no political organization, among them they do not form a class.[75]

Few sources of political education or experience existed for the working-class girl or woman. The slow permeation of individualistic values to their ranks was rather due to increased education, more opportunity for varied work and higher earnings and, above all, to the fall in the birth rate and the accompanying belief that it was possible to control their own fertility.

Given this basic pattern of working-class family life from the second half of the nineteenth century onwards, what were the effects of having been in service? One of the stock defences of domestic service for working-class girls had been the belief that it gave a training for married life, for the girl's natural transition to wife and motherhood. The fact that the key to efficient household management, the budgeting of money and materials, was usually not part of the servant's responsibility was overlooked, nor was it appreciated that the most overwhelming priority for wives was managing on an insufficient or, even more hazardous, a fluctuating income.[76]

The budgeting of time is more problematical. This was less directly taught to the girls than an attitude which they absorbed while in service, for in middle- and upper-class households by the first quarter of the nineteenth century, housework and childcare had been systematically allocated separate units of time. This change from a task-oriented to a time-oriented outlook as applied to personal and home life is one of the most important (and least explored) aspects of Victorian social life. Servants were instrumental to this development. 'As soon as actual hands are employed the shift from task orientation to timed labour is marked',[77] and this applied within the home as well as the workshop. Women who had had some experience of domestic service, particularly in larger households, undoubtedly absorbed at least part of this attitude. However, in their own home, it was the external time constraints of the husband's work, particularly shift work and, later in the century, the school, which created fixed time points in their day, not social ritual. In the limited framework of their lives, their singlehanded efforts to impose strictly fixed times to family life could be not only inappropriate but even counter-productive.

A few ex-servants were able to save money to use as a dowry or set up with their husbands in trade.[78] A few girls must have married into the master class, or more likely into the lower middle class; some may have been kept as mistresses by upper-class men. For the majority, however, who married into the working class, there must have been very great variations due not only to the diversity of households but to the length of time the girl stayed in service and her experience, if any, of other jobs. If she had accepted some of the preoccupations of order and social ritual already discussed but was not able fully to carry them out because of lack of money, time and space, she had to make do with what meagre external symbols she could, constantly striving to make up deficiencies with her own labour. The whitened doorsteps and net curtains, the struggle to keep children in clean clothes, the whole distinction between 'rough' and 'respectable' can partly be seen in these terms ('Pollution beliefs can be used in a dialogue of claims and counter claims for status'. Mary Douglas). Other working-class women with factory or shop experience were also caught up in the struggle against dirt and disorder but it is possible that these distinctions had particular saliency for ex-servants.

Many former servants had very ambivalent attitudes towards their past employers. A few probably maintained personal ties with them, or even more likely with their children with whom they may have had a special relationship. Some found their horizons widened by their experience of service, by having witnessed new ways of living, by having been introduced to new tastes, new forms of beauty in the furnishing, decorations, flowers and gardens of the houses where they worked.[79] Some of these ideas could in turn be passed on to their children along with ambitions for individual advancement.[80] It is even possible that here may be one of the sources of working-class conservatism.[81] It should be remembered, though, that others were deeply ashamed of their servile past: 'How could we have allowed ourselves to be ordered about so, and for that wage?'[82]

Such aspirations tended to be expressed in personal and individual terms for all their experience from early childhood had been of the same personal subordination.[83] 'They are confined within the limits of their imagination of the possible, the relationship is habitual. Insubordination must have not only alternative means of support but an alternative language.'[84] Whereas working-class men were beginning to find a tongue for their wrongs, there were few places where working-class wives could learn to speak of theirs; the Working Man's Club and the Public House were often not for them.

In weighing up the relative positions within a paternalistic relationship, the decisive point is what happens when the relationship is broken, given the fact that in theory it should last for life. Only when the servant or wife is abruptly removed from the household and the well-oiled wheels of domestic machinery grind to a halt does the superior realize just how important such services really are.[85] For the master/husband, the first reaction to the loss of the subordinate is outrage at both the inconvenience caused and the disloyalty implied. The depth of this outrage will partly depend on the ease of replacing lost services and this in turn will depend not only on his money resources but also the state of the domestic labour (and marriage) market, both in quantity and quality.

On the other side, the overwhelming fact is that the whole of life of the servant and wife, from material support to human surroundings, depends on the household of which she happens to be a member: its resources, physical setting, technical equipment and above all the temperament and tastes of the master (mistress)/husband. These resources determine the standard of living, the work load, the food and other rewards and even help to define the identity of the dependent. When this relationship is broken it is, therefore, bound to be more traumatic and to require greater adjustments for the subordinate.

For in the last analysis, in an industrializing society, particularly a capitalist society at the high tide of liberal economic doctrine, there was no place for those whose social identity was defined primarily in terms of personal relationships, neither servants nor wives. They had no roles to play in the great drama of market forces. In theory they did not exist or at most were residual categories. In reality they had to struggle for survival in what ever way they could, for in such a society, 'he who pays the piper calls the tune'.[86]

The majority of such positions have been filled by women, although I have deliberately stressed the fact that *both* men and women servants came into this category in order to demonstrate that this type of relationship is not necessarily linked to sex differences. The fact remains, however, that by and large submission to personal and unlimited authority has been the fate of a majority of women during the stormy history of industrialization.

Recently there have been renewed efforts to find women's place in that history. It is rightly felt that 'a people without a history is a dispossessed people'. Those who wish to seek out heroines, to make us aware that 'female hands ripped coal, dug roads, worked looms . . . that female will and courage helped to push the working class towards whatever decencies of life it has now'[87] are more than justified in doing so. But the heroines must be seen in context. Otherwise there is a danger that they will be frozen forever in the amber of a new feminist hagiology rather than taking their rightful place in the mainstream of human history.

ACKNOWLEDGEMENTS

Leonore Davidoff wishes to thank Howard Newby and Paul Thompson, Department of Sociology, University of Essex, for their helpful comments on this paper.

NOTES

1. D. Simon, 'Master and Servant' in J. D. Saville, *Democracy and the Labour Movement* (London, 1954).
2. L. T. Hobhouse, *Morals in Evolution: A Study in Comparative Ethics* (London, 1951), 231.
3. The point has been made in connection with slavery, that it is a mistake to make legal definitions and codes the basis of analysis. David Brion Davis's critique of Tannenbaum and Elkins 'points to the possibility of large gaps between the legal status of the slave and the actual working of the institution,' Anne Lane, *The Debate Over Slavery: Stanley Elkins and His Critics* (Urbana, Illinois, 1971), 8. This is an important warning against sociological naivety but should not push us to the other extreme of discounting legal conventions, especially court rulings, as historical sources.
4. Max Weber, (edited by G. Roth and C. W. Wittich), *Economy and Society,* Vol. 3 (New York, 1968), 1066.
5. Note that during this period Britain had neither an indigenous nor imported ethnically nor religiously disadvantaged population (with the possible exception of the Irish). Such groups often make up the majority of domestic servants and thus blur the effects of the master/servant relationship. Contrast with the American experience: Lucy Salmon, *Domestic Service* (New York, 1911).
6. In order to supplement the usual documentary sources, in my present research, I have used 200 employer and 75 servant 'autobiographies' both written and oral, including material from Paul and Thea Thompson's 'Family Life and Work Experience Before 1918', Social Science Research Project, University of Essex.
7. Akin to Genovese's basic meaning of 'treatment' in various slave societies. E. Genovese, 'The Treatment of Slaves in Different Countries: Problems in the Applications of the Comparative Method' in Laura Foner and E. Genovese, *Slavery in the New World: A Reader in Comparative History* (New Jersey, 1969).
8. C. B. MacPherson, 'Servants and Labourers in Seventeenth Century England', *Democratic Theory: Essays in Retrieval* (Oxford, 1973), 217.
9. It is also part of the 'pre-industrial' attitude to the use of cash as a work incentive; the belief on the part of employers that servants were only looking for a minimum subsistence income and once given that income any amount of work could be required in return. Sidney Pollard, 'The Creation of the New Work Discipline' in *The Genesis of Modern Management* (London, 1965), 190.
10. Part of the problem of the decline of family-based domestic and rural employment; see Ivy Pinchbeck, *Women Workers and the Industrial Revolution, 1750–1850,* Chap. V (London, 1969).

11. For a discussion of the same question at a time when industrialization began to provide alternative means of support for adolescents, boys and girls, see: Michael Anderson, 'The Phenomenal Level: Environmental Sanctions, Ideologies and Socialization' in *Family Structure in Nineteenth Century Lancashire* (Cambridge, 1972).

12. J. S. Mill, *On the Subjection of Women* (Everyman, London, 1965), 249. Logically, then, there should be no surprise at the discovery of 'serial marriage' in the 1970s.

13. Georg Simmel, translated by Kurt H. Wolff, 'Quantitative Aspects of the Group', *The Sociology of Georg Simmel* (Glencoe, Illinois, 1950).

14. A problem which has bedevilled the Elkins debate. Anne Lane, op. cit., Introduction.

15. Hence the importance of servants' quarters and kitchens separate from the house in colonial India and Africa. Aban B. Mheta, *The Domestic Servant Class* (Bombay, 1960). Large English houses did have a front and back stage divided by the 'green baize door', but in smaller houses physical separation was much more difficult. Erving Goffman, *The Presentation of Self in Everyday Life* (Penguin Books, Harmondsworth, 1972).

16. Mrs Loftie, 'Living in Flats', *Social Twitters* (London, 1879).

17. Georg Simmel, op. cit., 266.

18. M. G. Whisson and William Weil, *Domestic Servants: A Microcosm of 'the race problem'* (South African Institute of Race Relations, Johannesburg, 1971).

19. Peter Stearns, 'Working Class Women in Britain 1890 – 1914' in Martha Vicinus, *Suffer and Be Still: Women in the Victorian Age* (Indiana University Press, 1972).

20. In 1871, there were 68,369 male indoor residential servants.

21. C. Collett, *Money Wages of Domestic Servants,* Report of Board of Trade (Labour Department), P. P., xcii, Cmd. 9346, 1899.

22. Walter Allen, *Transatlantic Crossing: American Visitors to Britain and British Visitors to America* (London, 1971).

23. *Toilers in London,* British Weekly Survey, 1897.

24. The meaning of this dependency is described in Vilheim Aubert, 'On the Social Structure of the Ship', *The Hidden Society* (Totowa, N. J., 1965).

25. In weighing up the relative importance of cash versus food, clothes and 'extras,' note that domestic servants were specifically excluded from the Truck Acts of 1831 through 1887.

26. C. Collett, op. cit., 1899. Wage data from my 275 'memories.'

27. 'In England the rule is that the mere fact of service does not of itself ground a claim for remuneration, unless there be either an express bargain as to wages, or circumstances showing an understanding on both sides that there should be payment.' P. Fraser, *Treatise on Master and Servant,* 3rd Ed. (London, 1875).

28. Harold Perkin, *The Origins of Modern English Society 1780 – 1880,* Chap. II (London, 1969).

29. Dereck Hudson, *Munby, Man of Two Worlds: The Life and Diaries of A. J. Munby 1828 – 1910* (London, 1972), 310. Booth, in discussing the nature of domestic service in the 1890s, says that it is 'a relationship very similar in some respects to that subsisting between sovereign and subject . . . there is demanded an all-pervading

attitude of watchful respect, accompanied by a readiness to respond at once to any gracious advance that may be made without ever presuming or for a moment "forgetting themselves." ' C. Booth, *Life and Labour of the People,* Vol. 4 (1903), 225.

30. Howard Newby, 'The Deferential Dialectic,' unpublished typescript, 24.[The article was published (with slightly different wording) in *Comparative Studies in Society and History,* 17 (1975), 139 – 64; see p. 155.]

31. L. Davidoff, *The Best Circles: 'Society', Etiquette and the Season,* Chap. II (London, 1973).

32. J. F. C. Harrison, *The Early Victorians 1832 – 51* (London, 1971), 110. He notes that Rowntree in his study of York took the keeping of servants (or a servant) as the attribute for inclusion in the middle class.

33. 'Deference must actively be sought, it cannot be given to oneself', Erving Goffman, 'The Nature of Deference and Demeanor', *Interaction Ritual* (Penguin Books, Harmondsworth, 1967).

34. John Beatie, 'Ritual and Social Change', *Man,* No. 1, 60 – 74.

35. An emancipated middle-class girl who married into the aristocracy about 1914 was appalled to find that her lady's maid, after helping her into her nightgown, asked permission to go and tell her husband's valet to announce that her ladyship was ready. Ursula Bloom, *A Roof and Four Walls* (London, 1967).

36. A. De Tocqueville, 'How Democracy Effects the Relations of Master and Servants', *Democracy in America,* Vol. II (New York, 1955).

37. J. A. Banks, *Prosperity and Parenthood,* Chap. V. (London, 1954).

38. This is not to overlook purely physical problems of dirt control, e.g., new conditions produced by factory chimneys and urban living. Nor to deny the importance of the discovery of the germ theory of disease and related public health developments or even the connection of religious beliefs with ideas of purity. These all must be taken into account when discussing the history of the period but they are analytically separate from the above.

39. Mary Douglas, *Purity and Danger: An Analysis of Concepts of Pollution and Taboo* (Pelican Books, London, 1970), 12.

40. H. J. Habakkuk, *Population Growth and Economic Development Since 1750,* Chap. III (Leicester, 1971).

41. Servants and almost always female servants, dealt with the recurring by-products of daily life; excrement, ashes, grease, garbage, rubbish, blood, vomit. Such tasks are almost always also allocated to wives. 'Protection of the purity of upper strata is an important feature of caste societies.' Louis Dumont, *Homo Hierarchicus: The Caste System and Its Implications* (London, 1970).

42. At the Duke of Richmond's castle in Scotland, despite the number of men servants kept, 'on Friday morning an army of charwomen bore down on the place to assist staff with the "rough".' M. Beckwith, *When I Remember* (London, 1936), 73.

43. A. J. Munby, *Diary,* Vol. 7 (1860), 79, Trinity College Library. Munby's fixation extended to glorying in seeing his servant (whom he married in 1874) Hannah 'in her dirt' filthy from scrubbing; the dirtier her hands, the more smudged her face the more he valued her. His fascination with the 'degraded' seems to have included a strong sexual element centred around the themes of mastery and submission. I have deliberately avoided any discussion of servants and sexuality in this paper but this is

not to deny its importance as an element in the relationship. See L. Davidoff, 'Above and Below Stairs', *New Society,* 26 April, 1973.

44. *The Servant's Magazine or Female Domestics Instructor, 1839.*

45. Rev. A. J. Maddison, *Hints on Rescue Work: A Handbook for Missionaries, Superintendents of Homes, Clergy and Others* (Reformatory and Refuge Union, 1898).

46. Barbara Rowlands, 'Memories of a Domestic Servant in the First World War', *North East Group for the Study of Labour History* (Bulletin, Number 5, October, 1971).

47. 'I am of the opinion that a man cannot be the servant of several persons at the same time but is rather in the character of an agent'. (Rev. V. Goodbody [1838], 8 ct. 665).

48. J. Jean Hecht, *The Domestic Servant Class in Eighteenth Century England* (London, 1956), 155.

49. Lady Jeune, 'Domestic Servants' in *Lesser Questions* (London, 1894), 265.

50. Some mistresses feared losing control of the servant if they did not constantly find her 'something-to-do', i.e., to show that they owned all of the servant's time. Even on the eve of World War II the attitude was: 'with regard to industrial workers the problem is always how many hours they should work; with domestic servants it is how much time they should have off'. Minister of Labour, *Evening Standard,* February 14, 1938; Viola Frith, *The Psychology of the Servant Problem: A Study in Social Relationship* (London, 1925).

51. These have also been both the virtues and vices attributed to wives and slaves. Orlando Patterson, 'An Analysis of Quashee', *The Sociology of Slavery* (London, 1967).

52. Georg Simmel, op. cit., 186.

53. This ambivalence is even clearer under slavery. George M. Fredrickson and Christopher Lasch, 'Resistance to Slavery' in Anne Lane, op. cit.; George P. Rawick, *From Sundown to Sunup, The American Slave: A Composite Autobiography,* Vol. 1 (Westport, Conn., 1972), 95–7.

54. Lady Tweedsmuir, *The Lilac and the Rose* (London, 1952), 94.

55. Margaret Powell, *Below Stairs* (London, 1968), 156.

56. In a doctor's family where the two maids felt that they were over-worked and never given sufficient food, the master had accused them of stealing the kidney gravy at breakfast. Back in the kitchen, to spite him, one of the maids lifted her skirt and pissed in the gravy pan saying 'she'd see he had plenty o' kidney gravy'. Sybil Marshall, *Fenland Chronicle* (Cambridge, 1967), 240.

57. 'Lower class compliance might be more convincingly explained by their pragmatic acceptance of specific roles than by a positive normative commitment to society'. Mann also stresses the role of 'manipulative socialization', in our case through agencies such as Sunday Schools. Michael Mann, 'The Social Cohesion of Liberal Democracy', *American Sociological Review,* June 1970, 435.

58. P. and T. Thompson, Interview 115.

59. Eugene Genovese, *The World the Slaveholders Made* (London, 1970), 98, quoted in C. Bell and H. Newby, 'The Sources of Variation in Agricultural Workers' Images of Society', *Sociological Review,* May, 1973.

60. P. Stearns, op. cit.; L. Papworth and D. Zimmern, *The Occupations of Women* (Women's Industrial Council, 1914), 23.

61. Doreen Watson, 'The Problem of Domestic Work', typescript, University of Leicester, M.A. thesis, 1944.

62. K. Oliver, *Domestic Servants and Citizenship* (The People's Suffrage Federation, 1911).

63. T. H. Marshall, 'Citizenship and Social Class', *Sociology at the Crossroads* (London, 1963), 79. Paternalistic domination has always been given as a reason for denying the franchise; it was feared that total dependency would influence the vote. As long as slaves, servants and women were regarded as permanent 'grey-haired children' they could never be citizens.

64. Barbara Frankle, 'The Genteel Family: High Victorian Conceptions of Domesticity and Good Behavior', University of Wisconsin, Ph.D. thesis, 1969.

65. Charlotte M. Yonge, *Hannah Moore* (London, 1888).

66. L. Davidoff, 'Domestic Service in the Working Class Life Cycle', *Society for the Study of Labor History,* Bulletin 26, Spring 1973.

67. In this section I am speaking in the most general terms. There were variations in husband-wife relationships based on region, types of men's work, opportunity for women's work, degree of urbanization, level of income as well as over time. There were also working-class families with kinship ties to the lower-middle class as well as former members of the lower-middle class living on working-class incomes in working-class areas. Ex-servants would be represented in all these groups.

68. It was noted that servants won freedom from physical punishment by about mid-century. Who can *legitimately* beat whom is a social norm, and not based primarily on physical strength. This aspect of working-class marriage in contemporary America is discussed in Mirra Komarovsky, *Blue Collar Marriage* (New York, 1967), 227.

69. P. Reeves, *Round About A Pound A Week* (London, 1913); Alexander Paterson, *Across the Bridge or Life by the South London Riverside* (London, 1911); M. L. Eyles, *The Woman in the Little House* (London, 1922); N. Dennis, F. Henriques and C. Slaughter, 'The Family', *Coal is Our Life, An Analysis of a Yorkshire Mining Community* (London, 1956).

70. C. Rosser and C. Harris, *The Family and Social Change: A Study of Family and Kinship in a South Wales Town* (London, 1965); P. Wilmott and M. Young, *Family and Kinship in East London* (London, 1957); W. Greenwood, *There was a Time* (London, 1967).

71. E. P. Thompson, 'Le Charivari', *Annales: Economies, Sociétés, Civilisations,* March – April, 1972.

72. P. Stearns, op. cit.,

73. C. J. Collett, *Women's Industrial News,* February 1896. For a discussion on this point including family relationships seen as a system of exchange see: Michael Anderson, op. cit., 1972.

74. This isolation was growing towards the end of the century as improvements in transport and housing led to the growth of working-class suburbs. D. A. Reeder, 'A Theatre of Suburbs: Some Patterns of Development in West London, 1801 – 1911' in H. J. Dyos, *The Study of Urban History* (London, 1968).

75. Karl Marx, 'The Eighteenth Brumaire of Louis Bonaparte' in Lewis S. Feuer, *Basic Writings on Politics and Philosophy: Karl Marx and Friedrich Engels* (New York, 1959), 338.

76. 'The fluctuation of income makes the problem of housekeeping impossibly difficult for most of the women and the consequent discomfort and privations of the home drive the man to the public house, wear out the health, the spirit and self respect of the women.' Liverpool Joint Research, *How the Casual Labourer Lives* (1909), xxvi.

77. E. P. Thompson, 'Time, Work-Discipline and Industrial Capitalism', *Past and Present,* No. 38, 61.

78. Mayhew, quoted in Gareth Stedman-Jones, *Outcast London: A Study in the Relationship Between Classes in Victorian Society* (Oxford, 1971), 29.

79. Arthur Barton, *Two Lamps in Our Street* (London, 1967), *The Penny World: A Boyhood Recalled* (London, 1969). Barton's mother had been nursemaid in Lord Tennyson's family. She read poetry to her children and had his portrait on the wall. Richard Hillyer, *Country Boy: An Autobiography* (1966).

80. The importance of *mother's* aspirations in the achievements of children in the educational system is now being recognized. Frank Musgrove, *The Family, Education and Society* (London, 1966), 76 – 82. A parlourmaid who had worked in some of the large houses in Kensington during the 1890s described by her niece as 'quite the lady', sent her only son to Eton. Personal interview, Mrs K.

81. Servants as 'culture carriers' is an intriguing idea. It is particularly important in areas of private life, e.g., the adoption of ideal family size. The generation who were young servants in middle- and upper-class households in the late nineteenth century, where completed family size was declining, were the generation of working-class married women whose own family size fell in the beginning of the twentieth century. Of course no *direct* connection can be drawn between these two sets of facts. J A. Banks, 'Population Change and the Victorian City', *Victorian Studies,* March 1968, 287. For the eighteenth century see: 'The Servant Class as a Cultural Nexus', J. J. Hecht, op. cit.

82. Personal interview, Mrs F.

83. A striking contrast to the 'almost masculine' mateyness of the factory girl. C. Black, *Sweated Industry and the Minimum Wage* (London, 1907), 134 – 5.

84. Sheila Rowbotham, 'Woman's Liberation and the New Politics', M. Wandor, ed., *The Body Politic: Women's Liberation in Britain, 1969 – 1972* (London, 1972), 4. The relations of working-class married women with middle- and upper-class women were almost invariably in terms of patronage or charity. The employment of charwomen was often seen in this light. The contrast in attitudes to relations between men across class lines, who faced each other as employer and workman is brought out in James Littlejohn, *Westrigg: the Sociology of a Cheviot Parish* (London, 1963), 131 – 2.

85. When their old cook suddenly died, two grown-up sisters living with their father realized just how helpless they were, both practically and in that 'the "heart" had gone out of the house', Mrs Josiah Lockwood, *An Ordinary Life 1861 – 1924* (privately published in London, 1932).

86. Many Victorians were troubled by the results of the new system. Some of their reactions are discussed in Reinhard Bendix, 'Traditionalism and the Management of Labor', *Work and Authority in Industry* (New York, 1956). The creation of corporate schemes like Port Sunlight or hierarchical 'paternalistic' institutions like the railway companies whose 'servants' were given security of employment, pensions, bonus

schemes was partly an attempt to mitigate the harsh effects of early individualistic capitalism.

87. Jo O'Brien, *Women's Liberation in Labour History: A Case Study from Nottingham*, Spokesman Pamphlet No. 24 (1972), 15.

7

The Petite Bourgeoisie in Nineteenth-Century Britain*

GEOFFREY CROSSICK

The existence of a 'rural bourgeoisie' may be a matter for historical dispute, but that does not apply to the rural petite bourgeoisie. In many other European societies there existed a substantial group of small property owners in the countryside: most importantly a small-scale, landowning peasantry, but also the craftsmen and traders sustained by the village and small-town economy that went with it.[1] Any regional qualifications that one might feel obliged to make to this generalization shrink to secondary importance when compared with the British case, for there are two commonplaces about nineteenth-century Britain without which we cannot understand its petite bourgeoisie. The first is that Britain became an urban country very rapidly, and extremely early in international terms; the second is that it lacked a peasantry, a rural petite bourgeoisie. It is as an urban formation that the British petits bourgeois developed, and the significance of that fact will run as a thread through this essay.

This essentially urban force was not evenly distributed around the country. There were those ubiquitous petits bourgeois, the shopkeepers and, to a lesser extent, producers serving humdrum local consumption, and these would be distributed in rough proportion to the urban population. But there were also two kinds of concentration. The first is represented by those towns whose industrial structures gave particular emphasis to small enterprise—Birmingham and Sheffield are the most obvious examples. The second is towns with a substantial commercial and service function, where tertiary activities and small-scale consumer industries proliferated to give a distinctive character to the local social structure. Such towns ranged from the

* This is a slightly amended version of an essay originally published in Geoffrey Crossick and Heinz-Gerhard Haupt (eds.), *Shopkeepers and Master Artisans in Nineteenth-Century Europe* (London, 1984) and is reprinted by permission of the author and Methuen & Co. It is a substantially revised version of 'La Petite Bourgeoisie britannique au XIXe siècle', *Le Mouvement social*, 108 (1979), 21–61.

national capitals of London and Edinburgh, through regional centres such as Bristol, Newcastle and Leeds, to more locally oriented county and market towns such as Northampton and Newcastle-under-Lyme.[2] Indeed, those last-mentioned centres might be seen as the most satisfactory home for the petite bourgeoisie where, least threatened socially or even economically, they could occupy a significant place in local society.

This was not just an urban location, but an urban orientation as well. The universe of the British petits bourgeois tended to remain enclosed within their own towns and localities, marking out their social and cultural localism in a way quite different from the trend within the more substantial middle class. Their politics, their organizations, one might almost say their concerns, failed to take on a significant national character during this period. Urban orientation involved more than all this, however, for the economic functions of the petite bourgeoisie inserted it into a local economic structure and gave it a key function in the development of the nineteenth-century urban economy.[3] In part this derived from the place of small enterprise in providing the infrastructure of this economy—retailing, services, secondary manufactures—but it also grew out of the way petits bourgeois helped shape the structure and the fabric of the nineteenth-century town, most obviously in the finance and ownership of working-class housing.

From such arguments stem the need to re-assess the importance of the petite bourgeoisie within the expanding urban industrial economy of nineteenth-century Britain, yet neither its economic nor its social history have received substantial attention from historians. As a result, much of the research upon which such a re-assessment must rest remains to be done. In this general overview, I shall concentrate on certain themes: the changing economic position of shopkeepers and small producers; politics, organization and ideology; and some of the wider relationships of the petite bourgeoisie within urban society.

SHOPKEEPERS

Shopkeeping has a far longer history than it has been given credit for. Fixed shop retailing, traditionally portrayed as a product of the mid-nineteenth century and the subsequent decades,[4] was in fact widespread from the early years of the century, even in small towns and villages, but especially so in rapidly expanding commercial and manufacturing centres.[5] Indeed, shop provision in six northern towns rose faster than population in the first half of the century, only achieving a greater stability between 1851 and 1881,[6] as if conserving its strength for the new forms of competition that were to hit the traditional shopkeeper from the closing decades of the century. Two trends of the first half of the century need emphasizing. The first is the decline of the craftsman/retailer, a necessary unit for a poor transportation economy, and the emergence of specialist retailing. The other trend grew out of that, and that was the proliferation of small-scale retailers on the basis of highly local and individual initiatives. Fast urban and suburban growth made such activity particularly attractive, and it seems that only from the 1860s did a high and increasing association between shop location and population distribution introduce more intense competition.[7] In other words, although there was the inevitable and endemic instability of small retail businesses, competition remained limited in the first half of the century.

The general problems of small retailers began to emerge from the 1860s. It is difficult to be specific about the structural changes that occurred in British retailing during these years, for they have been little investigated.[8] One certainty, however, is the clear shopkeeper feeling that new and worrying forms of competition were developing, and that their novelty lay in both scale and capitalization. A shift towards more capital-intensive distribution methods can be traced back to the closing decades of the last century. Its origins have received but limited attention, though they must include the expansion of effective consumer demand that accompanied rising real incomes; the changing occupational structure, above all the emergence of a white-collar lower middle class; the increasing opportunities for standardized goods, with greater urban concentration and new outlets for advertising; and the availability of investment capital.

Department stores were a later development in Britain than in France, but by the 1870s were well established in London, and penetrating provincial towns. Selfridges in London, Lewis's in Liverpool, and the so-called 'civil service co-operatives' such as the Army and Navy Stores, and their many counterparts, all built their markets well beyond their immediate vicinity, with extensive use of delivery vans and mail-order selling. This last method was judged by one French observer to be more extensive in Britain than anywhere else in Europe.[9] Multiple retail chains appeared first in the food trades, but by the 1880s were spreading rapidly throughout retailing, and it was not just the size of these chains that was striking, but the range of trades affected. Both stood out in contrast to other European countries.[10] In the formation of new multiple companies and the deepening of capitalisation, the years between 1895 and 1903 seem a watershed.[11] Finally, there were the increasingly professional and expansive consumer co-operative stores, growing from the 1860s, but entering a new period of explosive growth in the 1890s. During that decade they seemed in many towns to be bidding for dominance, with the shift to main shopping street locations marking greater visibility, and a new level of product diversity hurting a widening range of retail trades. Membership rose from 100,000 to three million between 1863 and 1913, turnover from £2½ million to £88 million.[12] The quantitative impact of all these changes has not been satisfactorily measured, but they represented a major challenge to traditional retailing methods, in their level of capital, vertical integration, ubiquity and identifiability, and in their new style of selling. Their self-advertisement was distressingly public. How can the smaller retailers have felt when faced with the excitement of David Lewis's Liverpool store, with its model of Strasbourg Cathedral clock? Each hour it played melodies from Mozart, Rossini or Haydn, while the Cathedral doors opened and twelve Apostles marched into view.[13] Thomas Lipton's capacity for publicity and extravagance they could read of in their *Daily Mail* each morning, before eyeing anxiously his shop in the High Street. The psychological impact on petit-bourgeois shopkeepers is of importance in a way that simple calculations of market share cannot indicate.

Alongside such explicit pressures went a longer-term trend degrading the traditional skills of the shopkeeper and the premium placed upon them. These skills had required a knowledge of a wide range of goods, the ability to judge, to divide, process and prepare them. Price competition, proprietary goods, pre-packaging all undermined the pride and the craft-consciousness of the traditional retailer. So it was that apprenticeship had died out in the London grocery trade by the late nineteenth century. 'It is not wanted,' said one assistant, 'there is little or nothing to learn',[14] though a grocer's leader felt that such a view was a dangerous one. 'Many of these men set up for themselves and are ruined by their ignorance'.[15] Overall, though, W. B. Robertson observed in 1911 that 'knowledge of a shopkeeping trade is not nowadays considered nearly so necessary as purely commercial ability'.[16]

Yet however much we might talk of a retailing revolution that created a new degree of scale in a previously Lilliputian world, however much we might indicate the new types of shop and be drawn to investigate the venomous shopkeeper responses to them, it remains nonetheless true that shopkeeping was the home of the small man and woman throughout the century. Contemporary retailers almost certainly over-stated the new challenges, for a significant proportion of their problems were in fact due to the intensification of older patterns of retailing. Most of all, it was due to the increasing internal competition amongst individual retailers, as ease of entry and wholesaler support for new and increasingly-dependent retail ventures produced a level of prices and hours competition amongst ordinary shopkeepers that was a major reason for their late-nineteenth century unease. We really need to know a great deal more about such competition, and the structures of dependency within the 'traditional' sector. Many a large grocer in Manchester with a wholesale trade (and presumably not just there) would set up a married couple as small grocers in an outer part of the town.[17] Such dependency could appear in other ways. It had become common by the 1890s for failing retailers with relatively expensive stocks (above all small drapers) to get assistance from the wholesaler to whom the bulk of the debts was owed. The wholesale firm effectively took over the control of the business, some-times even using the debt as a means of acquiring a smaller shop (Josiah

Chater did this in Cambridge[18]). Taken together, then, the various forces discussed here made the quarter century that preceded the First World War a peak period of price competition in the retail trades as a whole. The small independent retailers were not declining, but they now faced new and intensifying difficulties. There were threats to their skill and pride, to their economic viability, most of all perhaps to their ambitions. The real extents of these problems may be unclear, but a sense of being embattled against the forces of size and competition prevailed amongst independent shopkeepers. The responses—organizational, political and ideological—were, as we shall see, marked by their paucity and ineffectiveness.

SMALL PRODUCERS

Industrialization in Britain produced no withering away of small-scale production. Economic necessity pointed to large-scale concentrated production in no more than a handful of specific sectors (mostly certain textiles and producers' goods), and the slow spread of powered machinery in Britain is merely generalized confirmation of that.[19] It is now clear that the Industrial Revolution generated a whole new set of possibilities for small producers, even if by the middle of the nineteenth century the context in which they operated was often very different and more constrained. They persisted most of all in a mass of consumer trades: clothing, leather, boots and shoes, food and drink, building, printing, cutlery, domestic hardware, hosiery, knitwear, lace, and much more.[20] Their position was certainly eroded by 1914, but in such a heterogeneous fashion as to confirm the remarkable diversity of these small producers.

Diversity of size must be recognized at the outset, for small producers were of varying degrees of substance, shading almost imperceptibly into an underemployed working class. We must try to distinguish the petite bourgeoisie from that layer of marginal producers hurled into existence by depression, underemployment or simple poverty, as unemployed journeymen and others sought to create or augment an income. This is a world of 'penny capitalism' whose aspirations seem to have been more desperate and fairly distinct.[21] Such marginal enterprises, seeking to survive in crisis or to add a little income to a wage, were even more common in shopkeeping.[22] Another form of very marginal producer appeared in many trades where intense sub-division and sweating generated a plethora of minuscule work units: amongst the 'little masters' of Sheffield, in building, in the late-nineteenth-century London shoe trade, in cabinet making, and in other depressed trades where outwork and the garret-master system flourished, if that is the word.[23] A distinction, however blurred in the sources and indeed on the ground, must be drawn between potentially viable petit-bourgeois producers and those workers exploiting one of the many methods other than wage employment by which nineteenth-century working people might obtain an income.

There was also a diversity of geographical distribution that was important for social and political relations. If all towns contained small producers, they were not necessarily a prominent element within the local economy. At one extreme stood such towns as Middlesbrough and Merthyr Tydfil, to which we should add Patrick Joyce's smaller factory towns,[24] where large employers dominated social as much as economic affairs. At the other were those industrial towns with a more broadly-based employing class, towns based on some species of workshop production. The best known examples are Birmingham, Sheffield and the traditional areas of production in London, but, as Behagg argues in his essay later in this book, it is a mistake to see the prominence of small producers as a sign of their continuing and unchanging independence.[25] To these must be added the larger commercial and manufacturing centres themselves: the rapid economic growth of early nineteenth-century Leeds saw not just large-scale factory production in textiles, but the exploding force of an increasingly specialized labour-intensive craft workshop sector.[26]

Finally, of course, there was a diversity of relationships to industrial and economic change. An essential starting point, in that it relates so pointedly to the social and political character of British small employers, is the absence from mid-century of a small master artisan class committed to its traditional place both in its craft and in local society, a group of small masters resisting change out of normative objections to the economic, social and political system as they saw it being transformed. The older craft framework did allow a response, as Behagg's work on Birmingham suggests, but it was one that was rapidly defeated in Britain, leaving to the bulk of masters a developing petit-bourgeois identity.[27] Long-established, even multi-generational, small firms embedded in a framework of values based upon a master artisan culture and its place in society seem increasingly rare in Britain. The absence of a corporate structure denied small producers even the myths of an idealized guild age to inform responses to change. Overall, the relations of small producers to industrial change were both more complex and more creative than the notion of a declining traditional sector would allow. We need to know a great deal more about the economic history of small-scale production in Britain, and its analysis will require close attention to such issues as capital concentration, the geographical organization of production, the technical division of labour, and the relation of that to mechanization. It is the variety of relationships of small producers to industrial change that stands out but, at the risk of being over-schematic, we can isolate three types of small producer in nineteenth-century Britain. Adding a chronological dimension to this framework means that any single industry might experience all three of these situations.

The first category saw the continuation of a small-producer sector without substantial change in either technology or unit size. Such apparent continuities, however, often hid fundamental changes in the organization of the industry which threatened the viability of individual small producers however much it supported small production as a general structure. The early re-organization of the tailoring trade of London, and the subsequent experience of the light metal industries of Birmingham and the Black Country, are the most obvious examples. By the 1860s these Midlands industries were characterized by a sub-division of trades and the advent of small hand-powered machines. Where steam power was advantageous, systems for power-sharing allowed a small master structure to accompany powered machinery. Alternatively, factory space and a concomitant access to a power supply could be hired from larger manufacturers, as in the cutlery and related trades of Sheffield by the 1860s, which were characterized by a high level of market integration, the division of operations, and a very low-level mechanization. The archetypal unit could thus remain the small firm.[28]

These Sheffield and Birmingham trades shared a more pervasive characteristic with light industrial towns elsewhere, and with other small, unrevolutionized manufactures: the integration of the producer into a larger structure of factoring on the one hand and subcontracting on the other. Most petit-bourgeois producers operated in sectors being transformed by the power of merchant capital, the new link between producer and expanding market. These became the basic method of organizing this category of small-scale manufacturing—or of re-organizing it. In trade after trade of this kind, the differential impact of the market, and its expression through merchant and wholesaler interventions, forced a divide between a viable small master class that sought to behave in a 'businesslike' fashion and accept merchant domination, detaching itself from the culture and custom of the craft community, and on the other hand a depressed body of marginal small masters whose independence became no more than notional, even where they survived. The Industrial Revolution was characterized more by commercial change than by factories, and nowhere more so than in the way in which it affected small producers. Commercial organization, factoring, and national merchant operations turned these small firms into new types of producer bound into increasingly-dependent relationships long before mechanization put different pressures upon them.[29]

The level of technology might have discouraged concentration in any case, but the factoring system perpetuated the very fragmentation upon which it depended.[30] With the merchant or factor organizing production and not merely distribution, often supplying raw materials and weekly financial advances, he not only bound the workshop owner into his operations, but threw the whole burden of fluctuations onto him. The factor's bargaining position was strong, knowing as he did the liquidity problems of the small masters, and their needs to sell goods to pay their wage and other costs. The dependence on credit was thus a critical force undermining master independence. Thus, as commercial advances took place—classically in the trades of Sheffield, Birmingham and the Black Country—the general economic logic behind small production was precisely the force determining the vulnerability of individual petit-bourgeois producers.

Those industries where small producers as a major element in production were actually created by the process of industrial and technological change form my second category. In a number of industries once characterized by domestic workers organized by merchant capitalists, the mid-century combination of market expansion and minor advances in a still essentially labour-intensive technology led to an upsurge of small firms. The shoe-making industry, where small enterprise was first created and then threatened by industrial growth, is the clearest example.[31] The early nineteenth-century shoe trade, above all in Northampton, was controlled by large-scale whole-salers organizing outworkers, supplemented throughout the country by traditional craftsmen/retailers working alone to supply local needs. The 1860s saw an expansion of demand, and the introduction of simple machines, notably the sewing machine. The combination stimulated the growth of mainly small firms, acting as both manufacturers and wholesalers, often combining small workshops with putting out. The 1880s brought depression, home-based competition, and price cutting. This was the classic situation in which the small producer would be squeezed in many industries, and the larger shoe manufacturers responded with a higher level of mechanization and factory rationalization, as well as by opening retail outlets of their own. The competitive advantages of the large manufacturers now accumulated, and by 1900 struggling small firms survived only by sub-contracting or becoming highly specialized producers.

Here is a good example of a small and simple machine element leading to the proliferation of small-scale workshop producers in a hitherto unmechanized industry. These are not traditional masters being squeezed, but largely new firms, in new activities, and substantially created by industrial change. We may find in this area further clues to the absence of a strong, craft-based, small-master ideology in nineteenth-century Britain: too few producers would have fitted that traditional characterization. There are other examples. In Sheffield, the application of small machines to the cutlery trades led to some shift from domestic production to larger workshop opera-tions. Early powered mechanization in the hosiery industry similarly encouraged a proliferation of small firms as factory production spread in Nottingham from the 1850s. Space and access to power could be rented, and small firms could readily buy second-hand machinery in an industry prone to bankruptcy.[32] The availability of lighter sources of power encouraged this process—at first the gas engine, but more significantly electricity towards the end of the century. Indeed, market conditions and technical sub-division of processes provided the context for electrical power to act as a stimulus to the emergence of small firms at a time when the trend towards concentration seemed to be set the other way.

The third and final category covers those industries which experienced marked concentration in the scale of production, but where small producers survived and were at times even stimulated by their relationship to the new and larger firms. As Kropotkin commented on Britain in 1912, 'each new factory calls into existence a number of small workshops'.[33] Small firms became an integral if dependent part of industries shifting towards more highly capitalized operations, and they often found the reason for their growth in that changing cost structure of their industry, with the commitment of large firms to continuing and high fixed costs finding relief in sub-contracting to small firms to meet periods of high demand, or to provide auxiliary services. Ready-made tailoring is one example, where the 1880s saw a massive increase in the number of large clothing factories in Leeds (from seven in 1881 to fifty-four in 1891), but that growth was accompanied by a boom in 'client' workshops taking on contracts from the great establishments.[34] There were other reasons for large and small firms to co-exist. There could grow up a more complex sub-contracting and buying-in-system amongst enterprises operating at a more marginal level, as in the Midlands brass industry, where large integrated units co-existed with small workshops, or in jewellery where 'the small businesses are in some sort the satellites of the larger ones, and move in their orbit'.[35] This was the more exploitative relationship, but the connections could have greater subtlety. Different sizes of firm could produce distinct types of product within a range, as with the edge-tool trades; chainmaking, where a factory would contract out to small workshops the lighter part of an order;[36] or van-building, where lighter vans for which there was a less regular demand were left to small employers.[37] This leads into the indistinct world where sub-contracting could merge into sweating and garret-masters, but if the line between these categories can never be rigid (indeed, the depressed garret-masters might be declined workshop owners) my concern is to stress that genuine small businesses often survived—and to a degree flourished—in this changing environment. Yet it carried with it a decline in independence, as petit-bourgeois producers, in this category as in the first, found themselves bound into increasingly-dependent business relationships.

In these three ways amongst others small production units survived, and were often encouraged by, industrialization and economic change. As I have stressed, however, small business in all three forms of persistence was experiencing increasing strain towards the end of the century. The need to increase investment in order to reduce costs at a time of depression and competition meant that the same business pressures that were stimulating the growth of larger firms provided for petit-bourgeois producers challenges with which they were ill-equipped to deal. Examples are the wood-screw industry in the Midlands, where expensive equipment had by the 1860s forced most small businesses out of existence; and the more dramatic decline of the small victualling brewer between the 1860s and the 1880s.[38] In times of declining trade, it was the small firms who more readily disappeared, and the more gradual trend towards a larger scale of enterprise is particularly noticeable during the Great Depression in many of the small metal goods industries. In this connection, it is important to distinguish the proliferation of tiny enterprises in economic crisis, as workers sought an income, from the role of depression during structural crises in eliminating once viable small firms. The 1890s seems to mark a critical moment in this respect, with the advance of capital equipment lifting onto a new level in many industries.[39]

All of this would be experienced as actual competition from larger and more efficient firms, which often themselves took over the role of factors. The advancing scale of retail organization intensified this by making small producers disadvantageously dependent on wholesalers who dealt with increasingly distant and cost-conscious markets. Under these combined pressures many small masters felt obliged to move into the factories within a no more than notional system of sub-contracting. G. H. Shaw of Sheffield observed in 1908 that 'a great many of these large firms are buying up the little masters, and instead of having these little masters, who perhaps employ a dozen or a score of men, and who supply some of these large houses, they buy a firm up, and appoint the little master as manager over a department, as a rule, to make that class of knife, or other article which he has been used to manufacture for the firm'.[40]

More diffuse social pressures encouraging a lack of confidence among small producers must be added to concrete difficulties such as these. The very towns in which they operated were coming to be dominated by large employers, especially the metal towns as new industries appeared (steel in Sheffield, engineering in Birmingham). This changing social context became generalized, as small producers sensed a national process of business concentration that fuelled a feeling of embattlement. As Joseph Brown commented about his small Birmingham tool-making firm, 'evidently we are destined to disappear before long'.[41] This must have been experienced through the declining opportunities open to small business, not so much to enter as to grow from small beginnings. Capital and technological requirements shut down the horizons for growth at this time in many sectors, perhaps well before small producers as such were generally endangered.

If we are to understand the paucity of organized small-producer resistance to these changes, then the ideological issues that will be analysed below must be linked to the complex picture of small-scale production outlined here. Three points must be emphasized in particular. Firstly, these firms were not generally traditional master artisans adhering to an older set of craft values. They became businesses, expanding or declining with the opportunities to do so. See de Rousiers' judgment of Joseph Brown in the 1890s: 'The trade which seems on the eve of slipping from him has not been in his case a time honoured refuge, in whose shelter he grew to manhood, but merely an opportunity of which he availed himself, as he would have done of any other'. The consequences were a reluctant resignation in the face of change. 'He is accustomed to rely upon himself and not on the fortunes of his trade, on his personal rather than on his technical aptitudes'.[42] The second point leads on from that. These were not generally long-established firms. On the contrary the limited evidence available suggests that small producers were characterized by a very high rate of turnover.[43] Thirdly, I have emphasized the responsiveness of the small-production sector to changing circumstances. The decline of opportunities in one area was matched by their expansion in another; the fate of individual producers was distinct from the persistence of small-scale production. Indeed, changing economic opportunities could provide the stimulus to which small producers, with their low capitalization and small adaptable technology, were often well-placed to respond. Thus the faltering small firms in the light-metal trades of the Midlands found new life in the 1890s when the bicycle industry sought parts for assembly.[44]

This is the starting point for an analysis of small producers in nineteenth-century Britain. We know all too little about them, and discussion is still over-dependent, as my own references will have suggested, upon the important economic histories produced in the early decades of this century. Only when we recognize the vitality and the complexity of small producers in Britain, and their diverse relation to capitalist industrialization, and stop viewing them as a declining pre-industrial sector, shall we be able to interpret their social and political role.

POLITICS, ORGANIZATION AND IDEOLOGY

In literary and even historical portrayal, the petite bourgeoisie in Britain has too often been the object of patronizing rejection, above all as culturally imitative, and that caricatured treatment comes frequently from writers such as H. G. Wells who were themselves from that background. Yet the caricature relates to the reality, for it seems that from the middle of the nineteenth century there was little distinctive or coherent about the voice of the petite bourgeoisie in British political life. Their politics and values came to seem fundamentally derivative. The characteristic rejection of both state and élites that had shaped the ideology that grew with dissenting religion survived wherever petit-bourgeois politics found expression, but they became subsumed within a blander liberalism that allowed many to move further towards social conservatism when faced with an increasingly organized working class.

The chronological emphasis there is important, for in the period from the late eighteenth century through to the 1840s, a vigorous petit-bourgeois radicalism had been more present in movements of militant opposition to the existing political system than historians' concentration on working-class politics has allowed. E. P. Thompson recognized this, and portrayed vividly a rationalist, individualist and democratic strand of radicalism that he identified with an artisanal and petit-bourgeois milieu.[45] In many towns through to the Chartist period, a section of the petite bourgeoisie (we can say no more precise than that) was a major radical voice confronting the older local élite, and limiting its ability to carry out its policies. It may be correct to see the reform of municipal government that stemmed from the 1835 Municipal Corporation Act as an attempt to shut down popular access to local politics and, with a weighted and often narrowed franchise, to incorporate the small propertied interests of the town within what was often a more restricted form of local government.[46]

This radical tradition is best understood through the notion of the *menu peuple*, the ordinary useful people, a radical conception that held at its centre a cultural and political rejection of opulence and oppression.[47] These notions structure so many early-nineteenth century movements of popular protest and struggle, to the extent that the language of 'capitalist oppression' that they talk is unwisely seen as a proletarian rejection of the new industrial capitalist order. We are beginning to understand how rooted that was in a *menu peuple*'s denunciation of privilege, oppression and parasitic wealth of a financial and speculative kind, rather than in a proletarian conception of capitalist exploitation. Their's was an ideology of modest means, hard work and independence as a solution to injustice and as an alternative to subordination. Therein lay the appeal of Cobbett and also, in a different way, of Paine and Thelwall to British radicals. Finance and speculation were the economic ogres, and for good reason. Credit and small-scale finance were continuing petit-bourgeois concerns—interest-rates were too high, access to finance too poor in local personalized capital markets, and the process seemed at the mercy of outside speculation. Condemnation of financial speculators in eighteenth-century Britain by those small borrowers who suffered most in panics, were thus rooted in practical experience and not just moral predilections. Credit certainly does not alone explain the radical analysis, far from it, but it shows the specific attractions of that analysis to those with small enterprises, and why they developed it as they did.[48]

Independence and the dismantling of economic and political monopoly were the aims of this radicalism, as political democracy and a particular economic morality intertwined in a way that gave priority to the former. We can observe the vitality of a shopkeeper and master artisan politics, often rooted in Painite democratic ideas, in the local politics of many towns between 1815 and the challenging Chartist experience of the early 1840s. Neale has characterized it as the 'rational anarchism of a community of small producers', concerned with democratic suffrage and the secret ballot, opposition to monopoly and the corn laws, civil and religious liberty, and national education. It was an expectant, optimistic radicalism, and its characteristics are becoming clarified by local studies. In Salford, an amorphous group of shopkeepers, teachers, and small manufacturers used a proliferation of local institutions to penetrate urban affairs;[49] the vestry radicals of London in the 1820s and 1830s had a very similar social base;[50] a radical petite bourgeoisie in Leeds used minor political institutions to gain a foothold in local politics from which to oppose narrowly based and wealthy élites, whether old or new.[51] Their rejection of dependency, of the client economy and politics, can be traced back to the eighteenth-century construction of an economic and organizational basis for independence among the 'middling sort' of the provincial towns. It was their mutual clubs and subscription societies which flocked to the support of Wilkes, and they read radical papers such as the *Middlesex Journal* which were directed specifically at them[52]. Their independence was to be important. A school proprietor in Birmingham who supported the Hampden Clubs during 1816 could not join for fear of offending gentlemen on whose custom he depended. But he noted in his journal that 'my brother Edwin who is a saw-maker and, of course, unfettered, is a member of the Hampden Club'.[53]

The ability of this petit-bourgeois radical milieu to cohere with a developing working-class politics, to create a world of popular politics that came under real internal pressure only from the 1830s, was made possible by the character of the traditional, older analysis of political oppression which held sway through to Chartism and in many ways within it.[54] That concentration on 'old corruption', taxation, representative government, and the conflict between productive and unproductive, formed the basis of a wider radical co-operation that broke down but slowly after the middle of the 1830s, as the older Painite radical formation splintered, though it was to leave a lasting imprint on the character of working-class politics. Prothero has persuasively demonstrated the interweaving of shopkeeper and master artisan radicalism with working-class politics in the radical movements of London between 1815 and the rise of Chartism, and his argument about the ideological and social roots of artisan politics is an implicit explanation of why such an alliance could have been possible. It was determined primarily by political not economic roles and analyses.[55] The substantial petit-bourgeois involvement in Chartist localities has been neglected by a historical emphasis which until recently has struggled to identify Chartism too exclusively as a proletarian movement. It was, in many ways, also the final *campaigning* commitment of the radical petite bourgeoisie to a democratic, liberal, anti-privilege and anti-monopoly ideology. Evidence for the Black Country, Wales, Bath, Nottingham and Halifax—where 'their values of independence and self-determination were the backbone of Halifax Chartism'—provides examples of this.[56] Where they were prominent in Chartist organization, strategy was at its most constitutional, though still radical and aggressive. In Leeds, the local government strategy of Chartists derived from the issue-based democratizing ideals of an essentially petit-bourgeois section of the local Chartist leadership. Its success depended upon its integration into long-established local radical traditions that were by no means exclusively petit-bourgeois.[57] Its bite derived not from policy, but from its belief in democratic control. That could readily draw upon the historically radical concerns of dissenters, and it often did.[58]

The substantial enrollment of petit-bourgeois special constables to handle the feared Chartist disturbances in London in 1848[59] does no more than symbolize the detachment of the small propertied from the radical movement, but the 1840s did see the decreasing viability of the older radical tradition. The rationalist belief in a consensual popular social order once corruption and privilege were eliminated was undermined for the petite bourgeoisie by social fear, conflict, and the intense experience of depression. It was an optimistic vision with declining prospects and, in a valuable case study, Morris has shown its hold on Samuel Smiles during the Leeds politics of that decade. Indeed, for Morris, the genesis of 'self-help' lay in the retreat into a purely individualistic struggle for self-development, and he labels it a 'petit-bourgeois utopia'.[60] That process, over the period since the early 1830s, denied 1848 its role as a turning point in the composition of the popular movement that it had in other countries. The change was more gradual in Britain. The subsequent years saw the development of a political liberalism that was to be critical to the relative stabilization of mid-Victorian society, and at its centre lay the fragile urban liberal community of local bourgeois, shopkeepers and small employers, and radical artisans; a community built around the often tense but viable assertion of notions of equality based on ideals that were narrowly individualistic and specifically political. The petite bourgeoisie was not simply drawn into it—it helped shape those ideals. It was embedded in local organizations. More strikingly, it led the struggle to oust Whig élites in places like the North-east where the struggle continued into the mid-Victorian period. It is this success of mid-Victorian liberalism that is vital to understanding the political limits within which the British petite bourgeoisie operated. The conflict between expanding bourgeoisie and a threatened petit-bourgeois sector elsewhere in Europe could weaken liberal co-operation of the British kind, and the low incidence of such tensions in Britain is important to an understanding of the political, and perhaps also social, development of the petite bourgeoisie from mid-century. Furthermore, if it was their experience and ideology as dissenters that helped shape earlier petit-bourgeois conceptions of the State, then the weakening of sectarian conflict within the state helped further this overall process.

Mid-Victorian liberalism as a local phenomenon[60] created a circumscribed area within which political conflict and even social dispute could operate. At its least settled level it drew in sections of the radical working class; at its most successful it drew the petite bourgeoisie into the political nation in a lasting and ultimately quiescent way. Joyce has shown that in northern industrial boroughs, as they became embedded in Liberal electoral organization, so the radical dimensions of their liberalism became weaker.[61] The success was in some ways the result of an effort by urban bourgeois élites to detach the petite bourgeoisie from its radical alliances. There are grounds for seeing many voluntary and benevolent institutions established by local élites in this period as directed as much at involving small propertied interests in formal associations as in shaping working-class behaviour. Success with shopkeepers was the most emphatic. The incorporation of small employers is less clear, because of the need to distinguish between that declining group enmeshed in an artisanal milieu that had helped give shape to their earlier radicalism, and those of different orientation who joined other small business interests at the heart of the liberal movement. The economic changes in small-scale production, the breaking of artisanal culture at the master level, the increasingly businesslike atmosphere and imperatives, and the activities of large-scale producers and merchants in encouraging these trends, were all central elements reconstructing the character of masters in small-scale production, and this helped lay the basis for the political and cultural changes that we can detect.

This ultimately became a drift towards a social—and eventually political—conservatism that emerged fully only after 1918. The move of the lower-middle class as a whole—white-collar as well as small-business elements—towards Toryism was slow but discernible, one facet of the declining viability of mid-Victorian community liberalism towards the end of the century. The petite bourgeoisie had helped bind together the liberal urban ideals, at times injecting them with a radicalizing attack on privilege and protection. As that declined in the changing social climate of the late nineteenth century, so the business élite's drift towards 'Villa Toryism' seems to have carried much of the white-collar and small-business lower-middle class with it.[62] The Tory organization in London, the London Municipal Society, was by 1905 reserving places on its local committees for representatives of property owners' and ratepayers' associations, though not all wanted that full identification.[63] The petite bourgeoisie was pressed increasingly into a small-business commitment to private property, laissez-faire, and the market that defined itself more in relation to labour than to big capital. It is significant that early socialist strategies from the 1880s sought to penetrate the administration of local government and the poor law—the very areas where the local interests of small property were most decisively represented. Local small businessmen like Frank Bullen were appalled: 'The doctrines I heard preached by the socialists in the open air simply filled me with dismay.

For it was nothing else but the unfit and incurably idle, the morally degenerate, at the expense of the fit, the hard-working, and the striving classes.'[64]

The politics of the petite bourgeoisie did not disappear after the 1840s, but it lost its distinctive presence as its focus and its concerns narrowed. The older positions did not vanish. We can see this in the way that the ratepayers of Bath and Great Yarmouth, and what has been called the 'cranky radicalism' of the West Midlands small-master belt, gave local organized support to the Administrative Reform Association in the middle of the 1850s.[65] We would probably find it in the Tichborne movement of the 1870s. And it was an independent and individualistic small business radicalism that led the struggle against the enclosure of a section of beach by the Pier Company at Southsea in the 1870s.[66] Hardly heroic causes, though still rooted in many of the old ideals and drawing upon their vocabulary. The petit-bourgeois political presence survived essentially as a ratepayer cause and became locally introverted, in significant contrast to developments within both the bourgeoisie and the organized working class. The national political framework is important here, for there were no attempts to mobilize the petite bourgeoisie against any subversive threats to the existing order. As a political force, they were not needed in Britain. No one tried to win, to bribe, or to appease them.

The very nature of petit-bourgeois problems outlined earlier in this essay encouraged this withdrawal into local and highly specific affairs. The distinctive interventions after mid century were largely limited to pressure group activities in support of precise interests, as the British petite bourgeoisie no longer sought any broader re-orientation of political or social practice. The unity of the German *Mittelstand* may have been illusory, but the ideal of the *Mittelstand* was not. No such formulation appeared as historical ideal or policy argument within British politics, where a petit-bourgeois presence became limited to the defence of sectional interests.

Such interest groups most commonly involved the petite bourgeoisie as shopkeepers, ratepayers or house-owners. Shopkeeper associations emerged from the 1850s, mostly at the town level but with the formation of national trade associations from the last decade of the century. I have examined the organizations and their ideology and activities elsewhere,[67] but what must here be emphasized is the limited demands of these associations, and the absence of either a political perspective or demands for government help. The principal efforts were to maintain 'free' competition, and to do that involved little in the way of national political organization. Services to members and local responses to issues provoked by municipal government prevailed. The way in which all these associations, and even the brief agitational movements such as those over co-operatives, eschewed any autonomous politics—in contrast to many petty commercial defence associations on the continent at this time—is striking evidence of the assumption that a distinctive political voice was not needed.

It was as cost-conscious ratepayers that a once radical petite bourgeoisie, fighting monopoly and privilege, now expressed its anxieties. Municipal investment in new sanitary schemes put pressure on the rates in the 1850s, and that decade saw the appearance of ratepayers' associations all over the country. The attack on the rich élite was there, as local shopkeepers and small masters organized to resist its profligate ways in the town's affairs. The evidence we have from Salford, Newcastle-under-Lyme, and most explicitly the Economy party in Birmingham, reflects a more widespread phenomenon. They were a continuing force in local affairs by late in the century and, if Offer's analysis of the unequal rate burden afflicting the small businessmen of London[68] is of wider validity, then their concern is explicable, however narrow its political perspective. Ratepayer concerns also characterized the house-owners' associations which, with their concern for local government rate demands and their anxieties over building and housing regulations, became widespread as the century progressed. Stable associations grew from the 1860s with a national federation established in 1888. Most associations seem to have been small, and could have organized no more than a minority of the myriads of small property-owners.[69] Englander finds in these property-owners' associations a sense of embattlement during the late-Victorian and Edwardian years, a feeling that economic and political developments were leaving them isolated.[70] A better comprehension of that atmosphere might come from an exploration of the social bases of landlordism, and its wider anxieties.

In none of these organizations do we see any weakening of the commitment to economic liberal assumptions on the part of British shopkeepers and small producers. They continued to visualize their future alongside, rather than dominated by, the larger bourgeoisie. The corollary of this commitment to economic liberalism is the absence of right-extremist political organizations growing out of or mobilizing small business interests. In Britain, the lower middle class as a whole remained committed to mainstream party politics. Organizations of a militantly right-wing complexion, such as the Liberty and Property Defence League and the Anti-Socialist Union,[71] were large-business backed groups concerned with opposing socialism and the threat of State intervention, and they never sought to appeal to the forces of the small man, to mobilize him with an alternative politics. Nor is there any evidence of a petit-bourgeois social base for nationalist organizations like the Navy League.[72] The unusual and virulently anti-socialist Cardiff Ratepayers' and Property Owners' Association set up in 1900 won little support.[73] Most interesting of all, perhaps, was the Middle Class Defence Organization founded in 1906 as an anti-socialist and pro-economy force directed at municipal affairs, for its propagandists talked a language familiar to students of movements of the *classes moyennes* on the continent. 'We are the buffer interest', noted one correspondent,[74] and there was much talk of those ground between capital and labour. Yet the sins of capital, when listed, were no more than its willingness to buy off labour by increasing taxes on the 'middle classes'.[75] There was no real infusion of the movement with petit-bourgeois concerns,[76] no distinctive identity in relation to capital.

In other words, petit-bourgeois politics in Britain stayed resolutely within the existing party structure, and there was no real pressure from the petite bourgeoisie or from outside political interests to break that. In part we are seeing the consequences of the absence of a distinctive petit-bourgeois ideology of a traditional kind. There had developed no body of economic or political ideas that distinguished small proprietorial aspirations and ideals from the dominant ideology of laissez-faire liberalism to which the British petite bourgeoisie remained resolutely wedded. An understanding of why there never developed in Britain, in the way that there did especially in Germany, but also in France and Belgium, a conception of the petite bourgeoisie as a stabilizing force in modern society would take us beyond those petits bourgeois and into larger questions of ideological and structural comparison. It is clear, though, that the lower-middle class as a whole (small business and white-collar groups) was given no wider political and social tradition to which to attach themselves and through which to develop a distinctive consciousness in relation to larger capital. The absence of a small-proprietorial peasantry might well be a central element in explaining that, but there was also the deeper hold in Britain of those competitive free trade ideas to which the petite bourgeoisie clung more persistently at the very time at the turn of the century when political and business leaders were relaxing the rigidities of non-intervention. The Birmingham tool-maker, Joseph Brown, for example, told de Rousiers of his deeply individualistic philosophy of life. Unhappy experiences had taught him that 'the best capital a man can have is himself', and that 'each man's life is a problem of which he must find the solution; . . . that each man must seek it for himself'.[77] The petit-bourgeois voice had none of the bite of the *Mittelstand* critique, and was characterized by an ideological diffuseness. That is why it was amongst such petits bourgeois in late nineteenth-century London that eccentric individualist concerns best flourished: anti-State fanatics, no-Popery extremists, political anti-clerics.[78] The combined effect of economic position and work situation, aspirations and anxieties, was to reinforce that faith in rational competitive individualism, and with it a view of the economic order that ascribed symbolic moral importance to the free enterprise system.

This narrow moral individualism might be viewed as the natural consequence of the work situation, vulnerability, and restricted capital resources of the petite bourgeoisie—though similar characteristics elsewhere in Europe were accompanied by a higher degree of mobilization and social association.

The differences are perhaps only of degree. Their's was an introspective way of life, and shopkeepers and small masters in Britain were reluctant to experience their problems except as individuals. Small enterprise was too fragile in its resources and its vulnerability to the pressures of credit, not to mention ill-health or family crisis, ever to feel secure. But the problems were individualized, as were the options for improvement. This must be a factor in the reluctance to organize. It must also explain the characteristic investment of any savings in secure and visible local forms, above all housing for rental. This helps us to see one of the most important features that distinguished these people from the more substantial bourgeoisie, and that is the specificity of petit-bourgeois property. Their belief in the rights of property became bound up, morally as much as economically, in a particular piece of property. Petit-bourgeois capital and property remained essentially immobile in practice—something well recognized by Cardiff councillors protesting against the threat that the shipping élite could simply shift to docks elsewhere.[79]

The anxieties that could flow from this were intensified by the problems of maintaining family status. How to ensure that those sons who could not hope to inherit the business entered suitable alternative occupations? What little evidence we have suggests a lower-than-average continuity between father and son in retailing.[80] The problem of suitable marriages for daughters could prove even more awkward for those with sufficient property to fear the threat to its security that was implied by a bad marriage,[81] but for much of the petite bourgeoisie such choices were probably not available and a family flow across the divide from the working class was inevitable. Provision for daughters who did not marry and for widows leads us back to investment in small property; it produced a very evident female *rentier* class in Victorian Britain.[82]

There were therefore many forces committing the British petite bourgeoisie in the second half of the nineteenth century to a lifestyle that focused on the family with an intensity that may have been less strong earlier in the century when a larger proportion of shopkeepers and small producers would have been involved in the popular world of the street and the *quartier*. The autobiographies of those born into shopkeeping families testify to the introverted world of their childhood, and oral history evidence supports that picture:[83] This was not a purely cultural introspection that grew out of fears of the rough world outside, but far more strongly one imposed by the economic and social necessities of a small enterprise that dictated its own lifestyle, its own sense of being tied to a demanding business. Yet a family-centred existence did indeed offer a means of separating such people from the working class that often lived around them, of preserving values and status. Helen Corke was born into a shopkeeping family of the 1880s, and had reached the age of eight before being allowed to associate with a neighbour's child or enter a neighbour's house. The Vincent family, with their shop and lodging-house in Cardiff, likewise coped with the poverty around them by turning in on the home. Yet they were at the same time an element in the community. More precisely, the father was, for 'when anyone died they'd come for him to head the funeral'.[84]

The resources with which to maintain that family-centred and respectable status for the next generation were very limited. As the problems of small enterprise grew in the late nineteenth century, and fuelled doubts as to the possibility and even the desirability of passing on such businesses, so we find petit-bourgeois parents all over Europe using education to obtain white-collar and minor professional careers for their sons. Status could thus be maintained, or so it was hoped. Education as a result came to assume great importance, for with limited financial resources to pass on, this offered a useful way to invest in their children's future.[85] In Britain, expanding white-collar employment (paradoxically based on that growth of state, commercial and financial institutions which so many petits bourgeois feared) thus proved an attractive solution to these perpetual petit-bourgeois problems, and evidence suggests that they were indeed taking it up.[86] Did such opportunities attenuate petit-bourgeois social frustration? And what was the consequence of the relatively limited availability in Britain of the State employment that carried so much more prestige to continental white-collar occupations? Whatever the answers, the prior problems of education itself remained real, for in contrast to France, where a hierarchy of educational institutions gave peasant and small business families potential access to professional and government service,[87] the counterparts of such people in Britain remained fairly well detached from the educational system of the upper-middle class. Indeed, the provision of education for petit-bourgeois families was to become a real problem in the closing decades of the century. An increasing section of the wealthier élite saw reform of education as a means by which to embed these people into an existing or reformed social and political order. Hence T. H. Green's scheme for Birmingham schooling, which concerned itself with the need to impregnate the petite bourgeoisie with a general culture from above, while simultaneously giving children of that group some real prospects for advance. He achieved little real success, and the difficulty continued. At the end of the century it was higher grade schools and the scholarship system, rooted in many ways in a petit-bourgeois quest for good and respectable education for their children, that made the problems even more explicit, for here was an attachment of such children to an educational system unconnected with that of the élite and not under the clear control of bourgeois culture and ideas. The setting up of a 'ladder of opportunity' with the 1902 Education Act was in part about the cultural co-option of these shopkeepers, small employers and traders, and clerks.[88]

The petit-bourgeois concern for advance or at least stability through education was the consequence of a status that lacked economic security or a more-than-limited potential for growth. The capital was usually too restricted and trapped. H. G. Wells's parents saw the poor prospects of their Bromley shop in the mid-Victorian period, 'but they had now no means of getting out of it and going anywhere'.[89] East Anglian trawling unexpectedly reveals exactly the same problem, the classic petit-bourgeois dilemma, as the fisherman-owner could neither realise his existing capital effectively nor find any alternative use for it. So he continued trawling.[90] In his *Confessions of a Tradesman* Frank Bullen articulates this sense of having to keep going, for even when the venture was going poorly he was trapped with it. For one reason, there was too much tied up in it. He went on not in hope, but because 'as far as my limited intelligence went I couldn't do anything else'.[91] All of these factors shaped the social localism and the moral individualism of the petite bourgeoisie.

While the established bourgeoisie would be marked out by its regional and even national contacts, there was something irreducibly local about much of the petite bourgeoisie. Further, if they were most publicly important in those small towns where a wealthier social élite was barely apparent, and where introspective communities in much of Europe might reinforce a small propertied identity,[92] then the British shopkeepers and small producers were in an especially difficult position in a society that urbanized both rapidly and early. Compared with a great deal of the continent, Britain was just not a small-town society. The localism would thus become less assertive. The parochial character of its culture must have severely impaired the ability of the British petits bourgeois to cope with change, and must have been responsible for much of the rigidity of values that only hardened as the period progressed.

A strict and conventional concern for respectability was one way to assuage these tensions. Helen Corke's father may have been stirred by the new bicycle craze, but he spent the money instead on a piano.[93] A symbol of the petit-bourgeois dilemma? An attachment to the values of a more prosperous bourgeoisie certainly characterizes these small-business people in the social as much as in the political sphere. See the growing separation of workplace from home in shopkeeping during the second half of the century, which not only dramatically altered the female involvement in the enterprise but signalled a purposeful identification with middle-class Evangelical ideas about the separation of spheres.[94] Status aspirations and social identity were essential, and they rested on a deep sense of economic independence, reinforced by the social ideals of religious nonconformity and the narrow dissenting historical culture that went with them. Did the passion for reading and for literature that some retailers seem to have passed on to their sons challenge that?[95] No culture can be purely imitative, but we know too little about that of the petite bourgeoisie. It does seem that personal effort, personal struggle and personal propriety were seen as the bases of access,[96] and in an economic milieu characterized by instability that must have been a disturbing ideology with which to interpret one's fate. The inability to imagine change or to organize for it derived not just from structural position but also from the specific ideology and values of the British petite bourgeoisie in the closing decades of the century. It was a view of the world that must have condemned many of them to a great deal of personal pain. Yet the ideology seems barely to have shifted to cope with a world which was, towards the end of the century, less and less favourable to them. There were, in any case, always new recruits for whom their position represented hope rather than despair. Instability of enterprises, instability between generations[97] must be one reason why they failed to develop what we might call a class experience, a cultural transmission of history and understanding.

SOCIAL RELATIONSHIPS AND THE COMMUNITY

The precise areas of integration of petits bourgeois into the economic and social structure and into networks of power and dependence might well prove to be the most illuminating way into an understanding of this group. Its economic significance has already been urged, but some of the other spheres of importance will at least be indicated—space permits little more—in the pages that remain: local government, the material fabric of the Victorian town, and relationships with the working class, notably over work, residence and retailing.

Local government in Victorian Britain enjoyed a degree of autonomy unusual in contemporary Europe, and the strong petit-bourgeois role in local administration is thus especially important. Each town had its own history in this respect. In some towns municipal reform led to liberal town councillors who were overwhelmingly traders, shopkeepers, minor professionals and small manufacturers from as early as the end of the 1830s: Stockport is one example.[98] Sometimes larger bourgeois involvement withered away early—by 1844 in Newcastle-under-Lyme—but often petit-bourgeois domination was the outcome of the eviction of larger business interests, as in Hull and Salford. According to the Salford local newspaper in 1868, the town's large businessmen were 'gradually compelled to give up all hopes or claims to posts of distinction in the town' by those from whom the inhabitants 'bought their beef and beer'.[99] The most striking case is that of Birmingham, with a continuing conflict from the 1860s between a municipally-minded dissenting élite and economy-minded small businessmen which produced a fluctuating balance of control.[100] None of this should be any surprise. Local government finance in Britain was derived exclusively from a tax on real property which gave those whose livelihood rested on the use of small property (shops or houses or workshops) a strong incentive to keep tight control on expenditure and therefore rates.[101] Petit-bourgeois strength in local government, resting as much on the willingness of a larger bourgeoisie to withdraw to a larger regional or national stage as on their actual displacement, was therefore a recurrent feature of town affairs. The fact that they could be permitted to occupy that position leads us back to the victory of liberalism amongst them: petit-bourgeois local government did not threaten liberal economic and social policy, certainly not until that changed with the rise of municipalism at the end of the century.

Self-interest could also drive small businessmen into local government. It was unlikely to have been a pure concern for public service that took three innkeepers and a pawnbroker onto Bridgwater Watch Committee in 1859,[102] and the drink trade was generally well-represented, as were builders concerned about both building bye-laws and contracts, and house-owners seeking control over public health officials and rate assessment. Retailers might have been anxious about excessive freedom for market traders, especially where the council controlled the town's market. Such a list could continue, but to attribute petit-bourgeois strength in local government to precise self-interest would be as mistaken as to present the professional and business élite as 'natural leaders'.[103] Indeed, it was the small businessmen who stayed on Salford council far longer than average.[104] If local commitment and identity, sharpened by the dissenting values of the liberal community, characterized the petite bourgeoisie; and if immobility of capital and the nature of the local taxation base engendered special anxieties; then the natural leaders of many communities might plausibly be seen as not the plutocrat or the lawyer in the villa beyond the fields, for whom the prestige of local office seemed increasingly insignificant, but the grocer, the draper and the small engineer whose local community was as much the centre of their lives as they were of its. Hennock has shown the cost-conscious yet inefficient character of petit-bourgeois local government, and when the Plymouth Medical Officer of Health complained in 1900 that 'the small shop element was what he disliked. Down with everything was their motto',[105] he was indicating their detrimental effect on municipal services.

It was not just through council inaction that the urban petite bourgeoisie could determine the character of local housing, for the small businessman stood at the centre of the provision and ownership of housing for the working class in most British cities. They could help finance house construction by making short-term credit available to speculative builders,[106] but they were more frequently the actual proprietors of houses that they let to working-class tenants. They might purchase new houses on completion, or purchase existing housing stock, and the shifting balance between the two investments is fundamental to the character of the housing problem. Even without that relative transfer, their specific investment needs could distort the local housing market. One contemporary attributed speculative over-production of houses in early-Victorian Sheffield to 'the petty capitalists . . . desirous of realizing a handsome percentage'.[107] The attractions of owning houses have already been stressed, and to that security was increasingly added the desire to invest capital for subsequent retirement, a pattern that seems to have been growing stronger by the 1880s.[108] The motives were complex, but their interaction with local capital and building markets left the men and women of small capital as the overwhelming force in working-class housing.[109]

House-ownership leads us into the ambiguous question of the relationship between the petite bourgeoisie and the working class, an ambiguity only partly attributable to the heterogeneity of the small business men and women and their social milieux. If, as Bechhofer and Elliott have suggested, the two social groups progressively separated as the century advanced,[110] then the control of housing constituted an important arena within which the divide opened up. The petit-bourgeois freeman's interest in the unenclosed burgess lands of Nottingham in the first half of the century, and their involvement in the housebuilding that followed enclosure, were two distinct mallets driving a wedge between the town's working people and its small-business class.[111] Housing was an area of particular vulnerability and insecurity, for tenants inevitably, but also for landlords, given their limited stature. It was the small house proprietors who were identified time and again as the worst of the landlords, least able to afford repairs or improvements, and least willing to afford them.[112] This behaviour was rooted in insecurity, and from that stemmed much of the tension of the housing relationship. The small landlord was dependent on his tenants for the return on his capital, and felt vulnerable to their non-payment and moonlighting. The working-class tenants—or a good proportion of them—depended on landlord credit as part of a strategy for survival, with arrears that accumulated in the winter being paid off as work prospects improved. It was for the property-owners to decide who might be allowed to defer their rent. In Englander's words, 'a bond of debt united landlord and tenant'.[113] Not all could be allowed that, at least not willingly, and the extraction of rents from reluctant and impecunious tenants, rents often high to allow for the inevitable defaulters, was a continuing source of irritation. Landlords sought greater legal support, and the Small Tenements' Recovery Act of 1838 made eviction a great deal simpler. Riot and disturbance over evictions became common in the early-Victorian period, and continuing tensions were engendered by the use of bailiffs and debt-collectors to distrain for rent.[114] None of this was made any easier by the close supervision that many a small landlord sought to exercise over his tenants. In the 1830s, the small shopkeeper and small proprietor of Derby 'invest their money in running up rows of little tenements, the rents of which they rigidly collect every Monday', while tradesmen in one Middlesex parish were pleased to possess such property, 'having the opportunity of personally looking after the occupiers'.[115] Not a great deal had changed in this respect a half-century on, for one Bristol observer confirmed that these small men who invest their savings in houses to let 'look very sharply after their tenants'; and that they liked to be able to collect their rents personally.[116] Concern for proper tenant behaviour, as much as pecuniary anxiety, inspired this closeness of inspection. Maybe the two motives cannot be separated in that way. 'Small capitalists' might even seek to use this control to influence their tenants' voting choices in local elections—that was certainly the claim of many witnesses to a 1859 parliamentary committee.[117]

These house-owners were often the local shopkeepers. Often enough, perhaps, to influence popular images of the petite bourgeoisie, whatever the reality. In this way could other sources of tension find reinforcement. Adulteration of produce was notorious amongst those retailers selling to the working class, and the credit system was the lynchpin- of their success. Irregular income meant that many working-class families needed a reliable structure of credit in order to survive. That usually entailed dependence on one shop where credit was available to the family. The shopkeeper secured a trapped clientele in return. A South Wales grocer in favour of cash only trading at the end of the period knew full well that 'the tradesman favours the credit system because it has a tendency to keep his customers under an obligation to deal with him'.[118] For many traders operating to tight and uncertain profit margins, the dependence allowed poor quality and short-weighting. 'All the small traders give credit', noted Frank Bullen. 'Of course, in this way much very inferior stuff is got rid of'.[119] It is unfortunate that we know so little beyond such generalizations about the daily relationship between shopkeepers and their customers. The self-evident abuses of this kind have to be counterbalanced by the power of the customers to shop elsewhere—and that generally rested on not needing credit. The practice of 'exclusive dealing' by popular radicals in the 1830s and 1840s was its most politicized expression, though there is disagreement as to the extent of its success.[120]

Against such tensions must be set the closeness and sense of identity that existed between small employers and shopkeepers[121] on the one hand, and sections of the working class on the other. The supposedly close relationship between masters and men in small workshop industries has provided the basis for a whole interpretation of the politics of Birmingham,[122] and that cohesion model has been extrapolated to other towns.[123] Little evidence is generally presented as to the content of this social cohesiveness, which tends to be assumed from political co-operation. It is an analysis of workplace relations that is too readily applied, irrespective of time and place. We know that later in the century the new kind of petit-bourgeois employer, who had lifted himself from a proletarian background, all too often regarded his workers with a critical superiority. Joseph Brown, the Birmingham tool-maker, had a 'poor opinion of men who find it hard to make a living for themselves and their families in a trade where he has been able to raise himself and his family to a good position'. A small employer's craft pride ('he still flatters himself that no smith in Birmingham can turn out better or quicker work') implied no necessary identification with his journeymen.[124] It is that fracturing of craft identity and cohesion[125] that is the key to the changing relationship, and it is a process that Clive Behagg has examined persuasively for the case of Birmingham.[126] That same capitalist restructuring of productive relations in the London artisan trades radically altered social relationships within small-scale production there too.[127] The economic difficulties of small masters, and the way that so many responded by intensifying work methods and behaving less and less according to the artisanal expectations of their trade, made increasing conflict between masters and journeymen unavoidable.

Small employers became notorious for paying low wages and maintaining poor work conditions. Even when workshop regulation grew in the 1860s, few localities had the staff of inspectors to enforce the law.[128] All of which should come as no surprise, for small enterprises were the most vulnerable to changing economic conditions, with their low capitalization, and tight credit and liquidity problems. Depression saw them suffer rapidly,[129] while in better times they found it hard to hold onto their best workmen. The Master and Servant Acts, compelling employers to fulfill contracts, were most frequently used by small manufacturers seeking to keep workers in order to complete orders. Staffordshire, the Black Country, Birmingham and Sheffield—the classic small-master districts—regularly saw more prosecutions than any other area.[130] Anyone who has worked through Victorian local newspapers will have seen the countless cases brought by building firms against recalcitrant craftsmen. So, even where social and workplace proximity might imply cohesiveness, the realities of small-scale production and its uneven transformation made for often tense relationships. It also made for those strike waves in such industries, movements about which we know too little. We find an early and ferocious example in the London tailoring trades of the 1820s and 1830s, as journeymen, together with some masters, sought to retain traditional modes of workshop production.[131]

The cohesion argument might prove to be an illusion that rests on a conflation of older master artisans rooted in the culture and assumptions of the craft, and newer small businessmen tied ever more closely not into the craft but into the world of business. There was, nevertheless, a degree of ambiguity to the workplace relationship quite absent from situations where shopkeepers and other small businessmen acted as middlemen in outwork and subcontracting. It was a classically petit-bourgeois activity to organize at a secondary level the putting-out system that abounded in British industry. During the first half of the century they increasingly owned the hosiery frames in Nottingham, and rented them out to knitters—an investment not unlike that in houses, and a good way for men of small capital to obtain a steady return without being involved in production itself. 'Foggers' was the Black Country name for those shopkeepers and publicans who acted as middlemen, notably in nail-making, and often gave part-payment in kind through their pubs and 'tommy shops'.[132] Publicans would often organize an industry. Many of the High Wycombe chair makers in the 1870s were publicans, controlling the manufacturing in the surrounding districts; while the 'lumpers' on the London docks were similarly organized by publicans and chandlers acting as sub-contractors of dock labour gangs.[133] Systems such as these proliferated in structures of production and employment geared to irregular or small-scale tasks. The organizational problems of industrialization were frequently overcome by such fragmentary means, and shopkeepers and small tradesmen rushed to play the middleman's part.

However, to press the tensions between working people and those small men who owned their houses, organized their work, gave them employment and sold them their food is to swim against a still resilient orthodoxy which has tended to stress the areas of propinquity and community that bound many small businessmen in Britain to the working class around them. The orthodoxy is not wholly wrong. Many a small master retained his trade union membership. John Watson, a pearl button maker with his own workshop, was actually secretary of the trade society.[134] They did so not just as an insurance against a return to wage employment, but as a sign of identification with the artisanal culture, the trade union and friendly society, and the public house.[135] In the context of nineteenth-century British society, the transition from wage-earner to small master was not *necessarily* experienced as upward mobility. It gave some freedom from wage labour, to be sure, but implied no automatic change of social identity or milieu. The power of popular sociability, of craft culture, of personal values, could all fundamentally shape the way that people experienced such change.[136] As the means to success or survival changed in small-scale production, as the traditional methods of production and distribution which partially insulated small masters against the competitive world of commercialized production declined, so the craft community was being fractured by economic change in more and more industries.

Those problems of differentiation within the world of small enterprise, and the implications for relationships with the working class, are just as great when we turn to shopkeepers. It is relatively easy to place the retailers whose custom was drawn from the middle class of the town, for their contact with the working class would become increasingly patrician as more substantial retailers inserted themselves into the structure of urban charity and voluntary associations that the wealthy were abandoning. The position of those who dealt with the working class in increasingly-segregated cities, where the retail petite bourgeoisie might be the only non-proletarian element left in inner districts, is more ambiguous. Many clearly felt at least sympathy and understanding for their customers, especially in depression or strikes. Robert Roberts's recollections of his mother's small grocery shop in a Salford slum before the First World War confirms the complex but close relationship with that neighbourhood of which she saw herself a part. She identified with local working-class struggles, and in times of crisis the granting of credit could prove a difficult decision, as her generosity and sense of identity fought with her instincts for self-preservation.[137] An oral history investigation of shop-keepers in East Brighton has shown the fragile and delicate operation that was the allowance of credit by small shopkeepers. 'There was a fine line between being too free with credit and taking on too many bad debts, and not being free enough and losing custom as a result'.[138] Giving credit in times of individual or community need was partly a business operation, partly a form of support or charity, and partly a source of what Melanie Tebbutt has called in relation to pawnbrokers 'an important source of authority and control'. She sees the result as 'a peculiar interdependence which impinged most directly upon the lives of women who were the retailers' main customers'.[139] It all tied at the daily level into the female world of the working-class community, struggling to make ends meet in ways often hidden from their husbands. Credit—and the ability to get it at short notice—was essential to that. It is hardly surprising that shopkeepers, ambivalently tied into the popular world around them, were so frequently the closest targets for out-bursts of fury. When political protest turned to riot, it was shops that were all too often the focus of attack, usually over issues apparently unconcerned with retail trade. Chartist protest in London was one example, but much more striking were the Tonypandy riots in South Wales over sixty years later.[140] The complex web of dependence, positive support and consumer aspiration, was woven with fragile threads, and the social explosion that crises could produce give us only a partial insight into relationships almost ignored by historians.

We return to the recurrent theme of the changing relationship between the shopkeepers, the small masters, and the working-class community around them, that has surfaced so regularly in this essay. R. J. Morris has suggested of the publican James Kitson in early-Victorian Leeds that he identified with the 'labouring classes', although as an innkeeper he was owning and managing capital in a bourgeois manner. 'Like many small shopkeepers and tradesmen he took his class identity from his customers rather than from his relationship with capital and property.'[141] If we distinguish the Roberts's sympathy from Kitson's class identity, we might merely be drawing attention to the changing definitions of class within the British social structure over the intervening three-quarters of a century. It is more likely that we are uncover-ing the relationship of petit-bourgeois identity to personal origins and family history, to political culture and social community, which introduced a myriad of distinctions within the social group itself. Against Kitson, against Roberts, stands the Corke family who feared and despised their inevitable contact with the working class. The very character of the British petite bourgeoisie means that so many of our unanswered questions are the most important: the precise questions of its relationship to the working class and to the larger bourgeoisie. If the shift in balance towards an identification with the latter is a general conclusion of this essay, that identification was never total and, more importantly, a dissection of the petit-bourgeois world would open up its own internal stratification. These were people whose changing economic and political character seem to have been shaped by forces, movements, transformations outside their own control, even influence. Yet the too-ready conclusion has been to see them as no more than the objects of history. This essay has sought to indicate their real historical and analytical importance for the study of British society in this period. Closer examination of the way in which different types of small producers and shopkeepers operated in relation to their communities, workforces and customers will enable us not only to differentiate more precisely within the small propertied groups, but also to understand their various relationships to the changing political and social structure of nineteenth-century Britain.

BIBLIOGRAPHICAL NOTE

More recent reading material includes the following: Michael Winstanley, *The Shopkeeper's World 1880–1914*, Manchester University Press, Manchester, 1983, is a useful but rather insubstantial survey. The oral evidence in the latter sections of the book is particularly interesting. For broader European comparisons see (in addition to the book of essays from which this one is drawn) my survey article 'The petite bourgeoisie in nineteenth-century Europe: problems and research' in Klaus Tenfelde (editor), *Internationale Forschungen zur Geschichte der Arbeiterschaft und Arbeiterbewegung*, Oldenbourg Verlag, Munich, 1984, and the references there.

NOTES

1. P. M. Jones, 'The rural bourgeoisie of the Southern Massif-Central: a contribution to the study of the social structure of *ancien régime* France', *Social History*, 4 (1979), especially 65–6. For other European countries see Geoffrey Crossick and Heinz-Gerhard Haupt (eds.), *Shopkeepers and Master Artisans in Nineteenth-Century Europe* (London, 1984).

2. Bédarida has calculated that small employers and shopkeepers formed nearly 10 per cent of the occupied population of London in 1851: F. Bédarida, 'Londres au milieu du XIXᵉ siècle: une analyse de structure sociale', *Annales E.S.C.* (1968), 292. For other towns see R. Gray, *The Labour Aristocracy in Victorian Edinburgh* (Oxford, 1976), 28; W. G. Rimmer, 'The industrial profile of Leeds, 1780–1840', Thoresby Society Publications 113, *Miscellany*, 14 (Leeds, 1967), 130–57; F. Bealey, 'Municipal politics in Newcastle-under-Lyme, 1835–1872', *North Staffordshire*

Journal of Field Studies, 3 (1963), 75; J. Foster, *Class Struggle and the Industrial Revolution: Early Industrial Capitalism in Three English Towns* (London, 1974), 76.

3. F. Bechhofer and B. Elliott, 'Persistence and change: the petite bourgeoisie in industrial society', *Archives européenes de sociologie*, 17 (1976), 81.

4. Cf. J. B. Jefferys, *Retail Trading in Britain 1850 – 1950* (Cambridge, 1954). The best surveys of the development of retail trading are D. Alexander, *Retailing in England during the Industrial Revolution* (London, 1970), and D. Davis, *A History of Shopping* (London, 1966).

5. R. Scola, 'Food markets and shops in Manchester, 1770 – 1870', *Journal of Historical Geography*, 1 (1975), 153 – 68; R. Scola, 'Retailing in the nineteenth-century town: some problems and possibilities', in J. H. Johnston and C. G. Pooley (eds.), *The Structure of Nineteenth-Century Cities* (London, 1982), 153 – 69.

6. G. Shaw and M. T. Wild, 'Retail patterns in the Victorian city', Institute of British Geographers, *Transactions*, 4 (1979), 280.

7. M. T. Wild and G. Shaw, 'Population distribution and retail provision: the case of the Halifax-Calder Valley area of West Yorkshire during the second half of the nineteenth century', *Journal of Historical Geography*, 1 (1975), 193 – 210.

8. The literature on increasing competition in the retail trades is dominated by the now rather dated, and in places speculative, study by Jefferys, op. cit. The only recent work is P. Mathias, *Retailing Revolution: A History of Multiple Retailing in the Food Trades based upon the Allied Suppliers Group of Companies* (London, 1967). See also the brief but valuable studies by F. G. Pennance and B. S. Yamey, 'Competition in the retail grocery trade 1850 – 1939', *Economica*, 22 (1955), 303 – 17, and B. S. Yamey, *The Economics of Retail Price Maintenance* (London, 1954), chs. 7 and 8. Contemporary work in Britain was very limited, but see H. W. Macrosty, *The Trust Movement in British Industry: A Study of Business Organisation* (London, 1907); and J. A. Rees, *The Grocery Trade. Its History and Romance* (London, 1910), vol. 2, 220 – 57. French social scientists were predictably far more interested in these questions. See Pierre Moride, *Les Maisons à succursales multiples en France et à l'étranger* (Paris, 1913), who has much to say on Britain, and L. Sénéchal, *La Concentration industrielle et commerciale en Angleterre* (Paris, 1909), chs. 8 and 9. For a close study of a single trade, there is only P. J. Atkins, 'The retail milk trade in London, c.1790 – 1914', *Economic History Review*, 2nd Series, 33 (1980), 522 – 37.

9. Moride, op. cit., 66 – 9.

10. 'In England, the rate of concentration by multiples has reached a quite remarkable degree of intensity', according to Moride, op. cit., 78. Shoes, grocery, pharmacy, bakers, booksellers, coal, dyers and cleaners, tailors, restaurants, milk, wine, tobacco all had major national chains. The most striking was amongst butchers, with no major chains elsewhere in Europe, while in Britain the three largest companies boasted 2,300 shops between them, ibid., 78 – 9. For the way that the multiples swept into one suburb in the 1890s, see H. J. Dyos, *Victorian Suburb: A Study of the Growth of Camberwell* (Leicester, 1966), 149 – 52.

11. H. W. Macrosty, *Trusts and the State: A Sketch of Competition* (London, 1901), 193.

12. Jefferys, op. cit., 16.

13. A. Briggs, *Friends of the People: The Centenary History of Lewis's* (London, 1956), 38.

14. Booth Collection (at the British Library of Political and Economic Science), B 133 f. 19.

15. Ibid., f. 34.

16. Cited in Jefferys, op. cit., 36.

17. Select Committee on the Shop Hours Regulation Bill, *Parliamentary Papers,* 1886, XII, Q. 274 – 82.

18. Booth Collection, B 134, f. 3; E. Porter, *Victorian Cambridge: Josiah Chater's Diaries 1844 – 1884* (Chichester, 1975), 63.

19. R. Samuel, 'The workshop of the world; steam power and hand technology in mid-Victorian Britain', *History Workshop*, 3 (1977), 6 – 72.

20. There are no systematic published data on size of firm in nineteenth-century Britain. In their absence, see J. H. Clapham, *An Economic History of Britain. vol. 2: The Early Railway Age, 1820 – 1850* (Cambridge, 1964 edn.), 33 – 5; P. Kropotkin, 'The small industries of Britain', *The Nineteenth Century*, 48 (1900), 256 – 71.

21. J. Benson, *The Penny Capitalists: A Study of Nineteenth-Century Working-Class Entrepreneurs* (Dublin, 1983).

22. An example of how tiny these operations could be is in J. Blackman, 'The development of the retail grocery trade in the nineteenth century', *Business History*, 9 (1967), 115 – 16; T. Vigne and A. Howkins, 'The small shopkeeper in industrial and market towns', in G. Crossick (ed.), *The Lower Middle Class in Britain 1870 – 1914* (London, 1976), 187 – 8.

23. G. I. H. Lloyd, *The Cutlery Trades: An Historical Essay in the Economics of Small-Scale Production* (London, 1913), 193; S. Pollard, *A History of Labour in Sheffield* (Liverpool, 1959), 157 – 8; H. Mayhew, *London Labour and the London Poor* (London, 1861); Dover edn. 1968, vol. 3, 228 – 29; E. P. Thompson and E. Yeo (eds.), *The Unknown Mayhew: Selections from the Morning Chronicle 1849 – 1850* (London, 1971), 390, 448 – 9; K. Brooker, 'The changing position of the small owner in the English shoemaking industry, 1860 – 1914', unpublished paper delivered to the 2nd Round Table on the European Petite Bourgeoisie in the Nineteenth Century, at the University of Bremen (1980), 4 – 5.

24. P. Joyce, *Work, Society and Politics: the Culture of the Factory in Later Victorian England* (Brighton, 1980).

25. G. C. Allen, *The Industrial Development of Birmingham and the Black Country 1860 – 1927* (London, 1929; 1966 ed.), 113. On London see G. Stedman Jones, *Outcast London: A Study in the Relationship between Classes in Victorian Society* (Oxford, 1971), 19 – 32, and Bédarida, op. cit.

26. Rimmer, op. cit.

27. Compare the German master artisans discussed by S. Volkov, *The Rise of Popular Antimodernism in Germany: The Urban Master Artisans, 1873 – 1896* (Princeton, 1978). C. Behagg, 'Masters and manufacturers: social valves and the matter unit of production in Birmingham 1800 – 1850', in Crossick and Haupt (eds.), op. cit.

28. On the London tailors see T. M. Parsinnen and I. J. Prothero, 'The London tailors' strike of 1834 and the collapse of the Grand National Consolidated Traders' Union: a police spy's report', *International Review of Social History*, 22 (1977), 65 – 107; on Birmingham and the Black Country, Allen, op. cit., and C. Behagg, 'Radical politics and conflict at the point of production: Birmingham 1815 – 1845. A

study in the relationship between the classes', University of Birmingham Ph.D. thesis, 1982; on Sheffield, Lloyd, op. cit.

29. On the business-like masters see Behagg in Crossick and Haupt (eds.), op. cit. Saddlers' and coachbuilders' ironmongers were one of the most nationally oriented of the factors referred to here. See Allen, op. cit., 130 – 1. For a helpful typology of the declining economic independence of craftsmen producers drawn into mercantile dependence, see H. D. Fong, *Triumph of the Factory System in England* (Tientsin, 1930), 9 – 11.

30. On London tailoring and furniture-making in the last quarter of the century in this connection, see Clapham, op. cit., vol. 2, 126.

31. For this discussion, see the paper by K. Brooker referred to already. I am very grateful to Keith Brooker for helpful discussions on this subject based on his doctoral research on the Northampton shoemaking industry.

32. Pollard, op. cit., 54; C. Erickson, *British Industrialists. Steel and Hosiery 1850 – 1950* (Cambridge, 1959), 94 – 102, 124. For workshop growth with small-scale machinery in the late nineteenth-century London clothing trades, see J. A. Schmiechen, 'State reform and the local economy: an aspect of industrialization in late-Victorian and Edwardian London', *Economic History Review*, 2nd Series, 28 (1975), 413 – 28.

33. P. Kropotkin, *Fields, Factories and Workshops* (London, 1912 edn.), 281.

34. Clapham, op. cit., vol. 3, 183. In cutlery-working, grinders and cutlers with a handful of employees took work from larger factories with excessive demand, Lloyd, op. cit., 196 – 7.

35. For brass see Allen, op. cit., 123 – 4. The words quoted are those of P. de Rousiers, *The Labour Question in Britain* (London, 1896), 95.

36. Allen, op. cit., 127, 136.

37. C. Booth, *Life and Labour of the People in London* (London, 1902 edn., Second Series), vol. 1, 234.

38. Allen, op. cit., 127, 140; Booth, op. cit., Second Series, vol. 3, 117 – 26; Clapham, op. cit., vol. 2, 122 – 3.

39. Pollard, op. cit., 202ff; Brooker, op. cit. On the impact of crisis, see G. Crossick and H. G. Haupt, 'Shopkeepers, Master Artisans and the Historian: the petite bourgeoisie in comparative perspective', in Crossick and Haupt, op. cit.

40. Evidence to the Fair Wages Committee, cited by Pollard, op. cit., 206.

41. de Rousiers, op. cit., 10. On business concentration see P. L. Payne, 'The emergence of the large-scale company in Great Britain, 1870 – 1914', *Economic History Review*, Second Series, 20 (1967), 519 – 42; L. Hannah, 'Mergers in British manufacturing industry, 1880 – 1918', *Oxford Economic Papers*, 26 (1964), 1 – 20.

42. de Rousiers, op. cit., 31.

43. For an example, see Geoffrey Crossick, *An Artisan Élite in Victorian Society: Kentish London 1840 – 1880* (London, 1978), 47 – 8. Of Northampton footwear firms failing in the years 1885 – 1912, 38 per cent had been in existence for less than two years, 60 per cent for less than five: Brooker, op. cit., 11.

44. Allen, op. cit., 294 – 5.

45. E. P. Thompson, *The Making of the English Working Class* (Harmondsworth, 1968 edn.), 781 – 915. Compare the abrupt dismissal by John Foster, who presents petit-bourgeois radicalism as little more than a response to working-class pressure on

vulnerable shopkeepers: Foster, op. cit., 131 – 3, 150.

46. J. Garrard, *Leaders and Politics in Nineteenth-Century Salford: A Historical Analysis of Urban Political Power* (Salford, n.d.), 20; T. J. Nossiter, 'Shopkeeper radicalism in the nineteenth century', in T. J. Nossiter (ed.), *Imagination and Precision in the Social Sciences* (London, 1972), 425.

47. This discussion of petit-bourgeois radicalism develops an argument presented in a comparative European framework in Geoffrey Crossick, 'The petite bourgeoisie in nineteenth-century Europe: problems and research', in K. Tenfelde (ed.), *Internationale Forschungen zur Geschichte der Arbeiterschaft und Arbeiterbewegung* (Munich, 1984).

48. J. Brewer, 'Commercialization and politics', in N. McKendrick, J. Brewer, and J. H. Plumb, *The Birth of a Consumer Society: the commercialization of 18th-century England* (London, 1982), 197 – 262.

49. Garrard, op. cit., 55 – 7.

50. J. Epstein, *The Lion of Freedom: Feargus O'Connor and the Chartist Movement, 1832 – 1842* (London, 1982), 24 ff.

51. D. Fraser, *Urban Politics in Victorian England. The Structure of Politics in Victorian Cities* (Leicester, 1976), 107.

52. Brewer, op. cit.

53. Behagg, 'Radical politics', op. cit., 337.

54. P. Hollis, *The Pauper Press: A Study in Working-Class Radicalism of the 1830s* (Oxford, 1970), 203 – 19; G. Stedman Jones, 'The Language of Chartism', in J. Epstein and D. Thompson (eds.), *The Chartist Experience: Studies in Working-Class Radicalism and Culture, 1830 – 1860* (London, 1982), 3 – 58.

55. I. Prothero, *Artisans and Politics in Early Nineteenth Century London: John Gast and his Times* (Folkestone, 1979).

56. D. Jones, *Chartism and the Chartists* (London, 1975), 25; J. T. Ward, *Chartism* (London, 1973), 96; R. S. Neale, *Class and Ideology in the Nineteenth Century* (London, 1972), 54 – 8; J. Epstein, 'Some organizational and cultural aspects of the Chartist movement in Nottingham', in Epstein and Thompson, op. cit., 227 – 32; K. Tiller, 'Late Chartism: Halifax 1847 – 58', ibid., 335 – 6.

57. J. F. C. Harrison, 'Chartism in Leeds', in A. Briggs (ed.), *Chartist Studies* (London, 1959), 65 – 98.

58. P. T. Phillips, *The Sectarian Spirit: Sectarianism, Society, and Politics in Victorian Cotton Towns* (Toronto, 1982), 24; R. J. Morris, 'Samuel Smiles and the genesis of *Self-Help*: the retreat to a petit bourgeois utopia', *Historical Journal*, 24 (1981), 97. For a valuable discussion of changing petit-bourgeois political ideology from these early nineteenth-century roots, see Bechhofer and Elliott, op. cit.

59. D. Goodway, *London Chartism* (Cambridge, 1982), 74 – 8.

60. Morris, op. cit.

61. Joyce, op. cit., 317.

62. J. Cornford, 'The transformation of conservatism in the late nineteenth century', *Victorian Studies*, 7 (1963), 65.

63. K. Young, *London Politics and the Rise of Party* (Leicester, 1975), 90.

64. F. Bullen, *Confessions of a Tradesman* (London, 1908), 158.

65. O. Anderson, 'The Administrative Reform Association 1855 – 1857', in P. Hollis (ed.), *Pressure from Without in Early Victorian England* (London, 1974), 275.

66. J. Field, ' "When the Riot Act was Read": a pub mural of the Battle of Southsea, 1874', *History Workshop*, 10 (1980), 152 – 63.

67. G. Crossick, 'Shopkeepers and the State in Britain 1870 – 1914', in Crossick and Haupt (eds.), op. cit.

68. E. P. Hennock, 'Finance and politics in urban local government in England, 1835 – 1900', *Historical Journal*, 6 (1963), 217; Bealey, op. cit., 74 – 5; Garrard, op. cit., 64 – 5; E. P. Hennock, *Fit and Proper Persons: Ideal and Reality in Nineteenth-Century Urban Local Government* (London, 1973), 31 – 3; A. Offer, *Property and Politics 1870 – 1914: Landownership, Law, Ideology and Urban Development in England* (Cambridge, 1981), 121 – 2, 288 – 9.

69. D. Englander, *Landlord and Tenant in Urban Britain 1838 – 1918* (Oxford, 1983), 55 – 7. For associations of this type, see T. C. Barker and J. R. Harris, *A Merseyside Town in the Industrial Revolution: St Helens 1750 – 1900* (London, 1959), 291; Garrard, op. cit., 66. See also the organizations of Blackpool lodging-house owners discussed in J. Walton, *The Blackpool Landlady: a Social History* (Manchester, 1978), Chapter 8.

70. Englander, op. cit., 69 – 70.

71. E. Bristow, 'The Liberty and Property Defence League and Individualism', *Historical Journal*, 18 (1975), 761 – 89; N. Soldon, 'Laissez-faire as dogma: the Liberty and Property Defence League, 1882 – 1914', in K. Brown (ed.), *Essays in Anti-Labour History* (London, 1974), 208 – 33; K. Brown, 'The Anti-Socialist Union', ibid., 234 – 61.

72. On these see Anne Summers, 'The character of Edwardian Nationalism: three popular Leagues', in P. Kennedy and A. Nicholls (eds.), *Nationalist and Racialist Movements in Britain and Germany before 1914* (London, 1981), 68 – 87.

73. M. J. Daunton, *Coal Metropolis. Cardiff 1870 – 1914* (Leicester, 1977), 165 – 6.

74. *The Referee*, 11 Feb. 1906.

75. Ibid., Feb. to Apr. 1906.

76. See the general nature of the suggested programme in *The Elector* (March 1909).

77. de Rousiers, op. cit., 33 – 4.

78. H. McLeod, *Class and Religion in the Late Victorian City* (London, 1974), 61 – 2.

79. Daunton, op. cit., 155 – 8.

80. B. Preston, *Occupation of Father and Son in Mid-Victorian England*, Reading Geographical Papers (1977), 31. For the struggle of H. G. Wells's parents to find an occupation for him of acceptable status, see his *Experiment in Autobiography* (London, 1934), 103 – 52.

81. The church or chapel community was one means of protecting the choice of marriage partner. See Foster, op. cit., 164 – 9.

82. B. Elliott and D. McCrone, 'Landlords in Edinburgh: some preliminary findings', *Sociological Review*, 23 (1975), 548 – 9, 559.

83. See especially H. Corke, *In Our Infancy. An Autobiography, Part I: 1882 – 1912* (Cambridge, 1975); Norman Nicholson, *Wednesday Early Closing* (London, 1975); N. Griffiths, *Shops Book. Brighton 1900 – 1930* (Queenspark Book, Brighton, n.d.).

84. Corke, op. cit., 38, 44–5; P. Thompson, *The Edwardians* (London, 1977 edn.), 125–8.

85. Case studies remain few, but see P. J. Dixon, 'The lower middle class child in the grammar school: a Lancashire industrial town 1850–1875', in P. Searby (ed.), *Educating the Victorian Middle Class* (Leicester, 1982), 57–70.

86. Preston, op. cit., 17–28; Crossick, *An Artisan Elite*, 115–16.

87. R. Anderson, 'Secondary education in mid-nineteenth century France. Some social aspects', *Past and Present*, 53 (1971), 121–46; P. J. Harrigan, 'Secondary education and the professions in France during the Second Empire', *Comparative Studies in Society and History*, 17 (1975), esp. 358–9.

88. On Birmingham, see D. Smith, *Conflict and Compromise: Class Formation in English Society, 1830–1914* (London, 1982), 180. Also see W. E. Marsden, 'Schools for the urban lower middle class: third grade or higher grade?', in Searby (ed.), op. cit., 45–56.

89. Wells, op. cit., 60.

90. T. Lummis, 'The East Anglian Fishermen: 1880–1914', University of Essex Ph.D. thesis, 1981.

91. Bullen, op. cit., 120, 172.

92. Cf. D. Blackbourn, *Class, Religion and Local Politics in Wilhelmine Germany. The Centre Party in Wurttemberg before 1914* (New Haven, 1980), 108 ff.; A. Corbin, *Archaïsme et modernité en Limousin au XIXe siècle, 1845–1880* (Paris, 1975), 305.

93. Corke, op. cit., 56–7.

94. C. Hall, 'The butcher, the baker, the candlestickmaker: the shop and the family in the Industrial Revolution', in E. Whitelegg *et al.* (eds.), *The Changing Experience of Women* (London, 1982), 2–16.

95. P. Searby, 'The schooling of Kipps. The education of lower middle class boys in England, 1860–1918', in Searby (ed.), op. cit., 123–4.

96. For this ideology in Edinburgh, see R. Q. Gray, 'Religion, culture and social class in late nineteenth and early twentieth century Edinburgh', in Crossick (ed.), op. cit., 149–50.

97. Some comments on the instability of small enterprise are in Bechhofer and Elliott, op. cit., 91.

98. Phillips, op. cit., 95.

99. Bealey, op. cit., and also his 'Municipal politics in Newcastle-under-Lyme, 1872–1914', *North Staffordshire Journal of Field Studies*, 5 (1965), 64–73; Hennock, *Fit and Proper Persons*, op. cit., 315; Garrard, op. cit., 91.

100. Hennock, *Fit and Proper Persons*, op. cit., 17–176.

101. In 1875 some 80 per cent of Edinburgh councillors were landlords: B. Elliott, D. McCrone and V. Skelton, 'Property and political power: Edinburgh 1875–1975', in J. Garrard *et al.* (eds.), *The Middle Class in Politics* (Farnborough, 1978), 103.

102. Select Committee on the Small Tenements Act, *Parliamentary Papers*, 1859. 2, VII, Q 138–9.

103. On house-owners, Englander, op. cit., 60.

104. Garrard, op. cit., 16.

105. Hennock, *Fit and Proper Persons*, op. cit., 316.

106. H. J. Dyos, 'The speculative builders and developers of Victorian London', *Victorian Studies*, 11 (1967–8), 641–90.

107. D. J. Olsen, 'House upon House', in H. J. Dyos and M. Wolff (eds.), *The Victorian City: Images and Reality*, vol. 1 (London, 1973), 335.

108. Select Committee on Town Holdings, *Parliamentary Papers* (1886), XII, Q 7875 – 76.

109. For evidence of this see J. Burnett, *A Social History of Housing* (Newton Abbot, 1978), 69; J. Treble, 'Liverpool working-class housing 1801 – 1851', in S. D. Chapman (ed.), *The History of Working-Class Housing. A Symposium* (Newton Abbot, 1971), 191 – 2, 213; J. Butt, 'Working-class housing in Glasgow, 1851 – 1914', ibid., 79; Elliott and McCrone, op. cit., 542; Pollard, op. cit., 21, 101; Daunton, op. cit., 114 – 21; R. S. Holmes, 'Ownership and migration from a study of rate books', *Area*, 5 (1973), 245 – 6. Evidence from all over the country for the early part of the century appears in Appendix B2 to the Royal Commission on the Poor Laws, *Parliamentary Papers*, 1834, XXXVI.

110. Bechhofer and Elliott, op. cit., 86.

111. S. Taylor, 'The political implications of urbanisation, with specific reference to the working-class housing market in Nottingham, 1830 – 1850', University of Essex M. A. thesis, 1977, 60 – 91.

112. Royal Commission on the Housing of the Working Classes, *Parliamentary Papers*, 1884 – 85, XXX, Q 6813 – 16; Pollard, op. cit., 101; S. Meacham, *A Life Apart. The English Working Class 1890 – 1914* (London, 1977), 34.

113. Englander, op. cit., 11.

114. Ibid., 15 – 16, 22 – 32.

115. Royal Commission on the Poor Laws, op. cit., 31, 171.

116. Royal Commission on the Housing of the Working Classes, op. cit., Q 6801 – 04.

117. Select Committee on the Small Tenements Act, op. cit., *passim.*

118. *The Grocer*, 6 Mar. 1909, 696.

119. Bullen, op. cit., 160. On the practice of adulteration in the mid-Victorian period, see the evidence to the Select Committee on the Adulteration of Food, *Parliamentary Papers*, 1856, VIII; Select Committee on the Adulteration of Food Act (1872), *Parliamentary Papers*, 1874, VI.

120. Foster, op. cit., 131 – 4; J. Vincent, *The Formation of the British Liberal Party* (London, 1966), 101 – 3; Nossiter, op. cit., 428.

121. On the diversity of small shopkeepers and their social situations, see Vigne and Howkins, op. cit., 184 – 209.

122. A. Briggs, 'Social structure and politics in Birmingham and Lyons (1825 – 1848)', *British Journal of Sociology*, 1 (1950), 67 – 80; T. R. Tholfsen, 'The artisan and the culture of early Victorian Birmingham', *University of Birmingham Historical Journal*, 4 (1954), 144 – 66.

123. C. O. Reid, 'Middle class values and working class culture in nineteenth-century Sheffield', University of Sheffield Ph.D. thesis, 1976; D. J. Rowe, 'The failure of London Chartism', *Historical Journal*, 11 (1968), 472 – 87.

124. de Rousiers, op. cit., 5 – 7.

125. I recognize of course that there is good eighteenth-century evidence of growing conflict within artisanal production—see C. R. Dobson, *Masters and Journeymen* (London, 1980). It is a matter of degree.

126. See Behagg's essay in Crossick and Haupt (eds.), and his thesis, both referred

to already, as well as his 'Custom, class and change: the trade societies of Birmingham', *Social History*, 4 (1979), 455 – 80.

127. See Parsinnen and Prothero, op. cit.; Prothero, op. cit.; Goodway, op. cit., 9.

128. Lloyd, op. cit., 195, 203; Booth, op. cit., vol. 5, 117; on inspection see Schmiechen, op. cit., 417 – 22.

129. P. E. Razzell and R. W. Wainwright (eds.), *The Victorian Working Class: Selections from the Morning Chronicle* (London, 1973), 183.

130. Select Committee on Master and Servant, *Parliamentary Papers*, 1866, XIII, Q 1372 – 80.

131. Parsinnen and Prothero, op. cit.

132. Report of the Truck Commissioners, *Parliamentary Papers*, 1871, XXIII, p. xxviii. On foggers, see Allen, op. cit., 128.

133. J. R. Oliver, *The Development and Structure of the Furniture Industry* (Oxford, 1966), 70. For shopkeeper middlemen in cabinet-making, see Mayhew, op. cit., 223, and as lumpers, ibid., 290 – 2.

134. Children's Employment Commission. *Parliamentary Papers*, 1864, XXII, 102 – 3; Crossick, *An Artisan Élite*, 114; E. J. Hobsbawm, *Labouring Men: Studies in the History of Labour* (London, 1964), 296.

135. For the way that many small masters stayed within an artisanal social world, see Gray, *Labour Aristocracy*, 134 – 5.

136. For a broader discussion of the problems posed by the petite bourgeoisie for the study of social mobility, see Crossick, 'The petite bourgeoisie'.

137. R. Roberts, *The Classic Slum: Salford Life in the First Quarter of the Century* (Harmondsworth, 1973), 81 – 2.

138. Griffith, op. cit., 53 – 60.

139. M. Tebbutt, *Making Ends Meet: Pawnbroking and Working-Class Credit* (Leicester, 1983), 35.

140. Goodway, op. cit., 114 – 16; D. Smith, 'Tonypandy 1910: Definitions of Community', *Past and Present*, 87 (1980), 158 – 84.

141. R. J. Morris, 'The rise of James Kitson: trades union and mechanics institution, Leeds, 1826 – 1851', Publications of the Thoresby Society, *Miscellany*, 15, 187.

8

The Victorian Middle Classes: Wealth, Occupation, and Geography*

W. D. RUBINSTEIN

The question of who earned the largest personal fortunes in Britain during the nineteenth century is one which has hitherto been neither asked nor answered. More surprisingly, neither has the larger question of which elements, occupational and geographical, predominated within the Victorian middle class been subject to serious research. Both of these are of considerable importance to the social and economic historian, for our common perception of British history during the nineteenth century rests upon several tacit assumptions which remain untested and which may or may not be correct. The chief among these are that the wealthiest men of nineteenth-century England, apart from the great landowners, were engaged in industry and manufacturing, in trades which were a direct part of the Industrial Revolution; that the nineteenth-century middle class consisted primarily of industrialists and manufacturers; and that the new towns of the north of England brought into existence a group of middle-class industrialists sufficient in wealth and numbers to constitute the dominant element in Victorian society. None of these assumptions, it will be suggested here, is correct, and any view of Victorian society which subscribes to them must stand in need of revision.[1]

This article emerges from research undertaken on the top wealthholders of Britain deceased between the early nineteenth century and 1939, based upon the valuation figures in the probate records at Somerset House, the Public Record Office, in Edinburgh, York, and Preston.[2] In the course of this research, a catalogue of all persons leaving £100,000 or more in Britain since 1809, when these sources begin in a usable form,[3] was compiled, although most attention centred on those wealthholders leaving £500,000 or more

* From *Economic History Review*, 2nd series, 30 (4) (1977), 602–23. Reprinted by permission of the author and the editors of *Economic History Review*. A fuller development of the topics treated here is now to be found in W. D. Rubinstein, *Men of Property: The very Wealthy in Britain since the Industrial Revolution* (London, 1981).

between 1809 and 1939, and on two groups of lesser wealthy, those leaving between £160,000 and £500,000 between 1809 and 1829, and those with estates worth between £250,000 and £500,000 in the period 1850 – 69.[4] During the nineteenth century until 1898 the probate calendars recorded the global value of the gross unsettled personalty of all persons, testate or intestate, leaving property in Britain (or within the jurisdiction of that probate court), while between 1898 and 1925 the valuation figure consisted of gross unsettled personalty and settled land.[5] Although imperfect in several respects, the probate calendars contain comprehensive and objective information on the personal wealth of the entire British population, and the purposes to which they may be put are manifold.[6]

Several methodological problems are involved in identifying personal wealthholding with estates left at death. Among these are the problem of gifts *inter vivos* or of deliberate estate duty avoidance; and the comparability of valuation conventions when applied to different types of assets, especially limited liability companies compared with private partnerships. There is an obvious possibility that either or both of these factors may have affected the findings of this article in the sense that, compared with other businessmen, manufacturers may, during their lifetime, have passed a significantly larger fraction of their business assets to relatives in the interests of their firm's continuity.

It must be realized that there is no precise way in which the accuracy of any of these contentions may be established, since the identity of wealthholders escaping the death duty net cannot be *comprehensively* traced from other sources. From 1881 account duty was levied on gifts *inter vivos* made three (later twelve) months or less before death; its yield was described as 'trifling' by Sydney Buxton and George Stapylton Barnes in *A Handbook to the Death Duties* (1890), p. 13. Although the accuracy of valuation conventions would surely have been affected by the spread of limited liability, in fact the final cohorts of wealthholders show the lead of commerce over manufacturing much as do those of the mid-century, a picture confirmed as well by the income-tax figures, which are derived from entirely different sources. If any group of wealthholders was likely to be under-represented here, it is not the manufacturers but the merchants and merchant bankers of London, whose businesses remain private partnerships or private limited companies to this day.

I

The first section of this article examines the occupational structure and geographical venues of Britain's wealthholders deceased between the early nineteenth century and 1914.

Between 1809 and 1914, the total of deceased male British wealthholders at each level of wealth discussed here and by period of death was:[7]

	1809−58	*1858−79*	*1880−99*	*1900−14*
Millionaires	12	34	69	89
Half-millionaires	62	120	177	206
	1809−29	*1850−69*		
Lesser wealthy	*192*	*186*		

The occupational distribution of these estates was not an even one, but clustered primarily among a limited number of fields. Ranked according to the Orders of the Standard Industrial Classification,[8] the distribution of the occupations in which these fortunes were earned[9] appears in the shape of a capital 'E', with Orders I, II, and III—agriculture, mining, and the production of food, drink, and tobacco—and Orders XIX, XX, and XXI—transport, distribution, and finance—containing the bulk of the wealthholders, and Order X—textiles—forming the crossbar. Yet even among these well-represented trades it is clear that the wealthy earned their fortunes disproportionately in commerce, finance, and transport—that is, as merchants, bankers, shipowners, merchant bankers, and stock and insurance brokers—rather than as manufacturers and industrialists. This is apparent in Tables 1 − 3, which record the occupations of the wealthholders according to

Table 1. *Distribution of Millionaires by S.I.C.*
(percentage of known, non-landed total in brackets)

Order		*1809−58*	*1858−79*	*1880−99*	*1900−14*
			Deceased		
I.	Agriculture	3	4	10	14
II.	Mining	—	2 (6.7)	2 (3.4)	2 (2.7)
III.	Food, drink, tobacco	—	1 (3.3)	14(23.7)	14(19.2)
IV.	Chemicals	—	—	3 (5.1)	2 (2.7)
V.	Metals	1(11.1)	5(16.7)	3 (5.1)	1 (1.4)
VI.	Engineering	—	—	1 (1.7)	3 (4.1)
VII.	Shipbuilding	—	1 (3.3)	2 (3.4)	2 (2.7)
VIII.	Vehicles	—	—	1 (1.7)	1 (1.4)
IX.	Miscellaneous metals	1(11.1)	—	1 (1.7)	—
X.	Textiles	2(22.2)	4(13.3)	5 (8.5)	8(11.0)
XI.	Leather	—	—	—	—
XII.	Clothing	—	—	—	—
XIII.	Bricks, glass, pottery	—	—	—	—
XIV.	Timber, furniture	—	—	—	—
XV.	Paper, publishing	—	—	1 (1.7)	—
XVI.	Miscellaneous manufacturing	—	—	—	—
XVII.	Construction	1(11.1)	1 (3.3)	3 (5.1)	1 (1.4)
XVIII.	Gas, water	—	—	—	—
XIX.	Transport	1(11.1)	1 (3.3)	3 (5.1)	7 (9.6)
XX.	Distribution	—	3(10.0)	7(11.9)	9(12.3)
XXI.	Finance	2(22.2)	12(40.0)	13(22.0)	22(30.1)
XXII.	Professionals	—	—	—	1 (1.4)
XXIII.	Other services	—	—	—	—
XXIV.	Government, defence	1(11.1)	—	—	—
	Miscellaneous, unknown	—	—	—	2
	Total categorized non-landed	9	30	59	73

Table 2. *Distribution of Half-Millionaires by S.I.C.*
(percentage of known, non-landed total in brackets)

			Deceased		
Order		1809–58	1858–79	1880–99	1900–14
I.	Agriculture	11	16	15	22
II.	Mining	—	1 (1.0)	7 (4.4)	11 (6.1)
III.	Food, drink, tobacco	1 (2.1)	3 (2.9)	23(14.6)	21(11.6)
IV.	Chemicals	1 (2.1)	—	8 (5.1)	5 (2.8)
V.	Metals	5(10.6)	12(11.8)	7 (4.4)	13 (7.2)
VI.	Engineering	—	1 (1.0)	4 (2.5)	4 (2.2)
VII.	Shipbuilding	—	—	—	1 (0.6)
VIII.	Vehicles	—	—	1 (0.6)	2 (1.1)
IX.	Miscellaneous metals	1 (2.1)	1 (1.0)	2 (1.3)	2 (1.1)
X.	Textiles	4 (8.5)	13(11.8)	23(14.6)	11 (6.1)
XI.	Leather	—	—	—	1 (0.6)
XII.	Clothing	—	—	—	—
XIII.	Bricks, glass, pottery	—	—	2 (1.3)	2 (1.1)
XIV.	Timber, furniture	—	—	—	1 (0.6)
XV.	Paper, publishing	1 (2.1)	4 (3.9)	4 (2.5)	7 (3.9)
XVI.	Miscellaneous manufacturing	—	—	—	—
XVII.	Construction	—	3 (2.9)	6 (3.8)	3 (1.7)
XVIII.	Gas, water	—	—	—	1 (0.6)
XIX.	Transport	2 (4.3)	5 (4.9)	9 (5.1)	13 (7.2)
XX.	Distribution	15(31.9)	25(24.5)	23(14.6)	44(24.3)
XXI.	Finance	10(21.3)	30(29.4)	34(21.5)	34(18.8)
XXII.	Professionals	1 (2.1)	5 (4.9)	4 (2.5)	4 (2.2)
XXIII.	Other services	1 (2.1)	—	1 (0.6)	—
XXIV.	Government, defence	5(10.6)	—	—	1 (0.6)
	Miscellaneous, unknown	3	2	4	3
	Total categorized non-landed	47	102	158	181

the Standard Industrial Classification. To make this point more concisely, it would help to assimilate the various Orders into a more convenient form. In Table 4, Orders II and IV-XVII (except for newspaper proprietors and publishers, classed according to the S.I.C. with paper manufacturers in Order XV) are termed 'industrial'; the 'food and drink' category here includes the brewers, distillers, foodstuff, and tobacco manufacturers of Order III, to distinguish them from the more strictly industrial categories.[10] Those wealthholders engaged in trades in Orders XIX-XXI are numbered in the 'commerce' category. Among the 'professional, public administration, and defence' wealthholders have been classed the newspaper proprietors and publishers.

It is evident from Table 4 that fortunes earned in commerce and finance were either the majority or the plurality of Britain's non-landed wealth among most of the cohorts in this study: indeed, of all the cohorts except among the nine millionaires deceased prior to 1858 and among the millionaire and half-millionaire groups deceased in 1880 – 99. Moreover, except among the first millionaire cohort, at no time did manufacturing in the strict sense

W. D. Rubinstein

Table 3. *Distribution of Lesser Wealthy by S.I.C.*
(percentage of known, non-landed total in brackets)

		Deceased	
Order		1809–29	1850–69
I.	Agriculture	32	32
II.	Mining	1 (0.7)	3 (2.2)
III.	Food, drink, tobacco	8 (6.0)	10 (7.2)
IV.	Chemicals	3 (2.5)	4 (2.9)
V.	Metals	2 (1.5)	4 (2.9)
VI.	Engineering	1 (0.7)	4 (2.9)
VII.	Shipbuilding	1 (0.7)	—
VIII.	Vehicles	—	2 (1.4)
IX.	Miscellaneous metals	—	3 (2.2)
X.	Textiles	5 (3.7)	17(12.3)
XI.	Leather	—	—
XII.	Clothing	—	—
XIII.	Bricks, glass, pottery	1 (0.7)	1 (0.7)
XIV.	Timber	—	1 (0.7)
XV.	Paper, publishing	1 (0.7)	2 (1.4)
XVI.	Miscellaneous manufacturing	—	2 (1.4)
XVII.	Construction	1 (0.7)	3 (2.2)
XVIII.	Gas, water	1 (0.7)	—
XIX.	Transport	3 (2.5)	4 (2.9)
XX.	Distribution	35(26.1)	37(26.8)
XXI.	Finance	28(20.9)	32(23.2)
XXII.	Professionals	17(12.7)	3 (2.2)
XXIII.	Other services	4 (3.0)	—
XXIV.	Public admin., defence	22(16.4)	6 (4.3)
	Miscellaneous	1	1
	Unknown	25	15
	Total categorized non-landed	134	138

Table 4. *Occupations of Wealthholders, Concise Ranking*
(percentage of known, non-landed total in brackets)

		Millionaires			
		1809–58	1858–79	1880–99	1900–14
I.	Manufacturing	5(55.5)	13(43.3)	22(37.3)	20(27.4)
	Food, drink, tobacco	0	1 (3.3)	14(23.7)	14(19.2)
II.	Commercial	3(33.3)	16(53.3)	23(39.0)	38(52.1)
III.	Professional, pub. defence, admin.	1(11.1)	—	—	1 (1.4)
		Half-Millionaires			
I.	Manufacturing	11(22.9)	32(31.7)	60(38.0)	59(32.6)
	Food, drink, tobacco	1 (2.0)	2 (2.0)	23(14.6)	22(12.2)
II.	Commercial	28(58.3)	60(59.4)	66(41.8)	91(50.3)
III.	Professional, etc.	8(16.7)	7 (6.9)	9 (5.7)	9 (5.0)
		Lesser Wealthy			
		1809–29	1850–69		
I.	Manufacturing	17(12.7)	44(31.9)		
	Food, drink, tobacco	8 (5.8)	12 (8.7)		
II.	Commercial	66(49.3)	73(52.9)		
III.	Professional, etc.	43(32.1)	9 (6.5)		

lead commerce as the origin of great fortunes, even in the 1880 – 99 period. Although the proportion of commercial wealthholders declined to as low as 39 per cent of the 1880 – 99 millionaire cohort, in the early twentieth century the significance of commerce in the wealth structure again increased and once more supplied the majority of top fortunes. Despite the Industrial Revolution, the most important element in Britain's wealth structure during the nineteenth century, apart from landed wealth, was commerce and finance.

Two aspects of the distribution outlined above require some special comments. One is the place of industrialists among the wealthy. There are numerous examples of immensely wealthy nineteenth-century manufacturers and industrialists—millionaires like Richard Crawshay (1739 – 1810), the Cyfarthfa ironmaster, Sir Robert Peel, 1st Bt (1750 – 1830), or Richard Arkwright (1755 – 1843)—but the typical successful manufacturer appears to have left an estate in the range of £100,000 after the mid-century, and rather less before. Among the well-known politico-industrialists at or around this level were William E. Forster (1818 – 86), who left £81,574; John Bright (1811 – 89), £86,289; Charles T. Ritchie, first Baron Ritchie of Dundee (1838 – 1906), £116,245; and Joseph Chamberlain (1836 – 1914), £125,495, as did the various members of the Ashworth cotton family deceased in this period.[11] Many successful industrialists left far less—for example, Anthony J. Mundella (1825 – 97), who left £42,619, or the Manchester umbrella-cloth manufacturer Frederick Engels (1820 – 95), who left £25,000. The level of wealth required to place a manufacturer firmly within the servant-keeping middle class was lower still, perhaps as low as a few thousand pounds.

The extraordinarily high percentage of early wealthholders, particularly those among the lesser wealthy deceased in 1809 – 29, engaged in the professions, public administration, and defence, also requires some comment. It will be seen that the percentage among these groups declined considerably between 1829 and 1850. This was Old Corruption, the beneficiaries of government contract and holders of government place, and their significance in the wealth structure virtually ceased after about 1840. Men like John, first Earl of Eldon (1751 – 1838), the celebrated Lord Chancellor, who left £700,000; the government provision contractor Sir Charles Flower (1763 – 1834), worth £500,000; or the army agent Alexander Adair (1739 – 1834), whose estate totalled £700,000, were as typical a part of the British wealth structure at this time as Hargreaves or Stephenson.

If it was on the commercial or financial side of the Victorian business world that the great fortunes were disproportionately to be found, it would seem to be a corollary that the centre of wealth-making in nineteenth-century Britain was London rather than the industrial towns of the north of England. This was, indeed, the case, although it would evidently be a gross oversimplification merely to identify London with commerce and the north with industry. Nevertheless, most top London fortunes were left by those in commerce and finance, while most of the fortunes of the north were earned in manufacturing, despite the wealth of merchants in provincial trade centres like Liverpool, Glasgow, Leeds, and elsewhere. Assigning each non-landed wealthholder to the locality or conurbation in which his fortune was earned—where his bank, factory, mine, or shops were located—a pattern of geographical distribution is indicated as favourable to London as the occupational distribution demonstrated the lead of commerce.[12] This is indicated in Tables 5 – 8.

Among millionaires, London was the venue for between about 39 and 63 per cent of the total number in each cohort; among half-millionaires, for between 38 and 64 per cent; while among the lesser wealthy London's lead was even clearer. The six conurbations making up the heart of industrial England in Lancashire and the West Riding accounted for no more than some 25 per cent of the most favourable millionaire cohort, and for between 18 and 27 per cent of the half-millionaire groups. As with the place of commerce in the occupational distribution, London's lead, although less marked at the close of the nineteenth century; was never lost.

Table 5. *Number of Millionaires, by Geographical Origin and Date of Death*

Area	1809–58	1858–79	1880–99	1900–14
1. City of London	4	14	11	24
2. Other London	1	2	9	15
3. Outer London	—	—	1	1
4. Greater Manchester	—	2	2	2
5. Merseyside	—	1	8	2
6. West Yorkshire	—	2	2	4
7. South Yorkshire	—	—	—	—
8. West Midlands	—	—	2	—
9. Tyneside	—	1	1	4
10. Clydeside	—	2	4	8
11. East Anglia	—	1	1	—
12. Bristol	—	—	1	5
13. South-west England	—	—	—	—
14. Other south England	—	—	—	—
15. Ribblesdale	1	—	1	—
16. Mid-Lancashire	—	—	1	—
17. Notts.-Derby-Burton	1	1	4	1
18. Other Midlands	—	—	2	—
19. South Wales	1	2	2	1
20. Tees-side	—	—	1	1
21. Humberside	—	—	—	—
22. Other north England	—	—	—	—
23. Edinburgh	—	—	—	1
24. Other Scotland	—	1	—	—
25. Belfast	—	—	—	1
26. Dublin	—	1	—	—
27. Other Ireland	—	—	1	—
Total	8	30	54	70

Table 6. *Number of Half-Millionaires, by Geographical Origin and Date of Death*

Area	1809–58	1858–79	1880–99	1900–14
1. City of London	15	37	40	40
2. Other London	9	9	19	22
3. Outer London	1	1	3	3
4. Greater Manchester	1	11	15	12
5. Merseyside	2	10	8	13
6. West Yorkshire	2	4	3	12
7. South Yorkshire	—	3	3	5
8. West Midlands	2	2	3	3
9. Tyneside	—	3	7	12
10. Clydeside	1	6	11	13
11. East Anglia	—	1	2	2
12. Bristol	1	1	2	1
13. South-west England	—	1	3	—
14. Other south England	—	—	1	2
15. Ribblesdale	2	—	2	2
16. Mid-Lancashire	—	—	1	2
17. Notts,-Derby-Burton	—	3	3	7
18. Other Midlands	—	—	6	3
19. South Wales	3	2	—	4
20. Tees-side	—	2	2	2
21. Humberside	—	—	—	3
22. Other north England	—	—	—	—
23. Edinburgh	—	—	3	3
24. Other Scotland	—	—	2	2
25. Belfast	—	—	1	1
26. Dublin	—	—	1	1
27. Other Ireland	—	—	—	—
Total	39	96	141	170

Table 7. *Number of Lesser Wealthy, by Geographical Origin and Date of Death*

Area	1809–29	1850–69
1. City of London	59	43
2. Other London	31	21
3. Outer London	2	1
4. Greater Manchester	6	14
5. Merseyside	2	5
6. West Yorkshire	2	—
7. South Yorkshire	—	—
8. West Midlands	4	4
9. Tyneside	2	3
10. Clydeside	—	3
11. East Anglia	4	1
12. Bristol	3	5
13. South-west England	3	1
14. Other south England	—	2
15. Ribblesdale	—	1
16. Mid-Lancashire	—	—
17. Notts.-Derby-Burton	3	7
18. Other Midlands	2	1

Table 7—*cont'd*

19.	South Wales	—	1
20.	Tees-side	—	—
21.	Humberside	—	—
22.	Other north England	—	—
23.	Edinburgh	—	2
24.	Other Scotland	—	—
25.	Belfast	—	—
26.	Dublin	—	—
27.	Other Ireland	—	—
	Unknown	22	13
	Total known	123	115

Table 8. *Largest British Fortunes (£2 m. or more), 1809 – 1914*

	Name, occupation, venue	*Valuation* (000)
1.	George, first Duke of Sutherland (1758 – 1833), landowner	'Upper Value'*
2.	Nathan M. Rothschild (1777 – 1836), merchant banker in London	'Upper Value'†
3.	James Morrison (1789 – 1857), warehouseman and merchant banker in London	*c*. £4,000 – 6,000‡
4.	Sir Isaac L. Goldsmid, 1st Bt (1778 – 1859), bullion broker and merchant banker in London	*c*. £2,000§
5.	William Baird (1796 – 1864), ironmaster in Lanarkshire, etc.	£2,000
6.	Richard Thornton (1776 – 1865), insurance broker and Baltic merchant in London	£2,800
7.	William Crawshay (1788 – 1867), ironmaster in South Wales	£2,000
8.	Thomas Brassey (1805 – 70), railway contractor	£3,200
9.	Giles Loder (1786 – 1871), Russia merchant in London	£2,900
10.	Baron Mayer A. de Rothschild (1818 – 74), merchant banker in London	£2,100
11.	Lionel N. de Rothschild (1808 – 74), merchant banker in London	£2,700
12.	Samuel J. Loyd, first Baron Overstone (1796 – 1883), banker in London	£2,119‖
13.	Herman, Baron de Stern (1815 – 87), merchant banker in London	£3,545
14.	Hugh McCalmont (1809 – 87), stockbroker and foreign merchant in London	£3,122
15.	John Rylands (1801 – 88), cotton manufacturer in Wigan	£2,575
16.	Sir Andrew B. Walker, 1st Bt (1824 – 93), brewer in Liverpool	£2,877
17.	Andrew Montagu (1815 – 95), landowner	£2,005
18.	John Gretton (1833 – 99), brewer in Burton	£2,884
19.	William Orme Foster (1814 – 99), ironmaster in Stourbridge	£2,588
20.	William R. Sutton (1836 – 1900), carrier in London	£2,119
21.	John, third Marquess of Bute (1847 – 1900), landowner	£2,067
22.	Samuel Lewis (1837 – 1901), money-lender in London¶	£2,671
23.	William, sixth Earl Fitz William (1815 – 1902), landowner	£2,882
24.	Harry L. B. McCalmont (1861 – 1902), stockbroker (not in trade)**	£2,279
25.	Sir John B. Maple, 1st Bt (1845 – 1903), furniture retailer in London	£2,153
26.	Edward Brook (1825 – 1904), sewing-thread manufacturer in Huddersfield	£2,181
27.	Edmund D. Beckett, first Baron Grimthorpe (1816 – 1905), barrister in London; banking family in Leeds and Doncaster	£2,127
28.	Sir Charles Tennant, 1st Bt (1823 – 1906), chemical manufacturer in Glasgow	£3,146
29.	Wentworth Blackett Beaumont, first Baron Allendale (1829 – 1907), landowner	£3,189
30.	John S. Schillizzi (1840 – 1908), foreign merchant in London	£2,089
31.	Charles Morrison (1817 – 1909), financier and warehouseman in London	£10,939
32.	Sir Frederick Wills, 1st Bt (1838 – 1909), tobacco manufacturer in Bristol	£3,051
33.	Sir Donald Currie (1825 – 1909), shipowner in London and Liverpool	£2,433
34.	Sir Edward P. Wills, 1st Bt (1834 – 1910), tobacco manufacturer in Bristol	£2,635
35.	Baron Sir John H. W. Schroeder (1825 – 1910), merchant banker in London	£2,131
36.	Henry Overton Wills (1828 – 1911), tobacco manufacturer in Bristol	£5,215

Table 8—*cont'd*

37.	William H. Wills, first Baron Winterstoke (1830 – 1911), tobacco manufacturer in Bristol	£2,548
38.	Peter Coats (1842 – 1913), sewing-thread manufacturer in Paisley	£2,562
39.	Sir James Coats, 1st Bt (1834 – 1913), sewing-thread manufacturer in Paisley	£2,548
40.	William Weir (1826 – 1913), ironmaster and colliery owner in Lanarkshire, etc.	£2,220

* Sutherland left a personal estate proved in the Canterbury Prerogative Court at 'Upper Value' in addition to a personal estate of £77,499 in Scotland. The precise value of his personalty, including the Bridgewater property he inherited, is not known, but Eric Richards, his recent biographer, recalls Greville's comment, 'I believe [he was] the richest individual who ever died'.—*The Leviathan of Wealth* (1973), p. 12. In 1883, the two heirs to his landed wealth, the Duke of Sutherland and the Earl of Ellesmere, were in receipt of a gross annual income of £213,000.

† Rothschild's fortune was estimated by contemporaries at up to £5 million.

‡ Sworn at 'Above £1 million'; this estimate was given by contemporary writers and in obituaries.

§ Sworn at 'Above £1 million', and estimated at this figure in the *Illustrated London News* of 11 June 1859.

‖ Overstone also owned land costing over £1.5 million to purchase.

¶ Lewis, who began life as a traveller in pen and watch materials, was a money-lender to the wealthy at Cork Street in Mayfair. 'Undoubtedly his terms were high,' commented on obituary, 'but probably no member of his profession possessed a larger number of clients among the upper classes of society.'—*Times*, 4 Jan. 1901.

** McCalmont inherited the bulk of the fortune of his great-uncle Hugh McCalmont (d. 1887), which had been left to gather interest for seven years after his death.

At the centre of London's wealth was the City, which was by itself in every period, and at every level of wealth, in these tables the single most important geographical unit, generally by several orders of magnitude over its nearest rival. Nearly all of the City wealthholders were engaged in commerce: only five City millionaires, for example, cannot be readily assigned to a commercial Order among the S.I.C.s. Many of the City's wealthholders obviously belonged to such celebrated financial or mercantile dynasties as the Rothschilds, Barings, Rallis, Sassoons, Gibbses, Montefiores, *et al*. But many others remain virtually unknown, and one important reason for the failure of economic historians to grasp the central importance of the City has been its relative neglect in business histories and industrial biographies. While everyone knows of the major figures of the Industrial Revolution, little attention has been paid to the careers of many of the City's wealthy men. It is likely that the richest commoner of the nineteenth century was the self-made textile warehouseman and merchant banker James Morrison (1789 – 1857), who left between £4 million and £6 million at his death, in addition to more than 100,000 acres of land. His eldest son Charles (1817 – 1909), a financier, left nearly £11 million, and was probably the second wealthiest man in Britain at his death; while eight other members of this family have also left fortunes of £500,000 or more. Yet the family remains unchronicled and largely unknown.[13] Unnoticed, too, are the vast, and typical, City fortunes of such men as Richard Thornton (1776 – 1865), an insurance broker and Baltic merchant who boasted that his signature was 'good for three million' and left £2,800,000;[14] Hugh McCalmont (1809 – 87), a stockbroker and foreign merchant worth £3,122,000; and Giles Loder (1786 – 1871), a Russia merchant who left £2,900,000. Such men were among the very wealthiest in the country, wealthier by several dozen times than the majority of successful industrialists. G. K. Chesterton's shrewd observation that the wise man hides a pebble on a beach, a leaf in a forest, is perhaps best illustrated by the invisibility of many of the City's richest men.[15]

London consisted of far more than the City, and its predominance in the British wealth structure was to a large extent the product of the variety and number of fortunes in its outlying districts. It is impossible to characterize these quickly. Brewing, retailing, and shipping fortunes were the most numerous, including among them dynasties like the Watneys and Charringtons, department-store owners like William Whiteley (1831 – 1907) and James Marshall (1806 – 93), art dealers like Sir Joseph J. Duveen (1843 – 1908), and shipowners like the Scruttons and Harrisons. Industrial fortunes were a minority, heavy industry represented by engineers and ship-builders like John Penn (1805 – 78) of Greenwich, chemical manufacturers like Frank C. Hills (1808 – 92), and builders like Thomas Cubitt (1788 – 1855) and Edward Yates (1838 – 1907). Most of the remaining London wealthholders were government placemen or London bankers.

Beside London, Manchester appears very much like the dog which did nothing in the night-time. Manchester will always remain a symbol and synonym for many things, from the doctrine of *laissez-faire* to the 'immizeration of the working-class', but its importance as a centre of British wealth is simply belied by the available facts. This may seem difficult to credit, but in the entire period between 1809 and 1914 only one Manchester cotton manufacturer left a millionaire estate, while only two others left fortunes in the half-millionaire class.[16] Of all the Manchester wealthholders deceased in the span of this study, only six were manufacturers or industrialists, while the remainder included seven cotton merchants, three bankers, a number of brewers, and a newspaper proprietor. It is to the outlying towns of Greater Manchester that one must look to find the textile manufacturing and industrial fortunes in this conurbation. Such wealth was to be found in the smaller towns like Oldham, with its nine cotton-spinners and three machinery manufacturers among the wealthholders, or among families like the Fieldens in Todmorden, the Peels in Blackburn, or the Bulloughs in Accrington. In these smaller outlying towns, every wealthholder without exception was a manufacturer or industrialist.

Liverpool, as the greatest of northern commercial cities, followed the London pattern in producing more wealthholders than Manchester. Here only two of the local fortunes were earned in industry—both in soap manufacturing—and the bulk of Merseyside fortunes were earned by its foreign traders, shipowners, and commodity merchants of various types. The West Yorkshire wealthholders were mainly in the industrial S.I.C.s, among them such families as the Fosters, worsted manufacturers at the Black Dyke Mills, and the Cunliffe-Listers, Barons Masham, silk-plush manufacturers. But the commercial life of the area was dominated by several old Anglican families based in Leeds, like the Fabers, Becketts, and Oxleys.

Each of the remaining centres of wealth requires some comment. The west Midlands had not by 1914 become of the first importance as the home of top fortunes; such as there were here were largely earned by ironmasters and colliery owners in the Black Country rather than by Birmingham men. On Tyneside the most lucrative sources of wealth were the coalfields of Durham and Northumberland and the engineering and shipping trades of Newcastle and Jarrow. Similarly, Clydeside rose to its leading place as a venue of wealth only among the cohorts deceased from 1880 onwards, on the basis of Glasgow's shipping and engineering, the nearby coal and iron seams, and the sewing-thread families of Coats and Clarks in Paisley. The situation in Bristol was unusual in that nearly all of its wealthholders belonged to two families, the tobacco-manufacturing Willses and the Frys, the Quaker sweets makers. There were virtually no fortunes here whose origins lay in the slaving and mercantile past of that town. Among the smaller towns and geographical areas, a considerable number of manufacturing and industrial fortunes were earned in much smaller localities, among families like the Claytons and Shuttleworths, the agricultural machinery manufacturers of Lincoln, the Arkwrights and Strutts in Derbyshire, or the Patons and Thomsons, who made woollens in Alloa, Clackmannanshire. With the exception of East Anglia, where dissenters provided a number of local banking dynasties of great wealth, it was a rarity for a merchant or banker not trading in a large conurbation to accumulate a vast fortune, while in smaller towns the leading manufacturer was likely to be its wealthiest man.

To turn from the general to the individual, an appreciation of the points made here may be gleaned from Table 8, which lists the largest individual fortunes—those of £2 million or more[17]—left between 1809 and 1914.

Of the 40 male British fortunes[18] at or above this level, four belonged to landowners and one to the railway contractor Thomas Brassey (1805–70), who cannot be assigned to a specific geographical venue. Of the remaining 35, however, no fewer than 20 were Londoners—16 from the City alone—while five were Clydesiders, four Bristolians, and the remainder spread among six other geographical areas. None was a Manchester man. Apart from Brassey and the ironmasters William Baird and William Crawshay, all of the non-landed millionaires listed here deceased prior to 1888 were Londoners, and it is only in the late Victorian period that provincial fortunes appear of a size sufficient to rival the largest among

Londoners. Eighteen of these fortunes were commercial, only ten industrial, and six of these were left in the last fifteen years of the study. Thus, not merely were large fortunes earned more readily in London, but the highest peaks of wealth were reached by Londoners, and especially by City men. In contrast, the fortunes earned in industrial Britain were fewer in number and relatively less lucrative.

II

The key question which must be asked of the occupational and geographical distributions outlined above is whether they were characteristic only of a handful of millionaires, or an important fact about the whole of Victorian middle-class society. In this section it will be contended that the geographical—and, by implication, the occupational—statistics offered above are the tip of an iceberg whose composition beneath the water is very largely similar to the visible portion, that the income of the Victorian middle class as a whole came as disproportionately from London as did the wealth of Victoria's millionaires.

Although the individual returns of nineteenth-century income-tax payers have almost certainly been destroyed,[19] there exists an immense variety of manuscript records in the Public Record Office of the assessment of the nineteenth-century income tax by schedule, by range of income, and by geographical area for every year during which the income tax was levied between 1799 and 1815, and from 1842 to 1911.[20] In addition, there are several remarkable returns in the Parliamentary Papers which have previously received no attention. Two of these will form the basis of the discussion in this section. The first is a county breakdown of Schedule D assessments in 1812,[21] the second, printed in April 1882, a listing of assessments under Schedules A, B, D, and E, as well as the amount of taxation paid under each of these schedules in each *parliamentary constituency* in the United Kingdom in 1879 – 80.[22] A comparison of these sources demonstrates the lead of London over the rest of the country, despite the growth of the great provincial towns after the Napoleonic Wars. A consideration of the geographical distribution of income-tax assessments is particularly useful in shedding light on the composition of the middle class, as the liability for payment of income tax was practically coextensive with the middle class as commonly understood, the minimum level of income being £50 or £60 p.a. in the period 1799 – 1815, and £150 p.a. at the time the 1879 – 80 return was compiled. In Table 9 are given the county assessments under Schedule D in 1812, and the assessments in 1879 – 80 of the London boroughs and all provincial boroughs with a population in excess of 100,000.

In 1812 of the United Kingdom total of £34,384,000 assessed under Schedule D, £13,349,000, or 38.8 per cent of the national total, was assessed in London, Westminster, or Middlesex. In contrast, no more than £4,046,000, or 11.8 per cent of the national total, was assessed in the six industrial counties of Lancashire, Yorkshire, Warwickshire, Staffordshire, Northumberland, and Glamorgan.[23] The place of London in these figures, moreover, is almost certainly understated in several important ways. First, the assessment in the Home Counties of Essex, Kent, and Surrey amounted to £3,883,000, or 11.3 per cent of the national total, and evidently the bulk of the income here represented industries located within the future municipal boundaries of London, or of London businessmen living and paying taxes there. This alone is sufficient to bring the London total to just under half of the national total assessed under Schedule D.

Furthermore, since only Schedule D is included in this table, no account is taken of income earned by owners of London ground-rents assessed under Schedule A, of the income from government funds, assessed under Schedule C,[24] which in the main probably accrued to wealthy brokers or *rentiers* located disproportionately in London, or of the income of office-holders under Schedule E. Practically all of this last category was paid in London. In 1814, the 'charge' (assessment) under Schedule E amounted to only £9,092 in the counties of Lancashire, Yorkshire, Durham, Northumberland, Staffordshire, and Warwickshire, while the charge in London, Westminster, and Middlesex totalled £915,310.[25] Finally, at this time the staffs of the Admiralty Court, the College of Arms, Court of Arches, Prerogative Court of Canterbury, and several other government offices in London were assessed under Schedule A at between £85,000 and £153,000 per annum.[26]

It is probably not surprising that more than half of Britain's middle-class income in 1812 should represent the income of Londoners. What is perhaps more remarkable is that the lead of London over Britain's other major urban areas persisted throughout the nineteenth century. This is demonstrated in the other geographical distribution offered in Table 9. In 1879 – 80, the 28 provincial towns with populations in excess of 100,000, whose combined population was 5,773,000, were assessed under Schedule D for £78,106,000, while the ten London boroughs, whose population totalled 3,453,000, were assessed for £87,674,000.[27] The place of commercial as opposed to manufacturing wealth at this time may be seen more clearly if the provincial trading centres like Liverpool—assessed at £11,014,000, more than any provincial city—Bristol, Edinburgh, and Dublin are considered apart from the manufacturing towns. There is evidently no definitive distinction between commercial and industrial towns, but were the predominantly commercial cities excluded, it seems likely that the assessment of the major provincial towns would be decreased by approximately three-sevenths. Moreover, as with the 1812 data, exclusive reliance on Schedule D excludes those portions of the middle class assessed under Schedules A, C, and E, and found more frequently in London than in the provincial towns. The amount for which tax

Table 9. (a) *Schedule D Assessments by Counties, 1812*

County	Assessment (£000)	County	Assessment (£000)	County	Assessment (£000)
Bedfordshire	96	Huntingdonshire	101	Suffolk	440
Berkshire	291	Kent	1,625	Surrey	1,660
Buckinghamshire	220	Lancashire	1,539	Sussex	365
Cambridgeshire	235	Leicestershire	300	Warwickshire	592
Cheshire	274	Lincolnshire	366	Westmorland	45
Cornwall	238	Norfolk	505	Wiltshire	366
Cumberland	164	Northamptonshire	181	Worcestershire	258
Derbyshire	196	Northumberland	474	Yorkshire	1,763
Devonshire	702	Nottinghamshire	293		
Dorset	203	Oxfordshire	305	Wales	419
Durham	238	Rutland	32	Scotland	2,314
Essex	598	Shropshire	279		
Gloucestershire	352	Somerset	1,223	City of London	6,697
Herefordshire	62	Southampton*	903	Westminster	2,678
Hertfordshire	256	Staffordshire	525	Middlesex	3,974

* The county of Hampshire.

(b) *Schedule D Assessments of Largest British Provincial Towns and the London Boroughs, 1879–80*

Borough	Population 1881 (000)	Assessment (£000)	Borough	Population 1881 (000)	Assessment (£000)
Birmingham	401	4,016	Swansea	106	628
Blackburn	101	384			
Bolton	106	682	Aberdeen	105	974
Bradford	180	1,921	Glasgow	488	8,148
Brighton	128	1,156	Dundee	140	1,182
Bristol	207	2,310	Edinburgh	228	4,807
Hull	162	1,218			
Leeds	309	2,480	Belfast	174	1,464
Leicester	122	909	Dublin	273	4,296
Liverpool	552	11,014			
Manchester	394	9,819	*London Boroughs*		
Newcastle-upon-Tyne	145	1,851	Chelsea	367	1,844
Nottingham	112	1,155	Finsbury	524	7,925
Oldham	153	799	Greenwich	207	933
Portsmouth	128	536	Hackney	417	1,898
Salford	176	859	Lambeth	379	3,317
Sheffield	284	2,020	London, City	51	41,237
Stoke-on-Trent	152	1,075	Marylebone	498	12,297
Sunderland	125	869	Southwark	222	4,857
Wednesbury	117	500	Tower Hamlets	439	3,063
Wolverhampton	164	436	Westminster	229	10,302

was assessed under Schedule E in 1879 – 80, *apart from* public office-holders (including the military and naval forces), was £5,934,000 for the ten London boroughs and £4,788,000 for the 28 leading provincial towns.[28] This income would largely consist of that of limited corporations and their employees, as well as non-business corporations such as churches.[29]

London's place among the leading British towns in 1879 – 80 was the more remarkable in view of the fact that the provincial cities examined here were 67 per cent more populous than the London boroughs in 1881. Thus it seems a plausible inference not merely that London possessed a larger total business income than all of the chief provincial towns combined, but that its middle class was richer *per capita* and almost certainly more numerous than that in the provincial towns.[30] The expansion of Britain's industrial base in the post-Napoleonic War period made London relatively somewhat less important than it had been, but it still remained considerably wealthier than the remainder of Britain's leading towns combined. The assessment of the City of London alone was twice that of Manchester and Liverpool combined.

An important question which must be asked here is whether the predominance of London is merely a reflexion of the fact that some provincial businesses were assessed there. Since the names of individual taxpayers remain unknown, the question cannot be answered definitely, but it is unlikely that even in 1879 – 80 many provincial businesses maintained their corporate headquarters in London, and possibly the major provincial towns would have attracted the assessments of outlying businesses in the same way. The 1860 return by parish detailed the place of assessment of the mines, railways, quarries, etc. which were listed separately. At that time, no income from mineral deposits was assessed in London, and the total of railways assessed in Middlesex was £3,475,000, of a total assessment of railways in England of £10,603,000. Further, the amalgamation of provincial banks into the 'big five' did not get under way until the 1890s. It is also the case that the income-tax and probate data are wholly independent of one another, yet support the same conclusion.

Another interesting question raised by these data is whether an analysis of those worth below £150,000 but above, say, £25,000, would show a similar distribution, either occupationally or geographically, to those at the very top. The Manchester cotton-lords and their kind must be found *somewhere* on the wealth scale, and if not at the very top, necessarily this was at a lower level. As suggested above, it seems likely that most successful manufacturers left around £100,000 after mid-century. Yet one should not really assume that there were not also a great many businessmen in commerce, or in commercial towns, at a similar level of wealth, perhaps plentiful enough to make the distribution at the lower wealth levels similar to that at the top. Some light is thrown on this matter by the income-tax records, where numbers of assessed income units (as noted above, not necessarily individuals) can be traced down to the lowest limits of tax liability. Table 10 indicates the regional and income distribution of individual units assessed for taxation under Schedule D in 1879 – 80.

Although it would be quite fallacious to infer more than a cautious minimum concerning the occupational distribution of Londoners from the

W. D. Rubinstein

Table 10. *Distribution of Individual Units Assessed for Taxation under Schedule D,*
1879–80

	Income range				
	£3–4,000	*£4–5,000*	*£5–10,000*	*£10–50,000*	*£50,000+*
Lancashire (total for county)	264	155	281	168	8
Liverpool	128	75	129	69	2
Manchester	90	56	94	61	3
Yorkshire	111	70	127	52	5
Warwickshire	54	16	36	16	0
Staffordshire	24	7	21	14	2
Northumberland	23	4	18	10	2
Middlesex, Metropolitan portion of	583	336	630	353	38
Surrey and Kent, Metropolitan portions of	51	32	53	32	4
Total Metropolis	634	368	783	385	42
City of London	318	181	373	232	25

Source: P.R.O. I.R. 16, 51.

bald figures for their assessed incomes, it can with considerable truth be asserted that where there was commerce, finance, or trade, money was made more readily than where there was manufacturing or industry. And standing above everything else there was London, the fixed point around which the Victorian middle classes revolved.

III

If it may now be accepted that commercial-based wealth and income exceeded that earned in manufacturing and industry during the nineteenth century, the central question which must flow from this is whether the distinction between the two forms of property is an artificial one, or whether it constituted a basic dichotomy in the nineteenth-century middle class as a whole. Might it not be useful to accept the possibility that two middle classes existed, quite distinct not merely in source of income but in attitudes and behaviour as well? This topic is a large one, and any suggestions must clearly be tentative; it ranges far beyond the scope of economic history. But in the space at hand it might not be irrelevant to the concerns of the economic historian to explore this question in light of the above data.[31]

In economic terms, the chief distinction between the London- and provincial-based middle classes was that one was largely capital- and the other largely labour-intensive. There were, of course, commercial industries which employed vast armies of workers, from the railways to the large retail shops, but even the largest bank or mercantile house employed only dozens where a factory or mine might employ thousands. Furthermore, although many employers in commerce or finance provided working conditions as bad or worse than anything in the north of England—merchant seamen and shop assistants were bywords for exploited labour—one may agree that what sociologists of labour term 'occupational ideology' was quite distinct in commerce and manufacturing. Even a menial clerk in the City was still a member of the middle class in some sense and enjoyed an income considerably higher than that of a skilled labourer. He worked fewer hours and could depend upon more fringe benefits.[32]

The chief social distinction between the two middle classes lay in their contrasting relationship with the traditional landed society. The London-based middle class was far closer to the old society than its provincial counterpart. Indeed, a not unimportant reason for the invisibility of this class was its failure to join in reform agitation, which, from Wyvill in the 1780s to the Jarrow hunger marchers, has typically possessed a provincial base: down the years a section, as well as an economic class, has felt itself aggrieved.[33]

The ties between London's middle class and the old society were many and varied. Two of the more important were in religion and in the education secured for its sons. Most London-based businessmen who were not aliens were Anglicans, and few were Protestant dissenters—a quite different profile from their northern counterparts. The Anglicanism of London's business class, together with its wealth, made its members far readier to send its sons to a major public school and Oxbridge than were the manufacturers. Most of the major public schools were located in London or the Home Counties and were of Anglican foundation. The leading historical study of public school alumni—that of Winchester, by Bishop and Wilkinson[34]—found that among 8,187 Wykehamists born between 1820 and 1922, the percentage of fathers engaged in finance or commerce was more than twice that of fathers engaged in manufacturing, a ratio which remained virtually constant throughout the nineteenth century. Similarly, down to 1914 more than twice as many of the Wykehamists themselves entered commerce rather than manufacturing.

In politics, the picture is similar, with London's middle class returning Conservative members earlier and with greater consistency than its counterpart in the industrial areas. By 1895 finance had replaced land as the most important single business interest among Unionist M.P.s,[35] while Liberals relied primarily upon industrialists and manufacturers, especially those with non-Anglican backgrounds. Much of the history of late Victorian Conservatism—for instance, the Liberal-Unionist split of 1886—may be interpreted as the movement of commercial wealth into the Conservative Party. Along with this movement went a parallel shift towards participation in City business life on the part of landed society. Society's opposition to the underworld of City life—to the Baron Grants and Jabez Balfours—vanished in the late nineteenth century, and with it vanished all reluctance to join the boards of public companies or the Stock Exchange. As early as 1866 the *Saturday Review* concluded that 'the City is rapidly becoming another branch of that system of relief for the aristocracy which Mr Bright denounces.'[36] In contrast, British industry possessed few such attractions for the aristocracy, and the number of aristocrats directly concerned with industry or manufacturing, apart from membership on boards of companies exploiting the minerals on their own land, was probably nil.

These social distinctions between élites were part of the larger dichotomy between finance and industry in Britain during the nineteenth century. The role of the City during the nineteenth century was largely to finance foreign and government loans. It did not act as a capital market for British industry until the very end of the Victorian period, if then. Manufacturing industry was either self-financed or financed by local banks whose directors had few City connexions. This was of the utmost importance to Britain's economic development: to no small degree the chronic underinvestment in British industry has been caused by the City's traditional role of financing foreign and government loans rather than domestic manufacturing. It was probably only in the 1930s that the merchant banks, driven by the lack of investment opportunities abroad, revised their attitudes towards financing home investment.[37] Even by 1914, as Prof. Payne has demonstrated, the role of the merchant banks as issuing houses was limited by the extremely patchy development of limited liability among major industrial firms in Britain.[38]

Obviously, economic historians are well aware of the central importance of London and, indeed, of finance and commerce in nineteenth-century Britain. Yet it is simultaneously true that the very dimensions of our common view of Britain's economic development in the past two hundred years have invariably been fixed by the central importance of the Industrial Revolution and the growth of those areas of the country where industry flourished. There is a common notion, held so deeply as to be almost subconscious, that British economic history in modern times has been about the growth of industry, and therefore about industrialists. It is doubtless easy to overlook or underrate the importance of any line of business which does not leave a hole in the ground, or make a noise, and to forget that a warehouse or mercantile office could prove as great a source of profits as a mine or a factory.

Several culprits have been at work here. The first in point of time has probably been Marxism. It is a tribute to the power of an idea, even of a dubious one, that the view of history embodied in dialectical materialism should have been tacitly accepted by many whose own politics are far removed from Marxism. Although in many of his writings Marx gave full weight to the importance of bankers and large-scale merchants as an element in the post-industrial bourgeoisie,[39] it can hardly be doubted that the interaction of industrial capitalists with their employees *per necessitum* constitutes the focal point of the class struggle; it is here that revolutions are made or aborted. This may be true, but it is surely a logical fallacy to infer from the central importance of industrial capitalism in the dialectical process the central importance of industrial capitalism for the bourgeoisie. Marx viewed mercantile capitalism as characteristic of an earlier and inferior stage of society than industrialism,[40] and by nature as being inherently representative of a more primitive state of society.

The effect of macroeconomics must also be noted. No *lèse-majesté* is implied in asserting that macroeconomic history is basically inappropriate to assessing the role of the middle class. The reason for this is simple: the statistical indexes of macroeconomics are influenced far more by labour-intensive than by capital-intensive industries. One has merely to compare the role of banking in the occupational distribution of the wealthy with its place in the net national product to appreciate this. The manufacturing, mining, and building sectors of the economy accounted for between 34.4 and 40.2 per cent of the total national income during each decade between 1831 and 1901, while the share of the trade and transport sector ranged between 17.3 and 23.3 per cent.[41] The difference between the lead of manufacturing over commerce evidenced in these figures, and the lead of commerce over manufacturing in the statistics of the wealthholders reflects the distribution of working-class incomes in the whole population. National employment statistics demonstrate that the difference at the top was made up at the bottom: 'commercial occupations' accounted for only 1.4 per cent of all employed males in 1841, while the various census categories of industrial and manufacturing trades were the fields of employment of 43.0 per cent of the total; in 1911 while commercial occupations still amounted to only 5.7 per cent of the male labour force, industry and manufacturing rose to 48.6 per cent.[42]

Quite clearly, no discussion of the middle class in Victorian society can be accurate which fails to take notice of the importance of London and of commerce, or which emphasizes the place of industrialists or manufacturers. The net effect of viewing the development of British society in the way suggested here is surely to make the fundamental break which the Industrial Revolution undoubtedly represented less important, and to make the continuities at the top of society between the Old Society and the New stronger and more tenacious. It may be that in viewing the middle class we have missed the woods for the trees, and the woods were traditionalist, Anglican, and, in a very real sense, conservative.[43]

ACKNOWLEDGEMENTS

In writing this article, I was greatly indebted to Profs. E. J. Hobsbawm, Harold Perkin, and David Spring, and to Dr Stanley Chapman, M. Didier Lancien, Miss Mary Chadwick, and Mr John Mercer for their helpful criticisms. Needless to say, none is responsible for its errors or inelegances.

NOTES

1. A typical exposition of these assumptions was made by G. D. H. Cole. He noted that:

[Great Britain] became capitalist in a new sense by the rise of the factory system. . . A new class of aristocrats—cotton-lords, coal-lords, iron-lords—grew up. . . It has often been suggested that the fear caused by the French Revolution put back the Reform movement for a generation. It did more than that: it made inevitable the final alliance between the old and the new lords of land and factory which is the basis of the English oligarchy of today.—*Life of William Cobbett* (1924), p. 4. .

In this article, it will be seen, the assumption is made that there is a direct relation between 'importance', business success, and personal wealth. There are evidently many other senses in which a businessman, or a business élite, may be 'important' for his society or for economic development. Among these are: control of the labour force, contribution to technological innovation, to investment, or to the dominant ideology of the age. In several of these senses, Victorian manufacturers were more 'important' than financiers or merchants. But it is quite incorrectly inferred that they were also wealthier, more numerous, and more powerful.

2. All property passing at death in Britain must be sworn for probate by the executor or administrator of the estate, and an inventory of property drawn up as part of the probate process. Since the mid-eighteenth century this has taken the form of a cash valuation. Prior to the establishment of the Principal Probate Registry in 1858 (located until 1874 at Doctor's Commons, London, and since then at Somerset House) estates might have been proved in any one of several dozen ecclesiastical courts in England and Wales, although the estate of a person leaving property to the value of £5 or more in two separate dioceses had to be sworn in either of the two Prerogative courts (York and Canterbury). The Bank of England required all funds in a testator's portfolio to be proved in the Canterbury court, and hence the great bulk—90 per cent or more—of the pre-1858 estates valued at over £100,000 were proved in the Canterbury court (which was located at Doctor's Commons). For this research, the Act Books of the Canterbury court (P.R.O. Prob. 8), and the indexes of the York Prerogative court, and the Chester Consistory court (containing those Lancashire estates not proved in a Prerogative court) were examined, as well as the printed probate calendars 1858–99 at Somerset House, the Scottish Calendars of Confirmation 1876–99, and the manuscript Scottish indexes 1824–75 (I.R.9) at the Scottish Record Office, and the Irish Calendars 1858–99. The largest twentieth-century wills have been printed annually since 1901 in the *Daily Mail Yearbook* and in newspapers like *The Times*. The authoritative guide to the probate records is Anthony J. Camp, *Wills and their Whereabouts* (rev. edn, 1974). On this topic see also W. D.Rubinstein and D. H. Duman, 'The Probate Records as a Tool of the Historian', *Local Historian*, xi (1974), and C. D. Harbury, 'Inheritance and the Distribution of Personal Wealth in Britain', *Economic Journal*, lxxii (1962).

3. Prior to 1809 estates valued at above £100,000 (£10,000 before 1803) were sworn in the Canterbury court records as 'Upper Value' rather than at a cash figure. It was only in that year that very large estates were given an approximate cash value. Estates at this level continued to be sworn to the nearest £50,000 or £100,000, rather than to a precise sum, until 1881 in England and Wales.

4. This was done primarily because of the dearth of very large estates in the early nineteenth century: only 12 millionaire estates were proved during the period 1809 – 58, for instance.

5. In Scotland, however, real property was not included in the probate valuations until 1964. It should be kept in mind that the personalty of landowners (and unsettled land in the period 1898 – 1925) has always been valued for probate, and numerous very large estates were left during the nineteenth century by landowners, consisting of their personalty. The percentage of wealthholders engaged in Agriculture in Tables 1 – 3 thus greatly understates the actual place of landowning in the British wealth structure.

6. Previous research taking the probate data as its basis has focused primarily on intergenerational social mobility, comparing the valuation of father and son. See Josiah Wedgwood, *The Economics of Inheritance* (1929); C. D. Harbury and P. C. MacMahon, 'Intergenerational Wealth Transmission and the Characteristics of Top Wealth Leavers in Britain', *Econ. Jnl.* lxxxiii (1973). It should be noted that the figures in the probate calendars differ from those published since 1894 in the *Annual Report* of the Inland Revenue, which largely form the basis of the debate on the contemporary distribution of wealth in Britain. The Inland Revenue's figures are anonymous, generally make use of the net rather than the gross valuation, and have always included both personalty and realty, as well as certain types of property not included in the probate calendar valuations, e.g. *inter vivos* gifts passed on before the three- or seven-year period prior to death had elapsed.

7. Women and foreigners leaving large estates in Britain have been excluded from all tables. Virtually all of the foreigners were engaged in commerce and had business interests in London. Of the 29 women wealthholders above the £500,000 level, the origins of the fortunes of 15 were in commerce or finance, only two in industry or manufacturing.

8. *Standard Industrial Classification* (H.M.S.O. 1958) has been used. (Henceforth S.I.C.)

9. Each wealthholder was assigned to the main field in which his fortune was earned, based upon biographical evidence. In only a handful of cases was there any ambiguity; here, the wealthholder was assigned to the trade in which he appeared to have possessed the larger interest, again based upon biographical evidence. Several groups of trades, especially shipbuilding/shipowning and iron/coalmastery, commonly produced wealthholders with overlapping interests within each group. But there was in particular virtually no overlap whatever between the classical City financier and the classical north of England industrialist. Descendants of businessmen were assigned to the field in which their family fortune originated, even if they were not actively engaged in trade, or if indeed no part of their portfolios appeared to be invested in their family firm. Conceptually it might be argued that such men ought to be classified elsewhere, but the aim of these tables is to identify the source of wealth of each wealthholder, not the occupation (or lack of occupation) he may incidentally have held. There is in addition the problem that many wealthy heirs continued to hold partnerships or directorships in their family firm which were largely nominal.

10. Socially, brewers, and especially the London brewers (e.g. the Whitbreads or Hoares, or, further afield, the Walkers in Liverpool or the Guinnesses in Dublin), were close to traditional society and readily accepted by businessmen as something higher than tradesmen.

11. See Rhodes Boyson, *The Ashworth Cotton Dynasty* (Oxford, 1970), Family Trees, facing p. 270. Dr John Foster regards a probate valuation of £25,000 as a convenient bench-mark to distinguish the capitalist *élite c.* 1851 in the industrial towns (Oldham, South Shields, Northampton) he has studied. See his *Class Struggle and the Industrial Revolution* (1974), pp. 161 ff. In 1830 the compiler of a Warwickshire directory estimated that in Birmingham there was at the time one individual worth £400,000, two worth £300,000, 12 between £100,000 and £300,000, and no more than 66 worth between £20,000 and £100,000.—William West, *The History, Topography, and Directory of Warwickshire* (Birmingham, 1830). This was a considerable increase on 1783, when William Hutton believed that only three Birmingham men were worth more than £100,000, only seven worth £50,000.—*History of Birmingham* (1781), cited in Asa Briggs, *The Making of Modern England, 1784 – 1867* (New York, 1959), p. 64. Among the more famous industrial dynasties, no Wedgwood, Kenrick, Marshall, or Greg ever left £500,000 or anything like it, in the period surveyed in this article.

12. I have been guided in this division of Britain into geographical units by T. W. Freeman's *The Conurbations of Great Britain* (Manchester, 1959). Most of these divisions are self-explanatory, but some require comment. 'Outer London' and 'Other London' correspond to the L.C.C. and G.L.C. areas respectively. 'Clydeside' includes the mineral fields in Lanarkshire, Renfrewshire, and Ayrshire, as well as Greenock. 'Mid-Lancashire' chiefly consists of Wigan and St Helens and the surrounding mineral areas. 'Ribblesdale' comprises Preston, Accrington, Blackburn, and Burnley. 'Nottingham-Derby-Burton' also includes the outlying mineral deposits and local cotton works. As with the assignment of wealthholders by occupation, much in these tables is necessarily arbitrary. Nevertheless, in the great majority of cases there was no question of the wealthholder's proper venue. Several types of wealthholders, however, could not be assigned to a particular locality and are excluded from this set of tables, most importantly foreign merchants trading abroad, multiple retailers with branches across the country, and contractors and builders not exclusively in local trade; landowners are also excluded. Thus the number of wealthholders in these tables is lower than in Tables 1 – 3. There is a time-honoured pattern of a family beginning in a small way in the provinces and then transferring its business to London as it grew in size. With few exceptions this is not reflected in the data in these tables. Most families experiencing this pattern had moved to London at least a generation before they produced a wealthholder; such wealthholders were Londoners, maintaining few if any links with their place of origin. Previous research on the geographical distribution of personal wealth or income in Britain is remarkably sparse. E. J. Buckatzsch, 'The Geographical Distribution of Wealth in England, 1086 – 1843', *Economic History Review*, 2nd ser. iii (1950 – 1), used only Schedule A (the tax on rents) of the income tax for the nineteenth century. A. D. M. Phillips and J. R. Walton, 'The Distribution of Personal Wealth in English Towns in the Mid-Nineteenth Century', *Transactions of the Institute of British Geographers*, 2nd ser. lxiv (1975), make use of Assessed Taxes (which fell on windows, carriages, armorial bearings, men-servants, horses for riding, game duties, etc.) and reach the same broad conclusions as this article. But it is open to the serious objection that men of wealth who chose not to possess some of the taxed items would be under-represented and that this would disproportionately affect the dissenting, manufacturing new men of wealth. This is an objection which cannot be raised against income tax or probate figures.

13. This is not for lack of surviving documents. Vast quantities of family and business papers survive, in the possession of a descendant, Mr Richard Gatty, J. P. of Pepper Arden, Northallerton, and in the London Guildhall Library.

14. See W. G. Hoskins, 'Richard Thornton: A Victorian Millionaire', *History Today* (1962), p. 578. Prof. Hoskins discovered Thornton and his immense fortune 'by pure chance in the official index of wills [at Somerset House] for 1865, while looking for an impecunious artist'.

15. The largest fortune ever left in Britain (until 1973, when his son left £52.2 million) was that of Sir John Ellerman, 1st Bt (1863 – 1933), the City financier and shipowner, whose estate, left at the bottom of the Depression, totalled £36.7 million.

16. The sole Manchester cotton millionaire was Edward R. Langworthy (1796 – 1874), who served as mayor of Salford in 1848 – 9 and 1850 – 1. At the half-millionaire level were Thomas Worthington (d. 1840) and Thomas Ashton (1818 – 98).

17. No distinction is drawn here between non-landed fortunes and those left by landowners in personalty or unsettled realty. It is worth repeating that since settled land is excluded, successors to, e.g. the dukedoms of Westminster, Bedford, Northumberland, and Portland, and to the earldom of Derby, who were undoubtedly worth far more than £2 million; are often excluded. For a full list of millionaire fortunes left between 1809 and 1949, see W. D. Rubinstein, 'British Millionaires, 1809 – 1949', *Bulletin of the Institute of Historical Research*, xlviii (1974). A perusal of this list raises several important questions related to inheritance and to the distinction between 'old' and 'new' wealth, as several families account for more than one top fortune. But the distinction drawn in this article between commercial and manufac-turing wealth would not seem to be much affected: both commercial dynasties, like the Rothschilds and the Morrisons, and manufacturing ones, like the Coatses and Willses, appear. It may well have been true, however, that there was a lower risk involved in maintaining an inherited financial than an inherited manufacturing fortune, which entailed continued entrepreneurial ability in subsequent generations, and it is main-tained below that for sociological reasons commercial heirs were less likely to leave business than those inheriting a fortune in manufacturing.

18. Aside from those listed in Table 7, several foreigners and women left fortunes at this level. They were the three 'Randlords' Barnett I. Barnato (d. 1900), £2.3 million; Alfred Beit (1853 – 1906), £8 million; and Sir Julius Werhner (1850 – 1912), £10 million; the French merchant banker Baron A. C. de Rothschild (d. 1900), £2.3 million; and the Canadian railway magnate Donald Smith, first Baron Strathcona (1820 – 1914), £4.7 million. Millionairesses at this level: Mrs Enriquetta Rylands (d. 1908), widow of John Rylands, £3.6 million; and Ellen Morrison (d. 1909), daughter of James Morrison, £2.4 million.

19. As is well known, the system of schedules in force after 1803 prevents any knowledge of the number of individuals paying income tax, or of the size of individual incomes, until the super-tax of 1914. A single individual would have been assessed under several or all of the five schedules if he received sufficient income from the requisite sources; 'individuals' included firms and businesses (except corporations, assessed under Schedule E). On this complicated matter, and on all other questions of the scope of the nineteenth-century income tax, see Josiah C. Stamp's peerless *British Incomes and Property* (1916). Briefly, Schedule A taxed the profits arising from

ownership of lands, houses, and other realty, Schedule B was the tax upon 'the occupier [of land] on the profits made by the occupier . . . from husbandry', i.e. upon farmers (ibid., p. 81), Schedule C taxed profits arising from government securities and funds, Schedule D was the tax upon the profits arising from business and the professions, while under Schedule E were taxed the salaries of public officials and the employees of any public corporation, including limited liability companies: thus in the late nineteenth century there was a constant 'drift' of assessed income from Schedule D to E.—Ibid. p. 266. Until 1867 – 8, profits arising from mines, quarries, iron-works, gasworks, waterworks, canals, docks, railways, market and fair rights, tolls etc. were anomalously assessed under Schedule A rather than D.—Ibid. p. 37. It is well known that the individual returns of the first income tax were assiduously destroyed. See Arthur Hope-Jones, *Income Tax in the Napoleonic Wars* (Cambridge, 1939), p. 4. It is more than likely that post-1842 returns were destroyed when no longer current. In 1857 a scandal occurred when it was discovered that London tax returns were sold as waste paper to wrap fish.—Parl. Papers, 1857 – 8, XXXIV. However, it appears that the names of individuals and amounts assessed during the first income tax survive for many Scottish parishes. See Hope-Jones, op. cit. pp. 128 – 30. There is a one-hundred-and-fifty-year time limit on the examination of confidential documents held by the Inland Revenue.

20. These include the hundreds of enormous sacks, containing records of defaulters and county and half-county assessments, which were sent to the King's Remembrancer in 1798 – 1815, and which are presently to be found at the Public Record Office (E. 182), and the manuscript books containing the details of the number, size, and venue of assessments by schedule (P.R.O. I.R. 16), running from 1845/6 – 1847/8 through to 1911/12.

21. *Account of Duty Arising From Profits* (P.P. 1814 – 15, X).

22. *Parliamentary Constituencies (Population)* (P.P. 1882, LII). An even more valuable return is that of April 1860, *Property and Income Tax* (P.P. 1860, XXXIX, pt II) detailing the gross value of property assessed under Schedules A and B, and the net amount of profits assessed under Schedule D in 1859 – 60 in every *parish* in Great Britain. Moreover, the income arising from railways, mines, quarries, et al. which were anomalously assessed under Schedule A until 1867 (when transferred to Schedule D) are each given separately by parish.

23. The assessment of Glamorgan was £109,474.

24. So far as I am aware, no survey of the geography of Schedule C taxpayers exists. Assessments were made through the Bank of England or the Bank of Ireland, not through individual taxpayers.

25. P.R.O. King's Remembrancer Manuscript, E 181, no. 42.

26. Hope-Jones, op. cit., 131 – 3.

27. The total of Schedule D tax assessed in that year in England and Wales was £209,318,000, and £249,489,000 in the United Kingdom. Apart from the London assessment £6,581,000 was assessed under Schedule D in eight county constituencies near London. Much of this would have been income earned in London.

28. It is unfortunately not possible to establish separately the geographical distribution of the Schedule E income of public office-holders, which would quite plainly add still further to the lead of London. The 1882 return only details at the end of each of its country divisions a global figure for all public office-holders not distinguishing

between military and civilian offices. For England and Wales this amounted to £13,983,000; for Scotland to £292,000; for Ireland to £896,000.

29. See Stamp, op. cit., pp. 263 – 71, for an explanation of these distinctions. A thorough comparison of the business incomes assessed under Schedules D and E after mid-century would be useful in ascertaining the growth of limited liability.

30. Among the manuscript sources referred to in p. 615, n. 2, are Schedule D assessments by range of income, arranged by the taxation districts employed by the Inland Revenue. In 1879 – 80 (P.R.O. I.R. 16, nos. 49 – 51), 385 individuals or business units reported a net income of £10,000—50,000 under Schedule D, and 42 others an income of £50,000 or more within the Metropolitan taxation districts, of which 232 and 25, respectively, were in City of London districts. The respective totals for some leading provincial taxation districts: Liverpool, 69 and 2; Manchester, 41 and 3; Birmingham, 13 and zero; Leeds, 11 and 1; Bradford, 8 and 1. In the United Kingdom there were 939 incomes in the range £10,000 – 50,000, and 82 of £50,000 or more. These figures are slightly at variance with those in Leone Levi, *Wages and Earnings of the Working Classes* (1885), p. 58.

31. In this section we are speaking of both the 'super-rich' wealthholders studied from the probate material and the middle class as commonly understood, including all businessmen liable to income tax. Yet it is here contended that the central occupational and geographical distinctions described above apply to all income or wealth levels considered here, and that both the 'super-rich' and the middle class can profitably be discussed together in this section.

32. On 'occupational ideology', see Theodore Caplow, *The Sociology of Work* (Minneapolis, 1954); J. A. Banks, *Marxist Sociology in Action* (1970), p. 159. There are few books, apart from George Grossmith's *The Diary of a Nobody* (1894), describing the world of the City clerk. One of the most entertaining is the auto-biography of H. G. de Fraine, *Servant of this House* (1960), who entered the Bank of England in 1886 as a sixteen-year-old clerk in the Bank-note Department and retired as principal of the Printing Department. De Fraine began on £42 p.a. rising to £80 p.a. after the second year. When Lord Cunliffe, known as the 'Terror of the City', became Governor of the Bank of England in 1913, he raised the hours of work for employees in the Bank's Printing Department from thirty-nine per week to forty-eight, to bring it more nearly in line with the fifty-two hours prevailing in the printing trade. In the Private Drawing room, a department of bored and underworked staff performing menial secretarial work for which they were too intelligent, absurd practical jokes flourished, and 'jokes shouted from one end of the office to the other, the singing of a line from some popular song, winding up with 'Amen' in a solemn cadence of about one hundred voices'. Everyone here had a nickname; his was 'Duck' since his home was in Aylesbury, and he was 'greeted with a chorus of quacks' whenever he returned to his old office in later years.—Ibid. pp. 161, 85, 88. On the paternalism of N. M. Rothschild & Co. see Ronald Palin, *Rothschild Relish* (1970), esp. pp. 42 ff. Palin rose from junior clerk to Secretary.

33. See Donald Read, *The English Provinces c. 1760 – 1960: A Study in Influence* (1964). Cf. Francis Place's celebrated explanation of London's idiosyncrasies to Cobden in 1840: 'London differs very widely . . . from every other place on the face of the earth. It has . . . a working population . . . who . . . are a quiescent, inactive race as far as public matters are concerned.'—G. Wallas, *Life of Francis Place, 1771 – 1854*

(1898), pp. 393 – 4. I discuss the class structure of Victorian Britain in light of this interpretation more fully in 'Wealth, Elites, and the Class Structure of Modern Britain', *Past and Present*, lxxviii (1977).

34. T. J. Bishop and Rupert Wilkinson, *Winchester and the Public School Élite* (1967), Table 5, pp. 104 – 8.

35. J. A. Thomas, *The House of Commons, 1832 – 1901: A Study of the Economic and Functional Character* (Cardiff, 1939), p. 25.

36. *Saturday Review*, 5 May 1866.

37. William M. Clarke, *The City in the World Economy* (1967), p. 129. On the Rothschilds' movement into domestic finance at this time, see Palin, op. cit. p. 104. An exception to this dichotomy has been insurance, where London houses dominated the field and contributed an important element to the stability and success of provincial industry.

38. P. L. Payne, 'The Emergence of the Large-Scale Company in Britain', *Econ. Hist. Rev.* 2nd ser. xx (1967). A considerable literature exists in Marxist and quasi-Marxist sources on the development of 'finance capital' and the dichotomy between manufacturing and finance, generally in the context of *fin-de-siècle* imperialism. The classical works are R. Hilferding, *Das Finanzkapital* (Vienna, 1910), which has never been fully translated into English, and Lenin's *Imperialism: The Highest Stage of Capitalism* (1916; English translation, 1933). Among contemporary elaborations, see Michael Barratt Brown, *After Imperialism* (rev. edn., 1970) and 'The Controllers of British Industry', in K. Coates, *Can the Workers Run Industry?* (1968); Andrew Glyn and Bob Sutcliffe, *British Capitalism, Workers, and the Profit Squeeze* (1969); and S. Aaronovitch, *The Ruling Class* (1961). It is especially unfortunate that this viewpoint has never been systematically applied to the whole of the British experience. There appear to be two reasons for this: the preoccupation with imperialism, and the fact that Britain was unique among industrial powers in that there was no merger between industry and finance until after the First World War. In my opinion the most salient feature of British élite group structure since 1918 has been the absorption of the manufacturing middle class and the landowners—the other élite hierarchies of the nineteenth century—by the City and finance.

39. e.g. ch. 6 of *The Eighteenth Brumaire of Louis Bonaparte*, in Karl Marx and Frederick Engels, *Selected Works in One Volume* (1968), p. 157.

40. George Lichtheim, *Marxism. A Historical and Critical Study* (1961), pt. 4, ch. 3, 'Bourgeois Society', especially pp. 155 – 9. The importance of 'finance capital' is, to be sure, fully recognized by Marx's successors.

41. Phyllis Deane and W. A. Cole, *British Economic Growth, 1688 – 1959* (Cambridge, 1969), Table 37, p. 166.

42. B. R. Mitchell and Phyllis Deane, *Abstract of British Historical Statistics* (Cambridge, 1962), p. 60.

43. Little has been said thus far of the place of landowning in the nineteenth-century wealth structure. Until the 1880's, half of the wealthiest men in Britain were landowners; earlier in the century the percentage was far higher. At the time of the Napoleonic Wars, perhaps seven-eighths of all persons worth £100,000 or more in Britain were landowners. It is now widely accepted, thanks chiefly to Norman Gash and D. C. Moore, that the 1832 Reform Bill did not fundamentally alter the balance of

power between the landed and middle classes. Insofar as wealth transmitted itself into political power, this corresponded to the realities of the day. Indeed, when the change did come later in the century, the political decline of the landowners may have preceded their decline in relative wealth.

9

Slums and Suburbs*

H. J. DYOS AND D. A. REEDER

I

Victorian London was a land of fragments. Yet the immensity of its mass and the bewildering tissue of its human associations argue for something quite different. To all appearances, its streets abutted each other with a stumbling logic and the names of the neighbourhoods they enclosed unrolled with a continuous rhythm across the map. By day, the great improvised structure could be seen to heave into operation like a piece of fantastic machinery set going by an invisible hand. By night, its operatives could be seen submitting with equal discipline to a different spatial logic as they redistributed themselves for sleep. The impression created by this daily act is of a kind of social contract being discharged by a society held together by a common purpose and conscious to some degree of being a community. Such a symmetry was not a complete illusion even in Victorian London. People commonly congregate in cities because they look for mutual support and they accept unthinkingly the commercial ethos ruling there as the first organizing principle of their working lives. The rule of the market was the original and most natural means of settling rival claims to all things in short supply, not least to space, and the population reshuffled itself by day and by night in tacit acceptance of the prevailing values laid upon the land. Whatever space they occupied was everywhere contracted for in some terms, whether by duly attested indentures or merely a nod upon the stairs, and this great interlocking bargain came daily into play. It was a contract of a kind.

But the irrigations of commercial capital that sustained it even in the smallest channels were not capable of keeping a larger sense of community alive when it was in danger of being crushed by sheer force of numbers. Whatever sense of that kind could be said to have lingered within living memory at the start of the Victorian period had been fractured by just such

* From H. J. Dyos and M. Wolff (eds.), *The Victorian City: Images and Reality* (London, 1973), 359 – 86. Reprinted by permission of the authors and Routledge & Kegan Paul PLC.

growth, and the animus that was replacing it already looked more like an instinct for survival. London was too vast, and the consciousness of the crowd too immanent, to admit the intimacy of a single community for the whole. There was instead the beginnings of a fragmentation that has never been reversed. This was only partly geographical. It was also social and psychological. The characteristic tensions being produced were not so much, perhaps, between class and class as between the individual and the mass, and between the individual's inner life and his outward behaviour. The characteristic shapes which these produced on the ground—the realities composed from their images, then and now—were of suburbs and of slums.

In the crudest model of their development with which we might begin, it is here that urban society most visibly diverged. Centrifugal forces drew the rich into the airy suburbs; centripetal ones held the poor in the airless slums. But the compelling pressures of expansion caused ripples of obsolescence, which overtook places once dancing with buttercups and left them stale as cabbage stalks. Suburbs begat or became slums, rarely if ever the reverse, and the two never coalesced. Whole districts lost ordinary contact with their neighbours, and London became, in the most indulgent terms, an island of villages; in the most heartless, a geographical expression of increasing vagueness. Yet this disintegration was not a disconnected process. The fact of the suburb influenced the environment of the slum; the threat of the slum entered the consciousness of the suburb.

We want in this chapter to look at some of the ways in which their individual characteristics were mutually determined. It is confined to London because the relationship between these two ways of life was not exhibited so clearly anywhere else in Victorian Britain. We concern ourselves chiefly with the narrow focus of the economic forces which were at work simply because we believe that, apart from the multiplication of the population, these were the most fundamental. And we have not the space to go beyond them.

II

We can see this London quite literally, then, as a great commercial undertaking. Here, even in 1815, was a million-peopled city articulated by commerce into a single gigantic enterprise, the supreme money market of the trading world and the most commanding concentration by far of people, industry, and trade to be found anywhere. This commercial metropolis was presently made more impregnable still by the concentrative power of the railways at home and the gains of imperialism abroad, and its capacity to stimulate new demands within the national economy was enhanced by its indomitable leadership in wealth and fashion. It was an enterprise supported by a labour force that was docile, abundant, and cheap, and by a capital supply that seemed more and more mobile and less and less exhaustible. Here was a formula for inexorable growth—of numbers, output, distances, elevations, mass.

It was a headlong business. What mattered most to a commercial metropolis was commercial success, whether on some remote frontier where money mattered less than existence or on its own doorstep, where it sometimes mattered a good deal more. Building and extending its own plant were inseparable parts of the whole field of operations, and investment in the necessary urban equipment—in houses and domestic amenities no less than in the means of locomotion or places of work and the storage of goods—obeyed as it could the first rule of the market place: buy cheap, sell dear. The housing of the poor, as of the rich, was an item of real property, capable of providing titles to wealth for a whole series of property holders; it was expected to yield profits commensurate with whatever were regarded as the risks of investing in it; and it was held to be quite as much subject to the ordinary pressures of the market as any other commodity put up for sale. As the manipulators of capital, the middle classes helped to make possible the expansion of house-building in the suburbs, the parts of the city in which they were shaping their own environment, but in diverting resources for these purposes they also helped to determine the environment of those left behind in the city centre.

It must be remembered here that the distribution of personal incomes and social disabilities in any society helps to determine not only the way in which power is used at the top but also the way in which weaknesses are shared at the bottom. The condition of the housing of the poor was a step through the looking-glass of the rich—a reflex of the allocation of political power and economic resources in society at large. It was no accident that the worst slums were generally found in places where large houses were vacated by the middle classes in their trek to the further suburbs. Such property could only be occupied economically by lower classes by being turned into tenements, but the rent for a whole floor or even a whole room was often too much for those eventually in possession, and the sub-divisions of space that followed usually meant the maximum deterioration in living conditions. It must also be recognized that the resources which might have made such a transition less dramatic were being ploughed heavily back into the commercial machine instead of being distributed in higher wages. It was tacitly accepted that, if better houses had been built to house industrial workers during the nineteenth century, the higher wages paid out to make this possible would have raised the costs of exports and reduced the capital being sent abroad, which would in turn have held back the growth of exports. More sophisticated economic reasoning might suggest that, so long as there were few substitutes for British goods abroad, paying higher wages and charging higher prices would actually have increased these receipts, but it did not look that way at the time. More matter-of-fact logic demanded that labour costs be cut to the bone. The slums were part of this argument for the economy of low wages, and one of their practical functions was therefore to underpin Victorian prosperity. The truth of the matter now seems to be that they embodied some of the most burdensome and irreducible real costs of industrial growth that might have been imagined.[1] When Henry Jephson wrote his classic study, *The Sanitary Evolution of London* (1907), it was, he said, 'the all-powerful, the all-impelling motive and unceasing desire' for 'commercial prosperity and success' that provided London's motive power. 'That indisputable fact must constantly be borne in mind as one reviews the sanitary and social condition of the people of London . . .' (pp. 7 – 8).

London's appetite for people had always been immense, but its commercial aggrandizement made it even more voracious. From just under a million inhabitants at the beginning of the century, its requirements had grown, by its close, to about four and a half millions within its own administrative boundaries alone, and a further two millions were distributed, less congestedly but within easy daily reach, in an outer belt of the conurbation—known for statistical purposes after 1875 as Greater London. London grew by sucking in provincial migrants because jobs were either better paid there or thought to be so; it also offered a more liberal array of charities, richer rewards for crime, a more persuasive legend of opportunity than could be found anywhere in the country.[2] So the net migration into London during the 1840s resulted in the addition of about 250,000 inhabitants, or almost one-fifth of its mean population for the decade—a rate of intake which declined appreciably over the next two decades while its absolute level continued to climb, but which surged up again in the 1870s, when almost 500,000, or over fifteen percent, were added to the natural increase. By 1901 Greater London contained one-fifth of the entire population of England and Wales, and in the preceding decade it absorbed, one way or another, one-quarter of the net increase in population of the whole country.[3]

How this provincial tribute was gathered and where it was harboured we cannot tell for certain. The paths of migration into Victorian London have not been traced sufficiently systematically, and whole decades of coming and going, of movements by the million, have dropped completely from our view. The traditional place for the stranger, the poor, the unwanted—for any threatening presence—was at the city gates, and the motley colonies that had accreted there since the Middle Ages remained the receptacles for the sweepings of the city until the space available within the walls was exhausted by the growth of urban society proper in the sixteenth and seventeenth centuries. The suburbs were the slums. The process of accretion that was already in motion around London at the beginning of the nineteenth century was quite different from this. The colonization of London's nearby villages by merchants and men of affairs in the eighteenth century had pre-empted a new middle-class ring of suburbs which, as it spread, congealed in the nineteenth century into a great continent of petty villadom. The new suburb had leap-frogged the older slum.[4] Before 1861 or so the growth of these outer districts, though often dramatic topographically, was not the most rapid or most important. The central districts, which had always belonged to both rich and poor, remained the chief focus of growth. It was here that the main influx of newcomers congregated, and it was here too that the slum was first given its modern name.

It was originally a piece of slang which meant among other things a room of low repute—a term which Pierce Egan extended in his *Life in London* (1821) to 'back slums', defining it in one place as 'low, unfrequented parts of the town'.[5] Dickens used it so when he wrote a letter dated November 1841: 'I mean to take a great, London, back-slums kind of walk tonight.'[6] Presently it took the form of 'slums' and began to pass into everyday use, though it took another forty years for the inverted commas to disappear completely. It was perhaps always an outsider's word, the lack of which did not necessarily imply that the thing it named was too esoteric for ordinary speech, but one too readily accepted to require a general pejorative term. That did not come about before the 1880s—when the assumed place names of the suburbs were first swept aside by the collective gibe of suburbia—and the all-too-real housing 'problem' began to take shape as a public issue. Precisely what a slum ever meant on the ground has never been clear, partly because it has not developed that kind of technical meaning which definition in an Act of Parliament would have given it: indeed, it still lacks this kind of precision and tends to be defined even nowadays in terms of the number of obsolescent houses which a local authority can clear rather than the kind of houses involved. This vagueness has in practice been aggravated by the failure of parliament or the courts to define at all clearly the chief characteristic of a slum, namely its overcrowding, or the actual basis of the medical judgment that a house was 'unfit for human habitation'.[7]

The implication of this is that, like poverty itself, slums have always been relative things, both in terms of neighbouring affluence and in terms of what was tolerable by those living in or near them. Such a term has no fixity. It invokes comparison. What it felt like to live in a slum depended in some degree, for example, on what it might feel like to live in a suburb. Yet there was no simple polarity. There were degrees of slumminess just as there were degrees of suburban exclusiveness, and there were many irregularities in the declension between them. To Patrick Geddes the whole lamentable process of city-building in the nineteenth century was of a piece: 'slum, semi-slum and super slum,' he wrote, 'to this has come the Evolution of Cities.'[8] The old order of slum had certainly insinuated itself as readily into the central purlieus of wealth in St James's as the new order was doing in the suburban ones of Bayswater or Camberwell.[9] Slums as well as suburbs had their moving frontiers and to try to define either too concisely makes very little sense. In terms of human values, the slums of Victorian London were three-dimensional obscenities as replete as any ever put out of sight by civilized man; in terms of the urban economy, they were part of the infrastructure of a market for menial and casual labour; in terms of urban society, they were a lodging for criminal and vagrant communities; in terms of real property, they were the residue left on the market, the last bits and pieces to command a price; in terms of the dynamic of urban change, they were the final phase in a whole cycle of human occupation which could start up again only by the razing of the site. The making of these slums was a process that began far beyond the reach of the slummers who packed into them. It is important to recognize that the unfortunates who occupied the central slums, and those only slightly more fortunate, perhaps, who occupied the slums of the inner suburbs or the embryo slums of the outer districts, were more than anything else merely the residuary legatees of a kind of house-processing operation which was started by another social class with little or no idea or concern as to how it would end.

We cannot here explain in detail what one reviewer of Mayhew called 'this locality of pauperization.'[10] The most general explanation for slum tendencies in particular places is that, without the kind of general control on the spatial development of the city that might have been given, say, by a rectilinear grid, there were bound to be innumerable dead-ends and back-waters in the street plan. A glance at Booth's maps show how often these introspective places were seized by the 'criminal classes', whose professional requirements were isolation, an entrance that could be watched, and a back exit kept exclusively for the getaway. They were not difficult to fulfil in scores of places in every part of Victorian London. A more careful reading of Booth's maps would show how some additions to the street plan—a dock, say, or a canal, a railway line, or a new street—frequently reinforced these tendencies. What often made them more emphatic still was the incense of some foul factory, a gas-works, the debris of a street-market, or an open sewer. They all acted like tourniquets applied for too long, and below them a gangrene almost invariably set in. The actual age of houses seldom had much to do with it, and it was sometimes possible to run through the whole gamut from meadow to slum in a single generation, or even less. Animal husbandry survived, of course, in caricature in some of these places, where pigs, sheep, cows, and other livestock were still being slowly cleared in the 1870s from the slums they had helped to create. One man who had spent twenty years visiting the poor of a riverside parish could write as late as 1892 of the donkeys, goats, and chickens which had as free a run of some of the houses by night as they had of the streets by day.[11]

It is possible, too, to trace the origins of slumminess in building scamped, whether legally or not, on inadequately settled 'made ground' or by virtue of some builder's sanitary blunder. The history of building regulations is a tale of the regulators never quite catching up with the builders, and of the piecemeal enlarging of the statutory code so as to reduce risks from fire and to health. The machinery for approving street plans and drainage levels took time to evolve and an incorruptible corps of local government officers to administer it.[12] No one can say with real confidence that the many hands required in building and rebuilding slum-prone neighbourhoods were under full and proper control in the public interest before the last decade of the century. Whatever was physically substandard was inclined to become socially inferior, too: the slummers themselves, though often adding the penalty of their own personal habits to the descending scale, seldom *created* such slums as often as they confirmed the builders' and others' mistakes. When this social descent began it was seldom, if ever, reversed, but went inexorably on—respectability taking itself a little further off, the sheer durability of such houses visiting the sins of their builders on the third and fourth generations of those that occupied them.

The more fundamental explanation of the slums, as of the distribution of all urban space before the era of zonal controls, rests, however, on the more basic commercial concept of supply and demand—of housing itself and of the capital and land which were its vital elements. Take first the dominant influence, the supply of housing at the centre. Here, as compared with the outer districts, were much stricter economic limits to an increase in houseroom at low rents, because the alternative uses of the land were capable of bearing a heavier charge for it. Economizing on land by building high was moreover inherently more costly per unit of space provided. Private capital was therefore shy of building flats on central sites for the working classes, and the working classes themselves had a horror of anything so undomesticated as a street standing on end. There was no real possibility of enlarging the housing capacity of the central districts. Indeed, it was impossible even to maintain it. The conversion of houses into offices and warehouses within the City alone began to force its total population down after 1861.[13] But the most draconian changes felt all over central London arose, as they had always done, in making way for a greater traffic in merchandise and fare-paying passengers, whether by sea, road, or rail; and the docks, street improvements, and railways being built in this period set off a whole series of detonations which could be felt not only on the spot but also in long chains of reactions which reached even to the suburbs.[14]

The connections between all this activity and the supply of living room became a commonplace among common people even though the scale of operations was never—nor perhaps ever can be—measured with real accuracy. In the history of the slums of Victorian London these 'improvements'—to use the generic term—had a special irony. They had always been hailed as the means of clearing the slums, though they had hardly ever failed to aggravate them, for their effect always was to reduce the supply of working-class housing, either absolutely or in terms of the kind of houses which those turned out of doors by their operations could afford or wish to occupy. 'Here was a continual pushing back, back, and down, down, of the poor', one slum clergyman told his lecture audience in 1862, 'till they were forced into the very places which were already reeking with corruption.'[15] This had been so, long before the Victorian period. It is possible to see, allied to the commercial zeal for wider streets and larger openings in the City since the eighteenth century, a restless opportunism for the demolition of the ugly, unhealthy, overcrowded—above all, commercially unjustifiable—bits of the ancient city.

Street improvement could even be justified on such grounds alone, for the 'perforation of every such nest', wrote one enthusiast for improvement in 1800, 'by carrying through the midst of it a free and open street with buildings suitable for the industrious and reputable orders of the people, would let in that *Eye* and observation which would effectually break up their combinations.'[16] Such a point of view was expressed literally over forty years later, when James Pennethorne pushed Victoria Street through the backstreets of Westminster along a line he chose solely for its effectiveness in puncturing Pye Street and its neighbouring slums, known locally as Devil's Acre. Not every pair of dividers that stepped across the map of London in this long age of street improvement between the 1780s and 1840s was guided solely by the topography of the slums: the Temple Bar improvers seem to have been practically oblivious of them; John Nash deliberately skirted them with his Regent Street; and to the arch-improver, James Elmes, the rightness of the line was settled primarily by reference to architectural principles. Yet by 1840 no stronger supporting claim for a scheme could be made than that it improved an unhealthy district; of marginally slighter importance only was the aim of the 'melioration of the moral conditions of the labouring classes closely congregated in such districts'.[17] Scarcely a scheme of street improvement in London failed to respond in some degree to this call of duty, or expediency, over the next sixty years. 'Courts, close, crooked, and ill-looking are in plenty; swarms of children . . . costermongers . . . the low night lodging-houses and ugly dens of Golden Lane,' was how one man saw such an opportunity as late as 1877. 'Let a good, broad, straight thoroughfare be cut through it from North to South: the whole district is at once opened up and plenty of elbow room given to the City.'[18] It was a deepening and pitiless irony that the 'moral condition' of those affected tended to deteriorate in processes like these.

London was being dug and re-dug with restless thoroughness by railway navvies, too, and would have been even more trenched by them, especially during the 1860s, if the struggle between the railway companies had not cancelled out some of the schemes. It was above all the railways' demand for land to carry their lines into or under the central districts that had the most direct effect on the dwindling supply of living room there, especially as they had, like the street improvers, every financial reason for choosing the poorest districts for their lines wherever they could. Until the 1870s or even the 1880s, their demolitions tended to evoke a mixture of barely modified censure and almost unstinted praise, except on the part of those directly affected, or their few champions. Scores of writers described what happened as the railways burrowed their way into the centre and swept aside whole neighbourhoods of densely packed houses: some were merely stupefied by engineering marvels or the new vandalism; some reflected on their unerring aim at working-class districts; some thankfully remarked on the supposed benefits of destroying slums so efficiently; some tried to tot up the real costs of operations which defied all normal accounting methods. Watching the trains come by became an almost routine assignment for journalists, ticking off the days 'to get out', picking their way over the rubble, counting the houses that had to come down, following in the footsteps of those turned out of doors to see where they had gone, estimating the further overcrowding of the already over-crowded. From the fifties to the seventies the press was full of this kind of thing.[19]

It is almost impossible to believe that the repercussions of all this random slum-clearance were not recognized at the time. 'Carts of refuse turn down one street and dirty families another,' explained one observer in the early 1860s in a book suggestively entitled *The Hovel and the Home*, 'the one to some chasm where rubbish may be shot, the others to some courts or fallen streets, making them worse than they were before.'[20] The notion that slummers turned out of doors could take flight for the suburbs, or that the shock of flattening acres of crowded houses could be absorbed by the surrounding areas without difficulty, was contradicted by brute facts so often, in every kind of newspaper, periodical, pamphlet, and public utterance, that one is driven to conclude that there was some deliberation in this kind of permissiveness. William Acton wrote: 'This packing of the lower classes is clearly not yet under control.'[21]

That is clear from the more or less bland acceptance, by select committees on railway bills and street improvement schemes before the late 1870s, of easy assurances by the promoters that no difficulty would be encountered by those displaced and of arguments which hinged on the facility of taking slum houses rather than factories or warehouses. At the back of this lay an over-tender but sharply legal regard for property compulsorily acquired, and a readiness of the courts to settle handsomely for property owners. Thus their lordships were told by the Metropolitan Board of Works' Superintending Architect, when examining the Bill for Southwark Street in 1857, that the course given to it enabled them to skirt several expensive properties (including Barclay Perkins's Brewery—'That was a property which it was desirable to avoid') and save £200,000, while displacing fourteen hundred people living in the slums of Christchurch and St Saviour's. 'No inconvenience is anticipated and the Bill does not contain any provisions,' ran the written statement. 'The surrounding district is much peopled with workmen engaged in the different factories and the Artizans are migratory and there is great accommodation for Artizans in the Borough—but the houses are dense and mostly too crowded for health, comfort and convenience.'[22]

Demolitions for docks, railways, and new streets added immeasurably to the slums that were spared, and exacerbated a problem they were powerless to solve without the most elaborate rehousing. The complete failure to do this was the prime reason why the West End Improvements—designed to carry Charing Cross Road and Shaftesbury Avenue, among other streets, through some of the worst slums at the centre—should nearly have been frustrated by a parliament which was coming to realize the need to rehouse those displaced. This was the first major scheme of its kind, outside the City, in which a proper attempt was made to prevent the multiplication of slums by the provision of alternative housing for those displaced, or at least for others who could afford the higher rents.[23] The failure even here to give permanent homes to the lowest grade of slummers displaced was also the major defect in the activities of the numerous charitable bodies which laboured to increase the supply of working-class housing in or near former slums. Their activities, puny as they were in relation to the problem, scarcely touched the principal classes involved.[24]

The other side to these market forces was the working man's inability to transform his need for living room at the centre into an effective demand for it. He could not outbid his employers in the rent they were prepared to pay for their premises where he went to work, nor could he follow them into the suburbs where they went to live. The reasons were almost entirely economic. Though we know far too little about family budgets, it is possible to relate slum or slum-prone housing to low and irregular incomes in a very general way. It is clear, for example, from a survey taken by the Registrar-General of about thirty thousand working men in different parts of London in March 1887,[25] that the scantiest living accommodation was occupied by the families of the lowest-paid and most irregularly-employed men and that the amount of living room increased roughly in step with money wages and security of employment: half the dock labourers, at one extreme, occupied a single room or part of one, while only 1 per cent of policemen occupied less than two rooms. As the proportion of men who were married did not vary significantly between occupational groups—the mean was 82 per cent—and the size of families appears to have been pretty constant, it seems reasonable to connect type of employment directly with room density. It is also fairly clear that, in general, the less a man earned the lower the rent he paid, the two sums bearing a rather surprisingly fixed relationship to each other, with rent coming out at around one-fifth of the income of the head of the family.[26] The picture is made still sharper by taking account of liability to unemployment in different groups. Very roughly, one may say that at one extreme (St George's-in-the-East) was a situation in which almost half the working men and their families in a whole parish occupied single rooms or less, with over a third out of work and over a quarter earning less than nineteen shillings a week; at the other extreme (Battersea) less than a fifth were unemployed, and around two-thirds occupied three rooms or more and earned over twenty-five shillings a week. This suggests that crowded living conditions were related to the general structure of the labour market.

So long as employment remained on a casual basis, with the number of available jobs fluctuating violently from day to day or hour to hour, not only for unskilled but also for some of the most skilled trades, working men were obliged to live within reasonably close walking distance of their work. The distance considered practicable varied between trades and might stretch to three or four miles, but there are many signs that working men often felt chained more closely to their workplaces than that.[27]

I am a working man [explained[28] one factory worker, who had a regular job]. I go to my factory every morning at six, and I leave it every night at the same hour. I require, on the average, eight hours' sleep, which leaves four hours for recreation and improvement. I have lived at many places in the outskirts, according as my work has shifted, but generally I find myself at Mile End. I always live near the factory where I work, and so do all my mates, no matter how small, dirty, and dear the houses may be . . . One or two of my uncles have tried the plan of living a few miles out, and walking to business in the morning, like the clerks do in the city. It don't do—I suppose because they have not been used to it from boys; perhaps, because walking exercises at five in the morning don't suit men who are hard at work with their bodies all day. As to railways and omnibuses, they cost money, and we don't understand them, except on holidays, when we have got our best clothes on.

The circle of knowledge of what work was going was in some trades a narrow one, and the prospect of making a journey for, rather than to, work shortened the commuting radius. Sometimes it was vital to be literally on call. In the docks or some of the East End trades, the connection between the worker's home and workplace sometimes had to be more intimate still, and it was in these circumstances of sweated labour and of insecure and poorly paid employment that creeping congestion either made a district ready for the complete descent into slum or more indelibly confirmed a condition that had already been sketched in. 'A slum', in a word, 'represents the presence of a market for local, casual labour.'[29]

The circle that closed over so much of the labouring mass was a spring for the middle classes. The wealth that was created in the commercial metropolis benefited them first, and they used it quite literally to put a distance between themselves and the workers. Whatever proportion of their earnings remained in their hands, once the capital requirements of commercial enterprise itself were satisfied, was invested in the manufacture of the city itself. Augmented by a certain amount of capital drawn in from outside, these resources were committed to a kind of self-generating expansion, a re-investment—to use economists' language—in the social overhead capital that was needed not only for the conduct of the enterprise City of London Ltd, nor even for so many safe-as-houses additions to personal portfolios, but also for making available to themselves those suburban parts of the city in which it was now thought desirable to live. Here was one of the most beautiful parts of the metropolitan mechanism. There were the business openings themselves: turning fields into streets brought large speculative gains to nimble dealers in land; keeping the suburbs supplied with building materials, fuel, and provisions was full of promise for the railways and the new multiple stores; transporting the commuters lifted the ceiling for street transport as well; buying and selling the property was endlessly rewarding for solicitors, auctioneers, banks, and building societies. It was for many a bonanza. These things apart, the middle-class suburb was an ecological marvel. It gave access to the cheapest land in the city to those having most security of employment and leisure to afford the time and money spent travelling up and down; it offered an arena for the manipulation of social distinctions to those most conscious of their possibilities and most adept at turning them into shapes on the ground; it kept the threat of rapid social change beyond the horizon of those least able to accept its negative as well as its positive advantages.

Within the analysis we are offering here, these suburbs were above all the strategic component in the housing of the whole urban community. It was the pace of their development and the amount of capital resources they consumed which determined not only the general scale of provision that could be made for the housing of the working classes but also the actual dimensions of their houses. In this sense the slums were built in the suburbs, and some of them actually were. These financial and logistical influences required their own kind of infrastructure—a new social order capable of transmitting by imitation the habits and tastes of the middle classes through their intervening layers to the upper strata of the working classes so as to form a continuum—in a word, suburbia. This had become a geographical reality by the last quarter of the century and the economic and social processes that sustained it have never lost their momentum. We must recognize that beckoning the middle classes and their imitators in their flight to the suburbs were images of many kinds. We are not disposed to succumb to their siren calls here, but it is important to see how beguiling they were.[30] The 'suburban quality' they sought, according to Henry James, was 'the mingling of density and rurality, the ivy-covered brick walls, the riverside holiday-making, the old royal seats at an easy drive, the little open-windowed inns, where the charm of rural seclusion seems to merge itself in that of proximity to the city market.'[31] For what filled their sails may well have been trade winds of irresistible reality, but what took hold of the helm were dreams of aspiration and even romance. It was the Englishman's practicality that found in the suburbs the solution to the essentially middle-class problem of escaping the snares of the city without losing control of it. It was his romantic idyll of pastoral bliss that wove in and out of all his plans for taking to the suburbs.

It was not merely that the central areas were becoming so clogged by commerce and infested by slums. These things assailed his sight, his touch, his smell. They undermined his health and his property. But what also became fixed in his mind was the realization that density itself spelt death and depravity on his own doorstep. The convulsions of the city became symbolic of evil tendencies in the best and in the worst writing of the day, while the serenity of the suburbs became a token of natural harmony. The undrained clay beneath the slums oozed with cesspits and sweated with fever; the gravelly heights of the suburbs were dotted with springs and bloomed with health. It did not greatly matter to the individual that neither the slum nor the suburb conformed in every case to its stereotype. What mattered to him was that here was his own way out of the urban mess, a protection for his family, a refreshment for his senses, a balmy oasis in which to build his castle on the ground.[32]

To return, however, to our own ground, we can see now that the middle-class suburb was both an invention for accentuating and even refining class distinctions, and a means of putting off for a generation or two the full realization of what was entailed in living in a slum. C. F. G. Masterman knew and shared these middle-class feelings, and his powerful imagery of the nether world across which the middle classes were carried daily on their railway viaducts towards the heart of the commercial metropolis conveys this well. The image of the working classes storming up the garden path was no more of a caricature to them than it had been, half a century before, to Ruskin, horrified at the cockneys tearing down the apple blossom and bawling at the cows.[33] To a society in which landed wealth, drawn though it increasingly was from urban revenues, was still underpinning great embankments of privilege and political leverage, as well as the smaller domains of parochial aristocracies, the slum people were like a sleeping giant. Reports of its size or its hideous appearance—even cautiously conducted inspections on foot—were as entertaining as a menagerie.[34] But when the thing stirred or broke loose it was as if those watching had seen a ghost. 'We are striving to readjust our stable ideas', wrote Masterman after one of these brief gestures of power by the multitude. 'But within there is a cloud on men's minds, a half stifled recognition of the presence of a new force hitherto unreckoned; the creeping into conscious existence of the quaint and innumerable populations bred in the Abyss.' That was written in 1902.[35] It was a premonition that the great days of the middle-class suburb were numbered. There were men in their fifties in certain suburbs who could not remember the time when workmen's tickets were not in use, and for twenty years this traffic had been planting new colonies of working-class commuters—at the behest of the Board of Trade if need be—around scores of suburban stations.[36] What had begun as a fugitive solution to the problem of rehousing slummers, turned out of doors where costs of new accommodation were prohibitive, was fast becoming by common consent the urban ethos of the twentieth century. It was now the turn of the suburbs to lose their immutability and for distance to lend less enchantment. To flight had been added pursuit.[37]

The means of making this mass exodus was a belated and perhaps dubious gift of the commercial system itself. Taine's native wits told him that the suburban trend of the 1860s implied 'large profits from quick turnover, an opulent free-spending middle class very different from our own'.[38] An earlier estimate had put commuters' incomes in 1837 at between £150 and £600 a year—'provided their business did not require their presence till 9 to 10 in the morning'.[39] What brought such giddy expectations nearer for the masses was not cut-price fares alone but advancing real incomes arising more than anything from the great fall in world commodity prices in the last quarter of the century, and by shorter working hours and securer jobs.[40] The employment of clerks, for example, rose geometrically in London after mid-century, and they went to live in their favoured inner suburbs—22,000 of them, one in eight of all London's clerks, were to be found in Camberwell, for instance, by 1901, when around 5 per cent of London jobs were in offices of some kind.[41]

It should not be overlooked, of course, that neither these plebeian places nor their more patrician counterparts were inhabited solely by commuting workers. Once established, these suburbs put on natural growth—perhaps accounting for up to a third of their overall expansion in the second half of the century—and they created employment locally mainly in the service trades. The longer the lines of suburban communications were stretched the more transport and distributive workers were needed to keep them open. This may help to explain how it was that by the 1860s outer suburbs beyond the reach of buses were growing markedly more quickly than their railway commuting services.[42] We might also add that when this tendency began to be augmented at all substantially by a growing volume of visitors to London on business or pleasure—something plainly happening from the 1850s—it helped to create a disproportionately large number of relatively badly paid jobs in London as a whole, and this reinforced the inherently depressing forces making the inner ring of places into potential slum.

It occasionally happened that this convoluted influence of the suburb on the structure of the city, and in particular on the slum, uncoiled itself as if to demonstrate beyond a doubt what was going on. Look for a moment at North Kensington, a district lying perhaps more off the line of fashionable progress beyond the West End than on it, but containing some of the more sublime as well as some of the more ridiculously ambitious suburban neighbourhoods to be found among the developments of the 1840s, 1850s and 1860s.[43] Among these were some where their builders had badly over-reached themselves and raised reasonably prepossessing houses for single families that never came, and which had had instead to be sub-divided immediately into tenements. Worst of all, as one of Dickens' reporters explained to his readers in *Household Words* in 1850, 'in a neighbourhood studded with elegant villas . . . is a plague spot scarcely equalled for its insalubrity by any other in London: it is called the Potteries.'[44] Here was a custom-built slum of seven or eight acres, nurtured by expediency, occupied by people made homeless by improvements in the West End or in the process of shifting in or out of London altogether, and sustained by a kind of bilateral trade with its affluent neighbours.[45] Its topography included a septic lake covering an acre, open sewers and stagnant ditches galore, a puzzle of cul-de-sacs and impenetrable settlement (especially on its most fashionable quarter), and a heap of hovels numbering under two hundred by mid-century. It was exceptionally low-lying, but made more of a gully for surface water from the surrounding district by having been extensively dug for brick-clay for the mansions round about, and left unpaved and unmetalled. In 1851 the population was returned as 1,177; pigs out-numbered people three to one. It was a nauseous place, but from it came a substantial supply of good quality bacon raised on middle-class swill, a profitable flow of rents for middle-class landlords, and a large pool of adult and juvenile labour for middle-class households—domestic servants, cleaners, wet-nurses, prostitutes, laundry-women, needlewomen, gardeners, night-soil men, chimney-sweeps, odd-job men, and builders. The return flow had to be reckoned not only in wages and charitable coppers but in things pilfered or pockets pinched. It was an impressive trade. Nor was it an isolated one. Agar Town in St Pancras and Sultan Street in Camberwell are similarly documented, and it is hard to believe that this uneven enterprise between suburb and slum was not being carried on in some degree in places barely known to historians even by name.

We have been speaking so far as if these migratory movements into the suburbs and the slums were taking place within closed frontiers, but it is clear that they were not. London, we noted earlier, was drawing off people from the rest of the country as well as redistributing them itself. The question naturally arises, where did these provincial migrants to London go? Were the inhabitants of the slums provincial in origin, drawn in perhaps at different times from overmanned farms or from under-developed or technologically obsolescent industrial towns? The evidence for the 1870s—to take a decade of high growth—does not suggest this. It is not possible to discover, by looking merely at the numbers enumerated at a particular census, which of those born elsewhere had arrived in the last ten years, nor is it possible to discover how many came and went. However, what the birthplaces of those enumerated on census night in April 1881 suggest is that, at a time when not much over one-third of London's population had been born elsewhere, the movement into London was producing in the most rapidly expanding suburbs a larger proportion of provincials than were to be found in districts nearer the centre. Mayfair was an exception in drawing practically 60 per cent of its population from outside London. Bethnal Green, by contrast, which had been three parts slum when Hector Gavin had rambled over it in the late 1840s,[46] and was by now one of the most extensive congeries of slum in London, contained little more than 12 per cent who had been born outside London, and the whole area of Whitechapel and St George's-in-the-East surrounding it did not raise the figure above 20 per cent; Seven Dials itself, plumb centre, had less than half as many inhabitants born outside London as had the most affluent parts of the same West End.[47]

This general pattern corresponds very closely with that prevailing in the Notting Dale Potteries as compared with the surrounding parts of Kensington. If we look simply at the birthplaces of heads of households in 1861, we see that just over half of them were born in London, whereas less than one-quarter of those in the entire district were—a disparity that appears to have increased as the area was being settled in the course of the preceding decade. Similarly, if we look simply at servant-keeping households for the same date in two long-developed districts of Bayswater—a very affluent quarter—we find the corresponding figures are 28 per cent and 35 per cent; whereas if we do the same for a district of quite new and less affluent settlement—to be quite precise, having exactly half the servant-keeping establishments (1·9 domestic servants per household as compared with 3·6 in Bayswater)—what we see is that the proportion of London-born was just over half.[48] By this date the proportion of London-born in London as a whole was dwindling below the half-and-half division of 1851. Charles Booth's calculations for the 1890s suggest that there was here an inverse ratio between the proportion of provincial immigrants and the poverty of a district, and if we look finally at the proportions of cockneys to provincials in what he regarded as one of the vilest slums he knew in London—Sultan Street in Camberwell—we can see just how true this is.

The birthplaces of the heads of the 104 households and their wives enumerated there in 1871, when the whole area had just started its social descent, divided in the proportion of six Londoners to four provincials and Irish, a ratio which widened considerably over the next three censuses: in 1881, 36 per cent of heads and wives were born outside London; by 1901 the figure had fallen as low as 26 per cent. Interestingly enough, the ratio of

London-born in Sultan Street increased very markedly during this period as compared with that in Camberwell as a whole, even though by 1901 this larger community was showing signs of deterioration in social class and, along with this, an increase in the proportion of Londoners to the rest. That only 8 per cent of the children enumerated in Sultan Street in 1871 should have been born outside London (and less than 2 per cent in 1901) supports the evidence of the more general statistics that the slums of Victorian London were mostly occupied by second or later generation Londoners, and that the suburbs were the ultimate destinations of the incoming provincials. The slums of Victorian London are therefore more properly thought of as settlement tanks for submerged Londoners than as settlement areas for provincial immigrants to the city.[49]

We get here another glimpse of that centripetal and downward movement in the development of Victorian London that needs to be set in relation to the more familiar one of the centrifugal deployment of another instalment of population into the suburbs. Here were two social gradients that sometimes intersected and sometimes even changed direction for a time—it all depends, as it commonly does, on where one is standing and how far one can see, and especially on when one is looking. In as general terms as we dare use, what we see is one such slope leading upwards and outwards, and the other leading downwards, if not inwards. The cultural slopes of Victorian London, which must be mapped one day more carefully than anyone has yet attempted, made no doubt an undulating plain of dull mediocrity—which is perhaps the natural condition of human society—relieved only occasionally by peaks or precipices of dramatic dimensions.[50] Moving up and down these slopes was always an exertion of some kind, whether to cut a better figure or to tap fresh credit, to escape the rent-collector, or even the police. How it all happened on the way up we know well enough: Wilkie Collins, Chesterton, Galsworthy, the Grossmiths, Thackeray, Trollope, Wells, describe some of the traverses and ascents; and Keble Howard, Pett Ridge, Shan Bullock, and unsung authors like Mrs Braddon and William Black, whose tedious novels were set in the suburbs because they were designed to be read there, echo some of the chatter that took place on the way.[51] Fewer people—Arthur Morrison, Israel Zangwill, Walter Besant, Gissing, and Kipling certainly among them—have told how it was on the way down or at the bottom.[52] Before we take a last look in a moment at the suburbs and the commercial ascendancy to be found there, it is worth measuring as dispassionately as we can the human ingredients of a slum as its slumminess intensified.

We must return to Sultan Street. Here was a street of around seventy six-roomed stock brick houses arranged on three floors, which had been virtually completed between 1868 and 1871. It was built, with an adjoining street, on a small plot of cow-pasture which for forty years had been completely enclosed by a heap of clap-board cottages on two sides, a row of modest villas on another, and by the long back-gardens of a decent Georgian terrace on the fourth. What gave to this ineligible building land still greater insularity was a railway viaduct, pierced by two bridges. The Herne Hill & City Branch of the London Chatham & Dover Railway was taken clear across the back-gardens of the terrace between 1860 and 1864 as part of the larger strategy that that company was using to get the better of its rival, the South-Eastern Railway, in its drive for the Continental traffic to Dover. The building of Sultan Street was therefore specially speculative, as nothing makes plainer than the speed with which the improved ground-rents were passed from hand to hand. The local influences at work on this place correspond closely with what was said earlier. Cowsheds and piggeries squeezed up with the surrounding houses, and a glue factory, a linoleum factory, a brewery, haddock-smokers, tallow-melters, costermongers keeping their good stuff indoors with them while leaving rotting cabbage-stalks, bad oranges, and the like on the street, created between them an atmosphere which, mingled with household odours, kept all but the locals at bay.[53]

Sultan Street was *not* badly built, but some of its houses became slums almost at once and the rest followed inexorably. By 1871 these seventy or so houses were packed out by 661 persons and almost a quarter of them were being made to hold between thirteen and eighteen occupants each, or more than two to a room. However, just over half of all the houses contained, in 1871, between seven and twelve occupants apiece, a situation which could not be described as one of overcrowding. In ten years the whole spectrum had shifted. The total number living in the street had grown by more than half as much again (57.4 per cent) to 1,038, over half of whom were now to be found thirteen to eighteen per house, while a further 14 per cent were living nineteen or more per house; only one-third of the inhabitants of the street were living, on the average, less than two to a room. The net effect of what had happened was that another forty-three families (197 persons) had come in and lifted the mean figure of persons per house from about nine in 1871 to fifteen in 1881. How many families had come and gone in the interval there is no way of telling precisely, but it seems clear enough from a statistical analysis of age-patterns at successive censuses that there was a big turnover in inhabitants, a process that produced by the 1890s a community that was distinctly older than it would have been if the younger people who had gone there at the start had stayed: the tendency was for older people to move in as the houses themselves aged.

As this was happening, the structure of households was changing appreciably. One noticeable feature was that relatives and lodgers were disappearing from the street. That lodgers should be declining is probably more revealing than that relatives should be growing scarcer, because families too poor to put up a nephew or a parent might be supposed to have taken in a lodger, provided room could be found: few indexes of poverty and overcrowding could conceivably be more significant than the inability to sub-let even sleeping-room. In 1871 the proportion of households with lodgers, almost 15 per cent, had been practically the same as the average for Camberwell as a whole, but by 1881 it had fallen to just over 4 per cent. By this date the whole pattern of Sultan Street society was beginning to diverge with statistical significance from that of the surrounding population in Camberwell as a whole. Three features make this plain: the marital status of the heads of households; the size of families; the occupational and industrial distribution of wage-earners. In all three respects Sultan Street society had in 1871 corresponded quite closely with that of Camberwell as a whole. By 1881, and still more markedly by 1891, there were signs that it was tending to become more matriarchal: relatively more widows, more married women whose husbands were 'away', and more single women as heads of households. So far as the size of both the household and the family are concerned, there was again virtually no difference between Sultan Street and Camberwell in 1871. By 1881, the average size of household had begun to diverge appreciably and before long the same was true of the size of families: both were larger in Sultan Street. Rather interestingly, although there seem to have been no significant differences in the number of children to be found in families of the different social groups in Sultan Street or outside it, in 1871, both skilled and unskilled workers in Sultan Street in 1901 had appreciably more children than the average for their class in Camberwell as a whole. The street seemed to be somewhat deficient in fathers and abundant in children, a situation which was liable to be open to only one interpretation. So far as jobs were concerned, the Sultan Street community already had many more labourers and domestic servants in 1871 than were to be found in Camberwell as a whole (80 per cent against 44 per cent), though the distribution between skilled and unskilled scarcely varied. It was this distribution which now proceeded to vary: the proportion of skilled to all labourers in Camberwell fell only slightly (62 per cent to 54 per cent between 1871 and 1901), but in Sultan Street it was halved in these thirty years (62 per cent, 46 per cent, 29 per cent, 32 per cent); actually, the disparity was at its greatest between 1881 and 1891, for Sultan Street was slightly redeemed in the nineties, whereas Camberwell at large deteriorated a little more rapidly than it had become accustomed to do. There were by now enough other slums in it to offset the effect of its middle-class residents in keeping its average status high. Across the northern reaches of Camberwell, at least, the menace of more general social decline was beginning to show. The suburb that had at the beginning of the nineteenth century contained 'few poor inhabitants and not many overgrown fortunes'[54] contained too few fortunes of any size and too many poor by its end. For it, as for other suburbs on the original frontier of London's expansion, the tide of middle-class settlement had rolled on. The erstwhile suburb had to take increasing care not to become a slum.

III

The dynamics of urban growth by suburban accretion had just such an irresistible momentum. The spread of the built-up area gave every appearance on its leading edge of an unstoppable lava flow; the encrustations that eventually cooled behind it seemed to take on the dull unworkability of pumice. The inhabitants of large cities begin to accept as part of the ground of their being the obduracy of these forces and see them almost as urban nature's way. And when we look at the suburban flux in the full heat of its making, there do seem to be relentless pressures demanding a release. It was there that money not only talked but also lived and moved almost under its own compulsion. The supply of middle-class housing in the suburbs was not simply a reflex of the demand for somewhere to live. It was the active quest for its own outlets that kept the supply of capital on the move. This was not the operation of some anonymous, inscrutable financial wizard who knew some special incantations. Anyone with a bit to spare could open sesame. Lending on mortgage was the passive 5-per cent way of taking part; going into the land market, getting some suburban land ripe for development, making it go, was the active, speculative, all-or-nothing way of doing so.[55] 'The formation of ground rents', one auctioneer's notice blandly proclaimed in 1856, 'has been the study and occupation of many of the most intelligent men of the day, and is accomplished by the purchase of freehold land, to be let on building leases.'[56] To this should be added innumerable supporting enterprises which were also creating their own demand, adding their weight to the engine of suburban economic growth: drainage schemes, gas and water undertakings, shops, schools, pubs, music-halls, parks, bus and jobmaster concerns, tramway and railway companies—the whole intricate web of agencies without which a suburb would have been a castle in the air.

The opportunities for this speculative enterprise were too numerous and too diverse, and their interpenetrations too tangled, to be described in any detail here. Nor can we draw up a balance sheet which would show their debit and credit sides. What mattered most was the *expectation* of gain. The tide ran too fast for the experience of loss to impede the flow. In fact, many were disappointed. Main-line railway companies in particular, compelled by their shareholders to get a share of the suburban market, had many regrets over their passenger accounts when they understood the economics of the rush-hour better.[57] Most of the money to be made out of suburban enterprise went to the men who dealt in·land, who were first on the scene, who leased or bought before the rise, who developed or sold it on the very top of the tide. What evidence we have about land values in the Victorian city suggests that land prices in the outer suburban districts appreciated by ten- to twenty-fold in the thirty years after 1840.[58] In this the railway played the role of inflating land values *en route* and offering windfalls to those quick or knowing enough to pick them up while still ripe. The Engineer of the Acton & Hammersmith Railway remarked in 1874: 'The moment a line is deposited and there appears a chance of carrying on, the speculative builders of London all rush to the ground to cover it with houses. Many cases have arisen where the Act has not gone through one committee before the builders were on the spot and commencing to sell.'[59] Those who courted ruin either moved in too soon or arrived too late, and occupied some salient easily outflanked by more desirably placed estates. These were the men who committed themselves to unsound schemes in the belief that they would share what others were known to have reaped, who kept doggedly on when their returns failed to rise, or tried to bolster the market by taking shares in railway companies when all their capital was locked up in bricks and mortar.[60]

Such men did not lose their nerve; nor did they normally run out of capital. By failing to sell their houses they fell short on the payment of interest on their loans and their creditors foreclosed on their security—the houses that had dragged their mortgagees down. There were too many undertakings, and too much was expected of them individually in the short run. In terms somewhat alien to the times, such investments looked too much for growth and too little for income. In the long run they made collectively very handsome holdings indeed, but the whole atmosphere in which they were created was charged with speculation and the operations themselves were hobbled by their scale. The supply of capital was never seriously depleted by other demands being made upon it—partly because the money market was more specialized than is often supposed—and even the counter-attractions of overseas investment merely had the effect of making funds more readily available when they were not going abroad, not of restricting them when they did.[61] The most palpable consequence of this in the suburbs was the sight from time to time of new untenanted streets of houses, a temporary fall in house prices, and an increase in bankruptcies among builders. The long-term trends in population growth and the supply of houses in London as a whole, on the contrary, scarcely wavered or diverged. All that these marginal alternations in the supply of capital did in the suburbs was to fix the reckoning day and to award the prizes. The estates that suited the tastes and the pockets of their middle-class adjudicators went on; those that did not were put on one side for more vulgar approval later on; and the housing industry re-formed its battalions for another campaign.[62]

The bowler-hatted field-marshals commanding these operations were the speculative builders—if by this term is meant not only those directly involved in erecting houses but also anyone capable of remaining solvent long enough to raise the carcass of a house and to find a tenant or a buyer for it. These were functions as readily discharged by men totally inexperienced in building as by men that were. The Forsytes' fortunes were based reputably enough on the success of a mason from Dorset, but there were speculative builders who had been tailors, shopkeepers, domestic servants, publicans: one District

Surveyor complained in 1877 of a clergyman-cum-speculative builder whom he remembered only too well because he had built several hundred houses and left the district without paying him his fees.[63] The big men were veritable entrepreneurs as much at home among the scaffolding as in the chambers of money-lending solicitors, men who were not only scrupulous businessmen but discreet vulgarizers of the fine arts, whose work was the stuff of dreams that would not fade, and whose plumbing was impregnable. But there were also others, not necessarily dishonest or incompetent men, whose business methods precluded such attention to detail or a guarantee of the best materials being used—men more skilled very often in raising money than raising houses. In any rapidly growing suburb of size there would be scores of such builders rubbing along on precarious credit from timber-merchants or brickmakers (something harder to obtain, incidentally, from the 1850s), mortgaging their houses floor by floor or pair by pair or terrace by terrace to a building society, a solicitor, or even to a bank. If they were lucky they would survive with virtually no stock-in-trade nor capital of their own, and skip from one take to another by finding buyers for their houses at the eleventh hour and transferring to their clients the mortgage they had raised on the house when the roof went on, in time to finance the first stages in the next operation. There were in this category some speculative builders who were little more than hirelings of the ground-landlord or the developer who had first laid out the estate, and who came almost inevitably and often very quickly into financial servitude to more powerful men. There were also builders' merchants and building societies which had to step in to complete a job on which they had been forced to foreclose. It was the kind of enterprise which tempted many men, not least the long-established family concerns of jobbing builders—father and son, brothers and brothers-in-law—who, when new houses did not seem to hang on the market above a week or two, could be seen measuring the leap into full-scale speculative building, and taking it.

These suburban outlets for capital were like a delta of a great river system, made fertile by deposits collected in distant places and carried along irreversibly by superior force. Landowners of London estates made advances in cash and kind—the prevailing leasehold system itself was but the means of transferring capital assets on credit—and were doubtless as ready to tap the resources of their country estates as to return them the proceeds of their urban ones. Cash left on trust in the country made its way into solicitors' hands in London, and professional men in particular knew such channels well. The intermediaries themselves also became the principals, and the legal system—despite its obscurity in the annals of economic history—became the axis for many of these movements of capital, especially after 1872, when advances to speculative builders by building societies began to flag. Thus the savings of the farmers and retired gentlefolk of Chippenham were channelled during the 1880s into the making of a seedy suburb in Paddington, and in

1874 some of Mr Speaker's money was combined in Lincoln's Inn with that of a reverend gentleman in Southampton to finance the building of a terrace in Walworth.[64] The most conservative of City institutions, the Royal Exchange Assurance, and several other insurance companies, along with two leading London banks, engaged in this disposal of loanable funds too, doing so in such a way as to accentuate the uncertainties of speculative building and, arguably, to make the employment of this capital more wasteful.[65] The standard instrument for all these transfers was the mortgage deed, the main outlet for surplus funds in the nineteenth century, but it was used to special effect by the building societies. Whether as channels for funds for occupying owners or for speculative builders, these highly parochial institutions per-formed the prime function of releasing the capital resources of one suburb for the development of a neighbouring one, just as the Church building societies were the means of transforming that wealth into places for prayer apart.[66] The crucial role of all these institutions was to convert the savings of the suburban communities into funds for re-investment in their own structure, into a hoopsnake of incomes and satisfactions that recycled what was earned in the tangible means of enjoying it.

But what of the slums? The mechanism that activated and populated the suburbs did not function for them in the same way. In the suburbs, a correspondent to the *Builder* was commenting as early as 1848, it was

as though one-half of the world were on the lookout for investments, and the other half continually in search of eligible family residences . . . There is a leaven of aristocracy in the parlour with folding-doors . . . The villa mania is everywhere most obtrusive . . . But the poor want dwelling-places. Whilst we are exhausting our ingenuity to supply our villas with 'every possible convenience,' we are leaving our working-classes to the enjoyment of every possible inconvenience, in wretched stalls to which men of substance would not consign their beasts of burden.[67]

It is indeed an interesting question whether the flow of private capital into suburban house-building has not always tended to be at the expense of invest-ment in lower-grade housing, unless moderated by public subsidies for working-class housing. The whole ethos of the 5-per cent philanthropy idea which was developed in the 1850s and 1860s to get private capital for this type of investment really evolved from a situation in which the returns on suburban house-building were not only setting the pace but also making the *idea* of securing comparable returns on housing the lower working classes, as distinct from the 'aristocracy', largely nugatory.[68]

Worse than this, it cannot be taken as an open question whether the people of the slums were not actually contributing to the environment of the suburbs. The lubrications of the money economy had made even these rusty parts revolve. 'There are courts and alleys innumerable called by the significant name of RENTS,' explained one sociologist, in all but name, of the 1840s. '. . . they are not human habitations . . . They are merely so many man-traps to catch the paying animal in; they are machines for manufacturing rent.'[69] It was profoundly true. The urban landlord already appeared to have become a kind of dinosaur across the water who took his tribute in flesh and blood. Whereas in the old pre-urban days, when the rent-receiver was often visible as employer or social better within a tolerable frame, and when the rent-night gathering might sometimes almost be said to have been celebrated 'as if the thing, money, had not brought it there',[70] the relations between landlord and tenant in the city were characteristically impersonal, conducted through agents called rent-collectors, and the rent itself seldom bore any demonstrable connection with the human container itself. The money that passed was the sum necessary to deny the space on the ground to some other use, and it soon bore, in the central districts, little relationship to the amenities available in the shape enclosing it. One enthusiast for garden suburbs for the masses, long ahead of his time, calculated in 1846 that a four-roomed cottage could be provided for half the rent of six shillings a week paid by working men for two rooms in town.[71] Little wonder, perhaps, that these extractions were so painful. 'Absentee-landlordism, subleases, rack-rents,' wrote Henry Lazarus in a diatribe hurled at the landlords of London in 1892, 'here is the trinity of England's land curse.'[72] Between tenant and landlord often stretched a whole chain of shadowy intermediaries, held in their contracted order by a series of subleases which divided responsibilities for the upkeep of the property and inflated the rents paid for it.

The direction in which these financial obligations led could scarcely fail to be outwards towards the suburbs. And when George Bernard Shaw first tried his hand as a playwright it was to these calculated connections between slums and suburbs that he turned. 'In *Widowers' Houses*', he explained after it was put on in 1892, 'I have shewn middle class respectability and younger son gentility fattening on the poverty of the slum as flies fatten on filth.'[73] The rent-collector describes his client's business:

LICKCHEESE. . . . I dont say he's the worst landlord in London: he couldnt be worse than some; but he's no better than the worst I ever had to do with. And, though I say it, Im better than the best collector he ever done business with. Ive screwed more and spent less on his properties than anyone would believe that knows what such properties are. I know my merits, Dr. Trench, and will speak for myself if no one else will.
COKANE. What description of properties? Houses?
LICKCHEESE. Tenement houses, let from week to week by the room or half room—aye, or quarter room. It pays when you know how to work it, sir. Nothing like it. It's been calculated on the cubic foot of space, sir, that you can get higher rents letting by the room than you can for a mansion in Park Lane.
TRENCH. I hope Mr. Sartorious hasnt much of that sort of property, however it may pay.
LICKCHEESE. He has nothing else, sir; and he shews his sense in it, too. Every few

hundred pounds he could scrape together he bought old houses with—houses that you wouldnt hardly look at without holding your nose. He has em in St. Giles's: he has em in Marylebone: he has em in Bethnal Green. Just look how he lives himself, and youll see the good of it to him. He likes a low death-rate and a gravel soil for himself, he does. You come down with me to Robbin's Row; and I'll shew you a soil and a death-rate, so I will! And, mind you, it's me that makes it pay him so well. Catch him going down to collect his own rents! Not likely!

TRENCH. Do you mean to say that all his property—all his means—come from this sort of thing?

LICKCHEESE. Every penny of it, sir.

That scene was enacted in 'the library of a handsomely appointed villa at Surbiton'. It conveys, as the most meticulous property ledger perhaps never will, the underlying logic of what another earlier Victorian commentator described as the 'terrible physiology' of the map of London.[74] The movements of capital in the making of the metropolis determined the social space available to its different users, and hence the relative wealth or poverty of its different districts. This is not to say that the living conditions which were produced by these commercial discriminations were necessarily inferior to, or their limits more extreme than, what had gone before. What was different was the geographical scale and the fact that with virtually no curbs placed on the way in which capital was allowed to spend itself—beyond the rather narrow limits set by legislation for the public health—the poor were quite literally starved of such finance. The curse of these poor was no greater than the poverty of any other, but it produced more visible ironies. The wealthiest parishes of London had the lowest municipal rates.[75] It was difficult at first to reverse the capital flows we have been describing within the boundaries of any one of them. Kensington, the wealthiest of them all, for example, reacted to efforts to do so on behalf of the Potteries as a healthy body does to some foreign matter embedded in it—by trying to evict it.[76] The effort to redress such unbalances, to equalize the rates, to steer capital where it would not normally go, was what the municipal socialism that found its voice with the establishment of a single government for London in 1889 was all about.[77] It was about the need, among other things, to make transfer-payments between suburbs and slums, to give the community a conscience, to put together again the fragments into which it had been shattered by the impact of its own growth. It was the start of a road that would never end.

NOTES

1. This argument was originally advanced in a paper from which some of the material for this chapter has been drawn: see H. J. Dyos, 'The Slums of Victorian London', *Victorian Studies*, xi (1967 – 8), 5 – 40. It has benefited since from the comments of Professor Lionel Needleman, to whom we are grateful. His own work, *The Economics of Housing* (1965), deals more theoretically with the subject, especially in regard to the supply and demand factors influencing housing.

2. For a discussion of the relations between London and the rest of the country, see H. J. Dyos, 'Greater and Greater London: Notes on Metropolis and Provinces in the 19th and 20th Centuries', in *Britain and the Netherlands. IV: Metropolis, Dominion and Province*, eds. J. S. Bromley and E. H. Kossmann (The Hague, 1972), pp. 89 – 112.

3. H. A. Shannon, 'Migration and the Growth of London, 1841 – 91', *Economic History Review*, v (1935), 79 – 86. These and other estimates of population growth given in this chapter have been calculated from the census returns.

4. For an account of this, see H. J. Dyos, 'The Growth of a Pre-Victorian Suburb: South London, 1580 – 1836', *Town Planning Review*, xxv (1954), 67 – 78.

5. Pierce Egan, *Life in London* (1821), pp. 274, 288, 343, 345 – 6.

6. To Daniel Maclise, 20 November 1840. For other contemporary definitions of the slum, see J. H. Vaux, *Flash Dictionary* (1812); Jon Bee, *A Dictionary of the Turf* (1823), p. 161; Henry Mayhew, *The Great World of London* (1856), p. 46; J. S. Farmer and W. E. Henley, *Slang and Its Analogues* (1890 – 1904), see 'slum'; *The Times*, 17 January 1845.

7. 'It may be one house', wrote Robert Williams in *London Rookeries and Colliers' Slums* (1893), p. 13, 'but it generally is a cluster of houses, or of blocks of dwellings, not necessarily dilapidated, or badly drained, or old, but usually all this and small-roomed, and, further, so hemmed in by other houses, so wanting in light and air, and therefore cleanliness, as to be wholly unfit for human habitation.'

8. Quoted by Lewis Mumford, *The City in History* (1961), p. 433.

9. See, for example, Revd Thomas Beames, *The Rookeries of London: Past, present, and prospective* (1851); Cardinal Wiseman, *An Appeal to the Reason and Good Feeling of the English People on the Subject of the Catholic Hierarchy* (1850), p. 30. Bayswater and Camberwell are dealt with below.

10. 'Ragged London', *Meliora*, iv (1862), 300. There is a large bibliography of contemporary writings on the slums in Dyos, 'Slums of Victorian London'.

11. [Thomas Wright], *The Pinch of Poverty* (1892), p. 187.

12. The only available history of building regulations in London during this period is C. C. Knowles, 'A History of the London Building Acts, the District Surveyors, and their Association', an unpublished MS. dated 1947 in the Members' Library, Greater London Council, County Hall, Westminster Bridge.

13. Corporation of London, *The City of London: A record of destruction and survival* (1951), p. 165 ff.

14. The large displacements in the vicinity of the new Waterloo station in 1858 – 9 for the Charing Cross Railway were augmented by the actions of landowners seizing the opportunity of re-shuffling their tenantry in the vicinity. The only step-by-step reconstruction of such a process is H. C. Binford, 'Residential Displacement by

242   *H. J. Dyos and D. A. Reeder*

Railway Construction in North Lambeth, 1858 – 61' (unpublished M.A. thesis, University of Sussex, 1967).

15. Revd G. W. M'Cree, *Day and Night in St. Giles* (Bishop Auckland, 1862), p. 6.
16. [C. G. Stonestreet], *Domestic Union, or London as it Should Be!!* (1800).
17. For a more extended account, see H. J. Dyos, 'Urban Transformation: the objects of street improvement in Regency and early Victorian London', *International Review of Social History (I.R.S.H.)*, ii (1957), 259 – 65.
18. Henry Chevassus, *Overcrowding in the City of London* (1877), p. 10.
19. See the references in H. J. Dyos, 'Railways and Housing in Victorian London', *Journal of Transport History*, ii (1955), 11 – 21, 90 – 100.
20. Ebenezer Clarke, Jr, *The Hovel and the Home; or, Improved dwellings for the labouring classes, and how to obtain them* (1863), p. 31.
21. William Acton, *Prostitution . . . in London and Other Large Cities* (1857), p. 180.
22. Quoted from the Demolition Statement submitted with its Bill by the M.B.W. under the provisions of a House of Lords Standing Order adopted in 1853 (House of Lords Record Office).
23. See Dyos, 'Urban Transformation', *I.R.S.H.*, 261.
24. See the references in J. N. Tarn, 'Housing in Urban Areas, 1890 – 1914' (unpublished Ph.D. thesis, University of Cambridge, 1961); C. J. Stewart, ed., *The Housing Question in London, 1855 – 1900* (1900); E. R. Dewsnup, *The Housing Problem in England: Its statistics, legislation and policy* (Manchester, 1907); J. S. Nettlefold, *Practical Housing* (Letchworth, 1908).
25. *Parliamentary Papers*, 1887, XV, Tabulation of the Statements made by Men living in Certain Selected Districts of London in March 1887 (C. 5228). The areas covered were the registration sub-districts of St George's-in-the-East, Battersea, Hackney, and Deptford. Despite the warning given that the details of the returns were 'of very small statistical value', there is a very general pattern discernible in them.
26. For a discussion of house rents in London in relation to the problems of housing the working classes, see A. S. Wohl, 'The Housing of the Working Classes in London, 1815 – 1914', in *The History of Working-Class Housing* (1971), ed. Stanley D. Chapman, pp. 15 – 54.
27. See E. J. Hobsbawm, 'The Nineteenth-Century London Labour Market', in *London: Aspects of change* (1964), Report No. 3, edited by the Centre for Urban Studies [University College, London], pp. 3 – 28.
28. John Hollingshead, *Today: Essays and miscellanies* (1865), II, p. 306.
29. B. F. C. Costelloe, 'The Housing Problem', *Transactions of the Manchester Statistical Society*, 1898 – 9, 48. The economic forces at work here have been brilliantly analysed by Gareth Stedman Jones, *Outcast London: A study of the relationships between classes in Victorian society* (Oxford, 1971), especially in part I.
30. These images can be discerned best from the numerous guides to the politer parts of the metropolis and the advertisements accompanying the 'well-advertised' building estates. See, for example, the Homeland Reference Books, *Where to Live Round London (Northern Side)*, ed. Freeman Bunting (1897, 1908).
31. Henry James, 'The Suburbs of London', *Galaxy*, xxiv (1877), 778.
32. For an explanation of these generalized statements, see H. J. Dyos, *Victorian*

Suburb: A study of the growth of Camberwell (Leicester, 1961), especially pp. 20 – 33.

33. C. F. G. Masterman, *The Condition of England* (1909), p. 72; John Ruskin, *Praeterita* (Orpington, 1886), I, p. 70.

34. See Dyos, 'Slums of Victorian London', 11 – 24.

35. [C. F. G. Masterman], *From the Abyss* [1902], p. 4.

36. The background will be found in H. J. Dyos, 'Workmen's Fares in South London, 1860 – 1914', *Journal of Transport History*, i (1953), 3 – 19.

37. For some discussion of the dynamics of suburban change in Victorian London, see D. A. Reeder, 'A Theatre of Suburbs: Some patterns of development in West London, 1801 – 1911', in *The Study of Urban History* (1968), ed. H. J. Dyos, pp. 253 – 71; and for an outline account of the rise and decline of a suburban district, see his description of Fulham in P. D. Whitting, ed., *A History of Fulham* (1970), pp. 150 – 64, 275 – 90.

38. H. Taine, *Notes on England* [1868 – 70], translated by Edward Hyams (1957), p. 14.

39. *Penny Magazine*, 31 March 1837, quoted in T. C. Barker and Michael Robbins, *A History of London Transport* (1963), I, p. 36.

40. William Ashworth, *The Genesis of Modern British Town Planning* (1954), ch. 6.

41. Dyos, *Victorian Suburb*, p. 62.

42. For a discussion of the relationships between suburban rail-travel and suburban development in Victorian London, see John R. Kellett, *The Impact of Railways on Victorian Cities* (1969), especially pp. 365 – 87, 405 – 19. Some account has been taken of the growth of low-paid jobs in the service industries by Mary Waugh, 'Suburban Growth in North-west Kent: 1861 – 1961' (unpublished Ph.D. thesis, University of London, 1968).

43. Reeder, 'Theatre of Suburbs', pp. 255 – 6, 264.

44. *Household Words*, i (1850), 463.

45. We are grateful to a former student for permission to use her work on this suburban slum. See Patricia E. Malcolmson, 'The Potteries of Kensington: a study of slum development in Victorian London' (unpublished M.Phil. thesis, University of Leicester, 1970).

46. Hector Gavin, *Sanitary Ramblings: being sketches and illustrations, of Bethnal Green. A type of the condition of the metropolis* (1848). See also R. J. Roberts, '*Sanitary Ramblings . . .* by H. Gavin', *East London Papers*, viii (1965), 110 – 118.

47. Stedman Jones, op. cit., ch. 6, deals more extensively with distribution of provincial immigrants in Victorian London.

48. These few calculations are derived from a larger study being undertaken by D. A. Reeder due to be published under the title *Genesis of Suburbia* by Edward Arnold in 1974.

49. These figures are also taken from a larger piece of work on the social organization of Victorian Camberwell, by H. J. Dyos. For a discussion of the methods being used to calculate these data, see H. J. Dyos and A. B. M. Baker, 'The Possibilities of Computerising Census Data', in *The Study of Urban History*, ed. Dyos, pp. 87 – 112.

50. For an attempt to work out some of the broad contours of this map for the mid-nineteenth century, see F. Bédarida, 'Croissance urbaine et image de la ville en

Angleterre au XIXe siècle', *Bulletin de la Société d'Histoire Moderne*, third series, No. 1 (1965), 10 – 14; also by the same author, 'Londres au milieu du XIXe siècle: une analyse de structure sociale', *Annales*, March-April 1968, 268 – 95. Interesting work has also been done on the internal movements of particular and easily identifiable ethnic groups. For example, Lynn Lees, 'Patterns of Lower-Class Life: Irish slum communities in nineteenth-century London', in *Nineteenth-Century Cities*, ed. Stephan Thernstrom and Richard Sennett (1969), pp. 359 – 85. See, too, Vivian D. Lipman, 'The Rise of Jewish Suburbia', *Transactions of the Jewish Historical Society of England*, xxi (1968), 78 – 103.

51. For example, W. M. Thackeray, *Vanity Fair* (1848); Anthony Trollope, *The Three Clerks* (1858); Wilkie Collins, *Hide and Seek* (1861); George and Weedon Grossmith, *The Diary of a Nobody* (Bristol, 1892); G. K. Chesterton, *The Napoleon of Notting Hill* (1904); W. Pett Ridge, *Mrs Galer's Business* (1905); Keble Howard, *The Smiths of Surbiton* (1906); Shan Bullock, *The Story of a London Clerk* (1907); H. G. Wells, *Ann Veronica* (1909).

52. See P. J. Keating, *The Working Classes in Victorian Fiction* (1971).

53. Dyos, *Victorian Suburb*, pp. 109 – 13.

54. J. C. Lettsom, *Village Society* (1800), p. 5.

55. For more extended accounts of these business operations and of the financial interests involved, see H. J. Dyos, 'The Speculative Builders and Developers of Victorian London', *Victorian Studies*, xi (1968), 641 – 90; D. A. Reeder, 'Capital Investment in the Western Suburbs of Victorian London' (unpublished Ph.D. thesis, University of Leicester, 1965).

56. From the notice of sale of the Gunter Estate including building land in Chelsea and Fulham (G.L.C.R.O.), 1856.

57. The economics of railway operations in Victorian London and other cities are discussed in: Barker and Robbins, op. cit., pp. 208 – 40; Kellett, op. cit., pp. 60 – 99, 388 – 405; H. J. Dyos and D. H. Aldcroft, *British Transport: An economic survey from the seventeenth century to the twentieth* (Leicester, 1971), pp. 215 – 19, 147 – 75.

58. Reeder, 'Capital Investment', pp. 104 – 9.

59. Minutes of Evidence, House of Lords Committee, Acton & Hammersmith Railway Bill, 1874, p. 208. For a discussion of the timing of estate development in outer west London after mid-century and for some examples of how development prospects were frequently over-estimated, see M. A. Jahn, 'Railways and Suburban Development: outer West London, 1850 – 1900' (unpublished M.Phil. thesis, University of London, 1970).

60. There was, for instance, the case of Charles Henry Blake, a retired Indian civil servant, who put savings of £116,000 into building thirty-six houses on the Kensington Park estate in the 1850s, lent heavily to unreliable builders, and plunged into railway speculation, before being hauled back from ruin by his solicitors in time to catch a boom that brought financial success. His large collection of papers are in G.L.C.R.O.: Ladbroke Estate.

61. The most comprehensive statements on investment in house-building in the nineteenth century are: H. J. Habakkuk, 'Fluctuations in House-Building in Britain and the United States in the Nineteenth Century', *Journal of Economic History*, xxii (1962), 198 – 230, and J. Parry Lewis, *Building Cycles and Britain's Growth* (1965). Among other writers whose work is indicated in Professor Parry Lewis's book, E. W.

Cooney was the first to discuss building fluctuations in London and S. B. Saul offers an explanation nearest to the interpretation offered by us. See, respectively, 'Long Waves in Building in the British Economy of the Nineteenth Century', *Economic History Review*, xiii (1960), 257 – 69; 'House Building in England, 1890 – 1914', *Economic History Review*, xv (1962), 119 – 37.

62. From the 1840s to the 1870s, 80 per cent of house-builders undertook six houses or fewer per annum, and very few built more than fifty. Following the boom that peaked in 1880 – 1, relatively depressed conditions forced the industry to rationalize somewhat, and at the next peak in 1899 a mere seventeen firms (3 per cent of the total) were building over 40 per cent of new houses in London; even so, 60 per cent of all builders were still undertaking six houses or fewer in a year, and they accounted between them for about one-fifth of all new houses (G.L.C.R.O., Monthly Returns of the District Surveyors, 1872 – 99).

63. *Builder*, xxxv (1877), 42.

64. Details of the Paddington estate loans are contained in the St Peter's Park estate records of the ground-landlords, the Dean and Chapter of Westminster, now the Church Commissioners; details of the Walworth transactions are contained in the property ledgers of Edward Yates, a speculative builder in South London, the only such business records known to us to have survived as historical records.

65. See P. G. M. Dickson, *The Sun Insurance Office, 1710 – 1960* (1960); T. E. Gregory, *The Westminster Bank through a Century* (1936); Barry Supple, *The Royal Exchange Assurance. A history of British insurance, 1720 – 1970* (1970).

66. The operations we are describing here have not been sufficiently researched as yet but we are confident from the two most helpful collections of building society records that we have examined—those relating to the Temperance Permanent and the West London Permanent Building Societies—that there is much more to be done by way of detailed investigations in this field. The best available general histories of the building society movement in the nineteenth century are: Sir Harold Bellman, *Bricks and Mortals* (1949); J. Seymour Price, *Building Societies, their Origins and History* (1958); E. J. Cleary, *The Building Society Movement* (1965).

67. 'The Building Mania', *Builder*, vi (1848), 500 – 1, quoting the *Morning Herald*.

68. See David Owen, *English Philanthropy, 1660 – 1960* (1964), pp. 372 – 93.

69. William Howitt, 'Holidays for the People. Michaelmas', *People's Journal*, ii (1846), 171.

70. Ibid., 170.

71. Andrew Winter, 'Country Houses for the Working Classes', *People's Journal*, ii (1846), 135.

72. Henry Lazarus, *Landlordism: An illustration of the rise and spread of slumland* (1892), p. 46. For the rise of urban land-reform movements at this time, see D. A. Reeder, 'The Politics of Urban Leaseholds in Late Victorian England', *I.R.S.H.*, vi (1961), 1 – 18.

73. *Plays Unpleasant* (1926 edn.), p. xxv. The following excerpt comes from Act II (pp. 33 – 4).

74. Winter, op. cit., p. 134.

75. For 'rates made' see the annual volumes of *London Statistics* from 1890 onwards.

76. Malcolmson, op. cit., ch. 4. For the law on this, see G. St Leger Daniels, *A*

Handbook of the Law of Ejectment (1900), which was designed to be 'specially useful to those landlords and their agents who often find the "getting rid of tenants" an unpleasant necessity'.

77. J. F. B. Firth, 'London Government, and How to Reform It', in *Local Government and Taxation in the United Kingdom*, ed. J. W. Probyn (1882), pp. 147 – 269; S. and B. Webb, *The London Programme* (Fabian Society Tract, 1891).

10

Working-Class Standards of Living in Barrow and Lancaster, 1890–1914*

ELIZABETH ROBERTS

This article examines some aspects of working-class standards of living in two areas of north Lancashire, Lancaster and Barrow-in-Furness, in the period 1890 – 1914.[1] It has two apparently distinct but yet interrelated themes. Firstly it reinforces the argument that there is a value in studying local and regional standards of living,[2] as significant differences have been discovered in those standards not only between this area of north Lancashire and the nation as a whole, but also between it and the nearest areas in geographical terms which have been studied in detail, York[3] and south Lancashire.[4] Secondly the article, using both oral and documentary evidence, suggests that there are very considerable difficulties in attempting to quantify these standards of living because so many unquantifiable factors affecting working-class patterns of earnings, expenditure, and consumption have been revealed.

The use of oral evidence by historians is, as yet, hardly established as an accepted activity and oral interviewing is necessarily undertaken therefore with great caution. But oral evidence cannot be lightly dismissed as unreliable: we should remember that, for example, until a decade ago it was possible to use oral evidence to send people to the gallows. Respondents, of course, cannot be treated as if they were in a court of law, but it is possible for an interviewer to use the same skills as a cross-examiner to detect and discard unreliable statements by establishing their improbability or inconsistency with other known and documented facts, by internal consistency, or by conflict of evidence with their contemporaries. In other words, oral historians do not claim that they have a new historical source, they consider oral evidence as critically as any written documentary evidence. Systematic,

* From *Economic History Review*, 2nd series, 30 (2) (1977), 306 – 21. Reprinted by permission of the author and the editors of *Economic History Review*. A fuller development of the topics treated here is now to be found in E. Roberts, *A Woman's Place: An Oral History of Working Class Women 1890 – 1940* (Oxford, 1984).

planned, and structured interviewing can elicit a mass of information which displays its own rationale, and both an internal consistency within a series of interviews with an individual respondent, and also an external consistency with the evidence of other respondents and the available documentary and literary evidence. Oral evidence also provides much information which is not available from any other source; working-class men and women rarely kept diaries, account books, bills, and letters.

A total of 90 old people has been interviewed but of these 15 either came to the area or grew up after 1914 and their evidence is therefore not included in this article.[5] These samples reflect and represent the various social, economic, and occupational groups within the working class in both towns. The chief industries in Barrow were the manufacture of iron and steel, heavy engineering, and shipbuilding. The nature of these industries required the employment of a relatively large proportion of craftsmen,[6] and this is reflected in the sample. Twelve of the 35 respondents' fathers were skilled men; two shipwrights, three moulders, one fitter and turner, one brass finisher, two boilermakers, one stonemason, one welder, and one blacksmith. The rest of the men earning over £1 a week were either semi-skilled men like the raftsman on the Timber Dock or shop or office workers. Those earning under £1 a week were labourers in the steelworks, the shipbuilding and engineering works, and on the docks and railways.

There were proportionately fewer skilled men in Lancaster because the two largest firms, both of which manufactured linoleum and oilcloth, required largely unskilled men. These labourers earned a maximum of £1.0s. 3d. a week. However there were some craftsmen employed by these firms as engineers, and the furniture and joinery manufacturing firm of Gillows, and the Lancaster Carriage & Wagon Company (which closed, after a series of company mergers, in 1908) did employ skilled men. Nine of the 40 respondents' fathers were craftsmen; one electric wirer, one wheelwright, two engineers, one bricklayer, one blacksmith, two joiners, and one tinsmith. As in Barrow the men earning more than £1 per week were semi-skilled (bakers, painters, etc.) or shop and office workers.

There can be no question that what men and women earned is of obvious and fundamental importance in any consideration of working-class standards of living. Respondents are in general very clear about their fathers' basic rates of pay, and where documentary evidence exists they are proved to be remarkably accurate in their memories. Some however recognize that there was considerable difference between their fathers' basic rate of pay and his actual money wages, and their difficulty in assessing money wages is shared by the economic historian attempting to estimate overall incomes in both towns.

There were factors which tended to depress wages so that a man's average weekly wage was less than his basic weekly rate. Three factors produced considerable unemployment in Barrow. The nature of shipbuilding meant that at each stage of completion of a ship some craftsmen were laid off until the next vessel to be built required their particular skills. (Labourers could more easily be found alternative work without creating demarcation disputes.) Some remained unemployed, others went off in search of jobs; mobility of labour was endemic to the shipbuilding industry which was probably the last large industry to retain relatively large numbers of tramping artisans.[7] There is considerable oral evidence about these patterns of migration. Fathers and respondents themselves moved between Barrow, the Tyne, the Mersey, the Clyde, Belfast, and the United States in search of work. These mobile workers could not be counted as long-term unemployed as they usually found another job within a few weeks. Yet their incomes were continuously and adversely affected by their frequent migration; if they left their families in Barrow they had the expense of maintaining a home and themselves in lodgings. Highly skilled craftsmen could not afford to send home much more than £1 a week. Those who took their families with them had the recurring expense of moving people and possessions about the country.

Secondly, both the iron and steel, and the shipbuilding and engineering industries were affected by labour disputes either between management and men about wages and conditions of work or between unions about demarcation disputes. Both, too, were adversely affected by miners' strikes which cut off vital supplies of coal and coke. Thirdly, there were violent cyclical booms and slumps in demands for the products of both industries. Both labour disputes and cyclical depressions in trade affected craftsmen and labourers alike; the latter suffered more because they had fewer savings and no union funds to assist them.[8] The seriousness of the unemployment created by these periodic crises is indisputable but it is not possible (because no Ministry of Labour returns were made until after the passing of the Insurance Act of 1911) to quantify it, and consequently to construct an index of possible earnings.

There was not such a serious problem of unemployment in Lancaster but it did exist. Large numbers of labourers and craftsmen were employed in various branches of the building trade.[9] Many of these men could not work in the winter and the son of a bricklayer remembers his father and his workmates being unemployed for as long as ten weeks in a bad winter. In 1908 when the Lancaster Carriage & Wagon Works closed down, an estimated 2,000 were out of work. There was serious unemployment throughout 1908 – 9, and relief works were established for the unemployed who were put to work levelling areas of the town moor to create playing fields.[10] Oral evidence shows that many woodworkers eventually moved to carriage works in Manchester and Birmingham, and a small group emigrated. The men working at the linoleum works[11] and more especially the labourers, suffered every year from the four weeks' compulsory annual holiday (at Easter, Whitsuntide, in August, and at Christmas) without pay. (These holidays were usually described as lock-outs by the workmen.)

There were other factors, in Barrow especially, which, rather than depressing wages, tended to increase them to a level above the basic rate of pay. In periods when demand for their products was high the firm of Vickers, in order to stimulate production, introduced elaborate systems of payment, three of which, after 1900, were in simultaneous operation: they were payment by time, a piece-work system, and a premium bonus scheme. The two latter forms of payment were the target of repeated criticisms by the ASE.[12] Some of the complexities of the system of payments is revealed by the ASE membership card for 1908.[13] Individuals and groups of craftsmen worked varying amounts of overtime depending on the nature of their craft and the general state of trade. The ASE Minutes for 1896 record men working 72-, 93-, and 95-hour weeks. One respondent kept a diary of his hours of work and the maximum number of hours he worked in one week was 110 (in 1914).

Because of these various factors, chronic and periodic unemployment, holidays without pay, and different systems of payment, it is difficult to be exact about actual money wages in either town.[14] In general, however, the labourers in both towns throughout the period earned £1 a week or less. Craftmen's wages showed greater variations; ranging in the earlier part of the period from a minimum of about 30s. a week to a maximum of £2 a week in 1914; but, it must be stressed, frequently falling below this level because of unemployment.

One of the difficulties economic historians have encountered when considering wage rates is to estimate what in fact constituted an adequate living wage; i.e. what was the level of wages below which a man could no longer provide his family with food, clothing, and shelter. This is a particularly pertinent question for both Barrow and Lancaster with their large numbers of labourers earning £1 a week or less, and with craftsmen periodically earning on average less than 30s. per week.

Charles Booth in his 1889 survey of life and labour in London[15] estimated that 30.7 per cent of London's population was in poverty, many of their basic needs being unprovided for, while B. Seebohm Rowntree in his 1901 study of York[16] wrote that primary poverty is 'earning insufficient to obtain the minimum necessaries for the maintenance of mere physical efficiency.' He collected and collated the daily menus of 26 families and concluded that it was possible to draw a poverty line at 21s. 8d. for a family of four to five persons.[17] Any family earning less than this was in primary poverty. Rowntree estimated that 9.9 per cent of York's population was in this position while another 17.9 per cent suffered from secondary poverty, with wages adequate for the basic necessities if nothing was spent on drink, travel, and other 'extras'.[18]

There were other rather less well-known surveys made at approximately the same time.[19] The value of these surveys is inestimable, for they show in considerable detail the domestic economics of some working-class families. No one need question Rowntree's considered view that the poverty line in York was 21*s*. 8*d*. but it would seem that attempts to deduce, from what were small regional surveys, a national poverty line for late Victorian and Edwardian England are fraught with difficulties and are likely to create more problems than they solve:[20] using budgets and menus from 115 families taken from the various surveys, D. J. Oddy has concluded that an income of 30*s*. a week was necessary for a family of four to five persons, if a diet adequate in terms of calorific value, and of adequate proteins, carbohydrates, and fats, was to be obtained. Whilst Oddy's evidence applies only to the period up to 1900, it raises questions about the whole period 1890 – 1914 for Lancaster and Barrow. Craftsmen's wages were very gradually rising, but for the whole of this period labourers' wages were less than the poverty lines drawn by both Oddy and Rowntree, and in depressed years craftsmen certainly earned less than 30*s*. per week. Moreover, Lancaster and Barrow families were larger than the 4.73 persons used by Rowntree and Oddy (with the exception of Lancaster in the 1911 Census).[21]

And yet it is doubtful if the working classes were quite as poor as one may logically conclude from these statistics about wages, poverty lines, and larger-than-average families. The statistics for death-rates per 1,000 of the population in both towns show that they were significantly lower than the national average.[22] And in 1912 the Barrow School Medical Officer of Health, in his third annual report, found 3.5 per cent of five-year-old boys and 0.33 per cent of five-year-old girls, and 3.3 per cent of 13-year-old boys and 1.1 per cent of 13-year-old girls malnourished.[23] These figures do not suggest a significant problem of malnutrition.

It is necessary to consider three factors, all interrelated, if this apparent paradox of a healthier-than-average population existing on earnings near or below the poverty line is to be explained. These factors are the economic role of the working-class married woman, family patterns of expenditure, and also patterns of consumption; it is in these areas that oral evidence has proved rather more illuminating than that from documentary sources. It has also seemed worthwhile to examine both towns together because, despite their differing industrial structures, their patterns of social life have proved very similar. The families from which evidence has been collected employed a variety of methods of defeating poverty and ensuring survival; none of these methods, however, can be quantified satisfactorily.

The local census figures show that very few married women were in full-time employment outside the home.[24] Oral evidence reflects these statistics; three Lancaster mothers were weavers, two did full-time domestic work, and one shop work. Only one Barrow woman worked full-time, as a cleaner, and she, like three of the Lancaster women, was a widow. Therefore only four of the respondents' mothers out of 75 earned a full second income for the family.[25] There were, however, 24 others employed on a casual part-time basis. Their occupations are not enumerated on the census returns but their financial contributions to their families could be of considerable significance. One took in dressmaking, two opened shops in their parlours to sell home-made pies and cakes, four helped their husbands in their small corner shops, three had lodgers, three did domestic cleaning, four were cooks and housekeepers (two of whom 'lived in' and had their families with them), two took in washing, one (who was quite illiterate but probably the most enterprising of all) bought items at the auction rooms, leaving them there and returning the next week to push up the bidding. She made enough money to buy each of her six children their own house.[26] The most hard-working were the remaining four who did more than one job, various combinations of baby-minding, taking in washing, housing lodgers, cleaning, dressmaking, and decorating houses. There is no way of quantifying these earnings; some women worked very hard like the washerwomen who washed every day (except Sunday) for customers, while others worked intermittently, possibly when their husbands were unemployed. Others again were not paid in cash but in goods.[27]

The second and third factors which need to be examined if the apparent paradox of low wages in Barrow and Lancaster combined with a healthier than average population is to be explained, are the interrelated ones of family patterns of expenditure and consumption. In these matters all working-class women had a vital economic role to play. It was their direct responsibility to see that their families were fed and clothed. Any consideration of working-class standards of living must inevitably take into account what people ate, for upon that largely depended their health, happiness, and general well-being.

Many criticisms have been made of the abilities of working-class women to select and cook food. In the matter of the selection they have been criticized for choosing either a limited, unbalanced diet or one which was nutritious but uneconomical because it relied heavily on animal protein. Rowntree regretted that the working class did not select a diet which was both economical and nutritious, but recognized that 'the adoption of such a diet would require considerable changes in established customs and many prejudices would have to be uprooted.'[28]

In 1904 the report of the Inter-Departmental Committee on Physical Deterioration (established to investigate the reason why as many as 60 per cent of volunteers for the Boer War, in certain areas, were rejected on medical grounds) stated that, 'a diet of bread and butter for breakfast, potatoes and herrings for dinner, and bread and butter for tea, enlivened by some cheap cuts of meat on Sunday and purchases from the fried-fish shop during the week, when funds permitted, was the normal working-class diet.'[29] The report also stated that the poor could have obtained a better diet in terms of calories and nutrients if less had been spent on animal protein. 'It is no doubt the case that with greater knowledge the poor might live more cheaply than they do.'[30]

Oddy writes: 'We know little about the status of foods in the nineteenth century, but there is a suggestion that certain prejudices against fruit, vegetables, and milk were retained until the beginning of the twentieth century.'[31] These criticisms of working-class choice of food are by implication criticism of the working-class woman, because as the controller of the family's budget and shopping it was she who created and sustained both her family's preferences and prejudices in their tastes in food. Criticisms of this woman's abilities as a cook have been less generalized. Eunice Schofield wrote bluntly: 'Many housewives did not know how to cook,' and 'they generally speaking had no training in the art of cooking.'[32] Margaret Hewitt commented: 'The truth of the matter was that amongst the working-classes generally the standard of domestic accomplishment was deplorably low.'[33] She quotes Victorian eye-witnesses to prove that the standards of cooking and housekeeping in general were very poor and argues that it is unfair to confine one's criticisms merely to the married cotton operatives of Lancashire. Dr Hewitt blames the lack of adequate teaching of cookery in schools for this depressing state of affairs. Robert Roberts, writing of Salford at the turn of the century said: 'In the poorest household through a lack of both knowledge and utensils little cooking of any kind went on except for the grilling on a fork before the kitchen fire of bits of bacon and fish. Many never cooked vegetables, not even potatoes.'[34]

Oral evidence for Barrow and Lancaster suggests that working-class women were rather more skilled than those criticized by the various authorities quoted, and that patterns of expenditure and consumption differed considerably from both national patterns and from those of York and cotton-dominated southern Lancashire. This evidence about patterns in local diet has been corroborated by virtually all the respondents; there were certain individual differences but they existed within a common framework of similarities. Oral evidence has also indicated the difficulties of constructing a price index, as no significant correlation has been established between the lists of commodities whose prices were quoted in the local press, and the actual patterns of consumption of the working class.[35]

The working classes were poor and they also worked hard physically; consequently for both economic and nutritional reasons they consumed large amounts of carbohydrates. All the Victorian surveys show that bread and potatoes provided the basis of working-class diets. Oddy's analysis of the data gives the mean per capita consumption of bread as 6.7 lb. per week and that of potatoes as 1.6 lb. per week.[36] Certainly these two items formed the largest part of working-class diets, although it is of course impossible at this distance in time to be exact about the amounts consumed in any family. However, as the mothers of all the respondents, without exception, baked their own bread, some can remember how much was produced each week and these memories suggest great variations between families in the amount of bread consumed. One family ate ten 2-lb. loaves a day, but much more usually women baked one or two stones of flour per week, suggesting that most local families ate less than the national average.[37]

There were many secondary sources of carbohydrates; pastries both sweet and savoury, suet dumplings and puddings, pasta and rice puddings, cakes, scones, and porridge. The nutritional value of the latter was enthusiastically canvassed by both Rowntree and the Barrow Schools' Medical Officer.[38] This enthusiasm was widely shared by the majority of working-class families in Barrow and Lancaster and their habit of putting treacle on the top gave them a valuable source of iron. For the main meal of the day (traditionally eaten at midday) the housewife did not rely on expensive animal protein except for Sunday, when the family usually had a joint. Instead there was a reliance on very cheap animal protein (bones, all kinds of offal, the cheapest cuts of meat, fish) and vegetables. Rowntree has shown that there was a basic prejudice against vegetables among the working class of York, where there are few references to vegetables in the menus given and only six recorded instances of a family eating soup.[39] On one of these occasions the soup had been given by a charitable organization and it is possible that this association with charity prejudiced the poor against soup; or possibly it was, as Rowntree himself argued, that soups and broths took a long time and some skill to make.

Barrovians and Lancastrians thought of vegetables very differently, regarding them as a cheap, nutritious, enjoyable, and essential part of their diet, as indeed they were providing iron, vitamins, and protein. 'I think in my own mind that vegetables is as good as if you've got a lot of meat.'[40] 'It was a good thing really, the vegetables, and I think that made us because we're all big-boned.'[41] A very wide range was eaten; potatoes, turnips, carrots, parsnips, leeks, onion, beans and peas (dried and fresh in season), lettuce, cucumber, tomatoes, celery, watercress cabbage, brussels sprouts, beetroot, cauliflower, and lentils, being the more usual ones. They were sometimes eaten alone in various vegetarian dishes, the commonest one being potatoes, carrots, and turnips, mashed together with butter. They could, however, be more elaborate like this vegetarian hot-pot: a layer of potatoes, a layer of tapioca, a layer of carrots and split peas, another layer of potatoes, onions, and tapioca, and seasoning. More usually, vegetables were added either to stock to make broth or to cheap cuts of meat to make stews, casseroles, and hot-pots of many different varieties. The most usual basis for the broths were ham or marrow bones, or sheep's head or heart. There were dumplings in the broth. The commonest basis for the other dishes were stewing beef, mince, neck of lamb, breast of mutton, black puddings, tripe, pigs' trotters, cow heel, and rabbit, used both alone and also in sometimes surprising combinations.

There was very little fried food; only fish and bacon are mentioned. The latter did not form a significant part of the diet; it was regarded exclusively as a breakfast food and was cooked in homes only where either father was a craftsman in full-time work or where there was a second wage from an older son or daughter. This relative absence of fried food (which had the merit of being quickly prepared but the disadvantages of being expensive and also, in quantity, harmful to health), contrasts with the evidence from Salford given by Robert Roberts.[42]

There was no reliance on convenience foods of any kind. Some housewives had definite prejudices about tinned food, believing it to be detrimental to health by either causing a general malaise or more specifically cancer. In no family did bought fish and chips form a regular part of the diet; they were an occasional treat. One respondent whose parents kept one of the earliest fish-and-chip shops in Barrow (beginning of the 1890s) believes that the usual customers for fish and chips were adults going home late at night from the theatres, music halls, and pubs. Some charitably minded women bought ready-cooked pies and hams from neighbours who were trying to earn some money. But basically working-class wives did not rely on buying ready-cooked food; it was considered expensive and many proud housekeepers believed that in buying it they somehow belittled both themselves and their culinary skills.

The historian using oral evidence does well to regard enthusiastic generalizations about the past with some suspicion. Respondents are unanimous in their enthusiasm for their mothers' cooking, recognizing that the only limitations placed upon her culinary achievements were those imposed by shortage of money. 'My mother was a very good cook. It was just a question of finance to get the ingredients to make them with.'[43] This enthusiasm could rightly be dismissed as pure nostalgia, but because of the widely corroborated evidence of the housewives' skills in making not only the above-mentioned dishes but also home-made jams and wines, pickles and potted meat, there is no reason to question their evidence that working-class women were good cooks. One begins to suspect that those historians who believed that traditional English peasant cooking disappeared with the Industrial Revolution might well be right about textile areas and large conurbations, but would be wrong about smaller urban areas where 90 per cent or more of married women did not go out to full-time work,[44] where it was possible for traditional skills to be continually handed down from mother to daughter, and where the women had the time to devote to dishes which required both long hours of cooking and of preparation. There is evidence from both towns that the domestic science taught in school was of little practical value, and this supports Dr Hewitt's view.[45] Women respondents claim, however, that they learned to cook by watching and helping their mothers. This was not possible in areas of cotton Lancashire where larger percentages of married women were at work.[46]

The housewife's skill in choosing her family's food, and cooking, is one explanation for the working classes of Barrow and Lancaster being rather more nutritiously and economically fed than their counterparts in both York and other areas of Lancashire.

There is also another factor, which again is intractable to quantification. In his survey of York, Rowntree concluded that free sources of food played a negligible part in sustaining the working classes.[47] Oral evidence from Barrow and Lancaster suggests that this was not the case, and that consequently it is not possible to equate patterns of expenditure with patterns of consumption. In years of depression, the soup kitchens provided a vital element in working-class diets—the soup kitchen in the iron-and-steel-works area estimated that it had fed two million people in twenty months in 1908 – 9.[48]

The working classes went to the soup kitchen only as a last resort, but there were many other sources of free food which were available to the poor and which did not carry the stigma of charity. Some ways were however less socially and morally acceptable than others: living on credit tended to be frowned upon by the socially respectable and aspiring members of the working class. There is, however, considerable oral evidence to suggest that many labourers' families had from necessity regularly to rely on credit. This was especially true in Lancaster during the four compulsory long holidays each year. 'The whole bill she ran up during that holiday week probably didn't come to 10s. but when you were paying it off at 1d. and 2d. it took a lot of getting rid of.'[49] Families like this one struggled to pay what they owed; some never settled their debts. 'You either owed the milkman, the coalman, the doctor, or you were in arrears with the rent. There were a lot of arrears in them days.'[50]

The problem of unpaid debts is frequently mentioned by respondents whose parents either owned or managed small corner shops, the chief suppliers of credit. Unfortunately the accounts of these small local shops have disappeared. The shopkeepers in turn lived on credit, and because debts were never paid off, the small local traders frequently went out of business; larger firms could presumably write off some of their bad debts out of profits. There seems to be no way of assessing the amount of credit acquired by the working classes in the period before the First World War, but respondents' evidence does suggest that a proportion of the food consumed by some families was not paid for. One's sympathy with their need to live on credit should not obscure the fact that the unscrupulous could and did develop the art of gaining credit from a large number of shops over a wide area, never settling more than a fraction of their debts, but usually just enough to persuade the shopkeeper to extend the credit further.

Acquiring food on credit was not of course obtaining food which was really free. Many men still acted out their old traditional roles as cultivators and even hunters, if only on a part-time basis. Of the 62 respondents so far asked, 31 had fathers with an allotment, and/or who kept poultry, six kept hens only, 18 grew fruit and vegetables, and seven did both. Most families used the produce of their gardens to supplement their purchased food, others relied on them for much of their basic food.[51] Others were able to sell their surplus eggs, tomatoes, and lettuces to neighbours, thus gaining extra income. Families who did not have their own allotment could and did benefit from other people's; relations and neighbours were always willing to give away surplus fruit and vegetables, and eggs or to sell them at prices well below market value. There is no way of putting a monetary value on the produce grown in these gardens, but there can be no doubt that the men who worked a 55-hour week and then laboured in their gardens deserved the fruit and vegetable harvest they had. It is surprising that so many found the strength and determination and genuine love of gardening needed to tend their allotments, yet here are signs of a deep working-class sentiment and attitude.

There was also a lot of living off the countryside: again it is impossible to quantify the benefits from this; at one end of the scale were little children going out once a year to collect a few blackberries, at the other end are families who obtained a significant second income from their efforts.[52] The countryside provided a useful harvest for those seeking it: rabbits, mushrooms, crab-apples, elderberries, nettles (for beer), bilberries, and samphire were all collected. But sources of more nutritious food were the River Lune and the sea and the shore at Morecambe (three miles from Lancaster) and Barrow. Children forked for eels in the Lune and collected cockles, mussels, winkles and crabs from the shores. Men and older boys trod for flukes, or laid down lines on the beach returning after high tide to remove the fish; some quite poor families in Barrow afforded boats and went fishing with nets in deep water.[53] Many more families than those whose fathers were fishermen benefited from their activities; relations and neighbours were given fish or were sold it at low prices.

The second necessity of life was clothing. Families who considered that it was not respectable to buy food on credit had no scruples about acquiring clothing and household linen through various clothing clubs. These were organized by local shops and also by the so-called Scotchmen, who were itinerant door-to-door traders, descendants of the old packmen. Each customer was allowed £1 of goods of which she paid 1s. a week for 21 weeks. These clubs were widely used and again it is difficult to begin to estimate the overall indebtedness of sections of the working classes.

These traders were, however, used only for such items as shoes, sheets, blankets, and 'special-occasion' clothes. The great majority of the working-class's clothes were not bought from ordinary retail shops, and this again makes the construction of a price index virtually irrelevant, for the clothes whose prices are listed in the local press were rarely bought by the working classes. Garments were bought from second-hand clothes dealers and most especially at jumble sales; the great majority of women made some of the family clothes, using material bought as cheap remnants in the market, or cutting-up or altering handed-down clothes. Very old clothes were cut up and converted into peg-rugs, the only carpets the great majority of the working classes owned. Others were made into patchwork quilts. Men who worked in the textile mills and linoleum works in Lancaster were given a weekly issue of cotton material to clean their machines, this was brought home and converted into babies' napkins, underclothes, sheets, and curtains, and foot bindings for the men who preferred them to socks. Several respondents have suggested that much of this cotton material was brought out illegally. More legitimately there was also the opportunity to buy remnants of cloth and linoleum from the works at very low prices. One is forced to the conclusion that a substantial part of the clothing and household linen and floor-covering used by the working classes of both towns was not bought in normal retail shops but was acquired in some other more economical way. Oral evidence about food and clothing indicates the many and various ways in which families were able to feed and clothe themselves both adequately and very economically.

The third necessity of life, housing, could not be obtained free unless the parents, like those of two respondents, were resident domestic servants. Nor, in the case of Barrow, was it even obtained cheaply. Leading Socialist politicians speaking in Barrow in the 1890s complained that house rents in Barrow were 2s. or 3s. more than in other similar areas.[54] Consideration of rents is restricted here, however, to Barrow and Lancaster. The levels of rents were basically unaltered throughout the period; respondents and advertisements in the local press show that working-class houses ranged from 3s. to 5s. a week in Lancaster, and 4s. 6d. to 7s. 6d. a week in Barrow.

Oral evidence indicates however that within this very broad generalization about levels of rent there were considerable individual differences in expenditure on housing, and that it is misleading to express the cost of housing as a certain proportion of income. Statistics on average rents do not indicate the wide differences in attitude towards the importance of housing, and consequently in the proportion of total income which was spent on it. The socially aspiring labourer spent a large proportion of his income on his house while the craftsman who enjoyed his drink did not. Although craftsmen were anxious to maintain wage differentials between themselves and other craftsmen and labourers, there was no distinction made in housing, craftsmen and labourers were very likely to live next door to each other and pay identical rents. Many families moved house frequently, and oral evidence suggests that while expenditure on food and clothing tended to be constant, that on housing was variable, depending on changes in the family's level of income. One of the most surprising pieces of evidence from respondents in Barrow is that of poor families placing such importance on housing that they managed to buy their own houses about the turn of the century. Four families did this.[55] The prices for small terraced houses were about £300. These home owners seem to have grasped the idea, later publicized by the Trades Council, that it was cheaper to buy a house in Barrow than rent it.[56]

One of the fundamental problems confronting the economic historian studying working-class standards of living is the problem of drink. Oral evidence shows some families forced into the workhouse because of the father's excessive drinking, and it shows many more 'kept low' for the same reason.[57] The stark choice facing many working-class people was expressed succinctly by one respondent. 'My mother was bigoted against drink and adamant that we did not take to drink because you cannot put down your own drink and food into your children's bellies at the same time.'[58] Any calculations about real wages and the number of families living below the poverty line are liable to be distorted by the father's drinking habits. Nationally there was a gradual decline in the annual consumption of beer from the extraordinary 1876 figure of 34 gallons for every man, woman, and child.[59] There are no figures of beer or spirits consumption in Lancaster and Barrow, but the annual reports of the Chief Constable of Barrow contain some revealing observations.[60] In his report for 1908 the Chief Constable suggested a reason why the number of convictions for drunkenness varied from year to year.[61] 'When employment is scarce drunkenness tends to diminish and these figures (i.e. for 1908) afford further proof if that were required of the acute distress in the borough.' Certainly the high figures for convictions in the years from 1898 to 1903 coincide with a boom time for trade, and similarly the low figures for the earlier years of the 1890s correspond with the years of depressed trade.[62] If this argument is valid it does suggest that high wages in prosperous years were fairly well accounted for in some families by a corresponding increase in the amount the father drank.

This article represents an attempt to indicate, using mainly oral evidence, some of the major factors affecting working-class standards of living in two specific urban areas during a limited period. It has been shown that the standard of living of every working-class family was substantially affected by one or more factors which at present are not open to statistically valid quantification; the casual wages earned by working-class women; eating habits which meant the choice of cheap but nutritious traditional foods, the supplies of free or cheap food and clothing, and variations in the proportion of income spent on housing and drink. Although it may be possible in the future to construct a real-wage index which takes into account the factors examined in the article, it would appear from the oral evidence collected that they should not be ignored when any retrospective assessment is being made of working-class standards of living.

APPENDIX I

Basic wages in Barrow[63]

(a) *Craftsmen*

1890	Joiners[64]	32*s.* to 33*s.*
	Carpenters[65]	32*s.* to 33*s.*
	Pattern-makers[66]	36*s.*
	Plumbers[67]	33*s.*
	Ironfounders[68]	34*s.*
	Engineers[69]	33*s.* to 36*s.*
1897–8	Fitters and turners[70]	35*s.* to 36*s.*
1908	Pattern-makers[71]	38*s.*
	Coppersmiths	38*s.*
	Turners	37*s.*
	Smiths	36*s.*
	Brass-finishers	36*s.* 6*d.*
	Fitters	36*s.*
	Planers, millers, shapers	33*s.*
	Drillers	30*s.*
	Capstan-lathe turners	30*s.*
	Shell turners	25*s.*

(b) *Labourers*

1892	Pulp-work labourer[72]	20*s.*
1896	Labourer's rate[73]	18*s.* to 20*s.*
1910	Labourers[74]	19*s.*
1911	Labourers[75]	18*s.* to 22*s.*

Basic wages in Lancaster

(a) *Craftsmen*

1890	Joiners[76]	6¾*d.* an hour for 55½-hour week
	Stonemasons[77]	8*d.* an hour
1891	Cabinet-makers[78]	32*s.*
1892	Joiners[79]	7¼*d.* an hour for 54½-hour week
1894	Masons[80]	35*s.*
1897	Plumbers[81]	9*d.* an hour for 53-hour week

APPENDIX I—*cont'd*

1899	Masons[82]	$9\frac{1}{2}$ *d.* an hour
1904	Joiners[83]	34*s.*
1914	Cabinet-makers,[84] polishers, wood-carvers	$9\frac{1}{2}$ *d.* an hour for 51-hour week

(a) *Labourers*

1890	Wagon works labourer[85]	17*s.* to 20*s.*
1892	Oilcloth labourers[86]	17*s.* to 18*s.*
1906	Oilcloth labourers[87]	18*s.* to 19*s.*
1909	Oilcloth labourers[88]	19*s.* to £1. 0*s.* 3*d.*

APPENDIX II

Number of cases of drunkenness per 1000 population in Barrow-in-Furness[89]

1890	11.3	1895	6.7	1900	13.7	1905	8.3	1910	5.8
1891	7.5	1896	9.3	1901	16.1	1906	10.9	1911	7.8
1892	6.4	1897	7.9	1902	12.5	1907	8.6	1912	6.1
1893	5.5	1898	11.3	1903	10.6	1908	4.7	1913	5.0
1894	7.4	1899	12.8	1904	7.9	1909	3.6	1914	6.7

NOTES

1. This research was supported by an S.S.R.C grant for the period 1974−6. Previously it was a pilot study assisted by a Nuffield Small Grant. The work has been carried out under the aegis of the Centre for North-West Regional Studies in the University of Lancaster and with the encouragement and helpful advice of Dr John Marshall, Director of the Centre. The project also covers the years 1914−30, but only the earlier period of 1890−1914 is considered in this article.

2. The need for regional and local studies of standards of living has been suggested *inter alios* by R. S. Neale, 'The Standard of Living, 1780−1844: a Regional and Class Study', *Economic History Review*, 2nd ser. xix (1966), 590; G. Barnsby, 'The Standard of Living in the Black Country During the Nineteenth Century', ibid. xxiv (1971), 220; and M. W. Flinn, 'Trends in Real Wages, 1750−1850', ibid. xxvii (1974), 395.

3. B. Seebohm Rowntree, *Poverty. A Study of Town Life* (1901).

4. Margaret Hewitt, *Wives and Mothers in Victorian Industry* (1958); Robert Roberts, *The Classic Slum* (1973 edn.).

5. A summary of the details of the familial, social, and economic backgrounds of the other 75 respondents is available from the author on request. Information about some respondents appears in footnotes.

6. Unfortunately it is not possible to determine the exact proportion of craftsmen to labourers as the census returns for 1891, 1901, and 1911 do not differentiate between them. *The Census of 1891*, vol. iii, Table 7, pp. 375−83, lists men under the heading

of the material with which they worked. *The Census of 1901*, County of Lancaster, Table 35, pp. 144 – 5, enumerates general labourers, but labourers in specific industries are counted with craftsmen, e.g. bricklayers, bricklayers' labourers—485. *The Census of 1911*, vol. x, Table 23, pp. 118 – 19, enumerates labourers and craftsmen in the same way as the 1901 Census.

7. E. J. Hobsbawm, 'The Tramping Artisan', *Econ. Hist. Rev.* 2nd ser. iii (1950 – 1), 299. D. Stark, 'Origins and Development of a One Industry Town, 1890 – 1910' (unpublished M. A. dissertation, University of Lancaster, 1972), p. 7.

8. Press reports, union records, and, after 1909, the annual reports of the Distress Committee show that the periods Sept. 1891 to March 1893, Jan. 1895 to Jan. 1896, 1897 to early 1898, 1905, and 1907 – 9 were times of particularly serious unemployment and distress caused by either trade depression or labour disputes, or both.

9. *The Census of 1901* (vol. cited), Table 35a, p. 178, enumerates 2,123 men in building and works of construction in the urban district of Lancaster. *The Census of 1911* (vol. cited), Table 34, p. 173, enumerates 3,359 thus engaged.

10. *Lancaster Guardian*, 5, 19 Sept. 1908, 3 Oct. 1908, 5 Dec. 1908, 9 Jan. 1909.

11. *The Census of 1901* (vol. cited); Table 35a, p. 178, under the heading 'All Other Occupations' enumerates 1,120 men engaged in floorcloth and oilcloth manufacture. *The Census of 1911* (vol. cited), Table 24, p. 173, enumerates 3,359 men thus engaged.

12. A.S.E. Minutes for the Barrow District Committee, 23 Aug. 1899, 5, 19, 27 Sept. 1899, 28 April 1904, 12 May 1904.

13. The card quotes, 'Overtime rates: members on piece-work working overtime must receive a shilling for the half day, three shillings for a whole night and two shillings per night for the night shift apart from piece prices. Night Shift: the rate for the night shift is to be seventy-five hours pay for $57\frac{1}{2}$ hours work.'

14. Appendix I lists the basic wage rates mentioned in documentary sources.

15. C. Booth, *Life and Labour of the People* (1889).

16. Rowntree, op. cit., p. 296.

17. Ibid. p. 296.

18. Rowntree, op. cit., p. 296.

19. *Family Budgets, being the Income and Expenses of Twenty-eight British Households, 1891 – 4*, published by the Economic Club (1896); D. N. Paton, J. C. Dunlop, and Elsie Inglis, *On the Dietaries of the Labouring Classes of the City of Edinburgh* (1901); Dr J. Oliver, 'The Diet of Toil', *Lancet*, 29 June 1895, 1629 – 35.

20. D. J. Oddy, 'Working-class Diets in Late Nineteenth Century Britain', *Econ. Hist. Rev.* 2nd ser. xxiii (1970), 314.

21. This figure was given as the national-average size of family in the Census of 1891. The averages for Lancaster and Barrow were as follows: *The Census of 1891*, vol. 1, Table 7, pp. 177, 179: Lancaster 5.58 persons, Barrow 5.61 persons. *The Census of 1901* (vol. cited), Table 12, pp. 64, 66: Lancaster 5.35 persons, Barrow 5.58 persons. *The Census of 1911*, vol. viii, Table 27, p. 197, and Table 27a, p. 216: Lancaster 4.39 persons, Barrow 4.95 persons.

22.

Death-Rates per 1000 Population		
England and Wales	*Barrow*	*Lancaster*
1890 – 9	18.34	15.54	16.2
1900 – 10	15.8	13.28	14.69
1910 – 14	13.76	13.62	13.19

These figures are taken from the Medical Officers' of Health Reports. The figures for Lancaster are taken from the Annual Reports of the Medical Officer of Health. Some are kept in Lancaster City Library. Others, including those in manuscript form, are kept by the Lancaster District Community Physician. The figures for Barrow are from the Annual Reports of Medical Officers of Health which are included in the *Borough Accounts of Barrow-in-Furness*. These were published annually from 1880 and are kept in Barrow Town Library.

23. School Medical Officer of Health, Annual Report for 1912, *Borough Accounts of Barrow-in-Furness* (Barrow, 1912).

24. *The Census of 1891* does not give these figures. *The Census of 1901* (vol. cited), Table 35a, p. 179, enumerates 5.8 per cent of married and widowed women at work in Barrow and 10.2 per cent in Lancaster. *The Census of 1911* (vol. cited), Table 23, p. 118 (Barrow), and Table 25, p. 176 (Lancaster), distinguishes between married and widowed women. The figures for the former were: Barrow 4.5 per cent and Lancaster 8.7 per cent. There were much higher percentages of widows in full-time work, 29 per cent in Barrow and 23 per cent in Lancaster.

25. Two of these women also did part-time work at home when not in full-time work.

26. Mr P.I.B. b. 1900, fourth of six children (code notation to preserve anonymity of respondent). Father was a labourer at the steelworks, wages 18s. basically but could be 24s, with overtime. Mother was a labourer in the jute works before marriage.

27. Oral evidence also shows that boys and men had part-time jobs which earned small but significant amounts of extra income for the family. Boys, before they left school, were employed as shop assistants, delivery boys, and newspaper sellers. A minority of men, despite their 54 – 5 hour week, worked on allotments, as barmen, and as odd-job men in the middle-class areas of the town. As well as money, butcher boys received joints of meat, shop assistants were allowed to buy cracked eggs very cheaply, and men were given fruit and vegetables from the allotments where they worked.

28. Rowntree, op. cit., p. 105.

29. *Inter-Departmental Committee on Physical Deterioration* (Parl. Papers, cd. 2175, 1904, XXX), p. 11.

30. Ibid. (P.P. 1904, XXXII), p. 224.

31. Oddy, loc. cit. 322; this suggestion was made also in J. C. Dummond and Anne Wilbraham, *The Englishman's Food* (1939), p. 379.

32. Eunice Schofield, 'Food and Cooking of the Working Class about 1900', *Transactions of the Historic Society of Lancashire & Cheshire*, cxxiii (1971), 106, 152.

33. Hewitt, op. cit. pp. 75, 78 – 80.

34. Roberts, op. cit. pp. 109 – 10.

35. Local market prices throughout the period 1890 – 1914 largely reflect prices of foods which did not constitute the main element in working-class diet. Certain quoted items, e.g. veal and chicken, were never bought by the working classes at all. The most useful prices quoted are those for potatoes.

36. Oddy, loc. cit. 318.

37. Mrs. S.2.B. b. 1895, third of ten children. Father was a labourer in the steelworks, wage 18s. Mother went out periodically helping newly confined mothers. She also took in sewing.

38. Rowntree, op. cit. p. 105; School Medical Officer's Report for 1912, *Borough Accounts of Barrow-in-Furness* (Barrow, 1912).

39. Rowntree, op. cit. ch. VIII *passim*.

40. Mr P.2.L. b. 1899, third of nine children. Father was a labourer in the linoleum works, wage £1.0s. 3d. Mother was a confectioner before marriage but had no work after marriage.

41. Mr M.I.B. b. 1892, fifth of 12 children (two died as babies). Father was a labourer on the railway, wage 18s. to £1 a week. Mother was a domestic servant before marriage but had no work after marriage until she took in lodgers during the First World War.

42. Roberts, op. cit. p. 107.

43. Mr. G.I.L, b. 1904, eldest of five children. Father was a labourer in the linoleum works but was frequently unemployed, wage £1. 0s. 3d. Mother was a domestic servant before marriage and took in washing after marriage and went out cleaning.

44. See above, p. 252.

45. e.g. respondents' views, and *Barrow Herald*, 8 March 1884; and see above, p. 253.

46. The Census of 1901 gives these figures of married women at work, aged 15 – 35 (the chief child-bearing age): Burnley 59.7 per cent, Preston 50.5 per cent, Blackburn 63.9 per cent, Bury 44.8 per cent. These figures are discussed in George Newman, *Infant Mortality a Social Problem* (1906), pp. 103 – 10. Roberts, op. cit. p. 107, writing on the married women at work in Salford, said, 'They had little time to cook or indeed to learn how to, since their mothers before them had often been similarly occupied in the mills. This I think contributed to the low culinary standards which existed in the Lancashire cotton towns before the First World War.'

47. Rowntree, op. cit. pp. 112 – 14.

48. *Barrow News*, 25 July 1909.

49. Mr G.I.L.—See above, p. 255.

50. Mr M.I.L. b. 1910, youngest of seven children. Father was a labourer in the linoleum works, wage £1.0s. 3d. He deserted the family when Mr M.I.L. was a small boy. Mother was a seamstress before marriage, she sold home-made pies to make money after marriage but was forced to rely basically on the wages of the older children.

51. e.g. Mr M.I.B.—See above, p. 254.

52. The most successful family which made a living off the countryside was the family of Mr P.2.L.—See above, p. 254. Depending on the season the father, helped by the older children, collected shell-fish, mushrooms, and blackberries, and poached rabbits. The family was fed first and the surplus was sold.

53. Respondents whose families had boats report that they were owned in a co-operative way by two or more male adults within the family.

54. Keir Hardie, in *Barrow Herald*, 18 Oct. 1892; Pete Curran (Labour's first Parliamentary candidate in Barrow in 1895), in ibid. 9 March 1895.

55. Mr M.I.B. (see above, p. 254), Mr P.I.B. (see above, p. 252). Mr F.2.B. b. 1900, youngest of three children. Father was a postman, wage £1. Mother before marriage was a housemaid (in 10 Downing Street). She had no work after marriage. Mrs M.I.B. b. 1898, youngest of five children. Father was a boiler maker, wage

35*s*.—£2. Mother was a domestic servant before marriage. She had no work after marriage.

56. Throughout 1904 the Trades Council advertised in the press arguing that if a purchaser could raise a deposit of £10 he could pay off his mortgage at about 12*s*. a month instead of paying at least £1 a month rent.

57. The most extreme example among the respondents of a family 'kept low' was that of Mrs B.I.L. b. 1888, youngest of five children. Father was a labourer in the mill, wage under £1. He was a drunkard and physically abused his wife. She was a weaver before and after marriage, having to work to support the children. The bailiffs twice took all the family's furniture. The mother died aged 32 and the father refused to take any responsibility for the children. They were brought up by the maternal grandparents.

58. Mr G.I.L.—See above, p. 255.

59. Roberts, op. cit. pp. 122 – 3.

60. Chief Constable's Annual Reports, 1890 – 1914. *Borough Accounts of Barrow-in-Furness*. The Lancaster reports have as yet not been discovered.

61. See Appendix II.

62. Stark, op. cit. *passim*.

63. I am indebted to Nigel Todd, a research student at Lancaster University, for much of the documentary evidence on wages. An exhaustive search carried out by Mr Todd who is researching labour movements in Barrow and Lancaster, has failed to reveal records for most of the trade unions.

64. *Barrow Herald*, 1 Jan. 1890.

65. J. D. Marshall, *Furness and the Industrial Revolution* (Barrow, 1958), p. 400.

66. Ibid. p. 400.

67. *Barrow Herald*, 2 May 1891.

68. Marshall, op. cit. p. 401.

69. Ibid. p. 401.

70. A.S.E., Minutes from the Barrow District Committee, 15 June 1897 and 3 March 1898.

71. All the information for 1908 is printed on the membership card issued to members of the A.S.E. It is in the possession of Mr M.6.B. who came to Vickers in 1913 from Tyneside to work as a shipwright.

72. *Barrow Herald*, Jan. 1892.

73. Barrow Trades Council, Jan. 1896.

74. *Barrow Herald*, 1 Feb. 1910.

75. Ibid. 10 Jan. 1911.

76. *Lancaster Guardian*, 3 May 1890.

77. Ibid. Nov. 1890.

78. *Lancaster Observer*, 4 Dec. 1891.

79. *Lancaster Guardian*, 12 Sept. 1892.

80. Ibid. April, 1894.

81. Ibid. Dec. 1897.

82. Ibid. Aug. 1899.

83. *Lancaster Guardian*, 1904.

84. Ibid. July 1914.

85. Ibid. 17 May 1890, 24 May 1890.

86. Ibid. 8 Oct. 1892.
87. Ibid. 7 July 1906.
88. *Co-operative News*, 27 Feb. 1909.
89. These figures have been calculated from the Chief Constable's Annual Reports, and the Medical Officer of Health Annual Reports, 1890 – 1914, *Borough Accounts of Barrow-in-Furness* (Barrow, 1890 – 1914).

11

Employers and Social Policy in Britain: The Evolution of Welfare Legislation, 1905–1914*

ROY HAY

I

The evolution of social policy in capitalist societies is exceedingly complex. Though it has often been treated in isolation, it is better appreciated as part of the whole political process.[1] Social policy may alter the distribution of income in a society in favour of certain defined groups, but it may also act as a means of social control or contribute to the efficiency with which resources are used in society.[2] Indeed for certain influential political groups the value of social policy may lie in its contribution in the latter two respects, not in the former. Therefore, explanations of the origins of modern welfare legislation, which is an important part of social policy, in terms of the extension of political democracy, humanitarian impulses, improved statistical knowledge or the workings of bureaucratic processes, are, in varying degrees, deficient. It is necessary rather to explain why social reform became acceptable to the political élites of advanced capitalist societies, or to significant and influential groups within these élites. Some recent research has shown that business interests played an important part in this process in Germany and the United States. In Britain, despite the attention given to pressure groups by historians, the attitudes of the business community to social welfare legislation have not been seriously examined. This gap is an important one because business interests not only helped shape the climate of opinion in which legislators operated, but also on occasion pressed for the implementation of specific measures of social reform.

The reasons why business interests wanted social reform have to be related to the social and economic context of the development of capitalist societies.

* From *Social History*, 4 (1977), 435 – 55. Reprinted by permission of the author and the editors of *Social History*.

It has been argued that as industrialization proceeded social welfare legislation 'became profitable from the point of view of productivity . . . to develop and maintain the capacity and the willingness to work. Social insurance became one of the means of investing in human capital'.[3] This aspect was widely recognized by employers in capitalist societies from the late nineteenth century onwards, particularly as international competition intensified.[4]

External challenges, which placed a premium on efficiency, were not the only threats faced by employers. In Britain, Germany and the United States an increasingly influential, articulate and potentially militant working-class movement developed. In all three societies groups emerged who appeared to employers to pose a revolutionary threat to the political and social structures of these societies. Hence employers increasingly realized that repressive measures to counter the revolutionary challenge had to be accompanied by social reform to meet some of the 'legitimate' demands of the working-class movement. They had to ensure that the mass of the workers would not be attracted to hasty, revolutionary solutions to social problems.

These ideas rather than an ideological commitment to *laissez-faire* or in favour of state intervention seem to have been the dominant motives in the minds of employers. Many of them viewed social reform, especially state social policy, not in isolation but as part of a spectrum of approaches to labour and the working-class movement. At one end of the spectrum was the repression of socialist movements and militant trade unionism, while at the other was the promotion of a moral and ideological consensus as to the inseparable links between capital and labour, and hence of the value of capitalism as a social system. In the middle stood the use of free labour, the promotion of internal and public welfare schemes and the encouragement of individual responsibility and self-reliance on the part of the worker.[5]

Research in Germany and the United States has shown clearly the importance of employers' influence on early welfare legislation. In Germany, the Bismarckian social insurance schemes were the product of the social and economic crisis of the early 1880s, which threatened to repeat the stagnation of the period following the collapse of the post Franco-Prussian war boom in 1873.[6] Bismarck's social programme was far more than the simple piece of anti-socialist bribery portrayed in the textbooks.[7] Many German employers had been providing social welfare schemes for humanitarian, economic and social control reasons for some time by the 1880s.[8] Bismarck was well aware of this, and saw social insurance as a means of social stabilization by a conservative extension of, rather than a radical break with, current practice.[9]

In America, too, the lead in the extension of social legislation, and in particular the Workmen's Compensation legislation of the 'Progressive' era from 1890 to 1917, was often taken by employers and not by labour organizations.[10] Arguments for such legislation only began to make headway when they were couched in terms of efficiency and the improvement of the productive process and not simply as measures to relieve poverty.[11]

II

British historians have not seriously considered the economic implications of social welfare legislation or the interests of employers in such measures from the late nineteenth century onwards. G. R. Searle's study of the campaign for national efficiency in the years after the Boer War is based largely on statesmen's papers, the press and periodical literature and does not discuss the attitudes of employers' organizations.[12] Even Gilbert's otherwise useful comments on national efficiency are limited to the pronouncements and influence of the ideologues of the movement, including E. E. Williams and A. Shadwell, rather than the business community.[13] J. F. Harris, in her study of unemployment as a political issue, mentions briefly the interest of a group of radical businessmen associated with Sir John Brunner of Brunner, Mond Chemicals, the precursor of I.C.I., in programmes of economic development to absorb surplus labour.[14] She also discusses the attempts by some deputations from employers' organizations to alter the details of Liberal legislation.[15] H. V. Emy has some brief passages on employers and emphasizes the opposition of the business wing of the Liberal Party to expensive programmes of social reform.[16]

The only exception to the generalization about limited study of employer attitudes to welfare is that the activities of certain Quaker businessmen and philanthropists like Charles Booth are well known.[17] There has, however, been no systematic study of the attitude of employers to welfare legislation, or of their influence on the evolution of social policy. The reason for this neglect may be the underlying assumption of most liberal historians that welfare legislation primarily benefits the working class and is thus largely to be explained by the pressure of the latter for legislation or by concessions by the political élite to such actual or potential pressure.

The traditional picture of British business in this period is of a hard-headed, unsympathetic group of short-term profit maximizing employers, together with a few progressive individuals, who provided welfare benefits for their workers and who themselves played leading parts in the movement for social reform.[18] The names which immediately spring to mind are those of Cadbury, Rowntree, Lipton, Lever and Booth. These men were often regarded, by contemporaries as well as by historians, as oddities and there was some ill-concealed amusement when their enlightened paternalism failed to pay its way.[19] Mathias has explained their appearance at this time as a consequence of the rise of new industries which required better and more efficient labour.[20] The workers earned high wages which enabled them and their families to form part of the expanding domestic market for mass-

Roy Hay

produced consumer goods. These industries faced little foreign competition and wage costs remained a lower proportion of total costs than in some other industries, which allowed employers greater leeway. As a result, employers in these industries, appreciating where their prosperity lay, supported high wages and internal and public welfare provision as a contribution to efficiency and well-being. Mathias contrasts their behaviour with employers in coal and heavy industry who took a negative line on both aspects of welfare.

In fact, some of the attitudes and activities, thought of as characteristic of only a few eccentric and 'philanthropic' employers, affected in varying degrees a wide range of British businessmen, many of whom faced market and labour situations very different from those of the 'new' and service industries. A large number of British employers, including many in coal and heavy industry, provided welfare benefits within the firm, and some went further and actively encouraged the state to introduce a greater range of public services in support.[21]

Employers who provided internal welfare services in Britain seem to have preferred informal schemes to formalized welfare institutions within the firm.[22] The former preserved for the employer the maximum degree of discrimination and control. 'Rough' or recalcitrant employees or ex-employees could be ignored, while the respectable and the efficient could be rewarded. Older employees, for example, could be retained in jobs which did not really pay as a form of disguised old age pensions.[23] The dependants of employees who died while in the service of the firm might be assisted by cash grants or more usually by aid in kind, including the education of children. As the scale of enterprises grew it became less possible to maintain these informal schemes, and, partly under pressure from the workers, more formal versions were substituted. In other cases, the regular and recurrent nature of calls on welfare schemes led to early institutionalization.[24] Some employers were worried by the trend of social legislation, particularly Workmen's Compensation Acts which threatened to reinforce the discrimination against the employment of older workers.[25] Some wished to see the Acts amended so that older workers could be contracted out.[26]

The reasons why employers supported state welfare schemes are not always simple and clear-cut. An analysis in terms of an ideological commitment to or against state intervention is quite insufficient.[27] Some employers were influenced by arguments about the declining relative efficiency of the British economy. Even though it may be true, as American revisionist historians have suggested, that the Victorian economy was not 'failing', this is beside the point.[28] At the time, there were many people who could see that, in relative terms at least, Britain was declining and, under the powerful influence of historical and social Darwinist arguments, they believed that unless something fairly drastic were done then this relative decline might well become absolute. This was the message of writers like Shadwell and Williams, of politicians like Joseph Chamberlain, and even of economists like Marshall.[29] It can also be found in different forms in the speeches and writings of leading businessmen.[30] The remedies ranged from Fair Trade or Tariff Reform to the encouragement of technical and scientific education and social reform.

Moreover, British employers and the ruling élite faced an internal challenge from the working class through its political and industrial organizations. Working-class groups were pressing for legislation on unemployment—the eight-hour day and the right to work—industrial accidents, old age pensions and more generally for a reduction of the risks and uncertainties of industrial life. The schemes put forward by socialists and trade unionists inevitably appeared costly and dangerous to some employers who became convinced of the need to deflect the attention of the mass of workers from them.

The efficiency and social control arguments for social reform are analytically separate themes, but the striking thing about much of the debate over welfare measures among employers is the way that they were regularly used in conjunction.[31] Support for state intervention was often based on internal measures developed by the firms themselves which employers found to be both productive and effective as means of social control. There was little idealistic philanthropy in this, more a practical appreciation that, in the context of the internal and external pressures on British society, social welfare, accompanied perhaps by more direct forms of social control, might serve the interests of society as employers saw them.[32]

Many employers, however, were worried about the cost of social welfare. They were concerned to minimize the burdens falling directly on them and consequently tended to favour schemes financed by workers' contributions. Some employers were clear that costs could be passed on in lower wages or higher prices, while others were not so convinced.[33] Therefore, the debate over welfare among employers involved considerations of efficiency, social control and cost and it was possible to take different views as to the balance of advantage and disadvantage in all three respects. These considerations formed the basis of an important split which occurred in the ranks of employers most notably in 1911 over the National Insurance Act.[34] Many leading employers, aware of the arguments on all three issues, seem to have supported the principle, if not the details, of social legislation. Rank and file members of organizations on the other hand, unaware perhaps of the preceding debates and discussions, seem to have been more concerned that short-run costs would outweigh any potential advantages.[35] It was this groundswell of backwoods opinion which caused some reconsideration on the part of the leaders, and which provided the support for organizations like

Sir Charles Macara's Employers' Parliamentary Association which opposed
social reform.[36]

It is not possible at this stage to say definitely why some employers were in
favour of welfare while others opposed it. Mathias's explanation crumbles in
the face of many contrary examples. In areas of small-scale employment,
with shortages of skilled labour, and often facing intense foreign competition, employers frequently tended to favour welfare legislation. The main
examples come from Birmingham and the Midlands. Where employment was
on a large scale, labour easily available and foreign competition less acute,
employers tended to be lukewarm about social welfare. This is true, for
example, of Glasgow and the North East. London and Sheffield stand in an
intermediate position. However, the extent and militancy of labour organization could cut across this spectrum and this might become crucial. Often in
areas where class differences were greatest formal measures of social control
were preferred, while in others informal means, such as welfare measures,
might appear more attractive. Such statements are, however, speculative
until a more detailed survey of employer welfare schemes and attitudes to
social legislation has been completed.[37]

III

The rest of this article attempts to demonstrate more clearly the extent of
employers' influence on the evolution of social policy. It tries to show how
employers were aware that the various aspects of social policy were inter-
connected. Particular attention is concentrated on the origins of the Labour
Exchanges Act of 1909 and the two parts of the National Insurance Act of
1911. Two main sources of evidence have been used. They are the records
of the Association of Chambers of Commerce of the United Kingdom and
some of its member Chambers and the Minutes of Evidence of the Royal
Commission on the Poor Laws of 1905 – 1909.[38] Neither is an ideal source for
establishing the opinions of the 'average' employer or the small businessman,
but they are almost perfect for determining the views and influence of those
employers who were most likely to come into contact with governments and
hence influence social policy. The Chambers of Commerce were regularly
in touch with governments over commercial and industrial legislation, and
their views were often sought by Ministers and civil servants or presented
unsolicited, sometimes with considerable vehemence.[39]

Before the First World War and the setting up of the Federation of British
Industries, the Association of Chambers of Commerce was the only national
organization representing employers' opinions from the whole range of
commerce and industry. Trade protection associations were usually
represented on the governing bodies of local Chambers, which sometimes
provided the secretariat for them.[40] The membership of many local

Chambers and of the Association was rising sharply in the first decade of the twentieth century, as employers faced problems which required more information and co-operation.[41] When contentious issues came up, most Chambers made strenuous efforts to sound local opinion. Therefore, the views expressed by the Chambers carry significant and increasing weight at this time.

Several groups of employers were in favour of specific welfare measures, particularly improved technical education, to increase efficiency. The activities of Sir John Brunner and his group of Liberal businessmen in support of Technical education are well known.[42] Sheffield Chamber of Commerce took up this issue in the Association of Chambers of Commerce in 1904.[43] They wanted an extension of vocational secondary education as a basis for an improved system of higher technical and commercial education. Fees were to be low and bursaries and scholarships were to be provided to bring it within the reach of boys of all grades. Such a system was necessary 'to maintain our industrial position and to introduce into this country such further industries as may be profitably developed'.[44] Sheffield Corporation was providing a model for this with its own technical schools.[45] The Association pressed the matter on the President of the Board of Education and its Permanent Secretary, Sir Robert Morant. The Marquis of Londonderry thought that the opportunities created under the Education Act of 1902 had not yet been fully exploited, and he felt that the main danger was that too much money might be spent on educating poor boys of only average ability, rather than that exceptional talents would fail for lack of opportunity.[46]

In March 1908, Hull Chamber of Commerce moved that the question of old age and unemployment be dealt with by a complete revision and alteration of the Poor Law.[47] The mover of the resolution pointed out 'that old age pensions, unemployment and the relief of the poor, whether necessitated by illness or accident, were really different phases of one great question: they were interdependent and could not effectively be dealt with by departments.' The resolution was seconded by Sheffield Chamber of Commerce, and both speakers agreed on the need for comprehensive schemes which would adequately provide for the deserving poor and re-establish control over 'idle and worthless people', perhaps through a contributory insurance scheme. After criticism from a Bolton member who pointed out that the exercise of individual tyranny by employers, particularly against older men, also caused pauperism, the resolution was carried.[48]

At this meeting, the next item but one on the Agenda was a resolution to limit the number of 'peaceful pickets' under the Trades Disputes Act of 1906 to prevent picketing from turning into riots and the breakdown of commerce, as was alleged to have occurred in Belfast during the dock strike of 1907.[49] This too was carried unanimously, after the member from Bolton had informed the conference that the 'best representatives of labour' also opposed mob law and wanted an extension of compulsory Boards of Conciliation to all centres of industry to bring capital and labour together. Thus social reform and the control of union militancy were closely linked in the minds of employers.[50]

Within the Association of Chambers of Commerce, however, the most consistent and active proponents of social legislation were the members of the Birmingham Chamber of Commerce. In particular they mounted a campaign for the adaptation of continental, especially German, social legislation to British conditions. For some, the mention of the Chamberlainite tradition of the late nineteenth century might seem a sufficient explanation of this interest, but it is very difficult to establish clear links between the leading personalities in the Chamber and the group surrounding Chamberlain.[51] Perhaps an alternative explanation is to be found in the social and economic character of Midlands industry by the early twentieth century. As Asa Briggs put it,

In the Midlands the pattern of relationships which emerged from the local industrial structure was not one of two opposing armies of employers and employed or even two sets of parallel peaceful interests, but one single, graduated hierarchy. In certain industries such as brass-working, friendly relations could be secured: in others, like bedstead-making, actual 'alliances' between employers and employed emerged, based on closed shop membership, agreed price lists, and a regular use of conciliation machinery. The alliances were particularly strong when a whole industry felt itself threatened by foreign competition.[52]

In such a situation social welfare measures, particularly those of the explicitly conservative German type, could be seen as one means of preventing the polarization between capital and labour which appeared to be developing in Britain in the early years of the twentieth century.

Whatever the precise reasons for their interest in social reform, members of the Birmingham Chamber were early in the field. In 1905 the Birmingham Chamber of Commerce Journal carried a leading article on unemployment, which argued that existing legislation had failed to get at the root of the problem.[53] It pointed out that the Board of Trade returns, based on information supplied by the Trade Unions, did not cover the vast mass of skilled and unskilled but unorganized men. Thus no accurate information was available on which to base a diagnosis of the extent and character of the problem. The article went on,

Before any really practical attempt can be made to prepare a national scheme—and only a national scheme can be deemed satisfactory—for dealing with the unemployed on sound lines, it is essential that permanent machinery be constructed for obtaining reliable information as to the number of persons out of work who are entitled to be classed as bona fide unemployed, that is to say, men who, through some cause over which they have no control, are temporarily out of work—men who will work when they have it to do. *These men are assets of the nation, and it devolves on the nation to see that they are not allowed to become pauperised.* With regard to the other class, the unemployable, the wastrel and the loafer, the sternest measures are necessary. Life has too long been made easy for this class, who thrive most when unemployment is greatest. It is desirable that they should be sifted out and then it would not be difficult to adopt measures for dealing with them.

We believe that the only possible way of obtaining the information which is necessary is to inaugurate a permanent system of labour registries under the control of the Board of Trade, and the bodies which naturally suggest themselves for the kind of work are the Chambers of Commerce.[54]

The article went on to commend the German system of labour registries as a model which could be followed in Britain. It stressed in particular the system of clearing houses which went beyond even the boundaries of the Empire. What was needed in Britain was a permanent system under the Board of Trade to ensure that it would not be regarded as having the remotest connection with the Poor Law.

This proposal was well in advance of expert opinion at the time.[55] William Beveridge, who is usually given credit for influencing Winston Churchill in the direction of a comprehensive Labour Exchange scheme in 1908, still regarded Labour Exchanges in 1905 as peripheral to the process of labour organization, and as useful mainly for elderly workmen.[56] The Central Unemployed Body, set up under the Unemployed Workmen Act of 1905, did not come out in favour of a national solution till February 1908.[57]

The General Purposes Committee of the Birmingham Chamber was asked to produce a report on the establishment of a system of labour registries, and this was transmitted to the Royal Comission on the Poor Laws in August 1906, together with a request to give oral evidence.[58] On 18 November 1907, the Secretary, George Henry Wright, appeared to put the Birmingham case.[59] Wright stressed the need for permanent national machinery under the auspices of Chambers of Commerce or, in their absence, associations having similar objects and functions. Committees set up to administer the registries should include labour representatives and the whole scheme should be co-ordinated by the Board of Trade.[60] Under questioning Wright maintained that the Chamber had no objections to municipal control of labour registries provided they were kept entirely separate from the Poor Law or Distress Committees. The idea of control by the Chambers in association with labour representatives was to ensure Labour registries were primarily commercial and industrial agencies. These registries should also have power and finance to assist workmen moving from one area to another in search of employment.

This well-considered scheme coming from the Chamber obviously took some members of the Commission aback. Professor Smart[61] questioned whether Wright's views were representative of employers in the Chamber and whether the scheme would not appear as a move by employers against workmen. Wright replied that the Chamber of Commerce had charged its Committee with the preparation of the scheme, and that the administration of labour registries should be handled by committees of workmen and employers. He thought that Trade Unions in particular would be glad to be relieved of the expense of maintenance of their own labour registries.

The Birmingham Chamber's proposal for a national scheme of Labour Exchanges was the clearest and most coherent put before the Commission. There were others who put forward suggestions on similar lines, most notably Beveridge.[62] Interestingly enough he stressed that Labour Exchanges should be tailored as far as possible to the needs of business and industry. The Commission, however, had more direct evidence on employers' opinions on this and other matters. At least sixty-three business firms or individual employers gave oral or written evidence to the Commission, while several of those who appeared as local councillors, representatives of Distress Committees or other local organizations were also employers.[63] The majority of these employers gave evidence as part of the Commission's inquiry into unemployment. Following Beatrice Webb's scathing remarks the inquiry has been treated with great condescension by historians.[64] In fact, after the debate among members of the Commission which led to the Webbs setting up their own research early in 1907, the Commission itself embarked on a wide-ranging, if not entirely scientific, study.[65] Letters were sent to interested parties inviting their views under a series of headings. A standard form was used and respondents were expected to confine their replies to those areas where they had special expertise.[66] Later that year, four separate and more detailed questionnaires were addressed to selected employers.[67] These covered the effects of the spread of machinery and modern developments on the demand for labour and labour mobility, and sought employers' opinions on the value of apprenticeships and technical training as the demands on the adult worker became more exacting. One question in three of the four schedules asked whether the greater complexity of economic conditions called for some public organization, such as Distress Committees or Labour Exchanges, to deal with unemployment. The narrowness of the focus of the questions obviously restricted the comments of some employers, but others used them as the basis for reasoned cases for or against wide-ranging state intervention to improve efficiency or reduce unemployment.[68]

The replies to the questions on technical education and measures to deal with unemployment are indicated in Tables 1 and 2.[69]

There are problems of classification and the sample is small, but over 40 per cent of the employers consulted were in favour of extended technical education, while a majority wanted Labour Exchanges, particularly if they could be separated from the existing Poor Law. The Commission obviously made some effort to sound employers' opinions and it is hardly surprising, in

Table 1

Technical education	Number of employers
In favour of technical education for most or all workers	= 7
In favour of technical education for limited groups only	= 3
In favour of apprenticeship only	= 4
Against technical education	= 2
No opinion expressed	= 8
	Total = 24*

* One employer in favour of both extended technical education and apprenticeship.

Table 2

Unemployment	Number of employers
In favour of Labour Exchanges or more comprehensive state action to assist the unemployed	= 12
Against Labour Exchanges	= 8
No opinion expressed	= 3
	Total = 23

the light of these results, that both the Majority and Minority Reports put Labour Exchanges at the forefront of their proposals to deal with unemployment, and both recommended improved technical education.[70]

There remains the difficult task of assessing the relative influence of employers and others on the Government and the Royal Commission.[71] Politicians, civil servants and Commissioners often professed to be trying to steer a middle course between the interest of capital and labour.[72] They may have preferred to accept evidence from an 'impartial' administrative source such as Beveridge. Beveridge's performance was, of course, carefully and discreetly orchestrated by the Webbs[73] and his proposals, based on his work for the Central Unemployed Body, were more detailed than those offered by any employers.[74] It should be clear from the preceding discussion, however, that the Birmingham Chamber's plans included all the essential elements proposed by Beveridge, and it remains very unlikely that the Commissioners would have been so positive in their recommendations had they not felt sure of strong support from the employers whose evidence they had heard.

The Government were preparing for the introduction of Labour Exchanges before the Commission reported, though not perhaps before the tenor of its views was known.[75] Churchill was clearly aware of the need for employers' active co-operation as he indicated to the Cabinet in his initial memorandum on Labour Exchanges and Unemployment Insurance early in 1909.

Unemployment is primarily a question for the employers. Their responsibility is undoubted, their co-operation essential. There already exists all over the country a great recognition on the part of the employing class of their duties towards their workmen and legislation is not required to inculcate any new doctrine, but only to give concrete embodiment and scientific expression to a powerful impulse of just and humane endeavour.[76]

Allowing for an element of window-dressing to convince a somewhat sceptical Cabinet this seems clear enough.

Government links with employers were not confined to general expressions of opinion about employer attitudes. Beveridge, who carried out much of the detailed planning of Labour Exchanges, was well aware of the commitment to Labour Exchanges expressed by the Birmingham Chamber of Commerce, though no hint of this appears in his autobiographical accounts.[77] Early in 1908 there was an attempt to get a system of Labour Exchanges set up in Birmingham and the Midlands.[78] The main requirements were that the scheme should be comprehensive, get Trade Union support and be compatible with the Government's own projected scheme. The planning meetings were held through the good offices of the Birmingham Chamber.[79] In March 1909, Beveridge himself went to Birmingham to meet representatives of the Chamber, the Lord Mayor and W. J. Morgan of the Trades Council to discuss, *inter alia,* the proper attitudes Labour Exchange officials should take to industrial disputes, representation on governing committees, connections between Labour Exchanges and Distress Committees and their influence on apprenticeship and technical instruction.[80]

So when the Liberal Government finally introduced Labour Exchanges as the first stage of their unemployment programme, the form they chose was very close to that set out originally by the Birmingham Chamber, though the scheme was to be completely administered and financed through the Board of Trade, since Churchill would not permit grants-in-aid to semi-autonomous local bodies. Harris, in her otherwise excellent discussion of the origins of Labour Exchanges, attributes them to Beveridge's work, but the Birmingham Chamber deserve as much credit for the idea, if not, of course, for its detailed implementation.

IV

The activities of the Birmingham Chamber of Commerce were not limited to Labour Exchanges. Late in 1906, they began to press for national insurance against sickness, invalidity and old age, on the German model.[81] They put their proposal to the Annual Meeting of the Association in March 1907, and called on the Government to receive a deputation from the Association which would make the case for a Royal Commission on national insurance.[82] In support of the motion, J. S. Taylor stressed that the future industrial efficiency of the country was at stake.[83] The Labour Party had decided views on the subject and some of 'their specious arguments' in support of welfare legislation were likely to be widely accepted if commercial men pursued a policy of drift. The Workmen's Compensation Act of 1906, which introduced compensation for trivial accidents and industrial diseases, was likely to prove an enormous burden on employers unless supplemented by a system of insurance to which the workers themselves contributed. Efficiency, social control and cost arguments were thus combined in support of the German scheme. Taylor did not envisage German methods being added to existing British arrangements, but wanted British practice to be assimilated to the German model.

Taylor was supported by speakers from Coventry, Dunfermline and the South of Scotland Chamber of Commerce, while representatives from Sheffield, Croydon and Oldham had reservations about the cost. The latter wished to ensure that the adoption of the German scheme would not result in an additional burden on top of the Poor Rates. After some debate the motion was lost by fifty-five votes to thirty-eight, but it was agreed to circulate copies of Taylor's speech to all Chambers and discuss the matter at a subsequent meeting.[84]

At the autumnal meeting in Liverpool in September 1907 Taylor once again moved the Birmingham resolution which was supported by delegates from Manchester, Kidderminster, Liverpool, Sheffield and Leeds.[85] Two amendments were carried, one dropping a specific reference to the 'working classes' on the grounds that they were not definitive of any part of the community,[86] and the other linking the resolution, not with a separate Royal Commission, but with the current inquiry into the Poor Laws which was to have its terms of reference extended and to be expedited. In this amended form the resolution was carried and became the official policy of the Association.[87]

A memorandum containing the resolution was sent to the Prime Minister and the Government's reply in October 1907 is worth quoting in full.

Sir Henry Campbell-Bannerman has given the subject of your memorial careful consideration and after consulting with the Home Secretary and the President of the Local Government Board, he is of the opinion that it would not be possible to extend the terms of reference of the Royal Commission on the Poor Laws, and that inasmuch as the subjects of old age pensions *and national insurance against accidents and sickness* are now engaging the attention of His Majesty's Government, no useful purpose would be served at the present by his receiving a deputation as you suggest.[88]

This is the first and clearest indication that the Government were considering national insurance against sickness and accident long before Lloyd George decided to extend the old age pensions scheme in the autumn of 1908. It is interesting too that, at this stage, the departments concerned are the Home Office and the Local Government Board. The former had been responsible for the Workmen's Compensation Act of 1906, which extended the principle of the worker's right to compensation for injury to all trades covered by contracts of employment. It also applied for the first time to a range of industrial diseases. During its passage, the Home Secretary, Herbert Gladstone, was faced with demands from various quarters for the extension of the coverage of the Act and its assimilation to German practice. There was also concern about the lack of compulsion on small employers to insure themselves under the Act. Gladstone, however, promised that as soon as the Bill was passed, the Government would take up the whole question of national insurance and decide on a form of inquiry into the matter.[89]

Now it might be objected that this promise applied only to Workmen's Compensation for accidents at work, but once the Act was extended to industrial diseases and, as employers put it, 'trivial' accidents, it inevitably raised more general questions about sickness and invalidity. For example, if a worker contracted an industrial disease and changed jobs at roughly the same time then serious problems would be raised in attributing responsibility to specific employers. The links between the Workmen's Compensation Act and a general system of accident and sickness insurance were clearly perceived by employers and some politicians.[90] It is reasonable to assume, therefore, that the extension of the Workmen's Compensation Act by a system of national insurance against sickness and invalidity was under intermittent consideration by the Liberal Government between 1906 and 1908. The Birmingham Chamber continued to press for the amendment of the Act and for national insurance throughout 1907. Gladstone was being overwhelmed by administrative routine at the Home Office, and by other Liberal legislation, and the Chamber recorded sadly in July 1907 that they had, so far, failed to move him.[91]

Meanwhile, other employers were putting forward proposals for state insurance against unemployment and ill health to the Royal Commission on the Poor Laws. D. M. Stevenson, City Treasurer of Glasgow and Chairman of the Coal Export Company, wanted a system of industrial matriculation (identity cards) and the organization of a national system of Labour Exchanges. But he also argued that the state should undertake the necessary organization of the unskilled for the purpose of insurance and that out-of-work wages should be made a charge on the industries concerned.[92] Similarly, John Macaulay, General Manager of the Alexandra (Newport and South Wales) Docks, recommended compulsory insurance against sickness and old age, with the Friendly Societies being amalgamated for the purpose and placed under state control. Child labour and sweating should be abolished, and laboratories for the study of criminal paupers and the defective classes set up.[93] Harris claims that the most radical proposals on unemployment insurance came from Thomas Smith, Mayor of Leicester and a retired Trade Union official, but his plans were very similar to those offered, albeit more briefly, by Stevenson and Macaulay.[94]

By late in 1907 other politicians were beginning to show interest in unemployment and ill health. Winston Churchill, on safari in Africa at the time, wrote to the editor of the *Westminster Review*.

However willing the working classes may be to remain in passive opposition merely to the existing social system, they will not continue to bear, they cannot, the awful uncertainties of their lives. Minimum standards of wages and comfort, insurance in some effective form or other against sickness, unemployment, old age—these are the questions and the only questions by which parties are going to live in the future. . .this is the sort of tune I think I will sing at Birmingham on the 23 January. 'Social Bulwarks'. 'Security'. 'Standardisation'.[95]

In the end, Churchill's speech did not mention all these ideas, perhaps because he had not received Cabinet approval at this stage. He concentrated instead on old age pensions, though he did mention the extension of proper training and apprenticeship to relieve the unskilled labour market, diminish casual labour, 'and to increase the productivity and healthy energy of British labour'.[96]

By March 1908 he was able to outline his plans more fully in a famous article in *The Nation*.[97] Churchill was then transferred to the Board of Trade and thereafter his direct interest in social legislation was concentrated on unemployment and minimum wages. Probably at Churchill's behest, early in 1909, the Board of Trade consulted various interested parties on their draft scheme for unemployment insurance, including Trade Unionists, economists and two employers, Sir Benjamin Browne and Henry Holloway.[98] Both had given evidence to the Poor Law Commission, though neither had expressed themselves in favour of national insurance.[99] Browne thought the Board of Trade plans would be extremely valuable for ordinary labour, but wanted skilled mechanics excluded as they already had the means of looking after themselves.[100] Holloway was more critical. He insisted that benefits should be handled independently of the Trade Unions, that contributions and benefits for skilled and unskilled should be graduated, and that the disciplinary clauses in the Bill should be strengthened.[101] Neither expressed serious opposition or suggested that other employers would do so. Churchill and his officials were thus convinced that there was considerable employer support for unemployment insurance on the basis of the opinions they had received.

While the Board of Trade were planning unemployment insurance, the discussion of a scheme of sickness and accident insurance had also begun. In the summer of 1908 the attention of the Government was centred on the passage of the Old Age Pension Bill, but in the autumn Lloyd George went off on his celebrated trip to Germany to study their insurance system. According to the *Daily News* report on the Chancellor's visit, Lloyd George seems to have been doing precisely what the Association of Chambers of Commerce requested. He was trying to discover whether the German

methods could be adopted in Great Britain.[102] Nevertheless the idea that
national health insurance sprang fully formed from the fertile brain of the
Chancellor of the Exchequer, following a brief visit to Germany, has always
seemed rather curious.[103] Lloyd George rather took over ideas which were
current in informed discussion inside and outside the Liberal Party, pushed
aside Herbert Gladstone who had belatedly resurrected his promise of a
Royal Commission on National Insurance,[104] and set about finding a scheme
which could be forced through the thicket of vested interests in the field
of sickness and accident insurance. Perhaps hardly surprisingly, the
Association of Chambers of Commerce did not react initially to Lloyd
George's rather insubstantial kites, though the Birmingham Chamber noted
with quiet satisfaction that their pressure seemed to have met with a
Government response at last.[105]

When the Government schemes for health and unemployment insurance
were outlined by Lloyd George in the 1909 Budget, the Birmingham Chamber
maintained its interest unlike many other employers' organizations. The
General Purposes Committee produced a report on unemployment insurance
although handicapped by the lack of detailed information from the President
of the Board of Trade on the Government proposals. The Committee were
not averse to unemployment insurance though they were concerned about the
cost to employers, which appeared to be additional to that already borne
under the Workmen's Compensation Acts. They preferred the German
scheme under which sickness and unemployment funds [sic] took the brunt
from the Workmen's Compensation fund. The report was sent to Churchill
but received only a formal acknowledgment. Throughout 1910 the Chamber
continued to press the Board of Trade and the Chancellor for details of both
health and unemployment bills, noting sourly that the Friendly Societies and
other organizations were being consulted, while the employers who were also
directly concerned were being ignored. As late as December 1910 Lloyd
George admitted that he had no definite scheme as yet but that he would be
prepared to receive the Chamber's views. Hamstrung by this official secrecy
the General Purposes Committee produced yet another report, which came
out in favour of health insurance provided that the burden on employers of
the Workmen's Compensation Act was recognized. They also wished to
ensure that workers were first compensated out of a fund, to which only
employees had contributed, for the first four weeks, to prevent abuse of the
system. This view was supported by Wakefield Chamber of Commerce in
March 1911.[106]

It was not till 4 May, when Lloyd George finally introduced the National
Insurance Bill, that more information became available. Even then many of
the clauses were blank. Chambers of Commerce who had paid less attention
to developments than Birmingham were forced to consider the matter again.
The initial reception was very mixed as employers in many areas realized that

they were being asked to contribute. On the whole health insurance was acceptable in principle. It was welcomed by the London Chamber who promptly got down to the business of detailed amendment to make the Act workable.[107] In Sheffield and Glasgow, however, reservations were expressed about employer contributions.[108] Some felt that employers should not contribute directly as was the case with old age pensions, though workers should be forced to do so. Others felt that contributions would fall disproportionately on certain employers according to the size of their labour force rather than their profits—it being assumed in these cases that the costs of insurance were not passed on to the consumer or to the worker in the form of a lower rate of wages.[109] Most Chambers expressed reservations about the haste with which the Bill was being rushed through.

There was, however, strong root and branch opposition to unemployment insurance in some areas. The Engineering Section of the London Chamber pointed out that a tax on employers for providing against unemployment must tend itself to bring about the unemployment. Unemployment insurance would also remove a necessary element of industrial discipline.[110] Even the Birmingham Chamber thought that this aspect of the Bill should be dropped pending a Royal Commission on the subject, though the Coventry Chamber came out in support of unemployment insurance.[111]

After representations had been made, the Chancellor agreed to receive a deputation from the Chambers in July 1911. The deputation asked for more time to consider the Bill but Lloyd George replied that national insurance had been part of the programme of the Government for three years. He could not permit further delay because this would be unfair to the Friendly Societies and the doctors.[112] Later, however, the Bill was delayed till an autumn session, but it then went through. The detailed work of amendment carried through by the Chambers in the course of 1911, though interesting in its own right, need not be dealt with here. The Associated Chambers carried several suggested amendments including one limiting the scope for extension of the Bill without Parliamentary approval. Though remaining lukewarm or hostile to many aspects of the Act in its final form, the Chambers refused to join in the opposition to the Act which was mounted by Sir Charles Macara's Employers Parliamentary Association.[113]

V

The conclusion of this argument is not that all or even a majority of British employers wished to see state welfare measures introduced in the first decade of the twentieth century, nor yet that welfare reform was a simple reflex of business interest and pressure. Rather it is that a significant and influential proportion of the business community did wish to see changes in the relationships between the employer, the employee and the state, which included measures of social reform as well as attempts to control the political and industrial activities of Trade Unions. These were not a few oddities, Quakers and crypto-socialists, but a wide range of industrial employers. The groups concerned did play a part in the change in the climate of opinion which was necessary before modern welfare measures could be introduced. As the Birmingham Chamber of Commerce Journal remarked in August 1908:

There is a chance that the system which has been consistently advocated by the Birmingham C. of C. during the past two years may be adapted to the circumstances of this country. The efforts of the Chamber have undoubtedly done much to mould public opinion.[114]

This was a modest but justified claim.

If it is granted, then there are certain consequential implications for the debate on the evolution of social policy. It has been popular in recent years, especially among administrative historians, to argue that welfare measures were unique solutions to specific social problems revealed, analysed and defined by social investigators or by civil servants. They have played down the ideological aspects to the point of extinction.[115] While it is true that social reform, especially in the 'New Liberal' phase after 1908, was carried through by a small group of radical politicians associated with Lloyd George and Churchill assisted by an equally small group of civil servants, this can easily lead historians to overlook the form and extent of a wider change in opinion among influential members of the ruling classes, a change which was far from being confined to those who were members of the radical wing of the Liberal Party. Many of them had become convinced that British society would best be preserved and strengthened against internal and external pressures by a series of measures which included social reform. The latter would not be enough by itself but it was an essential part of the programme. In this sense British social welfare policy, like British imperial expansion overseas in the late nineteenth century, was essentially conservative, even though it was carried through by radicals.[116]

More generally, however, the recognition that early social welfare legislation in Britain was introduced at least partly because of pressure from employers and partly to serve the interests of employers through increased efficiency, helps resolve some of the apparent paradoxes in the current debate about the effectiveness of the modern welfare state. Liberal legislation, despite some of the more florid public pronouncements of Lloyd George, was not designed to bring about a redistribution of income between social classes. He continually stressed to employers that they would be able to pass on the costs of insurance to the consumer, at the same time as he was, in public, declaiming about 'ninepence for fourpence'.[117] Welfare policy in Britain was initially designed to strengthen the basis of the existing structure of society in face of internal and external crises and it would be difficult to find a period when such motives ceased to be influential.

ACKNOWLEDGEMENTS

I wish to acknowledge the assistance of the Librarians of the Association of Chambers of Commerce and of the London, Birmingham, Sheffield, Leeds, Bradford and Glasgow Chambers. Professor T. C. Smout and Dr. T. R. Gourvish provided helpful comments on an earlier draft of this article. Keith Burgess, Bob Holton and Tony Slaven, assisted with comments and references, but they bear no responsibility for the content of this article.

NOTES

1. R. M. Titmuss, *Social Policy* (1974), 26.

2. V. George, *Social Security and Society* (1973), 15, 18 – 19.

3. G. V. Rimlinger, *Welfare Policy and Industrialization in Europe, America and Russia* (New York, 1971), 9 – 10.

4. Ibid., 68 – 70; E. C. McCreary, 'Social welfare and business: the Krupp welfare program, 1860 – 1914', *Business History Review*, xlii (1968), 40, 43; B.P.P., *Annual Report of Chief Inspector of Factories and Workshops*, 1914 (Cd. 8051), 31.

5. McCreary, op. cit., 48 – 9; J. R. Hay, *The Origins of the Liberal Welfare Reforms 1906 – 14* (1975), 27 – 36, 58 – 60.

6. H.-U. Wehler, 'Bismarck's imperialism, 1862 – 1890', *Past and Present*, xlviii (Aug. 1970), 132.

7. H. Rothfels, 'Bismarck's social policy and the problem of state socialism in Germany', *Sociological Review*, xxx (1938), 292 – 3.

8. McCreary, op. cit., *passim*; L. Cecil, *Albert Ballin, Business and Politics in Imperial Germany, 1888 – 1918* (Princeton, 1967), 35; H. Jaeger, 'Business history in Germany: a survey of recent developments', *Business History Review*, xlviii (1974), 38.

9. F. Stern, 'Gold and iron: the collaboration and friendship of Gerson Bleichröder and Otto von Bismarck', *American Historical Review*, lxxv (1969), 41; W. Manchester, *The Arms of Krupp* (1966), 180; McCreary, op. cit., 30; Rimlinger, op. cit., 112 – 18.

10. R. Asher, 'Business and workers' welfare in the Progressive era: Workmen's Compensation Reform in Massachusetts, 1880 – 1911', *Business History Review*, xliii (1969), 452 – 75; J. Weinstein, *The Corporate Ideal in the Liberal State: 1900 – 18* (Boston, 1968).

11. G. Kolko, *The Triumph of Conservatism* (Chicago, 1967 ed.), 197; Rimlinger, op. cit., 62 – 9. For a somewhat different analysis, see C. Woodard, 'Reality and social reform: the transition from laissez-faire to the welfare state', *Yale Law Journal*, lxxii (1962), 286.

12. G. R. Searle, *The Quest for National Efficiency* (Oxford, 1971); E. Wigham, *The Power to Manage* (1973) does not even discuss the attitude of the Engineering Employers' Federation to social legislation in his chapter covering the period

286 *Roy Hay*

1898 – 1914. They were obviously involved, and probably hostile, see p. 144.

13. B. B. Gilbert, *The Evolution of National Insurance* (1966), 62, 72 – 3, 81. In his 'Winston Churchill versus the Webbs: the origins of British unemployment insurance', *American Historical Review*, lxxi (1966), 847, Gilbert makes the extraordinary claim that unemployment policy was entirely a product of Government planning and owed nothing to outside pressures.

14. J. F. Harris, *Unemployment and Politics* (Oxford, 1972), 216 – 19.

15. Ibid., 291 – 3, 330 – 1.

16. H. V. Emy, *Liberals, Radicals and Social Politics, 1892 – 1914* (Cambridge, 1973), 58, 98 – 9, 124 – 5.

17. A. Briggs, *Social Thought and Social Action: A Study of the Work of Seebohm Rowntree, 1871 – 1954* (1961); E. Cadbury, *Experiments in Industrial Organization* (1912); B. Seebohm Rowntree, *The Human Factor in Business* (1921); T. S. and M. B. Simey, *Charles Booth* (Oxford, 1960).

18. See the discussion in E. J. Hobsbawm, *Industry and Empire* (1968), 149 – 63; P. Mathias, *The First Industrial Nation* (1969), 374 – 5; J. Amery, *Life of Joseph Chamberlain, Vol. 4, 1901 – 3* (1951), 393 – 4.

19. J. Child, *British Management Thought* (1969), 40.

20. Mathias, op. cit., 375.

21. K. Burgess, *The Origins of British Industrial Relations: the Nineteenth-Century Experience* (1975); A. Slaven, 'Earnings and productivity in the Scottish coal mining industry during the nineteenth century: the Dixon Enterprises', in P. L. Payne (ed.), *Studies in Scottish Business History* (1967), 223; see also below, pp. 271 – 3, 277 – 9, 282 – 3.

22. B.P.P., *R.C. on Poor Laws and Relief of Distress*, 1909 (Cd. 5066), Minutes of Evidence, Q. 88414, Evidence of Albert Hobson, senior partner in T. Turner and Co. and director of two other steel firms in Sheffield. Hobson was a leading figure in Sheffield Chamber of Commerce and became President in 1908.

23. Ibid., Q. 87722, Para, 10, and Q. 87952, Evidence of William Marshall, managing clerk of Vickers, Sons and Maxim, Ltd, Sheffield.

24. R. Challinor, *The Lancashire and Cheshire Miners* (Newcastle, 1972), 162.

25. It was claimed that insurance companies loaded the premiums of firms which employed older men.

26. *R.C. on Poor Laws*, Minutes of Evidence, Qs. 86258 – 68, Evidence of Sir Benjamin C. Browne, chairman of Hawthorn, Leslie and Co. Ltd, engineers and shipbuilders, Newcastle-on-Tyne. Browne thought the Act 'an enormous gain to the working classes and everyone else too'. But two of his three works had contracted out of the Act completely.

27. Child, op. cit., 33 – 5.

28. D. N. McCloskey, 'Did Victorian Britain fail?', *Economic History Review*, xxiii (1970), 446 – 59.

29. A. Shadwell, *Industrial Efficiency*, 2 vols. (1906); E. E. Williams, *Made in Germany* (1896); J. Amery, op. cit., 397 – 8; A. Marshall, *Principles of Economics* (8th ed., 1920), 596 – 8. Marshall was more sanguine about the prospects for the British economy, but he too recommended improved education, 'lavish' contribution by the state to the well-being of the poorer working class, and German paternal discipline for the residuum.

30. *Report of the Autumnal Meeting of the Association of Chambers of Commerce of the United Kingdom* (Sept. 1907), 68 – 70.

31. For example, in support of a proposal for compulsory attendance at Evening Continuation Classes up to the age of 17, the Association of Chambers of Commerce cited the following advantages which would follow: (i) Prevention of a great waste of public money. (ii) An improvement in the general education of the people. (iii) Diminution of idlers at our street corners. (iv) Cultivation at a critical age of wholesome discipline and restraint. *Report of the Annual Meeting of the Association of Chambers of Commerce* (1905), 53 – 4; see also P. L. Robertson, 'Technical education in the British shipbuilding and marine engineering industries, 1863 – 1914', *Economic History Review*, xxxii (1974), 233.

32. Sheffield Chamber of Commerce proposed compulsory military training in 1909, following a speech by Lord Newton in which he emphasized that this 'would increase a man's efficiency as a wealth producing machine'. Sheffield Chamber of Commerce, *Minutes of Proceedings*, 7 (1908), 141, 182.

33. Dudley Chamber of Commerce had a very thorough debate on the incidence of contributions. *The Chamber of Commerce Journal*, xxx (1911), 221. See also Leeds Chamber of Commerce, *Minute Book*, 6 (1909 – 21), 111 – 15.

34. See below, pp. 280 – 2.

35. London Chamber of Commerce, *Council Minutes*, 4(13 July 1911), Objections of the Manufacturers Section.

36. Emy, op. cit., 273; the support for the Employers' Parliamentary Association seems to have come mainly from the textile industries and from Lancashire. See the list in Sir Charles W. Macara, *Social and Industrial Reform* (Manchester, 7th ed., 1919), 255 – 8, and also Sir Charles W. Macara, *Recollections* (1921), 217 – 28.

37. Joseph Melling (University of Glasgow) is comparing Clydeside employers with those of the West Riding conurbation.

38. Cited hereafter as A.C.C. and *R.C. on Poor Laws*, Mins. Ev.

39. A. R. Ilersic, *Parliament of Commerce* (1960), 139 – 46. The author is apparently unaware, however, of the Association's efforts to encourage social legislation.

40. The Secretary of Birmingham Chamber was also Secretary of eight Trade Protection Societies in the city in 1913. *Cornish's Birmingham Yearbook* (1913), 296 – 308.

41. The membership of Birmingham Chamber of Commerce rose from under 200 in 1895 to 1700 by 1914, that of Sheffield from 266 in 1905 to 403 in 1913.

42. Harris, op. cit., 216 – 19; C. Hazlehurst and J. F. Harris, 'Campbell-Bannerman as Prime Minister', *History, lv (1970), 372.* S. E. Koss, *Sir John Brunner, Radical Plutocrat* (Cambridge, 1970).

43. Sheffield Chamber of Commerce, *Minutes of Proceedings*, 6 (5 Dec. 1904), 6.

44. *Report of the Annual Meeting of the A.C.C.* (1905), 18.

45. *R.C. on Poor Laws*, Mins. Ev., Q. 88430, Evidence of Albert Hobson.

46. *Report of the Annual Meeting of the A.C.C.* (1905), 19 – 20.

47. *Report of the Annual Meeting of the A.C.C.* (1908), 145.

48. Ibid., 147 – 8. The Bolton Member was R. Tootill, Secretary of the Bolton Trades Council and a member of the Labour Party. He was the lone voice of Labour at this A.C.C. meeting.

49. Ibid., 149 – 53.

50. Birmingham Chamber of Commerce, whose pressure for social reform is dealt with below, was in the vanguard of the movement to have the Trades Disputes Act of 1906 repealed. Failing that they wanted the number of pickets strictly limited, their role defined more clearly and notice given to the police before industrial action took place. Association of Chambers of Commerce, *Circulars*, 590 – 6 (13 June 1913 – 16 June 1914).

51. Several of the leading members of the Chamber including three successive chairmen, F. B. Goodman (1895 – 1905), J. S. Taylor (1906 – 10) and H. W. Sambdridge (1911 – 14) were Conservatives. Goodman took an active part in the elections of Sampson Lloyd and Randolph Churchill. G. H. Wright, the Secretary, was a friend of Neville Chamberlain. H C. Field, a member of Council, was educated in Germany and took a particular interest in social reform. He supported the idea of separate children's courts. Only one member of Council, Harrison Barrow, is clearly identifiable as a radical. He was a Quaker and a friend of the Cadburys. A detailed study of this group of employers is badly needed.

52. A. Briggs, 'The social background' in A. Flanders and H. A. Clegg (eds.) *The System of Industrial Relations in Great Britain* (Oxford, 1954), 17.

53. This was not the first occasion when a Chamber of Commerce advocated Labour Exchanges. The Exeter Chamber put a proposal to the Royal Commission on Labour in 1894. Exchanges were to be financed out of the technical education fund and supervised by the Board of Trade. They were to encourage emigration on the lines of General William Booth's 'Darkest England' scheme. Harris, op. cit., 280 – 1.

54. *Birmingham Chamber of Commerce Journal,* 3 (1905), 177 – 8. Emphasis added.

55. Harris, op. cit., 280 – 2, mentions several earlier suggestions for a national labour registry but concludes that they were not influential.

56. Ibid., 200. It is interesting that Beveridge's initial motive was not the reduction of unemployment, but the preservation of the efficiency of those who were unemployed.

57. Ibid., 210.

58. *Birmingham Chamber of Commerce Journal,* 4 (1906), 38.

59. *R.C. on Poor Laws,* Mins. Ev., Qs. 85021 – 85105, Evidence of George Henry Wright (1873 – 1929), secretary of Birmingham Chamber of Commerce, 1902 – 29. Also secretary to several trade protection societies and member of Birmingham Insurance Committee set up by the National Health Insurance Committee. He was a member of the Church of England and a Conservative.

60. Ibid., Q. 85021, Paras. 8 and 10.

61. William Smart, Professor of Political Economy, University of Glasgow (1896 – 1915).

62. *R.C. on Poor Laws,* Mins. Ev., Qs. 77831 – 78370; Harris, op. cit., 206, 286.

63. R.C. on Poor Laws, Mins. Ev., Appendix Volumes viii, ix, xi.

64. Harris, op. cit., 255.

65. Some account of its methods and the difficulties under which it was working is given in *R.C. on Poor Laws,* Majority Report, 1909 (Cd. 4499), 3 – 4.

66. A copy is in the British Library of Political and Economic Science, *Beveridge Papers,* ii b 5.

67. *R.C. on Poor Laws,* Mins. Ev., App. vol. xi. 2, 15, 34, 53.

68. e.g. ibid., 27, Evidence of George Hookham, Kynoch Ltd, Birmingham; 29, Evidence of G. B. Hunter, Chairman, Swan Hunter and Wigham Richardson Ltd, Wallsend-on-Tyne.

69. The questions were addressed to trade unionists, economists and others academics, but only the replies of employers have been used in the tables.

70. *R.C. on Poor Laws,* Majority Report, Part ix, 25 (b), 630 – 1; Minority Report, Chapter V, 1180 – 9. The proposals of the Minority had elements of compulsion lacking in the Majority suggestions.

71. Compare, for example, the different assessments of the origins of the Unemployed Workmen Bill in Harris, op. cit., 157 – 64 and K. D. Brown, 'Conflict in early British welfare policy: the case of the Unemployed Workmen Bill of 1905', *Journal of Modern History,* xliii (1971).

72. R. Davidson, 'War-time Labour policy 1914 – 16: a re-appraisal', *Scottish Labour History Society Journal,* viii (June 1974), 7.

73. So discreetly, in fact, that Professor Smart decided to take over the young Beveridge himself, and wrote a pompous letter offering to do so. *Beveridge Papers,* ii b 6, W. Smart to W. H. Beveridge (23 Aug. 1907).

74. *R.C. on Poor Laws,* Mins. Ev., Q. 77832.

75. Gilbert, op. cit., 259; Harris, op. cit., 262 – 3.

76. Public Record Office, *Cabinet Papers,* Cab. 37/96/159, Unemployment and Labour Exchanges (11 Dec. 1908).

77. W. H. Beveridge, *Power and Influence* (1953), 73 – 80; W. H. Beveridge, 'The birth of Labour Exchanges', Minister of Labour, *Minlabour,* xiv, 1 (Jan. 1960).

78. *Birmingham Chamber of Commerce Journal,* 7 (Jan. 1909), 5.

79. *Beveridge Papers,* ii b 8, Norman S. Chamberlain to W. H. Beveridge (19 Jan. 1909). Chamberlain was a nephew of Joseph Chamberlain and a Liberal Unionist City Councillor. He was active in social work in Birmingham and had been at Toynbee Hall.

80. *Birmingham Chamber of Commerce Journal,* vii (March 1909), 43. Morgan later became manager of one of the new Labour Exchanges.

81. Ibid., iv (1906), 177.

82. *Report of the Annual Meeting of the A.C.C.* (March 1907), 136 – 42.

83. J. S. Taylor (1849 – 1923) succeeded his father as chairman of the engineering firm of Taylor and Challen Ltd in 1875. Also director of Rudge Whitworth Ltd, Lanchester Motor Co. Ltd, and of the Midland Employers' Mutual Assurance Ltd. Chairman, Birmingham Chamber of Commerce, 1904 – 10. He was a Conservative.

84. *Report of the Annual Meeting of the A.C.C.* (March 1907), 143.

85. *Report of the Autumnal Meeting of the A.C.C.* (Sept. 1907), 40 – 1; M. W. Beresford, *The Leeds Chamber of Commerce* (Leeds, 1951), 51. Professor Beresford was puzzled by the support given by Leeds in 1907 since the Chamber was to criticize the National Insurance Bill in 1911. It can be explained, however, on the hypothesis outlined above, p. 271. In 1911, there was a deep division of opinion on the Bill and the Chairman of the Parliamentary and Legal Committee, Henry Barran, refused to support the critical recommendations of his Committee. Leeds Chamber of Commerce, *Minute Book,* 6 (1909 – 21), 117.

86. This was a neat expression of an aspect of the ideology of employers. They

professed to refuse to recognize that society was split into potentially antagonistic social groups.

87. *Report of the Autumnal Meeting of the A.C.C.* (Sept. 1907), 41.

88. Guildhall Library, *Minutes of the Executive Council of the A.C.C.,* 14, vol. 6 (12 Nov. 1907). Emphasis added.

89. *Parliamentary Debates (Commons)*, 4th series, clxii (1 Aug. 1906).

90. *Birmingham Chamber of Commerce Journal*, iv (1906), 170 – 5; Emy, op. cit., 148.

91. *Birmingham Chamber of Commerce Journal,* v (1907), 65 – 6, 72 – 3, 98 – 9; see also Harris, op. cit., 219 for Herbert Gladstone's interest in social reform before 1906.

92. *R.C. on Poor Laws,* Mins. Ev., Appendix vol. xi, 83.

93. Ibid., 66.

94. *R.C. on Poor Laws,* Mins. Ev., Qs. 86725 – 87013; Harris, op. cit., 301.

95. H. Wilson Harris, *J. A. Spender* (1946), 81; Emy, op. cit., 178 suggests that Churchill had been thinking along these lines since the beginning of 1905, citing R. Churchill, *Winston S. Churchill, Vol. II, The Young Statesman* (1967), 301. But the passage mentioned only refers to Churchill's interest in 1908.

96. *The Times* (24 Jan. 1908).

97. Gilbert, op. cit., 250.

98. *Beveridge Papers,* iii 37 A4, 6 – 8; iii 37 A5, 3; A7, 1 – 2; A8, 1 – 5.

99. *R.C. on Poor Laws,* Mins. Ev., Qs. 86220 – 86464; App. vol. ix, 28.

100. *Beveridge Papers,* iii 37 A4, 6 – 7.

101. Ibid., iii 37 A5, 3.

102. Gilbert, op. cit., 292 – 3.

103. It is repeated in K. O. Morgan, *Lloyd George* (1974), 65.

104. Bodleian Library, *Asquith Papers,* vol. 20, 169, Herbert Gladstone to H. H. Asquith (17 Sept. 1908).

105. Quoted in full below, p. 454.

106. Material in this paragraph is based on Birmingham Chamber of Commerce, *Minute Book* (1909 – 12), 141 – 89; and P.R.O., *Treasury Papers,* T/1/11284/1911/6955. G. R. Askwith to Treasury (6 April 1911), enclosing reports from Birmingham Chamber of Commerce.

107. London Chamber of Commerce, *General Minute Book,* no. 7. Special Committee re National Insurance Bill (25 May 1911), 88; see also *The Chamber of Commerce Journal,* 30 (1911), 218, 220 for initial approval in principle by Leeds and Sheffield.

108. Glasgow Chamber of Commerce, *Minutes (of Home Affairs Committee),* 1900 – 1913 (14 July 1911), 163. Sheffield Chamber of Commerce, *Minutes of Proceedings,* 8 (12 Dec. 1911), 24. In Glasgow rank-and-file opposition to the Bill did begin to build up and Glasgow demands for delay in implementation became increasingly vehement. *Minute Book of Committee of Directors,* 3 (10 Aug. 1911), 451 – 2.

109. *The Chamber of Commerce Journal,* xxx (1911), 219, 222.

110. London Chamber of Commerce, *General Minute Book,* 7 (9 June 1911), 93, Summary of objections affecting employers of labour.

111. *The Chamber of Commerce Journal,* xxx (1911), 160.

112. In this assertion Lloyd George did an injustice to Birmingham Chamber of Commerce which had been seeking information over the past three years to see if their support in principle could be translated into approval of the specific proposals of the Government.

113. London Chamber of Commerce, *Council Minutes,* 5 (11 Jan. 1912), 41. This was an important decision since Sir Algernon Firth, the vice-chairman of the A.C.C., had seconded Macara's resolutions calling for postponement of the Bill at a meeting in Manchester on 8 Dec. 1911. Macara, *Recollections,* 221 – 2.

114. *Birmingham Chamber of Commerce Journal,* vi (1908), 127.

115. Harris, op. cit., 362 – 6; R. MacLeod, *Treasury Control and Social Administration* (1968); R. Davidson, 'Llewellyn Smith, the labour department and government growth', in G. Sutherland (ed.), *Studies in the Growth of Nineteenth-Century Government* (1972).

116. D. C. M. Platt, 'Economic factors in British policy during the New Imperialism', *Past and Present,* xxxix (1968). Many employers, some Liberals, more Conservatives, opposed social reform because of its association with radicalism, others because of its cost or because they believed that social reform would weaken, not strengthen, industrial and social discipline. This was particularly true of unemployment insurance, which even with the most stringent safeguards seemed to some employers to be tantamount to encouraging 'malingering'. Those who opposed welfare, like Sir Charles Macara, were just as concerned to reduce labour unrest, but believed the best method was through conciliation machinery to unite capital and labour. Macara was the leading spirit in the Industrial Council set up in 1911. Macara, *Social and Industrial Reform,* 311 – 14; G. R.Askwith, *Industrial Problems and Disputes* (Brighton, 1974 edn.), 178 – 86.

117. Lloyd George often argued that any burden laid on employers would be more than compensated for by the improved efficiency of the worker. A.C.C. *Circular* no. 572 (1911), J. Rowland to Sir E. Fithian (23 Sept. 1911).

12

Popular Protest and Public Order: Red Clydeside, 1915–1919*

IAIN MCLEAN

During the first three months of 1919 unrest touched its high-water mark. I do not think that at any time in history since the Bristol Riots we have been so near revolution . . . On the 27th of January there were extensive strikes on the Clyde of a revolutionary rather than an economic character.

(Sir) Basil Thomson[1]

A rising was expected. A rising should have taken place. The workers were ready and able to effect it; *the leadership had never thought of it.*

William Gallacher[2]

Many observers, both at the time and later, thought that 1919 marked the high point for the prospects of the British revolution; and the Clyde, or more precisely the Glasgow munitions area, had gained during the War a reputation which events in the first two months of 1919 seemed to confirm. Labour unrest on the Clyde first attracted Government attention early in 1915, and on several occasions the apparent threat to public order was discussed at Cabinet level. The two most important were the 'dilution' crisis from January to March 1916, and the Forty Hours' Strike in January 1919, and it is to these that I intend to devote most attention.

The background to the dilution crisis has been examined elsewhere,[3] and I wish to mention only essential details here. 'Dilution' meant the substitution of unskilled or female labour for skilled labour in engineering, and particularly in munitions. The craftsman's job was to be split up, with those components which could be done by less-trained workmen, or women, being given to 'dilutees', and the craftsman being restricted to the tasks which could

* From J. Stevenson and R. Quinault, *Popular Protest and Public Order* (London, 1974), 215–42. Reprinted by permission of the author and George Allen & Unwin Ltd. A fuller development of the topics treated here is now to be found in I. McLean, *The Legend of Red Clydeside* (Edinburgh, 1983).

only be done by a fully-skilled man. From March 1915 until the end of the War, the Government was continually pressing for more dilution as an essential means of increasing the production of war materials. The 'Treasury Agreement' of March 1915 was signed between Lloyd George and the leaders of most of the craft unions, who agreed to suspend for the duration of the War their customary trade practices reserving certain jobs to craftsmen, in return for a promise that the Government would legislate to restore them after the end of the war. This agreement was given the force of law in the Munitions of War Act in July 1915, by which time the Ministry of Munitions had come into existence. One of the chief functions of its Labour Department was to impose dilution, a task in which it faced several opponents. Within Whitehall, other departments resented the fact that an upstart new ministry, created from scratch by Lloyd George, had taken over their responsibilities for industrial relations. In the munitions industry, neither the employers nor the unions were keen on dilution. The employers were unwilling to dilute for two reasons, one of which was sheer conservatism or incompetence. Dilution placed a heavy demand on line management at a time when many engineering employers had still not adapted to the rapid technical changes involved in mass production. Therefore, many employers were reluctant to initiate dilution schemes; 'some', according to a Ministry report, 'were frankly of opinion that women were unsuitable for engineering'. And, in the second place, employers knew very well that the agreement to dilution given by the craft unions, especially the Amalgamated Society of Engineers (A.S.E.) was at best very grudging. They regarded it as the Ministry's job, not theirs, to impose dilution. They were not prepared to pull Lloyd George's chestnuts out of the fire, and find themselves with strikes on their hands which could be avoided if dilution were quietly ignored. Ministry officials in Glasgow soon found out that merely issuing instructions to employers to introduce dilution was fruitless: 'It was hopeless to expect employers to take any action in the direction suggested until the Ministry of Munitions had brought the necessary pressure to bear on Trade Unions to secure the waiving in actual practice—and not merely on paper—of their restrictions'.[4]

As this indicates, the A.S.E. fought a long and dogged rearguard action to protect its craftsmen members against the effects of dilution. The position of the craftsman was being threatened by technological change, change which was rapidly accelerating under War conditions. As one of the shrewdest Ministry observers saw, the men's gut suspicion was that by the end of the war 'women will . . . have become so proficient that Employers will after the Munitions Act has ceased to operate employ them at a lower wage than and to the exclusion of the skilled men. This is the real difficulty in the case, and at the bottom of much objection to dilution.'[5]

The A.S.E.'s unwillingness to co-operate was a serious threat to the Ministry, both on its own account and because of the truculence it induced among employers, and it took more than a year from the signing of the Treasury Agreement for the Ministry to arrive at what it regarded as a satisfactory settlement. For a short part of this period, other bodies appeared on the union's left flank which posed a far more explicit threat to public order. Most celebrated of these was the Clyde Workers' Committee (C.W.C.), whose hey-day was from October 1915 to March 1916. Its declared objects were:

1. To obtain an ever-increasing control over workshop conditions.
2. To regulate the terms upon which the workers shall be employed.
3. To organise the workers upon a class basis and to maintain the Class Struggle, until the overthrow of the Wages System, the Freedom of the Workers, and the establishment of Industrial Democracy have been obtained.[6]

The committee's leaders were mostly revolutionary syndicalists of one kind or another, although it also featured opportunists who were 'determined to use the Munitions Act as a means for their own advancement . . . [and] came forward as champions of Trade Unionism to oppose the Act.'[7] Grassroots support for the C.W.C. came almost entirely from skilled engineering workers. What drew these groups together was condemnation of the unions for their 'act of Treachery' in assenting to the Munitions Act. Rank-and-file members did not know how hard the A.S.E. was in fact fighting behind the scenes against dilution; all they could see was that their officials were failing to protect their interests—their craft interests—in public. The C.W.C. was an uneasy coalition between revolutionary syndicalism and craft conservatism. By failing to realize that it was the latter which was its real driving force, the authorities (like many subsequent writers) were misled into seeing it as a much more severe threat to public order than it actually was.

The C.W.C. was the body which organized opposition to Lloyd George when he came to Glasgow at Christmas 1915 to encourage dilution. The visit spectacularly misfired. On Christmas Day, an impatient audience of shop stewards listened to Arthur Henderson explaining at some length the justice of the War on behalf of the 'brave and independent' Belgians ('Oh heavens! How long have we to suffer this?') and to Lloyd George asserting with passion that the responsibility of a Minister of the Crown in a great war was not a light one ('The money's good', and laughter). The socialist weekly *Forward* printed an accurate and unflattering account of the meeting, from which these comments are taken. In view of the damage the report might do to the dilution campaign, the Ministry suppressed the paper—certainly a mistake, which only highlighted Lloyd George's failure to impress the Glasgow munitions workers.

Nevertheless, after the *Forward* incident[8] the C.W.C. faded from the centre of interest for a couple of months. The Ministry of Munitions' immediate task was to break the A.S.E.'s opposition to dilution; its weapons were the three Dilution Commissioners who were sent to the Clyde in the middle of January. The obduracy of the union and the incompetence of the employers were their principal headaches, but from early February they began to become concerned about the C.W.C. They discovered that it was 'ostensibly a Socialist Organisation, if indeed it is not something worse. Its primary object is to overthrow all official Trade Unions on the Clyde and to supplant such effete organisations by a revolutionary propaganda of the international Anarchist type.'[9] Thereafter, two of the Commissioners sought a confrontation with the C.W.C. The third, a former union official and a professional arbitrator, sent a memorandum of dissent in which he argued that the Commissioners should attack the ' "old trade-union" bitterness, narrow and selfish'[10] of the pure craft conservatives rather than the C.W.C. But he was over-ruled, and the dramatic confrontation came in late March. On the 17th, men at the giant Parkhead Forge, in the East End of Glasgow, struck in protest at restrictions on the rights of David Kirkwood, their chief shop steward. They appealed to workers in other plants to join them:

Unite with us in demanding that during the present crisis our shop stewards in every workshop where dilution is in force shall have the fullest liberty to investigate the conditions under which the new class of labour is employed, so that this may not be used to reduce us all to a lower standard of life.[11]

The response was lukewarm, largely because C.W.C. leaders in other factories were suspicious of Kirkwood for having co-operated with the Dilution Commissioners. (He had produced a scheme of dilution for Parkhead which they approved without alteration.) Therefore, when Kirkwood's employer turned against him, C.W.C. supporters in other plants observed, somewhat smugly, that he had got his due reward. So only a few factories struck in sympathy. This did not stop the Commissioners from sending 'frenzied telegrams'[12] to the Ministry demanding action against the C.W.C. The Committee, according to them, had decided to cripple the war effort by bringing out on strike those of their supporters who worked in factories where howitzers essential for the Western Front or barges for the Mesopotamia campaign were being built.[13] The Ministry chiefs decided that 'We have been patient long enough,'[14] and deported ten of the leaders of the C.W.C., including Kirkwood, out of the Clyde munitions area. They were sent in the first instance to Edinburgh, where the workers were presumably regarded as impervious to revolutionary sedition-mongering.

Shortly afterwards, on 30 March, the Cabinet discussed the deportations:

It was shown that the principal danger of the situation depends not so much on the proceedings of the small (by comparison) number of workmen holding syndicalist views and revolutionary aims, as on the fear that the vastly larger body of patriotic and loyal trade unionists may be deluded by misrepresentation of the facts into expressing sympathy with the violent minority, believing them to be unjustly treated.[15]

By 4 April, the men on strike, including those who had joined out of sympathy for the deportees, were almost all back at work, and members of the Cabinet were congratulating each other that they had averted a major crisis.[16] It is not obvious, however, that one was ever in prospect. The Commissioners' claim that the C.W.C. was plotting to disrupt the War effort was sheer nonsense, and was painstakingly shown to be so by a Labour Party committee which later investigated the case.[17] It is possible that they decided to fabricate the story in order to force the Government to get rid of the C.W.C. It is much more likely that they simply took fright, and believed one of the scare stories which were constantly being passed on to them by agitated employers and self-appointed sniffers-out of German spies. At any rate, the Government took the Commissioners at their word. They took dramatic action against the deportees as they had against the *Forward;* the denouement appeared to be the government's success in scattering the members of a dangerous revolutionary organization, the C.W.C. But, like many later commentators, they grossly overestimated the C.W.C. by taking it at its own valuation. The Clyde Workers' Committee was not the harbinger of the revolution; it was a loose coalition of revolutionary socialists and craft conservatives. And it could thrive only when the craftsmen felt their position was at stake. Unlike (say) the Bolsheviks, the C.W.C. could make no effective appeal to the rest of the working class outside its own constituency. Its immediate appeal was to a group of craftsmen, and the threat to their status which they perceived came from women and unskilled men just as much as from 'the bosses' or 'the government'. They never received the support of the unskilled in their campaign; indeed, there is no reason at all why they should have done. Moreover, there is no way of knowing to what extent the C.W.C. leaders represented opinion even among the munitions workers from whom their strength was drawn. A supporter of the committee explained the position candidly to the Labour Party inquiry:

The Clyde Workers' Committee was a heterogeneous crowd which had practically no constitution. It was more a collection of angry Trade Unionists than anything else, which had sprung into existence because of the trouble which was going on on the Clyde. The Clyde Workers' Committee was the result of the trouble, the outcome of the trouble. . .

You must remember that it was not absolutely necessary for your Shop to send you; you could represent a minority in the Shop just the same as a majority, even though the minority was one.[18]

In spite of these drawbacks, the Committee seemed to have presented the Government with a revolutionary threat, and when it once again became involved in a major industrial upheaval, in 1919, the Government was again to make the mistake of taking it too seriously. In the intervening period, the reputation 'Red Clydeside' had acquired was enough to make the Cabinet jittery on several occasions. In August 1917, for instance, the Secretary for Scotland took fright at the notion of a Workers' and Soldiers' Council being formed in Glasgow as a result of the Leeds Conference in June, which had been called by the I.L.P. and the British Socialist Party in order to welcome the Russian Revolution and encourage the formation of local soviets. He brought the matter to the War Cabinet, which authorised him to ban the meeting, and announced that 'the Cabinet regarded the objects of such meetings as illegal, and would not permit them to be held'.[19]

Once again, Red Clydeside's bark was shown to be worse than its bite. When the Government announced the ban, the meeting of the Glasgow Soviet was transformed into a demonstration of protest at its prohibition. The Glasgow Trades Council, which had been in charge of the plans for a Workmen's and Soldiers' Council, recorded with pride that although 'quite 4,000' had attended for the meeting, there was 'not the slightest semblance of disorder', so that fifty plainclothes police who had been drafted in had had a 'holiday with pay'.[20] After two more months of abortive attempts to find a meeting-place for the Soviet which would be permitted by the Glasgow magistrates, the affair faded away. The revolution was postponed *sine die* because of the disapproval of the magistrates and the Secretary for Scotland.

The Leeds Convention and the outburst of enthusiasm for Workers' and Soldiers' Councils were perhaps untypical of wartime Labour politics, and normally cautious and bureaucratic bodies like the Glasgow Trades Council soon recovered from the burst of anarchic romanticism which had affected them. But there were individuals whose pursuit of the revolution was both more wholehearted and more consistent. Such a person was John Maclean, a Glasgow schoolteacher turned Marxist propagandist who had been sentenced to three years' imprisonment for sedition in 1916. He had been released on a ticket-of-leave in 1917 because his health, both physical and mental, had been deteriorating in prison. Far from ceasing his activities, however, he had stepped them up; after the October Revolution the Russians appointed him Soviet Consul in Glasgow. Munro, the Secretary for Scotland, was urged by several of his advisers to take action against Maclean. The Army's General Officer Commanding in Scotland, for example, expressed his annoyance with Munro for so much as raising the matter in the War Cabinet rather than simply imprisoning Maclean without further ado.[21] Less impetuously, the Lord Advocate suggested that there would be little point in doing anything beyond prosecuting Maclean and deporting his Russian secretary, Louis Shammes. But in the War Cabinet the note of alarm was sounded by H.A.L. Fisher: 'He learned from a reliable French source that there was an intimate connection between the more extreme Labour leaders in Glasgow and similar Labour leaders at S. Etienne. The latter were taking instructions from Glasgow.'[22] Rumours of close connections between Red Clydeside and unsavoury revolutionaries elsewhere were to disturb the Cabinet a good deal more in 1919, when served up more spicily by Basil Thomson and the Special Branch; but here they had at least a foretaste. The Lord Advocate was authorized to take proceedings against Maclean, as a result of which he was again tried and sentenced to five years' imprisonment with hard labour for breaches of the Defence of the Realm Acts.

Towards the end of the war, his supporters stridently took up the appeal to release him. Their efforts impressed George Barnes, the Labour member of the War Cabinet, and himself M.P. for the Gorbals district of Glasgow. 'Mr Barnes said he thought the continual agitation about this man constituted a serious danger for the government, and no good purpose was served by keeping him in prison. Maclean's supporters were threatening to take very drastic steps, e.g. cutting off the light on the Clyde, if his release were not brought about.'[23] The matter had been referred to the Imperial War Cabinet, which agreed to Maclean's release with only one dissenting voice, that of Cave, the Home Secretary, who thought it would be an undesirable encouragement to the revolutionaries of South Wales and London.

How justified was Barnes's alarm at Maclean's capacity for revolutionary disruption? There is no doubt that Maclean's prison terms made him a martyr in the eyes of many Clydeside sympathizers. The press, although totally hostile to his views, gave ample evidence of his popularity; the tumultuous welcome he received on 3 December 1918, on his return from prison, was prominently featured on the picture page of the leading popular daily.[24] But it is not at all clear that Maclean could have started a revolution. His aims sometimes (although not always) coincided with those of the C.W.C. But it is an exaggeration to claim that 'his agitation constituted the elemental driving force behind the whole revolutionary movement on the Clyde'.[25] A truer view of the relationship between the schoolteacher Maclean and his working-class audiences is that of another middle-class Marxist, Walton Newbold,[26] who said of him:

That forceful exponent of a fanatic evangel of revolutionary purpose could never take kindly to the thought that his audiences were motivated by material conditions rather than by the logic and urgency of his personal appeal . . . he was external to the life of the working class by reason of his professional work as a school-teacher of considerable academic distinction . . .[27]

In its assessment of Maclean, as with the C.W.C. in 1916, the Government was unduly impressionable. There is no solid evidence that either Maclean or the C.W.C. posed a real revolutionary threat. Both of these incidents, however, had been overshadowed by a much more spectacular affair, the Forty Hours' Strike of January 1919, which contributed more than any earlier incident to Red Clydeside's revolutionary reputation.

The origins of the strike lay in events which took place long before the end of the war. In 1917 and 1918, many labour leaders on Clydeside (and elsewhere) became concerned about the possibility of widespread disruption and unemployment at the end of the war, when demobilization and the end of munitions production were expected to throw millions of men and women into the labour market. They advocated reducing the length of the working week and spreading the available work round to ensure that everybody had some—a solution traditionally favoured by trade unionists and equally traditionally condemned as economically unsound by employers, newspapers, and governments.

One labour body which had discussed the problem was the Scottish Trades Union Congress. In 1918, its delegates resolved that 'the government should bring a Bill into Parliament to take effect on demobilisation, in enactment of a 40 Hour Maximum Working Week, preferably so arranged as to make Saturday a holiday, the hours worked to be 8 per day for the first 5 days of the week, with a break each day of an hour for dinner.'[28] Opposition to this came not from conservatives but from radicals who believed that it did not go far enough, for instance the Glasgow Trades Council, who urged a 30-hour week instead of a 40-hour one.

In one industry, at least, some progress towards shortening working hours was being made. Immediately after the Armistice in November 1918, the craft unions in engineering and shipbuilding negotiated a reduction in the number of hours in the basic working week from 54 to 47, with a corresponding increase in the hourly rate. The agreement took effect with the new year, and the A.S.E. reflected proudly on its achievement: 'The concession of a 47-hour week without reduction of wages will rank as one of the greatest triumphs of British Trade Unionism.'[29] In most parts of the country, this settlement was welcomed by union members (the total vote on the proposal by members of all the unions affected favoured it by two to one). In the Glasgow area, the majority vote was hostile among members of the A.S.E. and other unions (notably the iron- and brass-moulders) whose local officials were urging a 40- or 30-hour week. Popular hostility to the 47-hour week was increased when it was put into operation. The previous working period had involved a 6 a.m. start and a breakfast break at 9.15; the new one required a 7.30 start and continuous working through to 12.30. The psychological effect of this was that the men felt their work period was as onerous as before. They had to get up almost as early as ever, to eat their unaccustomedly early breakfast, and then had a long spell of continuous work to face before dinner. The arrangement aroused more resentment in Glasgow than elsewhere because of these long-established patterns of work, which in turn were made possible by the tradition of living in closely packed tenement blocks very near the workplace, and going home for meals.

There was nothing political in any of this, of course; it was the circumstances in which this occurred which made the Forty Hours' Strike so politically explosive. One relevant point was made by the local A.S.E.

Executive when they referred to 'the rebound from the pressures of the war-period which had prevented the workers from using the power, which the abnormal conditions had put into their hands, to secure [their] demands'.[30] Wartime negotiations had vastly increased the power of shop stewards. Labour was in a sellers' market; munitions production had brought in its train complex bonus systems and overtime arrangements. So shop-floor bargainers had greatly increased their power in negotiations at the expense of permanent union officials. At the end of the War this situation affected different groups in different ways. Militant shop stewards again took up the theme of 'betrayal' on which they had played profitably in 1915 and 1916. In this case it was easy to argue that union officialdom had 'betrayed' its Glasgow membership, which was against the 47-hour proposal. Thus the C.W.C. was revived, initially under the name of the 'Ways and Means Committee', to denounce the 47-hour system and to press for a 30-hour week. It is possible that, over and above their overt grievance, the militants suspected that their time was running out, that the end of the war would mean the end of their favourable negotiating position, and that union officials might be able to reassert their authority. This was certainly the view of many union leaderships, including that of the A.S.E., whose reaction to the Forty Hours' Strike was totally hostile: they suspended their Glasgow District Committee for supporting it. On the other hand, non-revolutionary trade unionists on Clydeside saw a constraint removed from their action. Men who had not been opposed to the War were unwilling to strike while it was in progress, for fear of being dubbed 'allies of the Huns' in the local press, or even of actually hindering the War effort. But once the War was over, many militant trade unionists who had previously been reluctant to show their strength thought the time had come for the workers to use their increased bargaining strength.

The result of this was that by January 1919 both moderates and extremists among local trade union leaders were in favour of a strike to pursue the 40-hour week demand. The involvement of the S.T.U.C. sprang initially from its commitment, dating from the 1918 Congress, to the principle of spreading the available work; in the first weeks of the new year, the Executive of the S.T.U.C. became more and more closely involved as it tried to keep the strike movement on course for 40 hours and away from the wholly impracticable 30-hours demand being made by the C.W.C. The terms on which the strike was called, for 27 January, represented a compromise between the two wings. It was for 40 hours, not 30; but the S.T.U.C. Executive, while asking its member unions to support the strike, called it 'hasty and unwise'[31] because its timing did not allow for proper preparations being made.

The organizers were reasonably satisfied by the numbers of men who came out on strike: 40,000 on the first day and 70,000 on the second.[32] But the strike had no sooner started than the moderates began to look for ways out of a position which had become acutely embarrassing because of the failure of national union executives to support the strike. The Ministry of Labour sent a chilly telegram to the S.T.U.C. executive in response to its appeal for intervention:

I am directed by the Minister of Labour to call your attention to the fact that the matter is one which should form the subject of negotiations between the unions and employers' associations concerned . . . In the meantime the Minister trusts that the Parliamentary Committee[33] of the S.T.U.C. will use their influence to support the unions in advising a return to work.[34]

It was in vain for the S.T.U.C. to protest that the 'Scottish movement for a 40 Hours' Week is general and cannot be dealt with by individual employers' associations'.[35] Neither the unions nor the Government in London showed the slightest sympathy for their case: '. . . the General Secretaries in London were strongly opposed to government action, [and] had used all their influence to prevent such intervention'.[36]

Government action was certainly being contemplated, but it was very different from what the strike leaders had in mind. On 22 January the War Cabinet considered the strike, but decided that for the meantime there was nothing for it to do:

Sir Robert Horne [Minister of Labour] said that . . . the position was rendered extremely difficult as the Government could not actively interfere in the settlement of these strikes over the heads of the Union Executives . . .

The War Cabinet requested the Minister of Labour to give to the Press at the latest on the following day the full facts regarding the present unrest, laying stress on the unauthorised character of the strikes.[37]

The Cabinet was sufficiently alarmed by the events of the next two days, however, to take a more active part. On the 29th, a delegation of the strikers met the Lord Provost of Glasgow with their demands, which he undertook to transmit to the Government for their reply. (For which he was furiously assailed by the *Glasgow Herald,* on the grounds that he was giving in to the strikers' threats. In fact, his motive was to alert the government to the seriousness of the situation, as he saw it. The intransigence of the strikers' demands did this job admirably.) The telegram ran, in part:

It was further stated [by the delegation of strikers] that they had hitherto adopted constitutional methods in urging their demand, but that failing consideration being given to their request by the government they would adopt any other methods which they might consider would be likely to advance their cause. They have, however, agreed to delay taking any such action until Friday in order that I may communicate your reply. I have just learnt from the manager of the electricity department that all men in generating stations have been compelled today to join the strike.'[38]

The Cabinet's reply to the request for intervention was to reiterate its flat refusal. But the Lord Provost's conjunction of the strikers' threats with the news of the total shutdown of electricity generation in the city (which was, in fact, untrue, although the Lord Provost probably wrote in good faith) alerted the War Cabinet to the risk of a serious threat to public order. Bonar Law telephoned to Lloyd George, who was at Versailles, about the Glasgow situation. Lloyd George said that he was prepared to come to London, but that he did not want to undermine Sir Robert Horne's authority. The War Cabinet therefore soldiered on without him. Bonar Law was the first to propose the use of troops in Glasgow to protect the 'volunteers' who might be found to run the municipal utilities. 'It was certain that if the movement in Glasgow grew, it would spread all over the country.' Most of the Cabinet agreed (an exception, interestingly, being Churchill, who thought that 'the moment for the use [of troops] had not yet arrived,' and advocated the use of the Defence of the Realm Acts against the strike leaders).[39] Accordingly, they turned to discussing the reliability of different forces of order for such an occasion. The spectre of police strikes and army mutinies clearly loomed large behind the discussion. The Secretary for Scotland argued for sending in 2,000 special constables, who, he thought, would be more reliable than soldiers. Sir William Robertson presented a gloomy picture of the troops available in Scotland: '. . . all sorts of men, old, young, convalescents, and men with wounds. As regards the officers, they were not very efficient.' Nevertheless, it was agreed to hold the military 'in readiness to give their services when requested by the civil authorities', and to send a senior Scottish Office official to Glasgow to provide liaison between the local authority and the government.

No sooner had this official arrived in Glasgow than he was plunged into further trouble. On Friday, 31 January, a large crowd had assembled in Glasgow and was waiting in George Square, outside the City Chambers, to hear Bonar Law's answer to the Lord Provost's telegram. In order to clear a way for the tramcars on one side of the square, the police mounted a baton charge on the strikers and spectators on that side. Next, they proceeded to clear other sides of the square.

with a vigour and determination that was a prelude to the extraordinary scenes which the Square was afterwards to witness, and to which the city, with all its acquaintance with labour troubles, can happily offer no parallel. A strong body of police . . . swept the crowd in front of them, raining a hurricane of blows which fell indiscriminately on those actually participating in the strike and on those who had been drawn to the scene merely through curiosity.[40]

This account is from the *Glasgow Herald,* a paper vociferously hostile to the strikers. It leaves no room for serious doubt that the riot on 'Bloody Friday', as the affair came to be known, was initiated by the behaviour of the police, not the strikers. A further point, not noticed at the time, is that the alleged reason for the baton charge was to clear the tramlines for traffic—but that after the first charge the police proceeded to turn up the east side of the square, next to the City Chambers, and then up a steep minor street opposite, neither of which contained any tramlines. It would be charitable to describe this as panic on the part of senior police officers; less charitable to call it a police riot, or a deliberate attempt to intimidate the strikers.

William Gallacher, at this time a leading shop steward but not yet a Communist, reacted to the *mêlée* not with revolutionary enthusiasm but with horror. Like most of the strike leaders, he was a pacific man who made militant speeches, not a tough-minded revolutionary. He shouted to the crowd to get out of the way of the police, to disperse, and to meet again on Glasgow Green. ' "Now, keep order. Understand that it has been a very unfortunate occurrence. March, for God's sake. Are you going to do that much for us?". (Cries of "Yes".)'[41]

The War Cabinet met again that afternoon, and the Minister of Labour informed them that

he had no details, but understood that foot and mounted police had charged the crowd in order to quell a riot, and casualties had resulted.

The Secretary for Scotland said that in his opinion it was more clear than ever that it was a misnomer to call the situation in Glasgow a strike—it was a Bolshevist rising.[42]

As steps had already been taken to move in the military forces—up to 12,000 troops, 100 motor lorries, and six tanks—the Cabinet had no further decisions to take. The first troops arrived at 10 p.m. the same day, and the rest arrived in the course of the weekend. By Monday morning the six tanks were stationed in the cattle market in the East End of Glasgow.

The rest of the history of the Forty Hours' Strike is anti-climax. The strikers began to drift back to work from about 4 February, as the effects of over a week with neither wages nor strike pay began to make themselves felt. The leaders of the strike—Gallacher, Emanuel Shinwell (at the time chairman of the Glasgow Trades Council), David Kirkwood and Harry Hopkins (district secretary of the A.S.E.)—had all been arrested on Bloody Friday, and no new leaders had been found to take their places. The only promise of sympathetic action from anywhere else in the country came from the London electricians, and they called off their proposed strike at the last minute although not before causing further alarm in the War Cabinet, which set up an Industrial Unrest Committee to deal with the situation. The Forty Hours' Strike was finally called off on 12 February. Later, the four leaders and eight others were tried at the High Court in Edinburgh on charges of incitement to riot and rioting. Eight of the defendants, including Hopkins and Kirkwood, were acquitted altogether; three including Gallacher, were sentenced to three months' imprisonment each, and Shinwell was given five months.

How serious a threat to public order did the strike and Bloody Friday actually represent? The local press, the Lord Advocate, most of the War Cabinet, and the Special Branch all took the strike with the utmost seriousness. At the time of the strike leaders' trial, the *Glasgow Herald* commented:

The tiresome and confused nature of much of the evidence was in significant contrast to the sinister simplicity of the main purpose which the whole case revealed . . . For the lightness of their sentences, they [Shinwell and Gallacher] have to thank, in the first place, the phlegm or hesitancy of the mass of those they led, and, in the second place, and more especially, the admirable self-restraint displayed by the civic and legal authorities and by the police force.

The formation of the Joint Strike Committee was . . . the first step towards that squalid terrorism which the world now describes as Bolshevism.[43]

In his speech to the jury, presenting the Crown case, the Lord Advocate had said dramatically:

The incidents on January 31st in George Square constituted the gravest imaginable menace to public order and security. There were not, thank Heaven, many incidents like them recorded in our time, and as incidents of that sort were not only in the highest degree criminal in themselves, but involved a menace to the foundation of public peace and security, he asked the jury by their verdict to express the guilt of those who instigated them . . . Every act of revolution was in progress, and could be traced to the previous incitement.[44]

The result of the trial itself cast some doubt on this view: neither judge nor jury was persuaded that Bloody Friday was the culmination of a violent and illegal conspiracy. But it was a view which undoubtedly had a part in persuading the Cabinet to take the strong action it did, because the whole tenor of the official intelligence reaching it was excitable and alarmist. A so-called 'Fortnightly Report on Revolutionary Organisations in the United Kingdom, and Morale in Foreign Countries'[45] was submitted to the War Cabinet by Basil Thomson, head of the Special Branch. Thomson (whose own assessment of the seriousness of the Forty Hours' Strike is printed at the head of this chapter) was Assistant Commissioner of the Metropolitan Police at the outbreak of war, when the activities of the C.I.D. had been combined with those of the Special Branch, so that Thomson found himself in charge of civilian intelligence relating to extremist political movements. (The Special Branch had been founded in the 1880s to deal with Irish terrorists but its brief had been widened to deal with all sorts of political extremism.) Halfway through the War, Thomson's bailiwick was extended by his takeover of the intelligence services the Ministry of Munitions had built up to deal with labour unrest affecting munitions production. The Ministry, Thomson wrote somewhat smugly, 'came to the conclusion that the work would be more efficiently and more cheaply done by professionals, and I was called up to take over the service with my own trained men'.[46] But Thomson's background as a policeman and (earlier) a colonial governor gave him no special insight into the nature of political extremism, and the quality of the information he supplied to the War Cabinet was often disastrously bad. It sometimes differed from the 'Red scares' of the popular press only in being printed on paper headed 'This Document is the Property of His Britannic Majesty's Government'. Indeed, one reason for the government's worse miscalculation of the labour situation in 1919 than in 1916 may be precisely that Thomson had taken over part of the intelligence service from the Ministry of Munitions. One of his wilder flights of fancy, for instance, was the notion that George Lansbury was the helpless dupe of a Bolshevik conspiracy:

The wirepullers behind him have not yet been disclosed, but the plan is, by holding a series of revolutionary meetings in what is regarded as a stronghold of the capitalist class, the *Royal*[47] Albert Hall, to test the strength of the revolutionary movement and fan the temper of the London workers with a view of [sic] preparing for action of a much more serious character. With this object Lansbury was primed with the scheme of turning the weekly *Herald* into a daily paper.[48]

He also gave advice on how to handle anti-Bolshevik propaganda:

Bolshevism in England.
The Ministry of Information and the War Aims Committee are now circulating information on the state of Russia under the Bolshevik regime. It is to be hoped that when they are giving details about the Terror they will not lay too much stress on outrages committed on the bourgeoisie, a matter about which the English extremists will feel unsympathetic, but will give ample details, especially in the Sunday news papers, of what working men have to suffer.
    . . . An exact translation of the world 'Bolshevik' is, I am told, 'out-and-outer'.[49]

Thomson's verdict on Bloody Friday itself was:

The plan of the revolutionary minority was to use the Clyde as the touchstone of a general strike and, if it proved to be successful, to bring out the engineers and the railways all over the country, to seize the food and to achieve a revolution. The scheme failed . . . It is now known that during the disorder on Friday, January 31st, the intention was to seize the Municipal Buildings in Glasgow, but the police were too strong for them.[50]

In January 1919 revolution seemed to be looming all over Europe. The Spartacist revolt in Berlin against the social-democratic regime there had been bloodily suppressed: Bavaria was degenerating into anarchy as various sections of the socialist parties fought for control. A Communist regime in Hungary lay only two months in the future. Above all, the Bolshevik regime in Russia appeared to be a very special kind of threat. So it is small wonder that the Cabinet reacted with nervous alarm to reports like Thomson's rather than to the cooler counsels of (for instance) Tom Jones, Deputy Secretary to the Cabinet. Jones wrote in a memorandum to Lloyd George: 'Bolshevik propaganda in this country is only dangerous in so far as it can lodge itself in the soil of genuine grievances . . . A definite reiteration by yourself of the government's determination to push forward with an advanced social programme is the best antidote.'[51]

One of the points on which alarmist views like those of Thomson and the *Glasgow Herald* were most consistently wrong was the degree of revolutionary purpose behind the strike. The C.W.C. was only one of the patrons of the strike; others, such as the S.T.U.C., could not possibly be accused of revolutionary tendencies. And even the most militant strike leaders had no very clear idea of what they wanted to do. Gallacher, for instance, writing in 1936 as an orthodox Communist, is explicitly self-critical for his lack of revolutionary purpose in 1919:

Had we been capable of planning beforehand, or had there been an experienced revolutionary leadership of these great and heroic masses, instead of a march to Glasgow Green there would have been a march to Maryhill Barracks . . . If we had gone there we could easily have persuaded the soldiers to come out, and Glasgow would have been in our hands.[52]

As we have seen, Gallacher's actual reaction to the riot was more that of a shocked pacifist than that of a dedicated revolutionary. The one strike leader who perhaps had more robust ideas was Emanuel Shinwell, who had been much the most outspoken in his speeches to 'mass pickets' at factory gates. 'When the workers in the power station knew that the strikers insisted on their participation, he believed they would not be at work in the morning. At the same time he recommended the police to take a holiday.'[53] Shortly before Bloody Friday, according to Gallacher, 'Manny had made a suggestion of a pretty desperate nature.'[54] If the suggestion was, in fact, that the workers should seize the City Chambers, then the behaviour of Gallacher and the other principals on the Friday was extremely good dissembling. It is much more likely that it was a plan to sabotage the electricity supply because the workers at one power station had not struck. But, whatever it was, it was not done. And in any case Shinwell was no revolutionary. He was one of those who had fought for a 40-hours, not a 30-hours strike, and he was an outspoken opponent of revolutionary speakers on the Glasgow Trades Council. His intention was surely to provoke Government intervention in the strikers' favour; the result was government intervention, but of a sort very different from what he had expected.

It is worth reviewing the fundamental weaknesses of the 40 Hours' Strike. In spite of the involvement of the S.T.U.C., hardly any union gave it official backing. Only the Electricians and two small moulders' unions were giving strike pay, and the A.S.E. was totally hostile—in sharp contrast with its connivance at the dilution strikes of 1916. No serious attempt was made to spread the strike outside Glasgow, and no sympathetic action followed elsewhere. Wartime resentments between skilled and unskilled men had by no means died down, and the unskilled men were suspicious at what seemed to them another craftsmen's strike. Two key 'unskilled' unions failed to join in: the Scottish Horse and Motormen's Association, and the Municipal Employees' Association, the union which organized the tramwaymen and the workers at the one power station which continued to work throughout the strike.

The strike movement of January 1919 was the final fling of the C.W.C., and it might be argued that its failure to reappear after the end of the Forty Hours' Strike justified the Government's firm stand. But this would be to ignore the catalogue of structural weaknesses just cited. The strike would certainly have collapsed, and discredited unofficial action, without any help from the Government. Indeed, the net effect of the tanks in the cattle market was probably the same as that of the policy misbehaviour in George Square: it gave the strike a romantic history which concealed, more or less successfully, an otherwise ignominious failure.

The Forty Hours' Strike ushered in a period of extreme government concern about industrial unrest, which lasted until the breakdown of the Triple Alliance of miners, railwaymen, and transport workers in April 1921. The most vivid account of ministers' anxieties at this time shows that they were continually obsessed with the problem and turning to unlikely remedies. In February 1920, for instance, Lloyd George raised with Sir Hugh Trenchard (the Chief of Air Staff) the question of the availability of the R.A.F. to deal with labour unrest. 'Trenchard replied that . . . the pilots had no weapons for ground fighting. The P.M. presumed they could use machine guns and drop bombs.' At the same meeting, 'Bonar Law so often referred to the stockbrokers as a loyal and fighting class until [sic] one felt that potential battalions of stockbrokers were to be found in every town.'[55] A similar concern about a possible breakdown in public order was paramount in Ministers' minds during the weeks leading up to the threatened Triple Alliance strike in April 1921.[56] One tangible result of this concern was the innocuously named Supply and Transport Committee. In February 1919 the War Cabinet set up an Industrial Unrest Committee which, after two changes of name, became the Supply and Transport Committee. This was reduced to a skeleton organization after the failure of the railwaymen and the transport workers to join the striking miners on 15 April, 1921, which led to the collapse of the Triple Alliance. But it was never entirely disbanded, even by the 1924 Labour Government, and it had its day in 1926, when it was the Government's means of organizing supplies during the General Strike.

The Committee was at its most alarmist right at the beginning, in the shadow of the Forty Hours' Strike. On 17 February, 1919, it was reported that 40,000 lorries and 100,000 motor cars had been earmarked for use in the event of a strike. In March, the Committee drafted a Strikes (Exceptional Measures) Bill which would have empowered the Government, *inter alia,* to arrest trade union leaders and to prevent unions from drawing on their strike funds by declaring a bank holiday. The proposal was too much even for the Cabinet of 1919, which turned it down.[57]

The Committee also turned its hand to political propaganda. During the 1921 crisis, for instance:

Briefs for the use of speakers and writers, but bearing no indication of their official origin, were issued two or three times a week during the critical period, and were distributed to about 1200 people through the good offices of the following Organisations: the Central Unionist Association, the Coalition Liberal Organisation, the British Commonwealth Union, the National Political League, the Middle Classes Union, and the Women's Guild of Empire.[58]

Admiral Sir Reginald Hall, the recently retired Director of Naval Intelligence, had earlier been helping the Committee by distributing propaganda through an unofficial (and secret) body called National Propaganda.[59] Like others mentioned in this account, Hall saw nothing improper in the identification of the national interest with the interests of the government of the day—provided that it was not a Labour one. His (probable) behaviour in the Zinoviev letter affair in 1924 presents an instructive contrast with his eagerness to help the Supply and Transport Committee in 1920.[60]

When the Committee's arrangements were reviewed by the first Labour Government, in 1924, the minister responsible (Josiah Wedgwood) commented: 'There has been an almost melodramatic air of secrecy about the whole business, as though a revolution were being combated, rather than a straightforward effort made to keep the essential services going'.[61] If the Labour Government had seen their predecessors' Cabinet papers, they would have been impressed by the extent to which members of the Committee did think they were trying to combat a revolution. However, the MacDonald Government continued the pruning of the Committee's powers which had been begun under Bonar Law and Baldwin, and left as its central feature the power to appoint a Chief Civil Commissioner (a Cabinet minister) and his eleven regional deputies (who were to be junior ministers). These officials were to be responsible for the maintenance of essential services in an emergency.

When the prospect of a general strike began to loom in 1925, the Baldwin Government had only to put this machinery into action. The Committee's attitude was much cooler and less feverish than in 1921, even though it was chaired by Sir William Joynson-Hicks,[62] and its machinery went smoothly into operation on 2nd May, 1926. It was a far cry from Sir Basil Thomson, and still further from Red Clydeside. Nonetheless, Red Clydeside played its part in the foundation of the Supply and Transport Committee. If the Forty Hours' Strike has had an enduring impact on history, it is as one of the catalysts of that committee, not as the harbinger of revolution.

NOTES

1. (Sir) Basil Thomson, *Queer People* (London, 1922), p. 276.
2. W. Gallacher, *Revolt of the Clyde* (London, 1936), p. 234. Emphasis in original.
3. *History of the Ministry of Munitions* (London, n.d.), vol. iv; J. Hinton, 'The Clyde Workers' Committee and the Dilution Struggle', in *Essays in Labour History, 1886 – 1923,* edited by A. Briggs and J. Saville (London, 1971); I. S. McLean, 'The Ministry of Munitions, the Clyde Workers' Committee, and the suppression of the *Forward:* An Alternative View', *Scottish Labour History Society Journal,* no. 6, December 1972.
4. Ministry of Munitions papers at the Public Record Office, Mun 5/73. Report by J. Paterson, Chief Labour Officer, Ministry of Munitions, Glasgow, 18 December 1915, in file marked 'Material supplied to the Minister before Tyne and Clyde visits'.
5. Mun 5/73. Commission on Dilution of Labour on the Clyde. Memorandum on the Progress of the Commission by Mr Lynden Macassey, 5 February 1916.
6. Quoted in, for example, W. R. Scott and J. Cunnison, *The Industries of the Clyde Valley during the War* (Oxford, 1924), p. 210.
7. Mun 5/73. Causes of unrest among munition workers on the Clyde and Tyne, by Lynden Macassey, 18 December 1915.
8. For further details of which see T. Brotherstone, 'The Suppression of the *Forward',* *Scottish Labour History Society Journal,* no. 1, May 1969; McLean, op. cit.
9. Mun 5/73. The Industrial Situation on the Clyde. Memorandum (incomplete) by Lynden Macassey, 9 February 1916.
10. Beveridge Collection on Munitions, British Library of Political and Economic Science, vol. iii, ff. 355 – 8. I. H. Mitchell to Sir H. Llewellyn Smith, 21 February 1916.
11. Manifesto from the Parkhead Forge Engineers to their Fellow-workers. Highton Collection, Glasgow University Department of Economic History. Also in Scott and Cunnison, op. cit., pp. 215 – 6.
12. C. Addison, *Politics from Within,* 2 vols. (London, 1924), vol. 1, p. 191.
13. See, for example, *History of the Ministry of Munitions,* 12 vols. in parts (London, n.d.), vol. iv, part IV, p. 130; (Sir) Lynden Macassey, *Labour Policy, False and True* (London, 1922), p. 79.
14. Addison, loc. cit.
15. From Lord Crewe's letter to the King reporting the meeting. Public Record Office, Cab 37/144. Reproduced from the original in the Royal Archives.
16. See, for example, Crewe to Lloyd George, 3 April 1916. Lloyd George Papers, Beaverbrook Library, London. D/16/9.

17. Labour Party, *Report . . . [on] the Deportation . . . of David Kirkwood and other workmen employed in Munitions Factories in the Clyde District* (London, 1918).

18. Labour Party, op. cit., para. 31.

19. Cab 23/3. War Cabinet 207 of the 8 August 1917. Cf. also Cab 24/22, GT 1625 of August 1917: Memorandum of Robert Munro (Secretary for Scotland) on the Prohibition of a meeting at Glasgow.

20. Extracts from the Minutes of the Glasgow Trades Council, 15 August 1917. Mitchell Library, Glasgow.

21. Cab 24/44. J. S. Ewart to Secretary, War Office, enclosed as appendix to GT 3838 of 7th March 1918: 'Revolutionary Agitation in Glasgow and Clydeside with special reference to the cases of John Maclean and others'.

22. Cab 23/5. War Cabinet no. 364, 12 March 1918.

23. Cab 23/42. Imperial War Cabinet 39 of 28 November 1918; cf. also Cab 24/70. GT 6379 of 26 November 1918.

24. *Daily Record and Mail* (Glasgow), 4 December 1918.

25. W. F. H. Kendall, *The Revolutionary Movement in Britain, 1900 – 1921* (London, 1969), p. 132.

26. Newbold was a Quaker turned Communist who became, briefly, Communist M.P. for Motherwell (1932 – 4).

27. Autobiographical TS Material (unsorted) in Walton Newbold MSS, Manchester University Library.

28. S.T.U.C. Annual Report, 1918, p. 37.

29. A.S.E. *Monthly Journal and Report,* December 1918, p. 18.

30. A.S.E. Statement by suspended Glasgow District Committee, February 1919, with request for reinstatement. Highton Papers, Glasgow University Department of Economic History.

31. S.T.U.C. Annual Report 1919, p. 44.

32. *Glasgow Herald,* 28 January 1919, p. 5; 29 January 1919, p. 7.

33. (i.e. Executive).

34. Quoted in S.T.U.C. Minutes of the Parliamentary Committee, 27 January 1919.

35. Ibid.

36. Ibid. 8 January 1919.

37. Cab 23/9. War Cabinet no. 521, 28 January 1919.

38. Cab 23/9. War Cabinet no. 522, 30 January 1919.

39. All quotations in this paragraph are from Cab 23/9: War Cabinet 522 of 30 January 1919. It may seem surprising that Churchill, 'the man who sent troops to Tonypandy', the scourge of the workers, the future editor of the *British Gazette,* should have been counselling moderation, but Churchill seems to have been consistently less agitated about the home front at this time than were most of his colleagues. Cf. Sir Maurice Hankey to Tom Jones, 17th January, 1920: 'The ministers . . . seem to have the "wind-up" to the most extraordinary extent about the industrial situation. C.I.G.S. also is positively in a state of dreadful nerves on the subject. Churchill is the only one who is sane on this subject, and on the subject of Denekin *he* is a nuisance.' T. Jones, *Whitehall Diary,* vol. I (ed. Middlemas, London, 1969), p. 97.

40. *Glasgow Herald,* February 1919.

41. *Daily Record,* February 1919.

42. Cab 23/9. War Cabinet 523. 31 January 1919.

43. *Glasgow Herald,* 19 April 1919.

44. Ibid., 18 April 1919.

45. Originally 'Fortnightly Report on Pacifism and Revolutionary Organisations in the United Kingdom'. They were not quite fortnightly (sometimes more frequent, sometimes less); not all of them appear to have reached the GT series of Cabinet papers in Cab 24.

46. Thompson, op. cit., p. 269.

47. Emphasis in original.

48. *Fortnightly Report* . . . 2 December 1918. GT 6425. Cab 24/71.

49. Ibid., 21 October 1918. GT 6079. Cab 24/67.

50. Ibid., 10 February 1919. GT 6816. Cab 24/75.

51. Jones to Lloyd George, 8 February 1919. Jones, op. cit., pp. 73 – 4.

52. Gallacher, op. cit., pp. 233 – 4.

53. *Daily Record and Mail,* 30 January 1919.

54. W. Gallacher, *Last Memoirs* (London, 1966), pp. 123 – 4. Earlier accounts of the same meeting are more reticent: neither T. Bell, *Pioneering Days* (London, 1941), nor Gallacher's *Revolt on the Clyde* names Shinwell in this context, although both refer to him.

55. Jones, op. cit., pp. 99 – 101. Lloyd George's comment may have been sarcastic: Jones thought that 'the P.M. did a lot of unsuspected leg-pulling as he does not believe in the imminence of the revolution' (p. 103). But Bonar Law, Long, the Geddes brothers, and other ministers were in deadly earnest.

56. Jones, op. cit., pp. 131 – 50.

57. Industrial Unrest Committee, 14 March 1919: Cab 27/59. War Cabinet, 19 March 1919: Cab 23/15. The Cabinet discussion was recorded in the separate 'A' series of secret minutes, which were duplicated instead of being printed because of fears as to the loyalty of the printers.

58. Cab 27/75. Meeting of the Supply and Transport Committee, 23 July 1921 (but reporting on activities during April 1921).

59. Cab 27/84. Supply and Transport Committee: Propaganda Sub-Committee, 9 March 1920.

60. L. Chester, S. Fay and H. Young, *The Zinoviev Letter* (London, 1967), Ch. 8, present strong circumstantial evidence that Hall tipped off the *Daily Mail* about the value of the Zinoviev letter as a stick with which to beat the outgoing Labour Government during the 1924 election campaign. Although an ex-intelligence man, Hall did not consider, or was prepared to ignore, the likelihood of the letter's being a forgery.

61. Cab 27/259. Supply and Transport Organisation: Emergency Committee, February – March 1924.

62. 'Jix', as Home Secretary from 1924 to 1929, was responsible for the prosecution of leading Communists under the Incitement to Mutiny Act, 1797, in October 1925, and for the raid on the Soviet trading company in London, Arcos, in 1927 in an abortive search for subversive documents.

Index

142–3, 176, 273 (on Clydeside, in World War 1 292–309; of domestic servants 136–9; for shorter hours 92, 108, 115); and respectability xxii, 67, 112–13, 142; social policy, pressure for 268, 270; Welsh 53–74 *passim*; *see also* class, labour, work
World War 1: on Clydeside 292–309 *passim*; and domestic service 138

Young, Arthur 2–3